DEDICATION

THIS BOOK IS DEDICATED TO MY SOUL MATE AND LOVELY WIFE, TRACY JO. SHE HAS BEEN A CONSTANT SOURCE OF LOVE, MOTIVATION, INSPIRATION, SUPPORT, AND INSIGHT IN MANY OF MY PAST LIVES AND NOW IN MY CURRENT LIFE.

◊ *Michael Jaco* ◊

Awakening of a Warrior: Past Lives of a Navy SEAL Remembered

SECOND EDITION

Intuitive Warrior Series :: Volume II

Published by the Consortium of Collective Consciousness Publishing™

As is common in a historic and reference book such as this, much of the information included on these pages has been collected from diverse sources. When possible, the information has been checked and double-checked. Almost every topic has at least three data points, that is, three different sources that report the same information. Even with special effort to be accurate and thorough, the author and publisher cannot vouch for each and every reference. The author and publisher assume no responsibility or liability for any outcome, loss, arrest, or injury that occurs as a result of information or advice contained in this book. As with the purchase of goods or services, caveat emptor is the prevailing responsibility of the purchaser, and the same is true for the student of the esoteric.

Library of Congress Cataloging-in-Publication Data: 2014906487

Jaco, Michael

THE AWAKENING OF A WARRIOR: PAST LIVES OF A NAVY SEAL REMEMBERED / Michael K. Jaco
p. cm.
Does not include index
ISBN 13: 978-1-888729-92-4 (Pbk.)
ISBN 13: 978-1-888729-93-1 (ebook)

1. Spirituality—Reincarnation. 2. Metaphysics—Historic Past Lives. I. Title Library of Congress Catalog Card Number: 2014906487

Printed in the United States of America.

10 9 8 7 6 5 4 3 2 1

AWAKENING OF A WARRIOR

PAST LIVES OF A NAVY SEAL REMEMBERED

MICHAEL JACO

SECOND EDITION

Consortium of Collective Consciousness Publishing
www.CCCPublishing.com • www.MichaelKJaco.com • www.UnleashingIntuition.com

AWAKENING OF A WARRIOR

CONTENTS

CONTENTS

continued

AWAKENING OF A WARRIOR

CONTENTS

ACKNOWLEDGMENTS

I'd like to acknowledge the contributions of Kevin Ryerson and his tireless efforts to enlighten humanity. This book would not have been possible without Kevin's invaluable service as a trance channel. Kevin is a trance channel, which means that when he works, he goes into a meditative state or trance and allows spirit beings to speak through him. Kevin has worked with the famous actress Shirley MacLaine for more than thirty years and is featured in four of her books. Kevin's own intuitive observations during our many enjoyable conversations together have also led me to research and uncover further past life insights.

I would also like to acknowledge my friend in several former lives, Ahtun Re. In my first channeled session with Kevin, Ahtun Re told me at the end of our conversation that we had been friends in previous lifetimes. Ahtun Re's last incarnation occurred approximately 3,350 years ago when he served as a high priest and adviser to Pharaoh Akhenaton in 1379-1362 BCE. Ahtun Re still seems like a friend to me, and I enjoy his humor and unique perspectives that have helped me grow my intuitive insights into past lifetimes.

I'd also like to thank Rebecca Shaw of Charleston Hypnosis Center in Charleston, South Carolina. Past life regression is easy and available to everyone, and Rebecca showed me just how rewarding a regression session could be. My regression sessions with Rebecca were instrumental in opening the doors to many of my past lives and continue to do so today. Rebecca's professionalism and easygoing nature put me at ease and were major factors in making this work possible.

Cover and book design by Mark J. Maxam, designer
2nd edition editor and image contributor Brad Olsen

FOREWORD

If we look at the perspective of any two people who witness the same event, they will invariably have a different view. This could be due to their different vantage points at the scene, different educational levels, their ability to articulate words, their upbringing, their political or religious views, as well as a myriad of other factors. Do not get wrapped up in my views because they are only meant to inform. Any reference to living families is not meant to draw favor or to get into any kind of relationship from former lives. I do not mean to intrude, insult, or draw any unnecessary attention to living relatives of my former lives. Nor do I intend to curry favor or influence anyone in anything other than to inspire and motivate others in their own personal search for past life information.

Many of the viewpoints from my own perspective of history may not fit with particular recognized stories or with the way history has been written. History is often written and shaped by the victors or by those with an agenda that does not include promoting what the truth really is. History is occasionally retold incorrectly or completely forgotten through suppression or fabrication. But we can make progress in discerning the truth amid the fog of time in which history has been forgotten, misinterpreted, or manipulated, if we are open to a variety of sources. Memories of former lives from many different people can come forth spontaneously or through different practices and may help to uncover the true history of an era or certain events. I believe, at some point in the near future, past life insights will be commonly recognized and considered a potential part of research into historical events.

Some of the lives I've lived are hard to trace, and specific proof is not always readily available by current scientific standards. I've tried, to the best of my ability, to hold all of my information to the light of truth. I have also tried, to the best of my ability, to triangulate from different sources, which include historical evidence, experts on the subject, and actual data that has survived through time.

My desire and my intent for writing this book are to spark an interest and perhaps stimulate an awakening in many to their own past lives and how these past lives have shaped and molded them over time. I firmly believe that our entire collective past lives have shaped and guided humanity in its entirety to this cur-

rent point in time. I did not write this book out of an egotistical need to show how I have lived the life of kings and great conquerors. I have used historically significant figures to draw interest and to show a pattern throughout many lifetimes that can be cross-referenced and validated for those that are skeptical. I am aware that my best efforts at convincing some will likely never be enough. My true desire is to educate humanity and further our collective advancement through a medium that is highly rewarding when approached with a desire to be informed.

So what does learning about past lives do for you personally? Think about your current life and how your experiences in this life have developed you into the person you are today. All of the challenges, frustrations, victories, joys, and moments of love and bliss are all part of who you are today. At unprompted times, some of these distant memories flash before you. A piece of your life will appear, and, if focused upon, a whole stream of memories will spill forth. Now think of the possibility that on the farthest side of your earliest memories exist even more memories. Myriad memories, in fact, and, if you could tap into these, they would reveal amazing things about who you are. Some of these memories would open up the possibility of skills and abilities that would vastly improve your life if you could tap into this treasure trove of information again.

You could possibly remember moments in history that have long been forgotten but would immeasurably improve the knowledge of humanity. This is actually starting to happen with many individuals all over the planet. You could remember an architectural technique that would allow homes to be built cheaper and last longer. Keep in mind that science still doesn't understand how many of the very ancient structures on Earth were built with such precision, and we are still in the process of decoding the sophisticated geometrical, astronomical, and arithmetical knowledge within the architecture of those structures. The list of possible uses of past life memories is long, and your imagination is the only limit as to what they could offer you and all of humankind as well.

The benefits are potentially many and can include everything from releasing past traumas that may be influencing your current life to achieving an understanding of why you are attracted to certain people, places, or things. Knowledge of a past life can give you insight as to why you are passionate and driven in certain areas and completely averse to other aspects of life. If we can come to a realization that we have had incarnations as people from many different races,

cultures, and religions, and that we have been poor, rich, noble, peasants, slaves, male, and female, would we still have the number of wars and conflicts with each other that we have at the moment?

The information in this book has taken me nearly half a century of research and introspection to come to. I'm completely convinced of reincarnation after having read dozens of books, had several past life readings, and experienced many synchronistic events that pointed me to my final conclusion that we all reincarnate. One of the aims of this book is to condense my own intensive personal research over the last several decades so that you can come to your own conclusions much faster than I did. I confidently believe that, if you don't currently believe in reincarnation, you simply have not investigated this topic thoroughly enough yet. Therefore, you have no cogent evidence, which is unfortunate because past life knowledge is extremely enlightening in a multitude of ways. This book will give you the proof if you are remotely open to it.

In my opinion and in the opinion of many advanced thinkers throughout time, the evidence is overwhelming and irrefutably in favor of spiritual transmigration. If we were to set up a trial of reincarnation in a court of law for perjury, which is defined as the deliberate and willful giving of false, misleading, or incomplete testimony under oath, it would be found not guilty. Whether you now believe in reincarnation, are curious but on the fence, or have no belief at all, you will find this book, at a minimum, entertaining, thought-provoking, and persuasive, if not downright enlightening and transformative.

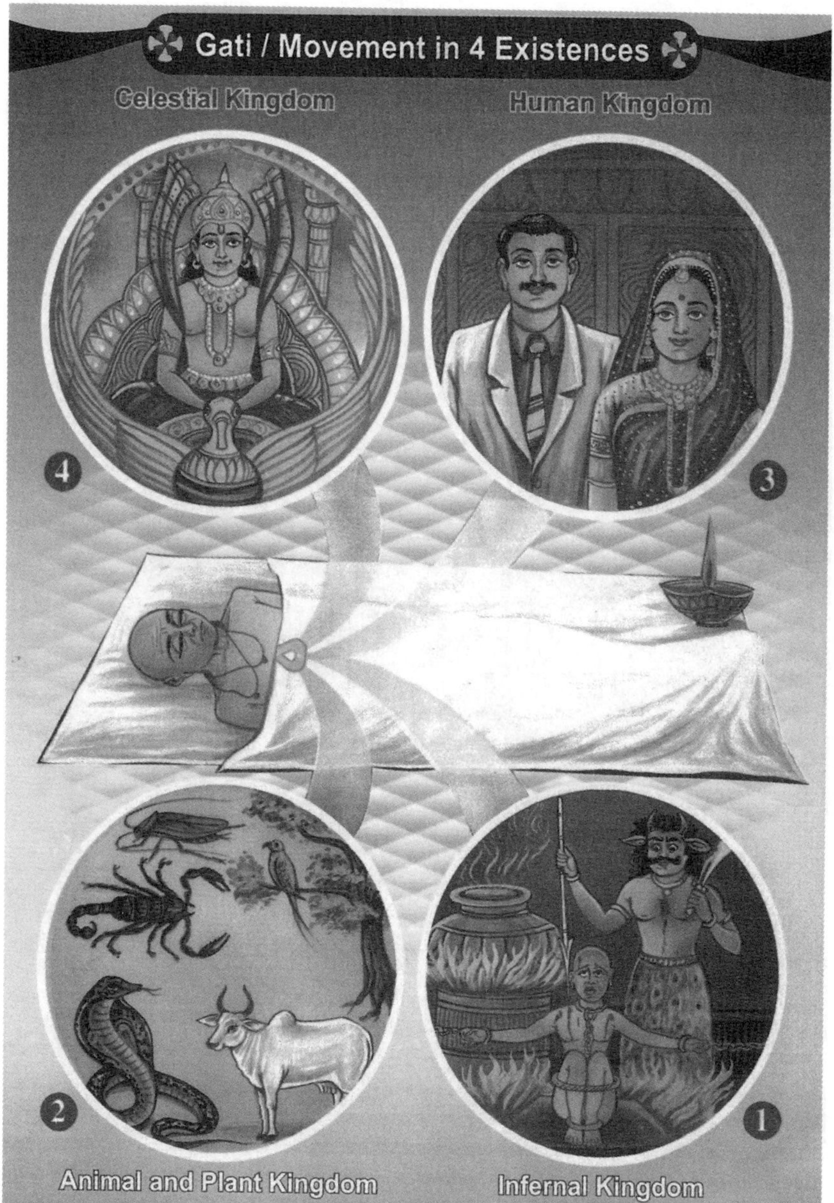

In Jainism, a soul travels in a spiritual transmigration to any one of the four states of existence after death depending on its karmas.

American army general George S. Patton was a strong believer in reincarnation, believing, among other lifetimes, he was a reincarnation of a legionnaire in France and the Carthaginian general Hannibal.

Ralph Waldo Emerson (1803-1882) **Henry David Thoreau (1817-1862)**

Ralph Waldo Emerson embraced the Eastern notion of Karma, the idea that all of our current actions are partly created and limited by past actions. As Emerson put it, *"the history of the individual is always an account of his condition, and he knows himself to be a party to his present estate."* Henry David Thoreau saw God as an ever present and constant force in life. He believed *"God himself culminates in the present moment, and will never be more divine in the lapse of all the ages"* as written on page 97 in his book Walden. Thoreau believed in the idea of an everlasting God. Additionally, similar to standard religion, he believed that God was an agent of good.

The visionary Henry Ford was also one of many great thinkers who was a firm believer in reincarnation; the transfer of souls from the mortal dead to the yet to be born. He said "I am in exact accord with the belief of Thomas Edison that spirit is immortal, that there is a continuing center of character in each personality. But I don't know what spirit is, nor matter either."

INTRODUCTION

I began to have thoughts about the possibility of past lives when I was quite young. Around age eleven, my parents allowed me to stay up late and watch the movie *Patton* with them on the televised Sunday night movie. George C. Scott's Oscar-winning performance as the American general and tank commander during World War II absolutely fascinated me. I was especially intrigued when he mentioned in the movie that he'd had past lives. Patton himself immortalized his feelings about reincarnation in a poem, whose verses are truly mesmerizing.

So as through a glass and darkly,
The age long strife I see,
Where I fought in many guises,
Many names, but always me.
So forever in the future,
Shall I battle as of yore,
Dying to be born a fighter,
But to die again, once more.

Reincarnation, which literally means "to be made flesh again," is the belief that the soul, after the death of the body, comes back to Earth in another body. My understanding is that, a new personality is developed during each life in the physical world, but the soul remains constant throughout the successive lifetimes.

As I matured, I continually came across literature and great works by many people from all times who had believed in past lives. Among them was the industrial trailblazer Henry Ford, who said, *"I adopted the theory of reincarnation when I was twenty-six. Genius is experience. Some think to seem that it is a gift or talent, but it is the fruit of long experience in many lives."*

Over time I found more interesting quotes from other well-known people that made me ponder the possibility that I may have had past lives as well. Powerful leaders, such as Mahatma Gandhi in India, would have me pause and meditate on quotes like, *"I cannot think of permanent enmity between man and man, and believing as I do in the theory of reincarnation, I live in the hope that if not in this birth, in some other birth I shall be able to hug all of humanity*

in friendly embrace The accomplished writer Ralph Waldo Emerson similarly stated, "*The soul comes from without into the human body, as into a temporary abode, and it goes out of it anew as it passes into other habitations, for the soul is immortal. It is the secret of the world that all things subsist and do not die, but only retire a little from sight and afterward return again. Nothing is dead; men feign themselves dead, and endure mock funerals— and there they stand looking out of the window, sound and well, in some strange new disguise.*"

Another contemporary of Emerson and one of my favorites as a boy, after I read the classic book *Walden,* was Henry David Thoreau who said, "*Why should we be startled by death? Life is a constant putting off of the mortal coil—coat, cuticle, flesh and bones, all old clothes.*"

Oliver Wendell Holmes served as an associate justice on the US Supreme Court from 1902 to 1932. Noted for his long service, his concise and pithy opinions, and his deference to the decisions of elected legislatures, he is one of the most widely cited US Supreme Court justices in history. Emerson's words deeply impressed him, as he said, "*Emerson was an idealist in the Platonic sense of the word, a spiritualist as opposed to a materialist. He believed, he says, 'as the wise Spenser teaches,' that the soul makes its own body. This, of course, involves the doctrine of preexistence; a doctrine older than Spenser, older than Plato or Pythagoras, having its cradle in India, fighting its way down through Greek philosophers and Christian fathers and German professors, to our own time.*" Many different leaders within several diverse and varied fields would come to deeper insights of our world and share them with us, like Jalal ad-Din Muhammad Rumi, an Islamic Sufi poet of the thirteenth century. Rumi, who is my favorite poet of all time, said, "*I died as a mineral and became a plant, I died as a plant and rose to animal, I died as animal and I was man. Why should I fear? When was I less by dying?*" Along these lines, he expressed his perspective on the idea that we migrated down as souls to the lowest denominator to experience all of existence through countless incarnations. In this manner, we work our way up through first mineral form, then plant, then animal, and now as humans. But even now as humans, we are still evolving into a higher form of existence. The evolutionary process is in a constant state of flux.

Among the earliest known religious teachings in the world today are the Vedic Hindu scriptures, which state that the soul is immortal while the

body is subject to birth, decay, old age, and death. An essential part of these scriptures are the Upanishads, where the term *karma* originated, which is intricately linked with the idea of reincarnation. In Christianity, the principle of karma is described in the saying *"as you* sow *so shall you reap."* Karma literally means action; it is the product of one's actions and the force that constantly determines one's destiny and sets the stage for the next reincarnation. The cycle of death and rebirth, governed by karma, is referred to as *samsara.* Many religious leaders throughout time believed in reincarnation and spoke openly of it with their followers.

Siddhartha Gautama, the man who became known as Buddha (563-483 Before Current Era, BCE), offered the following on reincarnation: "*Samsara—the Wheel of Existence, literally the 'Perpetual Wandering'—is the name by which is designated the sea of life ever restlessly heaving up and down, the symbol of this continuous process of ever again and again being born, growing old, suffering, and dying. It is constantly changing from moment to moment, as lives follow continuously one upon the other through inconceivable periods of time. Of this Samsara, a single lifetime constitutes only a vanishingly tiny fraction.*"

The current Dalai Lama, Tenzin Gyatso, is the leader of the Gelugpa lineage of Tibetan Buddhism. He is the fourteenth recognized reincarnation of the same soul and the inheritor of a rich tradition and culture, which started with Gendun Drup (1391-1474 Current Era, CE). This fascinating reincarnation story has been ongoing for over six hundred years! Before he dies, the Dalai Lama will meditate on his next incarnation and give the upper echelon of the Gelugpa monks clues as to what he sees through the eyes of his next incarnated self as a two- or three-year-old. After his death, the monks will start their own meditation on the location of the Dalai Lama's next incarnation, and then they will faithfully search for him. The monks correlate where he is located through previous clues and their own meditations over a two-to-three- year period. They will then travel to the general location and narrow down the potential children through a purposefully designed process of tests to find the true successor.

The monks then present several artifacts from the previous Dalai Lama's life to the children in question, such as an old worn toy that he had enjoyed, but they will also present a new and shiny one. The right child picks his previous toy and other artifacts such as prayer beads, staffs, and so on for a count of around ten different objects or questions. Satisfied, they ask for the child from the honored parents, and he is brought up as the new incarnation of the Dalai Lama. So far, this has always happened in Tibet, but the current Dalai Lama said that he would probably not reincarnate in what is now China and that he might even come back as a woman, *"but a beautiful one!"* he said jokingly.

The Dalai Lama wrote, in the preface of the book *The Case for Reincarnation* by Joe Fisher, that *"reincarnation is not an exclusively Hindu or Buddhist concept, but it is part of the history of human origin. It is proof of the mind stream's capacity to retain knowledge of physical and mental activities. It is related to the theory of interdependent origination and to the law of cause and effect."*

In all three Abrahamic religions, Judaism, Christianity, and Islam, there are several references to reincarnation. Josephus, the best-known Jewish historian from the time of Jesus, said that *"all pure and holy spirits live on in heavenly places, and in course of time they are again sent down to inhabit righteous bodies."* Other spiritual insights would follow from masters like Yeshua, who is commonly referred to as Jesus. In the account of John 3:3, he said, *"I tell you the truth, no one can see the kingdom of God unless he is born again."* In the Pistis Sophia, which is part of the Gnostic Gospels, Yeshua is quoted as saying that *"souls are poured from one into another of different kinds of bodies of the world."*

While fasting and in deep meditation in a mountain cave outside of Mecca, an area in present-day Saudi Arabia, the prophet Muhammad received messages from Allah through his messenger Archangel Gabriel. In the Holy Qur'an, we find the verses, *"And Allah hath caused you to spring forth from the Earth like a plant; Hereafter will He turn you back into it again, and bring you forth anew" and "God generates beings, and sends them back over and over again, till they return to Him."*

Scientific proof of reincarnation is also coming from many different sources. I have read many books by Dr. Ian Stevenson (October 31, 1918-February 8, 2007), who was the former head of the Department of Psychiatry at the University of Virginia. Before he passed, he was the director of the Division of Personality Studies at the University of Virginia and, over forty years, compiled several thousand cases of reincarnation from all over the world. In his

book *Twenty Cases Suggestive of Reincarnation,* he gives very credible accounts of children who remembered past lives that he had personally researched.

It is known that the Egyptians believed in reincarnation or the transmigration of the soul from body to body. This was one of the main reasons why they embalmed and preserved the body, so that it could journey along with "Ka," an animating force that was believed to be an energetic counterpart of the body, the equivalent to what we understand as the soul. This establishes the concept of reincarnation back to the ancient Egyptian religion in 3750 BCE, but many think the concept dates back even further.

A contemporary of Siddhartha Gautama was the Greek philosopher and mathematician Pythagoras, who taught that the soul is immortal and merely residing in the body, surviving its physical death. His teachings also held that the soul goes through a series of rebirths during which the soul rests between every death and rebirth, where it is further purified in the underworld. The purpose of this continuous process is for the soul to evolve to the point where it can eventually leave the transmigration or reincarnation cycle.

Countless philosophers have discussed the idea of reincarnation such as Socrates (469-399 BCE), who is one of the most acknowledged philosophers of all time. He stated that he was *"confident that there truly is such a thing as living again, that the living spring from the dead, and that the souls of the dead are in existence."*

Plato (427-347 BCE), another renowned Greek philosopher who was taught by Socrates and in turn taught Aristotle, shared similar views as Pythagoras about the eternal nature of the soul of man in that it is preexistent and wholly spiritual.

The early Christian philosopher Origen (185-254 CE), is considered one of the most prominent of all of the church fathers. In his *Contra Celsum,* he states, *"A soul enters into a body according to its former actions and then changes body."*

The Latin philosopher Saint Augustine (354-430 CE) was greatly influenced by neo-Platonism, which revolves around the idea of a single supreme being or source of goodness from which all other things in the universe descend. Neo-Platonists support the idea of a world soul, or *anima mundi,* which bridges the divide between the realm of forms and the realm of intan-

gible existence. Saint Augustine is deemed one of the most important figures in the development of Western Christianity, and in the *Contra Academicos,* he said, "*The message of Plato's reincarnation is the purest and most luminous of all philosophy.*"

Truth has a wonderful way of coming back full circle into the forefront of the collective consciousness. The knowledge of reincarnation and the self-realization that it initiates have been lost or suppressed for centuries in many cultures and religions, but now humanity's awareness is inexorably on its way to setting things straight. You may decide for yourself, as I did over time, that reincarnation is part of who and what we are as spiritual beings having a human experience over many lifetimes.

My thoughts on reincarnation and how we can benefit from our personal studies of past lives are multifaceted. Pulling in the added wisdom and experiences from another lifetime could help expand your horizon in many different ways. You might be able to figure out why you are actually here in this particular life and what you may need to do in order to progress and be more fulfilled. Learning what you have done wrong in past lives could motivate you to not repeat those mistakes in this life.

The awareness of past lives and my connection to them in this life have been part of my own spiritual awakening, a process of awakening that I believe everyone will eventually encounter as they progress on the spiritual path. To deny or suppress this integral part of spiritual ascension of consciousness is to impede or negate one's own right as a soul in passage through the human experience. It is with this concept of our rights as soul entities that I relate my own personal experiences in the hope that it will enhance or awaken your own personal spiritual development and intuition.

As Edgar Cayce wrote, "*In time, we who are trapped in the cycle of birth and rebirth can once again come to know our original state and purpose, and regain our celestial birthright as a companion to God. In time, we can again come to realize that the conditions in our current life are the result of our free actions and choices from past lives.*"

Page 14: *Reincarnation is the philosophical or religious concept that the non-physical essence of a living being begins a new life in a different physical form or body after biological death. This is an illustration of reincarnation in Hindu art.*

Rumi's imaginary on a tiling art from Yeni Qapi, Istanbul, Turkey.

Studio photograph of Mahatma Gandhi, London, 1931. the *Mahatma*, while often mistaken for Gandhi's given name in the West, is taken from the Sanskrit words *maha* (meaning *Great*) and *atma* (meaning *Soul*).

Edgar Cayce spoke in his trance messages the existence of aliens and Atlantis, and claimed that "the red race developed in Atlantis and its development was rapid." Another claim by Cayce was that "soul-entities" on Earth intermingled with animals to produce "things" such as giants that were as much as twelve feet tall.

The Buddha is revered by Buddhists as an awakened being whose teachings present and explain a path to freedom from ignorance, craving, rebirth and suffering.

The name "Dalai Lama" is a combination of the Mongolic word *dalai* meaning 'ocean' or 'big' (coming from Mongolian title *Dalaiyin qan* or *Dalaiin khan*) and the Tibetan word lama meaning 'master" or "guru.'

"EVEN THIS IS MY VOW STEADILY PURSUED, THAT I NEVER GIVE UP A PERSON THAT IS TERRIFIED, NOR ONE THAT IS DEVOTED TO ME, NOR ONE THAT SEEKS MY PROTECTION, SAYING THAT HE IS DESTITUTE, NOR ONE THAT IS AFFLICTED, NOR ONE THAT HAS COME TO ME, NOR ONE THAT IS WEAK IN PROTECTING ONESELF, NOR ONE THAT IS SOLICITOUS OF LIFE. I SHALL NEVER GIVE UP SUCH A ONE TILL MY OWN LIFE IS AT AN END."

◊ *King Yudhisthira* ◊

CHAPTER 1

KING YUDHISTHIRA DURING THE TIME WHEN THE MAHABHARATA AND BHAGAVAD GITA WERE WRITTEN, 3500 BCE

The setting was in ancient India in the sumptuous palace of the Pandava clan in the Northern city of Hastinapur. The malice of the rival Kaurava clan was displayed as they took advantage of the eldest clan member King Yudhisthira, who was involved in a deceitful game of dice. The game of dice was an ancient game that determined the direction a person's life was taking. If a person had an honorable and virtuous life, then that would reflect in the dice or cards. But if the dice were loaded, as was the case for this game, it wouldn't matter how virtuous or deserving one was. Yudhisthira, being a man of dharma, or in accord with cosmic law and order, had never lost at dice before. The materialistic Duryodhana of the Kaurava clan was using specifically cursed dice to foil and take advantage of the Pandavas.

Yudhisthira, thus, lost his kingdom, all his brothers, himself, and even the Pandavas' common wife Draupadi as he gambled on. The Kauravas then humiliated the Pandavas and even tried to publicly disrobe Draupadi, who could only be saved by their enlightened cousin Krishna. Dhritarashtra, who was the patriarch of the Kaurava clan, realized that the game had gone too far, and, in order to prevent his son from being cursed by Draupadi, he begged him to nullify the gambling score, but Duryodhana only agreed to one more game.

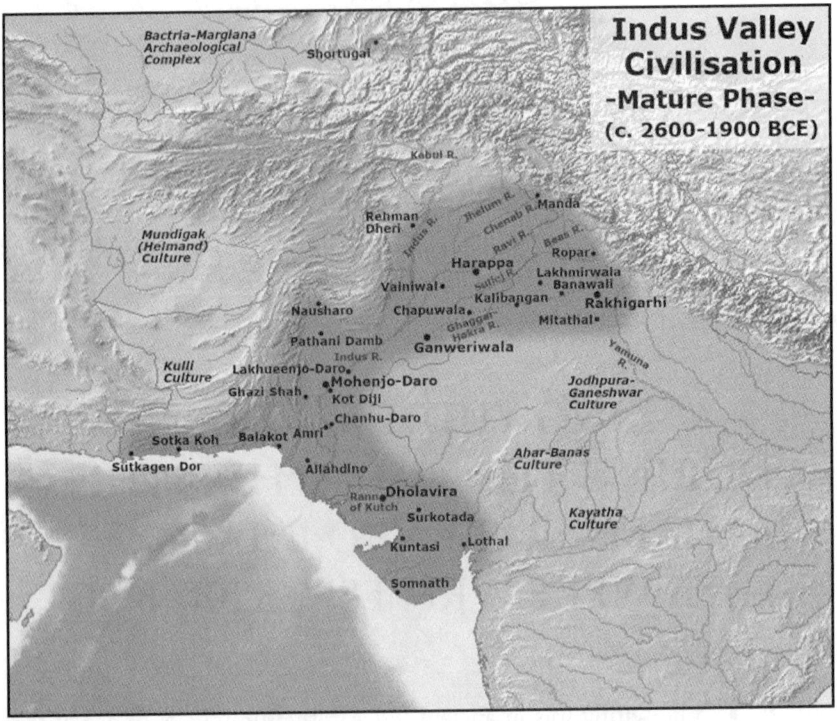

The loser would have to go into the wilderness, where he would have to stay twelve years in exile followed by one year hidden in disguise. If the other party should discover him during that year, he would forever forfeit all he had lost for the previous twelve years. As the dice were still loaded, Yudhisthira lost this game as well, and the Pandavas were driven into exile. Perhaps this is why I've never had a desire to gamble in my current lifetime! In fact, I have found no evidence of gambling throughout all the many lives I've researched. Some hard-won lessons last, not only for a lifetime, but also throughout eternity.

The story unfolds in the great literary work called the *Mahabharata,* the longest epic poem in the world and described as the longest poem ever written. About 1.8 million words in total, The *Mahabharata* is roughly ten times the length of the *Iliad* and the *Odyssey* combined, or about four times the length of the next greatest Indian epic, the *Ramayana.* The importance of the

Mahabharata to world civilization has been compared to that of the Bible, the works of Shakespeare, the works of Homer, Greek drama, or the Qur'an.

Krishna, an incarnation of the godhead, was a youthful prince and the cousin of both clans, but he was a friend and adviser to the Pandavas. Krishna was the divine incarnation in physical form of the supreme deity of Hinduism, Vishnu. He served as my brother Arjuna's mentor and later as his charioteer in the great war against the Kauravas. Within the greater work of the *Mahabharata* is the *Bhagavad Gita,* which focuses on the thoughts of Arjuna and his discussion with Krishna before the great battle of Kurukshetra. One of the great gifts for humanity to be derived from the story in the *Bhagavad Gita* are the many life lessons and philosophical insights into human behavior that are interwoven within the greater story.

I've personally found, while reading the *Mahabharata,* that it is not just another tale of endless human drama, but it is filled with a treasure trove of political wisdom, philosophical insights, and religious beatitudes, and it is an overall captivating work of literary art.

In an earlier account, it is said that, prior to the Kurukshetra War, the two heroes meet the god Vishnu after flying across oceans in Krishna's chariot. Krishna and Arjuna had both been *rishis* or wise sages together in a previous lifetime. Krishna told Arjuna that they had been brought together again to restore dharma on Earth. Vishnu then spoke and said that Krishna represented wisdom and Arjuna was action. One without the other was useless. Wisdom was useless without action, and action was useless without wisdom. You can only succeed in a battle when both are utilized in synergy.

Easily the most dramatic figure of the entire *Mahabharata,* Krishna was considered the supreme personality of the godhead himself, descended to Earth in human form to reestablish his devotees as caretakers of Earth and teach the practice of dharma. These godlike men would incarnate periodically throughout the ages in different cultures to help advance mankind.

Dharma is regarded as natural law and is a concept of central importance in Indian philosophy and religion. It is a concept that has run throughout every religion throughout time. As well as referring to law in the universal or abstract sense, dharma designates the behaviors considered necessary for the maintenance of the natural order of things. Therefore dharma may encompass ideas such as duty, vocation, religion, and everything that is considered correct, proper, or decent behavior.

The idea of dharma as duty or propriety derives from an idea found in India's ancient legal and religious texts that there is a divinely instituted natural order of things. Justice, social harmony, and human happiness require that human beings discern and live in a manner appropriate to the requirements of that order. For Krishna, there cannot be dharma without the spirit of generosity, because laws and rules are worthless without genuine love.

Once exiled to the forests, the five brothers of the Pandava clan are assisted throughout the story by various gods, sages, and Brahmins, including the great sage Krishna. During this journey, after they have lost everything, they turn within themselves for answers and learn many lessons of spiritual significance in the secluded and beautiful forests. This contrasts markedly with the Kaurava clan that is materialistic and has no dharma in the pursuit of outer pleasure and gratification. This has parallels throughout time.

Who were the five Pandava brothers and what have been their incarnations throughout time? As the eldest brother, I was Yudhisthira. The strong and powerful Bhima would be the future incarnations of Hercules and more recently General Patton. Arjuna would be the future incarnation of Alexander the Great. The twin brothers Nakula and Sahadeva are currently alive as motivational speakers and successful authors of self-help books. They have even appeared on stage together in a television special featuring their work as new age spiritual masters.

The Pandavas managed to remain undetected for the entire thirteen years and then set out to claim their rightful kingdom. They tried to find a peaceful and diplomatic way to get this accomplished, and Krishna's elder brother Balarama advised the Pandavas to send an emissary to get the support of the elders of the family. The Kauravas were brought a message saying, "Let us avoid armed conflict as much as possible. Only that which is accrued in peace is worthwhile. Out of war, nothing but wrong can issue."

While the emissary was in the Kaurava court, the Pandavas wisely began with war preparations. They realized that Duryodhana would probably not be willing to be true to his word after he had cheated and conspired against them before. They also sent messages requesting assistance to a number of neighboring kingdoms. Their ambassador of peace was insulted and turned away

by Duryodhana, who was absolutely intent on war, defying the counsel of the elders like Bhishma, who had agreed with the reasoning behind the Pandavas' proposal. After several failed attempts at peace, war seemed inevitable.

As a last attempt, Krishna traveled to the capital city of Hastinapur to persuade the Kauravas to embark upon a peaceful path with him, but, at the formal presentation of the peace proposal by Krishna at the court of Hastinapur, his peace proposals were ignored, and Duryodhana publicly ordered his soldiers to arrest Krishna. Krishna laughed and displayed his divine form, radiating intense light. The soldiers then refused to arrest Krishna and did not stand in his way as he left.

The Kurukshetra War lasted only eighteen days, eighteen conch shells were blown before the battle, the text has eighteen chapters, and eighteen groups of soldiers were involved, eleven on the side of the Kauravas and seven on the side of the Pandavas. The cross total of eighteen is nine, which in numerology is a completion number and could be a clue to this having been the end of one age and the start of another. Many sages have said that the end of the Kurukshetra War was the start of the fourth age or Kali Yuga. The Kali Yuga is supposedly the darkest age for humanity and is ended with a return to a golden age. I believe we are just entering the faint edges of a new golden age in our present day.

Kurukshetra was purposefully chosen as the battleground, because, if a sin was committed on this holy land, it was forgiven on account of the sanctity of the land. A number of ancient kingdoms would participate as allies of the rival groups, and overall each army consisted of several divisions of which the Kauravas had eleven while the Pandavas controlled seven.

Each division was under a different general, apart from the commander-in-chief, who was the head of each respective army. A division included 21,870 chariots and chariot riders, 21,870 elephants and riders, 65,610 horses and riders, and 109,350 foot soldiers, for a ratio of 1:1:3:5. The combined number of warriors and soldiers in both armies was approximately four million.

Let me give you an idea of the magnitude of the number of combatants involved. If you took *all* of the two largest military forces in the world, China and the United States, in the period of January 2014 and combined their *total* numbers, it would still be several hundred thousand shy. That is *all* the army, navy, air force, and marine personnel of both sides; if you put them all on one battlefield, plus another three hundred thousand allies, you would finally reach the four million of the Pandavas and Kauravas.

Because the Pandava army was smaller than that of the Kauravas, it relied on strategy and surprise. At various times during the Kurukshetra War, the supreme commanders of both armies ordered special formations. Each formation had specific defensive or offensive purposes as well as specific strengths and weaknesses. These battle formations had been developed on Atlantis after thousands of years of tactical warfare. Later in this chapter, I will go into more detail about the significance of the Atlantean history in regard to the events in India.

Today we know only the names of the formations and can only guess what they were exactly. My memories are that they were designed for large numbers of forces fighting in unison and displayed the shape or the characteristics of the different animals or other items they were named after. At times, it was common for animals to join forces with men to fight wars. We all know about the use of elephants and horses in warfare, but, in the course of history, almost every species of animal has become involved in some way.

The Mahabharata lists the following battle formations: heron formation, crocodile formation, tortoise or turtle formation, trident formation, wheel or discus formation, lotus formation, eagle formation, ocean formation, galaxy formation, diamond or thunderbolt formation, box or cart formation, demon formation, divine formation, needle formation, horned formation, crescent or curved blade formation, and garland formation.

Julius Caesar also mentions using the turtle formation in his commentaries, which was formed by interlocking shields on the top and along the sides. It was a defensive move inspired by the hard shell of the turtle, which protects the animals' soft inner tissue from predators, hence the name. The Korean navy also used "turtle ships" shaped like the shell of a turtle effectively from the fifteenth through the nineteenth centuries CE.

During the Kurukshetra War, the weapons used included bows and arrows, which were the weapons of choice for Arjuna and Bhishma; the mace, chosen by Bhima and Duryodhana; and the sword and the spear chosen by Yudhisthira. I have chosen the spear or lance in many lifetimes as a weapon of choice. The twins Nakula and Sahadeva were both skilled swordsmen.

Before the battle began, my brother Arjuna had misgivings on waging

war and confided his deep-seated hesitations to his chariot driver, Krishna. From their conversations within the greater work of the *Mahabharata* is the more famous and recognizable *Bhagavad Gita*. Within this particular work are described the reasons for the Kurukshetra War and the duty and honor that Arjuna would be recognized for by having fought. Krishna explains that, without the war, the barbaric actions of the Kauravas would throw the world into deeper levels of darkness that would take even more effort to overcome in future ages. This has echoes throughout history with the most recent being Nazi Germany's Third Reich.

The Kurukshetra War was characterized by numerous individual combats, as well as mass raids against entire enemy divisions. The victor or the vanquished on each day was determined, not by any territories gained, but by the number killed. This was a war to the death. The survivor would be the victor. If the text is taken to be chronologically accurate, this was one of the bloodiest wars in the history of mankind. Only a few warriors from each side would remain, meaning that close to four million combatants were killed in only eighteen days.

Indications are that many of the surrounding cities and regions of India were also involved; my estimation is that the casualty rate could have easily been as high as several million people there as well. We can tell, through recent archaeology, that more than one million people could have inhabited cities in India's ancient past. If we look at the population today, throughout the entire region, it would be well over this figure. So it is not impossible to believe that, at one time, this area was able to support these numbers as it does today.

I believe that the high number of casualties in the surrounding regions is due to the fact that their cities were attacked with nuclear weapons or, at least, something similar. I'm fully aware of the implications of this statement, and I will present substantial evidence supporting this claim. But first I want to cover more of the actual accounts in the texts. Try to keep an open mind when considering that our very distant ancestors would not have used the same terms for advanced technology that we use today, simply because we invented the terms we currently use—but maybe we were not the first to invent these technologies.

For instance, one account on the third day tells us that Bhishma arranged the Kaurava forces in the formation of an eagle with himself leading from the front, while Duryodhana's forces protected the rear. Bhishma wanted to be sure to avoid any mishap. The Pandavas countered this by using the crescent formation with Bhima and Arjuna at the head of the right and the left wings, respectively. The Kauravas concentrated their attack on Arjuna's position, whose chariot was soon covered with arrows and javelins. Arjuna, with amazing skill, built a fortification around his chariot with an unending stream of arrows from his bow. This sounds like a description of some type of force field technology that is only science fiction today, but who knows what we may come up with in the future or what is already being developed in secret?

Another fantastic story with indications of high technology occurs on the fourteenth day of the war when Ghatotkacha was summoned by Bhima to fight on the Pandava side. Invoking his magical powers, he wrought great havoc in the Kaurava army. In particular, after the battle continued on past sunset, his powers were most effective. Ghatotkacha had received the ultimate boon from Krishna that nobody in all the worlds could match his magical capabilities, except Krishna himself. So it seems that the text is referring to the use of aircraft with advanced weaponry and night-vision capability because apparently it worked better at night.

At one point in the battle, the Kaurava leader Duryodhana appealed to his best fighter, Karna, to kill Ghatotkacha as the whole Kaurava army was coming close to annihilation due to his ceaseless strikes from the air. Karna possessed a divine weapon called Indrastra, granted by the god Indra. It could be used only once, and Karna had been saving it for his archenemy Arjuna, the best Pandava fighter.

But unable to refuse Duryodhana, Karna used the Indrastra against Ghatotkacha and killed him. Ghatotkacha increased in size and fell dead on the Kaurava army, killing thousands of them. This is considered to be the turning point of the war. After his death, the Pandava counselor Krishna smiled as he considered the war to have been won for the Pandavas now that Karna no longer had a divine weapon to use in fighting Arjuna.

Another indicator of remaining Atlantean technology was that the craft was also able to singlehandedly destroy so much of the Kaurava army. Karna fired what appears to be one of the last remaining surface-to-air missiles. When Ghatotkacha's craft crashed down, it increased in size and killed thousands. It appears to have contained some type of advanced weaponry that had a tremendous blast radius when it was destroyed.

The references in the *Mahabharata* to technologically advanced flying chariots are absolutely abundant. They are referred to as the *vimanas,* and they are also mentioned throughout the Vedic epic *Ramayana,* which predates the *Mahabharata* by thousands of years. There it reads, "The Pushpaka chariot that resembles the sun and belongs to my brother was brought by the powerful Ravan; that aerial and excellent chariot going everywhere at will ... that chariot resembling a bright cloud in the sky ... and the king [Rama] got in, and the excellent chariot at the command of the Raghira rose up into the higher atmosphere."

Adding up all the different ancient sources, there were, at least, four different types of *vimanas,* some of which were said to be saucer-shaped and others like long cigar-shaped cylinders. They were also described as double-decked, circular, cylindrical aircraft with portholes and a dome. They flew with the "speed of the wind" and gave forth a "melodious sound." Ancient Indian texts on *vimanas* are so numerous that it would take several books to relate what they all have to say. The *Vaimanika Shastra,* the "treatise on *vimanas,*" has eight chapters with diagrams describing the operation of *vimanas,* including information on the steering, precautions for long flights, protection of the airships from storms and lightning, and how to switch the drive from a free energy source, which sounds like "antigravity," to "solar energy." It outlines the features of three types of aircraft, including apparatuses that could neither catch on fire nor break. It also mentions thirty-one essential parts of these vehicles and sixteen light- and heat-absorbing materials from which they were constructed.

The Vedas describe the *vimanas* as the flying chariots of the gods that they used to transport themselves not only around the skies but also to other planets. The word airplane is commonplace in Vedic literature, as you can see in the following passage from the Yajur Veda where it says, "O royal skilled engineer, construct sea-boats, propelled on water by our experts, and airplanes, moving and flying upward, after the clouds that reside in the midregion, that fly as the boats move on the sea, that fly high over and below the watery clouds. Be thou, thereby, prosperous in this world created by the Omnipresent God, and flier in both air and lightning."

In the Sanskrit Samarangana Sutradhara, it is written, "Strong and durable must the body of the *vimana* be made, like a great flying bird of light material. Inside one must put the mercury engine with its iron heating appa-

ratus underneath. By means of the power latent in the mercury, which sets the driving whirlwind in motion, a man sitting inside may travel a great distance in the sky. The movements of the *vimana* are such that it can vertically ascend and descend, movement could be accomplished by slanting forward and backward. With the help of the machines human beings can fly in the air and heavenly beings can come down to Earth."

Not far from India, in the Euphrates Valley, a Jewish ethnologist, Yonah ibn Aharon, who was conversant with all the basic dialects upon which most languages of eastern Eurasia are founded and who produced the first and only Basrai-Aramaic dictionary, discovered two remarkable documents. The oldest document is Babylonian and is believed to be seven thousand years old, forming a part of the Hakaltha, the "holy laws," and containing a passage saying, "The privilege of operating a flying machine is great. The knowledge of flight is among the most ancient of our heritages, a gift from Those Upon High. We received it from them as a means of saving many lives."

A little more than ten years ago, the Chinese discovered some Sanskrit documents in Lhasa, Tibet, and sent them to the University of Chandrigarh in Punjab, India, to be translated. There Dr. Ruth Reyna of the university found out that the documents seemed to contain directions for building interstellar spaceships. Their method of propulsion, she said, was "anti-gravitational" and was based upon a system analogous to that of *laghima,* a mysterious power of the ego existing in man's physiological makeup, "a centrifugal force strong enough to counteract all gravitational pull." According to Hindu yogis, it is this *laghima* that enables a person to levitate.

Dr. Reyna said that on board these machines, which were called *astras* by the text, the ancient Indians could have sent a detachment of men onto any planet, according to the document, which is thought to be thousands of years old. The manuscripts apparently also revealed the secret of *antima,* which is the art of becoming invisible, and *garima,* the ability to "become as heavy as a mountain of lead."

Indian scientists did not take the texts very seriously, but then they became more positive about their value when the Chinese announced that they were looking into utilizing certain parts of the data for their space program. This was one of the first instances of a government admitting to researching antigrav-

ity technology. Today, the Chinese have sent astronauts into space and safely landed them and are now close to sending astronauts to the moon. Have they been utilizing some of the ancient information in their rapid mastery of space?

The manuscripts did not explicitly say that interplanetary travel was ever made, but did mention a planned trip to the moon, though it is not clear whether this trip was actually carried out. However, the Ramayana does contain a highly detailed story of a trip to the moon in a *vimana,* or *astra,* and in fact details a battle on the moon with an airship of the Asvin. This is but a small bit of recent evidence of antigravity and aviation technology used in ancient history. Many very accomplished archaeologists, of whom Klaus Dona is a wonderful example, discovered stunning artifacts all over the world that account for a high degree of advancement, sometimes surpassing our current manufacturing abilities, and also include models of many different types of aircraft.

To really understand this ancient technology, we must go much further back in time. The Rama Empire of northern India and Pakistan developed at least fifteen thousand years ago on the Indian subcontinent and was a nation of many large, sophisticated cities, many of which are still to be found in the deserts of that area. Rama existed parallel to the Atlantean civilization, which was located in the Atlantic Ocean and ruled by "enlightened priest-kings" for thousands of years, who governed the different cities of this now sunken continent. The recent findings of a team of scientists are consistent with the theory that an extraterrestrial body impacted Earth in that area approximately 12,900 years ago.

My own past life memories reach back to Atlantis and even farther to the ancient continent of Lemuria in the Pacific Ocean. There I remember being a priest-king when humanity was still mostly spiritual and when there were no wars. Lemurian priest-kings were androgens or hermaphrodites, meaning they embodied both genders simultaneously. The shift away from the androgynous human was the beginning of the shift away from the archetypal priest-king to the warrior-king, as the balance of masculine and feminine was harder to maintain in a separated body. This conflict, unless balanced internally, was the beginning of external conflict and its resolution through war.

In her book *The Camino,* Shirley MacLaine describes a process that she recalled from a past life where she was a Lemurian androgen that split its male and female bodies in a sacred ceremony in Atlantis. I was one of the scientist

priests involved in that event. During several of my Atlantean incarnations, I was a priest-king on the island of Poseidon and later incarnated as scientist-priests, and, toward the end of Atlantis's days, I reincarnated as a warrior-king. Science and spirituality were inseparable in the earlier part of Atlantis's long history.

When the separation between the two started, the wars began. In one lifetime as a scientist-priest, I was in charge of what were called the fire crystals. These crystals had an innate intelligence and were used to power cities and run healing devices. In that lifetime, I was approached by the militaristic faction of Atlantis and was asked to use the fire crystal technology for destructive purposes. I refused, but I knew that they would eventually get control of the fire crystals and cause cataclysmic events that would destroy Atlantis, which they did.

Because the crystals had a consciousness of their own, they could not long tolerate the negativity they were being used for. Eventually a destructive force was initiated by the misappropriation of the power of the fire crystals that caused several natural disasters on the continent of Atlantis. The complete sinking of the remaining major islands as the fire crystal technologies were continually abused and ultimately followed a breaking up of the continent into several islands. I had made a vow in that lifetime that I would insert myself into future lifetimes to help mitigate the destructiveness of war. As you can tell, humanity's warlike tendencies provided the ground for many more conflicts to come where we would experience and learn much more about the possibilities and effects of warfare.

My own memories of the *vimanas* during my lifetime as Yudhisthira are that they were basically leftovers from a golden age several thousand years before when India was a colony of Atlantis. The epic *Ramayana* dates from this earlier time frame and chronicles a war with the Atlaneans when India rebelled against their oppressive rule. Toward the later days of Atlantis's history, it had been bent on tyrannical world domination by force. In that distant time, more than twelve thousand years ago, the *vimanas* were far larger and more numerous than they were during my lifetime as Yudhisthira.

Of the few remaining and workable airplanes, we had a few options available to us during the time frame of the *Mahabharata*. Most of the craft remaining were one- or two-seat models. There were only a couple of craft remaining that could hold several people for transportation purposes. The parts

and fuel were an issue for some of the models, and we had to constantly take parts from other models to keep fewer and fewer up and running.

Many of the *vimanas* were fueled by a solid propellant, whereas the more advanced ones were antigravity vehicles, which only the pilots with the most advanced psychic abilities could run. You literally ran them with your mind, and rarely were they used for combat because there were usually no weapons mounted on these vehicles, making them worthy only for transportation or as observation platforms. If your thought processes were not correct or not of an altruistic intent, the craft would not work.

An added benefit of the thought-controlled *vimanas* was they also enhanced and heightened your metaphysical capabilities. Among the feats that could be accomplished when inside a *vimana* was the ability to remotely influence other aircraft. Other powers that would manifest over time and with training were the abilities to see into other aircraft via remote viewing or to make your own craft invisible.

Very skilled pilots could even make jumps instantaneously from one location to another. Krishna was one of the few pilots that had this ability. His *vimana* was exceptional because, while it was moved by thought, it could also utilize weapon systems. To operate such a craft, you had to be a master of the physical as well as the nonphysical worlds simultaneously, because you had to maintain a certain state of mind to run the vehicles. If you got excited or angry, the vehicle would not fly. It would just hover and stand still unless you were relaxed and calm.

The movie *Firefox* featured Clint Eastwood as an American pilot who was inserted into Soviet Russia to steal an advanced aircraft. The aircraft was invisible to radar and the weapon system was controlled by thought. Believed to be science fiction at the time of its release in 1982, it is virtually a recognized reality more than thirty years later.

I remember that the central control mechanism of the mind-regulated vehicle was located under the driver's seat; you just sat down over it and communicated and guided it with your thoughts. In the fueled vehicles, you had a joystick, but all of the airplanes could also be controlled with body movements. If you tilted your body a certain way, you could maneuver the aircraft because the gyroscope mechanism under the seat could read your body move-

ments. The maneuvering capability with the joystick and gyro control made the *vimana* extremely quick in turns, flips, and twists.

Two people would often operate the planes with weapon pods, but it was not absolutely necessary to have a weapons controller as the pilot could also fire the missiles. Inside a *vimana* you would not experience any gravitational force, even if you were flying upside down or doing rapid spins. You would not be pulled or pushed a certain way, and, other than some dizziness, if you didn't focus your eyes correctly, there were no ill effects to the occupants.

The metal of some of the more advanced aircraft would change shape according to your thoughts. Watching or remembering *The Terminator* science fiction movie series can help in deriving a visual image of what I'm trying to relate. In the second movie, the Terminator robot could shape shift its liquid metal body into whatever form it needed to accomplish its mission. The aircraft I learned to fly would change shape to fit whatever mission I needed to fly. It could even change shape during flight. The metal was silver colored but could change to green if I flew close to Earth where green trees were located so that it could blend in. It could also turn blue to match the sky so that those on the ground could not see it. Because it used a free energy source, no spent fuel trails were visible.

During a long period in the jungle during our thirteen-year seclusion, we learned how to use the advanced systems that were secreted in caves. The advanced priests, or *rishis* as they were then known, lived deep within the seclusion of the jungle. They trained us in the correct techniques of mental and physical self-control that was necessary to interact with the advanced technology.

Apart from "blazing missiles," the *Mahabharata* records the use of other deadly weapons that appear to be powerful lasers. "Indra's Dart" operated via a circular "reflector." When switched on, it produced a "shaft of light" that, when focused on any target, immediately "consumed it with its power."

References to flying *vimanas* can be found in forty-one places in the Mahabharata. Of these, the air attack of the Asura king Salva on Krishna's capital Dwaraka deserves special notice. Salva had an aerial flying machine known as Saubha-pura in which he came to attack Dwaraka. He began to shower hail and missiles from the sky. As Krishna chased him, he went near the sea and landed in the high seas. Then he came back again with his flying machine

and gave a tough fight to Krishna staying about one *krosa,* approximately four thousand feet, above ground level.

In one particular exchange, Krishna is pursuing Salva in the sky, and Salva's *vimana* is made invisible in some way. Undeterred, Krishna immediately fires off a special weapon, described by him saying, "I quickly laid on an arrow, which killed by seeking out sound." This powerful weapon hit Salva's craft in the middle, so that it broke into pieces and fell into the sea. This vivid description of an air attack between flying vehicles occurs in the *Bhagavad Gita* also.

Other passages speak of things hauntingly similar to nuclear weapons carried on the *vimana:* "Gurkha, flying a swift and powerful *vimana,* hurled a single projectile charged with all the power of the universe. An incandescent column of smoke and flame as bright as ten thousand suns rose in its entire splendor ... it was an unknown weapon, an iron thunderbolt, and a gigantic messenger of death, which reduced to ashes. The entire race of the Vrishnis and the Andhakas ... the corpses were so burned as to be unrecognizable. Their hair and nails fell out; pottery broke without apparent cause, and the birds turned white. After a few hours, all foodstuffs were infected. To escape from this fire, the soldiers threw themselves in streams to wash themselves and their equipment."

This wash down with water is a standard procedure today to decontaminate personnel and equipment of radioactive fallout. One of my jobs as a sailor in the US Navy was to set up stations to decontaminate personnel and equipment with special detergents and water. I was also responsible for putting on protective clothing and monitoring and measuring the radioisotopes before and after decontamination with special Geiger counters.

"Dense arrows of flame, like a great shower, issued forth upon creation, encompassing the enemy ... a thick gloom swiftly settled upon the Pandava hosts. All points of the compass were lost in darkness. Fierce wind began to blow upward, showering dust and gravel. Birds croaked madly ... the very elements seemed disturbed. The ground shook, scorched by the terrible violent heat of this weapon. Elephants burst into flame and ran to and fro in a frenzy ... over a vast area, other animals crumpled to the ground and died. From all points of the compass, the arrows of flame rained continuously and fiercely."

Recent excavations at Mohenjo-Daro in northern India add credibility to the notion of atomic weapons use, as they revealed that this city had been

completely destroyed quite unexpectedly. There were no traces of natural disasters or wars in that area. Mohenjo-Daro was a well-planned city laid out on a grid with a plumbing system superior to those used in Pakistan and India today. They found the streets littered with "black lumps of glass."

In 1979, scientists David Davenport and Ettore Vincenti published a major clue to the Mohenjo-Daro mystery. The thousands of black lumps intrigued them, and when they analyzed them, they turned out to be fragments of pottery fused together by extreme heat. According to the scientists' updated calculations, the clay vessels had been exposed to a blast of heat measuring between 1,400 and 1,600 degrees centigrade. Davenport and Vincenti then studied the site of Mohenjo-Daro in some depth and pinpointed three distinct waves of devastation, which had spread out up to one mile from the epicenter of the explosion.

The scientists put forward a theory saying the ruins had all the marks of a nuclear explosion as they found big stratums of clay and green glass. Similar stratums of green glass could also be found in the Nevada deserts after every nuclear explosion test.

When the excavations of Harappa and Mohenjo-Daro reached the street level, they discovered skeletons scattered across the cities. Many were holding hands and were sprawled in the streets as if some instant, horrible doom had taken place. People were just lying unburied in the streets of the city. These skeletons have been found to be at least thousands of years old by traditional archaeological standards. What could have caused such a thing? Why did the bodies not decay or get eaten by wild animals? There are no apparent indications of physically violent deaths like in combat, but these skeletons are among the most radioactive ever found, on par with those at Hiroshima and Nagasaki. Other cities have been found in northern India as well that show signs of explosions of great magnitude.

One such city found between the Ganges and the mountains of Rajmahal also seems to have been subjected to intense heat. Huge masses of walls and foundations of the ancient city are fused together, literally vitrified, and since there is no indication of a volcanic eruption at Mohenjo-Daro or at the other cities, the intense heat to melt clay vessels can only be explained by an atomic blast or some other unknown weapon. These cities were wiped out entirely.

While the skeletons have been carbon dated to 2500 BCE, we must keep in mind that carbon dating is based on measuring the amount of radiation

remaining after it decays or is lost over time. When atomic explosions are involved, massive amounts of radiation are left over. This makes highly radioactive sites seem much younger than they actually are.

Another example in the area of Rajasthan, India, features an area of three square miles covered in radioactive ash. Researchers began to test the area after locals were experiencing a high rate of birth defects and cancer. The levels of radiation they found were so high that Indian officials quarantined the entire area.

Archaeologists have since found evidence of an ancient city that, between 12000 and 8000 BCE, could have supported approximately half a million people. This fits in with my idea that the *Ramayana* also depicts a nuclear war with Atlantis before the cataclysmic sinking of that continent and the wiping out of Rama with atomic weapons. Only at some point after this nuclear war did the world collapse into what mainstream scholars see as the final period of the Stone Age. Archaeological evidence suggests that atomic explosions during the war between the Atlanteans and the Ramans destroyed a lot of their progress, which was later followed by another setback after the Kurukshetra War.

In the years that followed the war, Dhritarashtra, his queen, Gandhari, and Kunti, the mother of the Pandavas, lived a life of asceticism in a forest retreat and died with yogic calm in a forest fire. Krishna departed from Earth thirty-six years after the war. A hunter, who mistook him for a deer, shot him in his one vulnerable spot, his foot. Yudhisthira had been crowned king of Hastinapur at the end of the war and renounced the throne after ruling for thirty-six years, passing the crown on to Arjuna's grandson Parikshit.

When they learned of Krishna's departure, the Pandavas believed it was time for them to also leave this world, so they embarked upon the "Great Journey," which involved walking north toward the polar mountain that is toward the heavenly worlds, until one's body dropped dead. Yudhisthira thus left for the Himalayas with Draupadi and his brothers in what was to be their last journey.

One by one Draupadi and the younger Pandavas died along the way until Yudhisthira was left alone with a dog that had followed him all the way. Yudhisthira made it to the gate of heaven and there refused the order to drive the dog back, at which point the dog was revealed to be an incarnate form of the god Dharma who was Yudhisthira's actual physical father and who was there to test Yudhisthira's virtue.

Once in heaven, Yudhisthira faced one final test of his virtue, when he was shown only the Dhritarashtra clan in heaven and told that his brothers were in hell. He insisted on joining his brothers in hell, if that were the case. It was then revealed that they really were in heaven and that this illusion had been one final test for him.

I have no memories of this final part of the story and believe it to be an artistic flourish. A hero's ascension is a common theme in legends and religious stories. Ascension is a possibility for everyone, however. The real stories of ascension are often not so colorful and obvious as we would like to believe.

In 1815 the British army used a secret weapon called "rockets" in the Battle of Waterloo against the French army of Napoleon. They had learned firsthand of these terrible weapons while fighting in India. The Indians had used the weapons with great success against the British, who didn't quite understand them and were not nearly as effective. Where did the Indians learn their rocket technology?

Julius Robert Oppenheimer (April 22, 1904-February 18, 1967) was an American theoretical physicist and professor of physics at the University of California, Berkeley. He is often called the "father of the atomic bomb" for his role in the Manhattan Project, the World War II project that developed the first nuclear weapons. The first atomic bomb was detonated on July 16,1945, in the Trinity test in New Mexico. Oppenheimer remarked later that it brought to mind words from the Bhagavad Gita: "Now I am become Death, the destroyer of worlds."

Later, a student asked Oppenheimer, "How do you feel after having exploded the first atomic bomb on Earth?" His reply was, "Not the first atomic bomb, but the first atomic bomb in modern times." Oppenheimer strongly believed that nuclear weapons were used in ancient India.

Fact can be stranger than fiction at times. I hope that you are beginning to see that these are not stories that I randomly dreamed up. I'm a very centered and rational thinker who is a truth seeker, so making up casual stories for sensationalism would be abhorrent to me. I stake my reputation on these revelations, and I do my utmost to keep them well- researched and accurate.

Why share this particular incarnation? As I've mentioned, it is a major turning point in human history. A further sinking into the abyss would need players that would soften the trauma of an event. I will often do this throughout history—be at key points in history along with members of my soul group.

We have, throughout time, lessened the potential severity of many negative events' magnitude or would hold back the tide in barbarism. I am a harmonizing soul that incarnates into out-of-balance environments to help humanity achieve or maintain its poise and equilibrium.

It will become apparent in my outline of future incarnations that this particular life as Yudhisthira is a landmark lifetime that set the stage for future lifetimes. A thread of our many incarnations exists within each one of our lives. The sum total of all of our lives comes together in our "now-life" to shape the mortal cloth we currently wear. I will eventually incarnate as Ananda, cousin and supporter of Buddha in the same area of India as this life, and, then again, as Ashoka the Great, who would unify India and spread Buddhism. The center of the flag of India today has the symbol of Ashoka's chakra, which symbolizes dharma. Remember that Yudhisthira's life symbolized righteousness or dharma.

Buddha, who remembered all of his past lives and the lives of those around him, could also see into the future lives of people he met. He once told Ananda that he would either ascend or be the first king of a united India. I guess I chose to be king over ascension. By doing so, I helped spread the work and ideas of Buddha through Buddhism. Ashoka's life is an interesting one of conflict, battles, and romance, but such is life. I will share Ananda's story in a later chapter in this book and Ashoka's in a follow-up book.

The *Mahābhārata* is the longest epic poem known and has been described as "the longest poem ever written. It narrates the struggle between two groups of cousins in the Kurukshetra War and the fates of the Kaurava and the Pāndava princes and their successors. It also contains philosophical and devotional material, such as a discussion of the four 'goals of life' or *purusārtha*."

The *Bhagavad Gita* is set in a narrative framework of a dialogue between Pandava prince Arjuna and his guide and charioteer Krishna, the Supreme Personality of Godhead. At the start of the Dharma Yuddha (righteous war) between Pandavas and Kauravas, Arjuna is preoccupied by a moral dilemma and despair about the violence and death the war will cause in the battle against his kin.

Mohenjo-daro has a planned layout with rectilinear buildings arranged on a grid plan. Most were built of fired and mortared brick; some incorporated sun-dried mud-brick and wooden superstructures. The covered area of Mohenjo-daro is estimated at 300 hectares. Regularity of streets and buildings suggests the influence of ancient urban planning in Mohenjo-daro's construction.

The Trinity test of the Manhattan Project was the first detonation of a nuclear weapon, which led Robert Oppenheimer to recall verses from the Hindu scripture *Bhagavad Gita*: "If the radiance of a thousand suns were to burst at once into the sky, that would be like the splendor of the mighty one ... I am become Death, the destroyer of worlds."

Krishna is worshipped as the eighth avatar of Vishnu and also as the Supreme god in his own right. He is the god of protection, compassion, tenderness, and love; and is one of the most popular and widely revered among Indian divinities.

The massive Pushpaka vimāna is seen flying across the sky. Vimāna are mythological flying palaces or chariots described in Hindu texts and Sanskrit epics.

"PAST LIFE REGRESSION IS CONSIDERED ONE OF THE MOST POWERFUL TOOLS AVAILABLE FOR TRANSFORMATION IN THE FIELDS OF INTEGRATIVE MEDICINE, PSYCHOLOGY, AND SELF-AWARENESS."

◊ *International Association for Regression Research & Therapies* ◊

CHAPTER 2

HOW TO ACCESS YOUR PREVIOUS INCARNATIONS

An October 19, 2010, radio show and poll about reincarnation on *Coast to Coast AM* with host George Noory indicated that 55.47 percent of 8,446 people surveyed believed that we all experience a succession of lives to advance and grow. There were 26.13 percent who felt that intriguing evidence for past lives existed, but were not fully convinced though still open to other explanations. Only 18.4 percent felt that reincarnation was just a made-up concept and that there was no real proof for it at all.

It has to be taken into account that *Coast to Coast* revolves around information and topics that are beyond the mainstream with an audience that is generally rather open-minded, but, since it is one of the biggest radio shows on the planet with more than 3.5 million listeners per week, I would assert that the poll results are significant and a close representation of the overall view on reincarnation. Over half of those polled unequivocally know about or believe in the transmigration of the soul, over a quarter are nearly convinced, and less than a fifth have not yet discovered enough information to side with this idea. So we see that over 80 percent of people are generally going along with the idea of reincarnation.

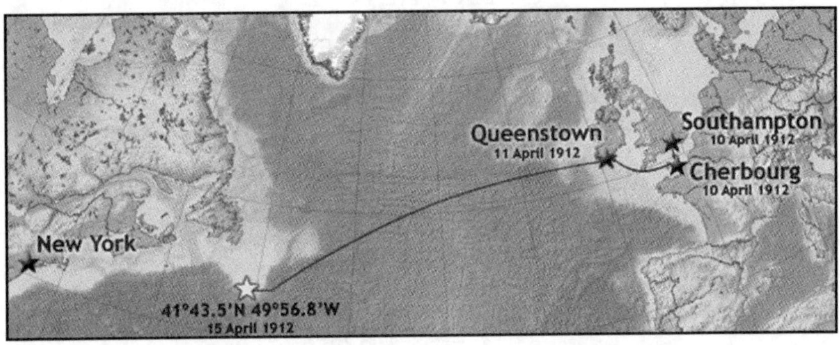

I feel that never before has it been as important to acknowledge and integrate the reality of past lives and reincarnation into our current awareness. Fragments left in other lifetimes leave unresolved issues and need to be brought to the surface so that they can be solved. By connecting with past lives and settling issues, we become whole and non-fragmented. When we clear past karma and resolve karmic debts, we can connect with our true soul essence. Karma refers to the energy created as a result of our actions and relationships during our current and past lives.

Karmic debt refers to entanglements, whether in this life or previous lives, that must be addressed, brought to a conclusion, and released. This release can happen in the present or at some point in the future, but they must be addressed before you can release the effects on your soul. Once karma is released you can continue on to enjoy your life more fully and freely. My own view of karmic debts is that they are simply life lessons that continue to manifest to us in one form or another life after life, until we learn what it is we need to balance our energies and then move forward. For instance, I once read of a past life regression wherein the soul lived through one thousand incarnations before the person worked through the negative emotion of jealousy.

We can also tap into information and skills at a more rapid pace once we consciously connect with past life abilities that we have developed over many lifetimes. A proclivity for any endeavor that we choose could be because we are tapping into the potential of formerly developed capabilities. By accepting this possibility, we can even further accelerate our development in any given venture.

Between incarnations we usually take time to review the life we've just lived. Every word, every deed, and every thought from every life is recorded

and can be reviewed. The information for all of our lives is contained within the akashic records *(akasha* is a Sanskrit term meaning sky or ether). These records are described as containing all knowledge of human experience and the history of the cosmos. They are metaphorically described as a library; other analogies commonly found in discourse on the subject include a "universal supercomputer" and the "mind of God."

People who describe the records assert that they are being constantly updated automatically and that they can be accessed between lives *and* in our current lives. People who are trained or gifted can access the information in the akashic records from our present dimension. To train in this yourself, you need to get into a meditative state and be open to the images and scenes that may come to you, if you request and venture to see them. It is a highly demanding challenge to finally get to the point where one is sufficiently stalwart and composed to really open one's intuition and look into the past without bias or blinders, and even into our possible timelines for the future.

It is mostly the conscious or subconscious aversion toward the intense emotional upheaval that blocks the average human today from looking into all that right away, this and the disregard or the distrust in the existence of one's direct connection to the akashic records. To bring yourself into a position where you can access them on your own, you must know that it is your divine right to do so, and be intent to look at the truth, whatever it is you may find. Really setting out on this endeavor is not to be taken lightly, and be assured that there are guides that you can call on to help you. In essence, the steps on your journey have to be taken by yourself, but there will always be help along the way.

This help can come in the form of your personal guardian angels or other entities. For some people, communication with them is realized more naturally and easily than the establishment of an immediate connection to the akashic records, and that is fine also. In any case, whether you choose to directly access the living library or if you choose to ask somebody to read it to you, discernment is always key. Be vigilant and prudent when scrutinizing information that comes to you in whatever way or form.

Sometimes the influx of such information can come rather unexpectedly, as the case of Suzanne Ward shows. For most of her life, she never had any particular interest or training in the metaphysical, yet currently she has

written several books that deal with the afterworld and what we do and experience in that realm. Her books and messages contain information gleaned from her son Matthew, who died in an accident at age seventeen. It was relayed to her independently by several different psychics after her son's death that he was still observing her and would talk to her telepathically at some point.

Suzanne was particularly impressed by the amount of personal information brought forward by the psychics that they could not possibly have known or come up with on their own, but it was only fourteen years after Matthew's physical death that the predictions really manifested. Since then Matthew and Suzanne have communicated over many things, beginning with his experiences in the afterworld, which she has shared in many excellent books. Matthew relates that the correct term for heaven is nirvana, and he also shares information about what we can all expect to encounter in that environment between lives. Of course it has to be noted that simply because one is physically deceased and dwelling in the heavenly abode, this doesn't mean that one's discernment is suddenly impeccable. As above, so below; just as we are in a learning process while in human form, so is everybody in other realms, but their insights from their vantage points can surely be a great inspiration and guide stones.

There are also living human helpers who can assist you in getting into the meditative state necessary to access your past lives. For instance, in his books *Journey of Souls: Case Studies of Life Between Lives* and *Destiny of Souls: New Case Studies of Life Between Lives,* Michael Newton, a hypnotherapist who has worked with subjects in deep meditative states, has collected many accounts of the akashic records or the "Book of Life." Another renowned practitioner in this field is Dolores Cannon, author of *Between Death and Life* and *The Convoluted Universe,* who found herself very surprised in the early phase of her work as a hypnotherapist in the 1960s when her clients were bringing up memories from previous lifetimes, sometimes not even as a human on this planet, all of which was completely unfamiliar to her back then. But unlike some of her colleagues, she would continue with the therapy. This is a virtue of any good therapist and past life regressionist—to assist and protect the client along his way through the vastness of his memories so that potentially unsettling memories may be processed constructively without any negative effects on the present life of the client.

Integrating and growing through the awareness of the vast information pool available to us is at the core of our evolution and applying the knowledge one can gather in a responsible and sagacious way are what it takes to live this knowledge into wisdom and to consciously expand our awareness through the myriad levels of existence. We can then truly realize the interconnectedness of everything, not merely as an idea that one is sympathetic of, but as a very distinctly experienced reality. In most religions, heaven is a realm in which we exist on a higher dimensional level, a plane of existence that is, of course, different from our three-dimensional reality in which we abide while we are incarnated on Earth.

It is from this other plane of existence that we usually review the impact of everything we did in our previous life after the death of our physical container, or even during our current lifetime when we tap into higher states of consciousness. Because both planes are permanently interwoven, you don't have to die physically to connect to other levels of existence. You can also do it by intentionally changing your focus, which sounds very simple but actually takes a tremendous amount of inner discipline.

Another possible and rather harsh way to connect to the higher realms of existence is the near-death experience. There is a massive amount of congruent and independent documentation on the specifics of those experiences, clearly indicating that there is a very substantial reality behind them. One of the researchers who was inspired by such an experience was Betty J. Eadie, who has written several books that offer excellent insight into the life between lives. I read her book *Embraced by the Light* many years ago when it was first released and was deeply inspired by the account of her near-death experience and interactions in heaven where she reviewed her life. There she realized that not only her deeds but also her thoughts affected those around her and their lives in different ways depending on whether her thoughts and deeds were positive or negative. Betty explains how this creates a ripple effect, where we affect the people around us, and, in turn, they affect the people that they interact with, and, in turn, those people affect the people that they interact with ad infinitum.

Throughout this chapter, I've already given clues about the attitude necessary to connect with previous lifetimes and the akashic records right now, and I also mentioned concrete ways to accomplish this. To condense and summarize it now, I have broken it down into three categories that can be used individually or together, in any order or combination. It's the process that I used for confirming and investigating my own past life incarnations.

Intuitively exploring your own past life memories and connections.
Contacting a reputable psychic or trance channel.
Past life regression, PLR, sessions with a certified PLR practitioner.

First of all, try to connect with a historical period that you have been drawn to in your current lifetime. It can be anything from a few years before your birth to very ancient times. As a small boy, I was always drawn to World War II. I would be glued to the television or any movie about this topic. Now that I have learned that my most previous incarnation before this one was during World War II, I can see why I had the strong connection to that period. I was curious how it turned out because I died before the end of the war. Over time, as this curiosity was satisfied, I moved on to other periods of time I was always fascinated with, among them Egypt, Greece, and Rome. And again, through reconnecting with past lives, I began to understand where the pronounced interest for these eras came from.

Once you recognize a connection with a time period, contemplate what most fascinates you about it. Look at pictures from that time period. Do an Internet search and just let whatever comes up that interests you lead you along a path of discovery. Now that I know about particular past incarnations, what I often find is that, when I read articles and books about the relating epochs or do research on the Internet, I find myself either nodding my head in agreement or shaking my head in disagreement to certain events described. Often I don't have any logical explanation for why I agree or disagree until much further research. It has become kind of fun to get these intuitive flashes that go against the academically recognized and taught history about certain events and to have them later justified.

One occasion where this has happened to me was when I immediately felt very certain about the fact that Pharaoh Tutankhamun was actually the son of Pharaoh Akhenaten. On some level, I just *knew* it, and I said for years that they were genetically related as son and father, even though no proof existed. But it has now become a recognized fact through DNA sampling that this is indeed the case. I have no doubt that much of what I speak of throughout this book that is not currently accepted as fact or part of the established history will

eventually be proven sound. Perhaps some of the information in this book will even motivate others to do further studies on their own. By allowing yourself to be guided by your intuition and your past life connections you may also find similar proofs as I did and uncover more yet unestablished historical facts.

You may have experienced a connection with an event in time where the official account of it didn't quite seem right to you. Over a period of time, new evidence may have come out about that time frame that really got your attention. New revelations may have provided for an "aha" moment, helping you to fully connect with the actual reality and giving you a sense of relief.

I believe that James Cameron's 1997 epic romance and disaster film *Titanic* had exactly that effect on hundreds of millions of people who watched it. The movie is based on a fictionalized account of the sinking of the RMS Titanic that sank after hitting an iceberg on its ill-fated maiden voyage across the Atlantic from Britain to America. The movie *Titanic* was an enormous critical and commercial success; it was nominated for fourteen Academy Awards, eventually winning eleven, including those for best picture and best director. It became the highest-grossing film of all time with a worldwide gross of over $1.8 billion—the first film to reach the billion dollar mark—and remained so for twelve years until *Avatar,* again directed by James Cameron, surpassed it in 2010.

Production on the film began in 1995 when Cameron shot footage of the actual *Titanic* wreck. A reconstruction of the ship was built at Playas de Rosarito, Baja California, for filming purposes. I remember passing by this site on my way down to Rosarito beach restaurants from my home in Coronado, California, where I was stationed as a Navy SEAL at that time. The grilled and fried lobster was deliciously amazing, and at the time the beachside restaurants were little known or discovered.

I would marvel at the scale models of the *Titanic* as I passed by during the day on the coastal Mexican highway and wondered excitedly what the highly anticipated movie would reveal. On my return trip to San Diego, I would again pass by the dark mock-up of the ship under a clear starry night sky. I tried to get an image of what it must have been like on that sinking ship long ago under a similar starry sky with the orchestra playing on deck as the cold dark waters of the Atlantic relentlessly rose up the sides of the vessel. What must have gone through those people's minds?

Apart from the scale models, computer-generated imagery was also used to re-create the sinking for the film, and, before its worldwide release, several documentaries described how the *Titanic* had broken up when it sank. Scientific proof and analysis of why the unsinkable ship had sunk and what had happened to the metal structure as it sat on the bottom of the cold Atlantic were all covered, much of which had not been generally known previous to that. The depiction of the sinking in the movie promised to be historically accurate with never-before-seen footage of the *Titanic* on the bottom of the ocean.

My thoughts are that many of us had been incarnate during the sinking of the *Titanic* and that we had never been fully satisfied with why the ship had sunk. I don't mean to imply that we were all passengers, although some were, but that we were part of the vast humanity that was shocked and mystified at reading or hearing about the tragedy during that lifetime. That feeling of unresolved trauma that we had intensely felt for the victims of the *Titanic* carried over for many of us into this life.

I even know of one young man named Evan Justyn whom I met through my website for *The Intuitive Warrior.* Evan was a student at the College of Charleston, South Carolina, who contacted me to express his admiration for the book. Evan was extremely interested in becoming a Navy SEAL, and, in the process of mentoring him, we have become good friends.

Not surprisingly it was Evan's mother, Daria Justyn, who initially gave Evan the book, thinking that he would connect with the powerful message of how we can use the positive power of intuition and love in every situation in life including war. Daria is a successful intuitive and author of the beautifully written book *Angels Whisper to Us: Decoding the Messages in Daydreams* and she had me on as a guest speaker in 2010 on her popular BlogTalkRadio show *Medium in Our Midst,* where we discussed the power of intuition.

Like many women who are connected with their intuitive side and have come across my book, Daria believed that the book would help create a bond of common interest between herself and Evan, because Daria felt that Evan's own advanced intuitive abilities would not be crushed by becoming a warrior if he connected with the information in the book. I believe Daria is correct, and, if Evan decides to pursue a Special Forces career, he will bring a level of intuitive skill that will help in the transformation of humanity from one focused on war to one of peace.

During a conversation one day at a seafood restaurant in historic Charleston, Evan told me how ironic it was for him to be interested in becoming a Navy SEAL. I will let Evan describe his fascinating story and how events unfolded that led him to the realization that he was one of the passengers on the actual *Titanic* who died on that fateful night.

"Up until I was three years old, whenever I was speaking, no one could understand anything that I was attempting to say. My mother, Daria, claimed it sounded like a foreign language. She took me to see speech therapists that ended up having me doing ridiculous things like blowing bubbles, but to no avail. She would just sit there and cry as this happened.

"One day when I was about three and a half years old, my mother and I were driving over a canal bridge in Point Pleasant, New Jersey. While we were driving over the bridge, I looked down at the water, and I said to her as clear as could be, 'I fell off the bridge and drowned, but I was the daddy that time.' Those were the first intelligible words I ever spoke. From that moment on, I spoke clear enough as a child of that age to be understood with no problem. Growing up I also had a tremendous fear of water. When I was an infant, anytime my mother attempted to wash my head, I would scream. Later, when I was a toddler, I was afraid to sit down in the bathtub and was terrified to get my head washed or let water be poured over it. As I grew a bit older, my family got an aboveground pool, and I would go so far as to go up the ladder but refused to get off of it and go into the water. I was quite happy just letting my toes dangle in the water.

"During this time, my great-grandfather was still alive and living with my grandmother. He had a subscription to *National Geographic* magazine, which he loved to share with me. One day the shipwreck of the *Titanic* appeared on the cover of an issue that featured information on how they had developed the technology to find the *Titanic* and what they had uncovered there since. From that point, I became completely obsessed with anything that had to do with the *Titanic.* There was also a documentary my grandmother had taped for me about the discovery of the *Titanic,* and I would spend my time watching it over and over. This was all quite mysterious, but a major piece of the puzzle fell into place when my mother held the copy of that particular issue of the *National Geographic* in her hands; that was the first time in her life that she saw actual images from the *Titanic.* She immediately made the connection that it wasn't a

bridge over water I had fallen off of, but the bridge of the *Titanic.*

"We lived around the corner from the library. We spent a lot of time there because my mother taught art classes there. I got to know all of the librarians and they knew me, because I had requested every book in the Ocean County library system on the *Titanic* shipwreck. In fact, I would go over to all the libraries whenever I would get a chance searching for anything on the *Titanic* I hadn't seen before. It was because of my obsession with the *Titanic* that almost every librarian knew me by my first name.

"Eventually, James Cameron's *Titanic* came out in theaters. I was about ten years old at the time, and my family managed to get tickets to see it on opening night. Unfortunately I do not remember anything of that experience nor of the rest of the night. I am told that I sat there physically motionless throughout the whole movie and that I didn't say a single word. That night I got into bed, and, when my mom came into my room to say good-night, as always I was already half asleep and somewhat dreaming. She tucked me in and asked me what I thought about the movie. She says I replied, 'The rooms were much smaller than they appeared in the movie.'

"She also said that I pulled on the collar of my pajamas and said, 'Those collars felt really stiff and were tight around my neck.' Following this statement, I just kind of shivered, maybe picking up on how cold it was on the voyage. Asking my mom about it now, what struck her most about my responses to how I felt about the movie was that they seemed like something I really experienced as opposed to something I had only seen on the movie screen.

"One other important factor during all of this was that I had some horrible problems with my lungs as a child. I had serious asthma and had to have a portable inhaler for when I woke up in the middle of the night struggling to breathe. It wasn't until the time that the movie came out and I started getting adjusted by a chiropractor that it cleared up and disappeared. I have not had lung problems since nor had to use an inhaler to help me breathe."

Evan's testament is just one out of many examples illustrating the significant influence that events from past lives can wield in our present lifetime. When we connect with past life traumas, we can then proceed to release the hold they have on us in our current life, which is one of the values of connecting with past lives. Fortunately for Evan, his mother was open, patient, caring,

and, best of all, a gifted intuitive who was able to help him work through the past life trauma that was influencing him in his current incarnation.

I personally remember, as a teenager in the mid-1970s, going with my mom to our local museum in Columbia, South Carolina, to see the *Titanic* exhibit that was traveling around the country. We were both very excited. We were in awe of the artifacts from the wreck, as well as the videos that showed the ship being built and the launch of the maiden voyage. Decades later and several years after the movie came out, there was an even more comprehensive exhibit, and synchronistically Evan had visited it. He shared with me another insight into a further release that he had after he experienced his release that came with watching the movie *Titanic*. The new exhibit was very realistic and to scale with the original ship's dimensions; it also held more actual artifacts recovered from the wreck itself.

"I was fortunate to go to the new *Titanic* exhibit that's been touring the country. It was on *Ghost Hunters* due to some of the artifacts being haunted, and it's currently one of the world's largest collections of *Titanic* artifacts.

"I went with my mother, and it was cool, but it also felt very strange at the same time. The exhibit plays a little game with you when you buy your ticket to get in. They give you a replica of a real-life ticket with an actual passenger's name and information on it. My ticket was a man who had been on a book tour throughout Europe and was on his way back to America with his wife in second class.

"I think my mother's character was a woman in first class and the second richest person on the ship. When you get to the end, they have a huge passenger manifesto with people by name and class split into two categories, as perished with the ship or survived. Unfortunately my guy died, but, in the iceberg room, there was a quote from him on a banner that his wife, who survived the sinking, had disclosed to reporters. He told her, 'For the love of God, it's the last lifeboat! Get on it.' This really impressed me.

"The whole exhibit was absolutely astonishing; they had it set up as a gigantic ship. I believe they had the original companies who built the rooms for the *Titanic* build the rooms for the exhibit. You walked onto a reconstructed dock, then through steerage, second class, first class, the sun decks, and so on. They also had the iceberg room where they made a huge block of ice you could touch to feel how cold it was in the water. The interesting part about this is that saltwater has a lower freezing point than freshwater. The water the *Titanic* sank in was saltwater, which means that in order for the iceberg not to melt, the water had to be below freezing. Just touching the iceberg sent shivers through my spine. Not the best of feelings.

The entire time you are in the exhibit you are surrounded by objects brought up from the wreckage. Many of the artifacts are perfectly preserved since the area on the ocean floor was so cold, dark, and under enormous pressure. A suit with original stitching, a glass jug that still had cooking oil in it, a leather fanny pack filled with experimental perfume that still had scents to it, and a steamer trunk the size of a fridge were all perfectly preserved and on display.

I honestly did not know what to expect while traveling to this exhibit. I was excited but at the same time I was pretty quiet during the car ride. It felt like I was going back to a traumatic event, so I didn't really know how I would react or what to expect. Going through the whole re-created ship and seeing everything in its original state felt like looking at old items you once had. You could sense that emotions were very subdued in the re-created Titanic; it was very quiet instead of it being like a regular museum with comparatively high energy and people talking.

It was very fascinating for me to experience how, in certain parts of the museum, I was struggling to breathe and had to stand still for a few minutes. In the end I felt like I needed it. It was like the sheer act of going through all this lifted a weight off of me. I got the feeling that a lot of the other visitors experienced something similar there, too. It gave me a lot of closure, and I felt that many people were affected in a very similar way."

My thoughts are that Evan's mother was his daughter in the *Titanic* lifetime. He lovingly saw her off in safety and was not able to rejoin her and went down with the ship. In their current life, she has returned the love by bringing him safely into this world and helping him overcome the trauma of the *Titanic*'s sinking that he carried through into this lifetime.

I believe that, at different times throughout our lives, we are all affected by past life traumas. They can manifest in many different aspects of our lives, whether it is in relationships or business dealings, or among siblings or parents. We will often switch roles from one life to the next in order to learn and grow in wisdom. As one example, there could be a mother in one life becoming the

daughter in the next life and vice versa, as is the case with my wife, Tracy Jo, and her daughter, Christy, who had opposite roles in a previous life. When you closely examine it, you can see the justification for this role reversal, the challenges that are presented, and the lessons that can be learned by both parties.

Virtually any issues or traumas that were experienced in previous lives can be rectified and released in our current life, as we have seen through the example of Evan and his mother, Daria. Fortunately Daria was open and lovingly supportive of the idea that Evan was possibly being affected by a previous incarnation.

Often synchronistic events will show up, like Evan's grandfather showing him the *National Geographic* magazine and documentary video that sparked an intense curiosity in Evan. Another powerful syn- chronicity was Daria making the connection with Evan and the *Titanic* when she picked up the same *National Geographic* magazine that had so mesmerized Evan. If we open up to the idea that there really can be an influence on our current life ensuing from past lives, then we can heal from these events and move on to more productive lives. A mysterious or an unusual connection to historical times, cultures, and geographical locales that attract an unusual amount of interest from us can be possible connections with past life times.

Imagine where Evan would possibly be today if he had not experienced the release of the trauma of his death during the sinking of the *Titanic.* He would most probably not even think of going to Navy SEAL training. He might also suffer from inexplicable anxieties as well. I believe that Evan could find even further release if he could find out who he actually was on the *Titanic.* I'm sure that from the several clues he has gotten over the years that he may be close.

After the tremendous successes of the movie *Titanic,* many people were finally ready to let go of the fear and confusion that had held the collective consciousness for more than eighty years. James Cameron provided a tremendous gift and service to humanity by making this film. At least hundreds of millions of people have now seen it, and the veils of mystery and confusion are finally being lifted. The ghosts that have haunted so many are quietly fading and drifting away to a much- deserved rest.

The second thing I would recommend for connecting with the idea of past lives is to contact a reputable psychic or advanced Reiki practitioner who specializes in past life therapy in your area. You can often find out about a good psychic by asking others who have visited a local psychic or Reiki practitioner. Internet searches are good as well and will often contain reviews and recommendations. Many books on reincarnation contain stories of how people have begun past life awareness through psychics. Intuitive individuals have helped people connect with their past lives through their readings, catalyzing a psychological release or opening the door to fascinating discoveries. Often psychics and trance channels will be mentioned and referenced by name, location, and contact information in these books. This is how I got in contact with Kevin Ryerson, whose information and website I found in an excellent book called *Return of the Revolutionaries: The Case for Reincarnation and Soul Groups Reunited* by Dr. Walter Semkiw. Kevin Ryerson's own work and insights are contained in his book *Spirit Communication: The Soul's Path,* which I still find invaluable and refer to often.

Kevin is a trance channel, who works in cooperation with Ahtun Re, an Ascended Master from ancient Egypt. Ahtun Re is an interesting character and will often ask what you are feeling and what your thoughts are for a particular lifetime, when he accesses information from his location in the higher dimensional spirit world. He is not always forthcoming in revealing information, but Kevin believes that in our sessions he has been revealing an unusual amount of information to support me with my work that is dedicated to helping enlighten and empower humanity. Ahtun Re will usually either confirm your intuitive insights or redirect you to what actually happened and what your relationship was to a particular time frame or historical figure. This procedure helped me substantially with uncovering my memories from many different lifetimes, as you will be able to see throughout this book.

Once you've decided to contact an intuitive to give you a past life reading, find out if the person will record your session or if you will need to provide a recording device. Kevin Ryerson, who lives more than one thousand miles from me, fortunately does his readings over the phone and recommends you record your own session. If the person doing the reading will record the reading, I recommend that you still use or bring your own device as a backup. You will definitely want a recording of your reading so that you can refer back to it. Often the information provided can be overwhelming in its revelations and you may miss valuable dialogue as you ponder some profound point that has been revealed to you.

I still refer often to my recorded past life sessions to gather clarity and

further information that I have missed or did not fully grasp. Some of my recordings are now over a decade old, and I still receive insights from them.

I remember the first time, many years ago, when I learned that I was incarnate during the lifetime of Jesus and had actually interacted very closely with him during his final ministry. I was astonished when I initially heard it, but, on a deeper level, I *knew* it was correct. As I drove back to my place in Virginia Beach after my first-ever psychic reading from Mary Roach, I was in tears for much of the drive. My initial past life regressions had the same effect. When you are reconnecting with very intense, long-lost, and often suppressed emotions, you will likely have some powerful releases. These releases are very rewarding because they unravel pent-up energies.

A release will often be followed by a clarity that can bring forward a powerful flood of past life memories and deeper understandings of the nature of your own existence. I have often felt a deep gratitude for connecting with my own past lives. On many occasions, I've experienced a profound sense of joy and awe upon finding new revelations of past life recall. Like all new experiences that are of an emotional nature, you gradually condition to the release of information. I'm rarely shocked by the magnitude of revelations that come forth these days, and I've found that allows even more material to come through.

The third thing I recommend that you can do to connect with past life memories is to contact a person that does past life regression therapy. Arguably one of the most famous past life regression (PLR) practitioners is Dr. Brian L. Weiss, the author of *Same Soul, Many Bodies* and *Many Lives, Many Masters.* He has written numerous excellent books that I can really recommend if you are going to consider PLR research. He has also produced several very effective meditations CDs that can help you get into a meditative state to do your own PLRs. Dr. Weiss also does seminars all over the world but is unfortunately unavailable for personal PLR sessions; however, he does group regressions during his seminars.

After several years of searching for the right PLR practitioner, I came across some information that listed certified PLR practitioners throughout the United States. I searched for someone in my area, and that's how I found Rebecca Shaw of the Charleston Hypnotherapy Center in Charleston, South Carolina. I would later learn that Rebecca and I had crossed paths in previous lives, and, to be quite honest, such synchronicities aren't even so much of a surprise to me anymore; they're rather something to be expected once you really set out to uncover the mysteries of life and to work for the highest and best good of all. The universe has magnificent ways to let things fall into place when you align with this greater focus. So having found someone that I had worked with in previous lives to help me uncover past life memories now makes perfect sense to me. My first few sessions were absolutely amazing and were far more than I had expected. I had vivid recall of my past lives under regression. PLR works because you go through a deep, guided meditation process that allows the intuitive side of the brain to fully come forward. Once you are deeply regressed you are able to open the door to any past life. Rebecca was very intuitive in this whole process and guided me into several lifetimes during many sessions that revealed an amazing amount of information.

I was fortunately guided expertly under deep meditation, and, because Rebecca is very intuitive and aware, she was able to help me gather much of the information for this book. In my first couple of sessions, I had a very strong emotional response. I had tears streaming down my face, but I learned to allow these emotions to surface and dissipate more easily with multiple PLR sessions. I was also more open to allow information to surface as I learned to navigate while regressed in a particular life. At first, like with anything new, you may be in awe of what you are experiencing. I surely was, but you will settle down as you get more PLRs. Rebecca was my guide while in the deep meditative state and seemed to know the perfect time to ask questions and prod me in a new direction. I was moving within a transcended state of no time and accessing multiple incarnations during my regressions.

In one of my favorite regressions, I examined a lifetime during the era of the Spartan King Leonidas and the Battle of Thermopylae. Kevin Ryerson, through his communications with Ahtun Re, also confirmed much of what I had strongly felt over multiple sessions concerning my experiences during my Spartan lifetime, and much more information was revealed in my own intuitive meditations and in other past life sessions with psychics, whether channeled or PLRs.

All of the past lives that I write about in this book have had multiple confirmations. These confirmations were made without the different parties knowing any of the prior information that I had been exposed to. This multiple-source validation over time has strengthened the entire body of work that

I'm writing about in this book. I'm not trying to impress or draw acclaim from a famous past life incarnation.

I have had a fairly humble life this time around, and, in many ways, it serves me better to play out of the limelight. Being a king or extremely wealthy can have just as many drawbacks as benefits. Imagine trying to write books about former incarnations if I was the president of the United States or the king of England. It wouldn't go over well. Being a decorated former Navy SEAL gives me some credibility. I'll take a little flak; I'm sure, but I've survived a lot of years in combat zones, so I'm pretty thick-skinned at this point.

My own past life research is still ongoing and will probably last for the rest of this life. The reward and satisfaction of researching, discovering, and then further investigating my own past lives has held many benefits, which will become more apparent throughout this book. I have also begun to notice the people around me in former incarnations, and it gives me insight into my relationships with others that would never come through without such insight. I sincerely hope that the ideas outlined in this chapter are just as useful to you as they have been for me. I trust that you may uncover and explore your own past life memories more clearly and deliberately after reading this book. Now let's journey through time together.

Sigmund Freud's couch for patients, known for Psychoanalysis, including the theories of id, ego and super-ego, oedipus complex, repression, and defense mechanism.

Colossal statue of King Amenhotep IV/ Akhenaten, Egyptian Museum in Cairo, Egypt.

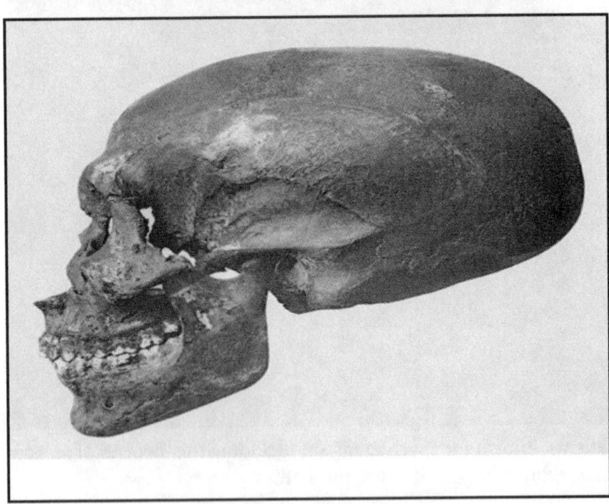

Recent genetic tests have conclusively demonstrated that this individual was the father of Tutankhamun. The JAMA eSupplement from Feb. 17, 2010 concludes that "the results demonstrate that the mummy in KV55 is the son of Amenhotep III and father of Tutankhamun, leading to the assumption (also supported by the radiological findings) that the mummy can be identified as Akhenaten."

The famous burial mask of King Tutankhamun on display at the Egyptian Museum in Cairo, Egypt. The 24-pound (11-kilogram) mask is made of gold, glass, and precious stones. The nemes headdress features a vulture, symbolizing sovereignty over Upper Egypt, and a cobra, symbolizing sovereignty over Lower Egypt.

Well over one thousand people were still aboard the ship as it broke apart and foundered. Just under two hours after Titanic sank, the Cunard liner RMS Carpathia arrived on the scene, and took on board an estimated 710 survivors.

"REBIRTH IS AN AFFIRMATION THAT MUST BE COUNTED AMONG THE PRIMORDIAL AFFIRMATIONS OF MANKIND."

◊ *Carl Gustav Jung* ◊

CHAPTER 3

PHARAOH MENES'S NUBIAN HEAD CHARIOTEER, 3100 BCE

My very first reading with Ahtun Re, who had also experienced a cycle of reincarnations on Earth, was very surprising. Here was a genuine Ascended Master, whose last incarnation was during the time of Pharaoh Akhenaten in the fourteenth century BCE, in which he had completed his personal human curriculum and therefore ascended. Ahtun Re has been watching humanity evolve ever since, serving as a teacher of mankind from the spirit realm. I first read a number of his communications in several of Shirley MacLaine's books, of which *Out on a Limb* had tremendously helped me expand my own view on reincarnation. But it was Ahtun Re's prominent appearance in Dr. Walter Semkiw's *Return of the Revolutionaries* that then eventually prompted me to contact Kevin Ryerson. As a trance channel, Kevin allows Ahtun Re to connect with his spirit and to utilize his body in order to communicate with humans, which is why Kevin jokes that as a channel he serves as a "human telephone," connecting the spirit world with the human race.

It took me a little while to fully grasp that an Ascended Master of the likes of Jesus and Buddha was chatting with me about the mysteries of life and my

past lives. It compels respect and humility, but by no means do I think that I was at any time the exclusive recipient of such guidance. As time and space are really relative constructs that are perceived and experienced very differently on different levels of existence and even in different states of consciousness, Ascended Masters can inspire and communicate with countless humans simultaneously. Of course, that doesn't take away anything from anyone's personal experience, but it helps to put things in perspective. As I spoke with Ahtun Re over the phone, his easy conversational style and humor quickly put me at ease anyway.

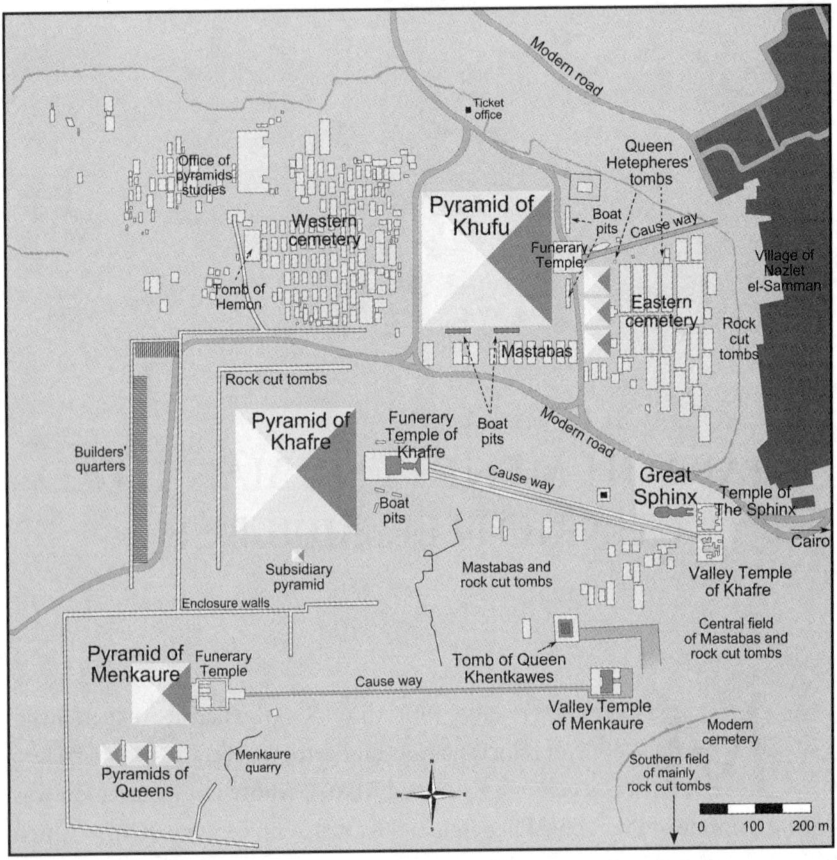

The information that he conveyed matched what I had heard from other psychics, what I had found out in past life regressions, and what I had gleaned intuitively during my meditations, without anyone involved having collaborated or shared any information prior to that. He also helped me to connect with informa-

tion that I had not yet been fully aware of. For example, at the end of our first conversation when he volunteered, "Oh, and by the way, we had two lives together as friends." One of those had been with Pharaoh Menes, in which both of us had been Nubian warriors. Ahtun Re told me that he had been the head general of the pharaoh's armies, and that I had been the pharaoh's general of the chariots. The chariot drivers, Ahtun Re related, were the equivalent of today's Special Forces warriors.

Nubians were a dark-skinned people and descendants of a great civilization situated south of the first cataract of the Nile. Their territory used to be the gateway into the rest of Africa for the Mediterranean cultures, but as a consequence of the same great deluge that destroyed the continents of Atlantis and Lemuria, their magnificent cities now lie buried under the sands of the Sahara desert. Survivors escaped to the mountainous regions or underground shelters near and far, and thousands of years would elapse before humanity would regain even a remote resemblance of a civilized society.

Some of the more advanced survivors would return and once again bring forth much of the knowledge gained before the cataclysm to help speed up the return of humanity to a point above survival level, but it would be a slow process. Because of their enormous impact on the rebuilding of civilization, many of them were viewed as saviors or even gods and were immortalized through time in stories and carvings all over the world. Most were just survivors of the cataclysmic event who had simply come out from their sanctuaries; however, some of those saviors would be from off-planet worlds such as Sirius, which is why the Nubians as well as the Egyptians had a similar affinity within their cultures for the star system of Sirius, but they were not the only ones.

In the American Indian culture of the Hopi, there is the prophecy of the Blue Star Kachina, and many researchers believe that it refers to Sirius as well. The Hopi connect its coming to a period of uplifting and purifying changes, and mainstream science tells us that Sirius is indeed moving closer to Earth over the next sixty thousand years, gradually increasing in brightness and being the brightest star in the nighttime sky for the next 210,000 years. When looking at this projected time frame and while considering the incontrovertible fact that modern science really allows us to observe and examine portions of the cosmos in some detail, we should also take into account that there is still much that we don't see and much that may be misinterpreted.

Another culture with a clear affinity to Sirius are the Dogon people of West Africa, who believe that the starting point of their creation is a star that revolves around Sirius and is known as the Digitaria star. It is not even visible to the naked eye, and so the existence of this star that we know today as Sirius B was only proven after astronomers had rediscovered it in 1862 through the use of telescopes. The Dogon in ancient times already believed in the existence of this star; they said it is small, but heavy, and it contains the primary elements of creation. Modern scientists have only very recently discovered the truth of the information relayed by the Dogon.

Their ancient traditions contain highly precise astrophysical information about the orbits in the star system of Sirius, like the fifty-year elliptical orbit that Sirius B has around Sirius A. The Dogon also believe that there is a third star in the Sirius system, which is neither accepted nor ruled out by mainstream science today. Its existence was seemingly confirmed by modern astronomy in 1995, when the French astronomers Daniel Benest and J. L. Duvent published the results of years of study in the *Journal of Astronomy and Astrophysics,* stating that a red dwarf star, Sirius C, existed. This hypothesis was then again challenged and refuted, but the existence of a third star could still not be ruled out. It seems that, if it exists, it must be orbiting Sirius A even more closely than formerly assumed, in an area that has not yet been explored thoroughly, as claimed by Andy Lloyd, author of *The Dark Star,* who among others suggests that Sirius C could actually be a brown dwarf star.

The initial discovery of this treasure chest of knowledge in the culture of the Dogon was first made by two French anthropologists, Marcel Griaule and Germaine Dieterlen, who studied the Dogon people in the isolated mountainous region of Bandiagara, south of the Sahara Desert in Mali. Griaule wrote about their discoveries in his book *Conversations with Ogotemmeli,* published in 1947. Ogotemmeli was the tribe's griot as was his father before him. He states that we were created by beings that genetically engineered our DNA, an amphibious hermaphrodite race called the Nommo. In fact, he said that our DNA was manipulated three times and that our creators designed three different versions of humans, which was due to failed experiments. Their oral history relates how those aliens from the Sirian star system landed on Earth "with great noise and wind" in a three-legged spacecraft, and how they combined their DNA with the DNA of single-sexed animals—meaning with ours!

I'm convinced that Earth has been visited by intelligent beings from Sirius in the distant past, and that they have left behind precise information about their star system. But not only that, much of the currently unfolding advanced scientific information that we believe we are discovering for the first time, such as atomic, quantum, and string theory, has parallels in Dogon mythical narratives, as Laird Scranton points out in his book *The Science of the Dogon.* Robert Temple, an astronomer and scholar of Oriental studies, gives a detailed analysis of many of the facts surrounding the evidence of Sirian contact in his book *The Sirius Mystery,* where he also presents an intriguing analysis of the Sphinx.

He says that the Sphinx actually doesn't depict a lion, but Anubis, the Egyptian jackal god guarding the entrance to the realm of the afterlife. Accordingly it was the purpose of this giant statue of Anubis to be the guardian of the Giza Necropolis. Temple also states that the Sphinx was surrounded by a pool of water, which would explain its lowered position on the Giza Plateau as well as the water erosion on the Sphinx, as there was simply not enough rainfall in the officially estimated time frame of its existence. But the raising and sinking of that water around the Sphinx during the seasons as well as its sinking when the sand was regularly being cleared out of the pool could explain the massive erosion. This pool, called the Jackal Lake, was also an important element during a ritual in which a deceased pharaoh's son would wash the entrails of his father to free his spirit, making the Sphinx also a focal point of the pharaonic resurrection cult. The Sphinx originally being modeled as a jackal with a jackal head would also explain its current disproportionately small human head, which seems to be an alteration that was made later in its existence.

The Nommo also taught the Dogon about reincarnation, as Ogotemmeli related. According to him, the Nommo reincarnated consciously, meaning without the massive loss of memory that most humans experience. He said for them it's like when a snake sheds its skin, and they allegedly also used the genetic hybrid of their making as a vessel to reincarnate in. As with the Dogon, both the Nubian and the Egyptian belief system entailed the concept of reincarnation, as well as the prominent role of Sirius. The goddess Isis, who had shared origins in both cultures, was said to be from the star system of Sirius, and many of the ancient structures in both countries had alignments to Sirius.

My current life wife in the lifetime of Menes was a beautiful Nubian prin-

cess, and, like many royal descendants during that time, she was an advanced initiate in the sacred mysteries. In particular she was initiated into the wisdom of the goddess of Isis, which was one of the reasons why she had been a great inspiration to me. Groups of souls often incarnate together or arrange to get together at some point in their incarnations to help each other advance in spiritual development and to accomplish the greater missions that we're all here for.

Meeting my wife in my current lifetime was again a powerful stimulus that opened yet another chapter in both of our soul journeys. We have been soul mates throughout time, coming together at various times throughout history. We always help each other advance when we do. Ahtun Re once told me that we have been together throughout time. In the future we intend to do a joint book from the perspective of a couple in several different incarnations.

The goddess principle, the feminine energy of love, and the connection with the Earth were very important and sacred in Egyptian and Nubian life. Whenever there was an imbalance regarding the male and female aspects in something, it was often the energy archetypally represented by the goddess of Isis that would help pull it back into balance. This was essential not only for the continuance of the human race through reproduction, but also for the fertility of nature, the planting of crops, and all the other large and small constituents of human civilization.

During that time in Egypt's history, every year around July 23, when Sirius began to rise, the waters of the Nile would begin to flood, and it was up to the Egyptian priests, who attended to the calendar, to sight the first rising of Sirius. At the ancient temple of Isis-Hathor at Denderah, there is a beautiful statue of Isis located at the end of an aisle flanked by large columns. The statue was oriented to the rising of Sirius, and priests would place a jewel in the goddess's forehead so that the light from the returning star would fall on the gem. When the Egyptian priests saw the light of Sirius upon the gem on the statue of Isis, they would announce to the people that the New Year had begun.

It was believed that Isis was the great mother of the gods, the lifeblood of fertility. Our solar system was born from Isis's womb, and I contest that the Egyptian myth is based on actual facts, meaning that the star system of Sirius is really older than our solar system. This claim may sound outrageous to you, since mainstream science asserts that our solar system is around 4.5 billion years old, while the Sirius star system is supposedly only around 240 million years old.

But as I alluded to before when mentioning Dewey Larson, it seems that mainstream science has its understanding of stellar evolution wrong—in fact, backward! So their models seem consistent, but under a completely false premise. If you have an interest in astronomy, I highly recommend reading into Dewey Larson's excellent work to discover a new point of view in that regard. Sirius B, which is the planet assigned to Isis, is made of iron, and the iron of Sirius B is the same as the iron in our blood and the iron of the crystalline core of the Earth, which is why we resonate to that star system and its position in the cosmos.

In that lifetime I was an advanced initiate into the teachings of the goddess Sekhmet, originally the warrior goddess of Upper Egypt. She is depicted as a lioness or as a woman with the head of a lioness, which connects to the fact that the female lion was the fiercest hunter known to the Egyptians. She was the fiery eye of Ra, the sun god, which he sent out against his enemies. In this form she also appeared as the cobra on the brow of the king, rearing to protect him. Sekhmet literally means "she who is powerful," which suits her function and abilities. She was also given titles such as "the one before whom evil trembles."

To pacify Sekhmet, festivals were celebrated at the end of a battle, so that the destruction would come to an end. During an annual festival held at the beginning of the year, a festival of intoxication, the Egyptians danced and played music to soothe the wildness of the goddess while they drank great quantities of beer. This ritual was to imitate the extreme drunkenness that once stopped the wrath of the goddess as she lapped up beer secretly mixed with blood. Sekhmet had almost destroyed humanity when she became mad with blood from a battle in which she had participated and could not control herself. The beer then made her drunk, and she had passed out. When she awoke, she was herself again and vowed to always follow a battle with a drinking festival so that she would never go into the rapture of another bloodlust again.

Although often portrayed as a war deity, Sekhmet could also be compassionate. Most of the statues of Sekhmet were made of ebony granite, because black can absorb everything. Sekhmet could thus be whatever mankind most focused on; if mankind wanted war, then Sekhmet would come out in incredible wrath and destructiveness. If mankind focused on love and compassion for others, then Sekhmet was capable of the most intense expressions of these emotions as well.

In the massive temple complex of Karnak located on the banks of the Nile River is a small temple of the god Ptah, who was also a favorite deity during Pharaoh Menes's time. In that lifetime, Ahtun Re and I were both ardent followers of not only Sekhmet but also of the god Ptah, who was said to have fashioned the universe through sound harmonics and thought. This creation story was part of Egyptian culture thousands of years before a similar story was written in the Old Testament. In the first chapter of Genesis is the story of God speaking his creations into existence just as Ptah had done. Ptah began his creations by first thinking of them and then speaking them into existence through the sound harmonics of his voice.

This surely seems fantastic, but when you look, for instance, at how sound frequencies can move sand on a plate in visible sound and vibration studies called cymatic experiments, you may begin to readjust your thinking in this regard. There were many highly advanced technologies known in ancient Egypt that relied heavily on etheric energy and subtle forces, aspects of nature that are almost entirely disregarded by contemporary mainstream science today.

Another very powerful of these advanced technologies is hidden in a symbol that was very popular in ancient Egypt—the ankh. It looks like a cross with a handle, and it's a symbolic representation of the unity of male and female energies, as well as of a circular movement of etheric energy through the body. This particular circuit boosts longevity, which is why the ankh is associated with immortality. The effects of applying this circuit are very pronouncedly observable especially in men, because it is accompanied by a reversal of the sperm flow, whereby the energy contained within it gets transformed and dispersed throughout the body; this phenomenon is today known as multi-orgasmic potential within men. Some men do this naturally, but everybody can learn this; it's really a wonderful way to do something positive for yourself, your partner, and your relationship.

Drunvalo Melchizedek contends that this technique had already been known in Lemuria, where couples applying it were creating an immortal offspring and were becoming immortals themselves. He describes it in some detail in his book *The Flower of Life*. This energetic circuit is also known in other cultures around the globe, like in Tantra or Taoism. In China there is the legend of Huang-di, the Yellow Emperor, who was allegedly taught this technique by three highly

intuitive concubines. Consequently he felt inspired to write the *Huangdi Neijing*, also known as the *Yellow Emperor's Inner Canon*, which is the core foundation of traditional Chinese medicine. But although the knowledge of this energetic circuit had already been discovered in ancient China, it has only gained wider public attention in the last few decades through books like *Awaken Healing Energy Through the Tao: The Taoist Secret of Circulating Internal Power* by Mantak Chia, who has trained with monks, martial artists, healers, and spiritual scholars for most of his life. Chia dubbed this energetic circuit the "microcosmic orbit."

In ancient Egypt, pharaohs often carried the ankh during ceremonies, and, in carvings and paintings, it's almost always depicted in one of their hands along with a scepter in the other hand. It's a powerful symbol, also known as the "key of life," originally created by the Nubians, but what it represents is, of course, as old as creation. The ankh can also be found in connection with Sekhmet and Ptah in a small temple in Karnak that is dedicated to Ptah. It contains an ebony statue of Sekhmet standing in a small back room holding a lotus to her heart in one hand and the ankh in the other hand.

When gazing into the eyes of Sekhmet, you would be overcome by an intense emotion of compassion. In the past, only the most fearless of warriors would dare gaze upon Sekhmet's eyes. On the advice of Ahtun Re, I have actually visited and entered a small chapel in Luxor in this lifetime to see an exquisite statue of her. The effect of gazing into Sekhmet's eyes was once again quite amazing and indeed triggered many inner processes, which made this experience a key turning point in the reawakening of my abilities to thwart war in this life.

In this past incarnation, I would use compassion inspired by Sekhmet to calm war. In turn the harmonics of thought learned through Ptah were utilized to transmit these compassionate thought forms to others throughout the kingdom and along our borders. Now in this lifetime I have again brought forward these abilities to be utilized once more to help put an end to warfare in all the countries where I've been deployed as a SEAL and as an independent contractor. And although there is still a lot of turmoil in many regions all over the world, most of which is artificially instigated, I was always able to make a significant difference in my direct environment and thus also in the bigger picture. In my opinion this is really the way to go, because everybody who applies this in his or her life is pushing the envelope and helps to facilitate the often-quoted hun-

dredth-monkey effect. It is a hard way, but it's absolutely worth going it, as it will be the way in which humanity will eventually manifest a new renaissance.

One of the skills often developed by Nubian warrior priests was communication with animals. Advanced warrior priests of Sekhmet could call whole prides of lions or cheetahs into battle with them. I was told that, in one battle, I had two lions yoked to a chariot and a pride of lions with me as we attacked. But Nubian warriors were also gifted runners and would even run into battle with lions. Elephant herds could also be called forth for use in battle.

On some occasions Nubians would call all the animals of an enemy's city out during the night, so that on the next morning the city would awaken with all of the animals having deserted them. They would assume that their deity had abandoned them, and as they looked out over the walls of the city they would see all of nature allied and gathered with the pharaoh's army against them; even nature was calling them to justice. It's kind of funny, but the old Tarzan movies, which were a favorite of mine as a young boy, were perfect examples of this ancient ability to enlist the help of nature against a negative consciousness.

The training in the Nubian warrior priesthood was intended to develop a mind-set within one that is focused on respecting and keeping a balance in nature. Becoming a sacred warrior priest did not only focus on the mastery of weapons and chariots, it also pertained to the mastery of the sacred cycles of nature, inside and outside of oneself. During that lifetime in Egypt, I was erudite in the art of binding the lower and upper chakras of the human body, which was among the real duties of the priests. When it comes to the more explicit warrior skills, Nubian archers were famous for their abilities, and hieroglyphs often depicted the Nubians as a bow. Nubian warriors would be recognized for their formidable skill and courage in battle for thousands of years. The pharaoh's special warfare warriors were often Nubian archers in horse-drawn chariots, which, when combined, would prove to be a great weapon combining high speed, strength, durability, and mobility that could not be matched by infantry.

During the unification wars, the pharaoh's army practiced sacred warfare, which refers to the act of calling back to consciousness a city filled with people that have gone astray and fallen into negativity. The idea was to bring about a change in consciousness by a vibratory resonance that was induced through drumming, trumpeting, and singing while a city was surrounded.

Those playing musical instruments and singing or chanting would be marched in spiral form around the city walls to increase the vibratory resonance. One of the gates of the city would be left open so that people could leave the city freely. Warriors stayed away from this gate so that as people were drawn back into consciousness they would be more inclined to leave. So in effect we were calling back our kinfolk to a higher state of consciousness.

The last stage before the occupation of a city was accomplished by pitting warrior against warrior. The remaining corrupt leadership, military commanders, priests, and merchants would go to trial and would be retrained if found guilty of corruption and manipulation. The city itself would be deconstructed or ceremonially cleansed and then rebuilt. Cities of that time were made of adobe bricks, and, just like with the cycle of nature and life, there would be a process of death and rebirth. This deconstruction process, not to be confused with destroying a city and salting the Earth, would remove old negative patterns and facilitate a genuine renewal in support of the true empowerment of a population.

The archetypes of mankind were known at this time and discerned as a way of understanding the greater pattern of progression toward enlightenment. Archetypes are models of personalities or behaviors that are important to be identified within oneself. As your current archetype is revealed you can see where you are in the ascension process in your lifetime. Archetypes are stepping-stones to a higher spiritual consciousness, awareness, and intuition. The archetypes can also help you to comprehend where others are at in their own journey. Awareness of others' journeys inspires compassion because no one state of mind or state of affairs ever seems to be ultimate or unchangeable. Whatever archetypes one is embodying, there are always opportunities and challenges to learn and comprehend particular lessons and to apply certain virtues. Reflecting on this can also show you if you are stuck in one of the archetypes and what your next step is. The following is a possible succession of archetypal motives throughout a lifetime:

Eden—This is considered the primordial archetype, where everything is absolutely whole and perfect. You are considered innocent until you leave it to explore what else is there.

Orphan—You experience pain and feel wounded after the separation from Eden. Feeling that pain, you search for truth. Once you discover a truth that you believe in, then you often become a warrior to protect it.

Warrior—Often the same truth and wound that motivated you to become a warrior may also be motivating your enemy, and this will move you to become a healer. When you realize that what you are warring against is often a reflection of what is within you, then you wish to become a healer.

Healer—Healers must be cautious not to become a healer warrior, who strives to heal the world by making war on evil, always looking for something evil to heal. The transition from a healer warrior to a healer comes mainly through transcending inconsiderate actions.

Alchemist—This is the synergy of all the previous archetypes. An alchemist's presence begins to alter the environment, more subtly accessing the underlying fabric of reality. The nature of warfare will stop and a rejuvenation process can begin.

Sage—At this stage you are genuinely able and willing to call people to consciousness as a communicator of the wisdom and truth of spiritual ascension.

During one's transition through archetypal phases, it always happens that at some point we leave behind seemingly essential parts of ourselves to embrace new ways of thinking and new modes of operating. Just like the cycle of death and rebirth, this process of letting go and embracing something new seems to be unremitting.

There is a victory stela of Menes still in existence today that illustrates this idea, but only advanced initiates could comprehend its deeper meaning. You can find pictures of this stela on the Internet under the Narmer Palette. Carved on this stela or stone slab is a depiction of Pharaoh Menes with a club raised over his head, gripping the top of the head of a bound person on his knees. This is often described as the king smiting his enemies in battle, and to the average person this explanation would appear to be perfectly sufficient.

On a deeper level, it is a depiction of the death of the ego, the victory of the soul over materiality. Then on even deeper levels of wisdom and knowledge this palette represents the binding of the negative side of ourselves, as well as the joining of the lower and upper chakras, similar to the joining of Lower and Upper Egypt, one of Menes's accomplishments. Chakras are spinning wheels of energy located throughout our bodies.

There are seven main chakras, starting with the lower chakras located at the base of the spine, in the sexual organs, and solar plexus. The upper chakras

are located in the heart, throat, and pineal gland, and lastly the seventh or crown chakra is located at the top of the head. This is just to explain the bare essentials; there is a lot more to this, like the fact that they all correspond to a variety of things such as colors, frequencies, or glands and organs in the body.

Reaching and maintaining a balanced and efficient flow through your chakra system is really like cultivating a garden, with all the different influences that have to be considered and the arduous efforts it takes to make it flourish and thrive. There is abundant information about chakras on the Internet and within a myriad of books. I want to remind you to always use your intuitive abilities along the way to sense and cultivate the flow of energy through your chakra system.

Menes would create temples along the Nile that would correspond to the seven chakras. Interestingly, if you were to take a child's body and look at the spinal position while it was still in the womb and then superimpose it on the topography of the Nile you would see a similarity in the two. The first cataract of the Nile would be the location of the base of the spine, the pyramids of Giza would represent the third eye or the pineal gland, and ancient Heliopolis near present-day Alexandria would represent the crown chakra, which is often depicted as a lotus blossom. Rituals and sacred ceremonies would be instituted in each temple that would cleanse and purify the chakras of the initiates until they were ready to progress to the next chakra farther up the Nile toward the delta.

At the bottom of the stela, you can see the purifying waters washing away the sins or cleansing the lower chakras, and, right next to Menes, you can see a man holding a pail in the shape of a pinecone. This pail signifies the opening of the pineal gland, which is located between the two lobes of the brain and is shaped like a pinecone. Above the bound warrior is a lotus blossom, which signifies the opening of the crown chakra to allow the flow of information to and from God depicted as the falcon above the lotus blossom. The falcon is clutching the former binding cord and sets man free when he connects with God.

The imagery on the stela thus illustrates how the old self is overcome so that a new self may emerge. The war club can be seen as a scepter that is used to raise the vibratory frequency of a person, not to literally kill. By looking at the stela and interpreting its meaning, you would hold a psychic tension between the material world of lower consciousness and the spiritual world of higher consciousness. Similar seemingly brutal and explicit metaphors can

be found in other ancient wisdom teachings as well. Jesus is quoted as having said, "To enter the strong man's house, first you must bind him," which is a parable describing sacred warfare. The disciples that Jesus directly taught this inspired information to were often far more than the twelve mentioned in the Bible. Many women, including the women in his family, were also followers of Yeshua, the Aramaic name of Jesus. During Yeshua's lifetime, my current wife was also incarnate and belonged to this extended group of female disciples who were known as the Magdalenes, many of whom who had also been priestesses or initiates of the Egyptian goddess Isis.

At the top and middle of the stela is the name Narmer, which literally means hammer. It is another name that refers to Menes, who was coming to hammer you as in "bring you and your city back to consciousness." Menes's reign was a long sixty-two years, and, during that time, a number of names were given to him that are sometimes falsely believed to denote other kings. One such name was the "Scorpion King," which was derived from a mace-head that belonged to Pharaoh Menes and that had a scorpion figure on it. Another name confused with another king but actually referring to Menes is Hor-Aha, which was the spiritual name given to Menes, signifying that he was at one with Horus.

Pharaoh Menes's son was Athothis, who would rule for fifty-two years after his father died. Athothis's nickname was the Wild Bull, which is one of the reasons for the many bull ceremonies in Egypt, Crete, and Spain, where he established colonies.

Also at the top of the stela is the depiction of two bulls, which represent the god Apis as well as a time frame between 4286 and 2143 BCE, the age of Taurus the Bull in the precession of the equinoxes. The Egyptians were very well versed in astronomy and knew that the stars and constellations appear to slowly rotate around the Earth, which is, of course, caused by the Earth's own rotation within the greater mechanics of the universe. The Earth also has a slight wobble in its rotation, like a wobbling spinning top. The orientation of the Earth's axis is slowly but continuously changing as it traces out a conical shape over approximately a 25,776-year grand cycle. About every 2,148 years, the sun rises in the preceding zodiacal constellation, moving through all twelve traditional constellations of the zodiac at a rate of about 50.3 seconds of arc per year, or one degree every 71.6 years.

Each zodiac sign has thirty degrees (12 * 30 = 360). One degree or 71.6 years times 30 degrees equals 2,148 years per zodiac sign. Every 2,148 years per zodiac sign times twelve zodiac signs equals 25,776 years or a grand cycle.

During the time of Menes, the structures on the Giza Plateau were already ancient. The arrangement of the Giza pyramids and their relation to the Nile were aligned with the Belt of Orion in relation to the Milky Way at around 10,500 BCE, as Robert Bauval and Adrian Gilbert point out in their book *The Orion Mystery*, suggesting that this may have been the time that the pyramids were built. I actually have memories of helping to build the pyramids in this time frame by levitation of the stones. Sound technologies were used in this era not only to move the stones but also to shape them, as I alluded to earlier in this chapter. Bauval and Gilbert also compare how star brightness and pyramid size are related. The Giza Plateau consists of two almost equally tall pyramids and a smaller one that is only 53 percent of the height of the other two. Orion's Belt consists of two almost similarly bright stars, and one with only half of the brightness of the other two. The smallest pyramid is the one that deviates from the diagonal, as does the dimmest star! Look up into the night sky and find Orion's Belt and see for yourself.

Bauval and Gilbert made many interesting observations concerning Egyptian pyramids: "More pyramids in Egypt fit the picture of the sky; the two large pyramids at Dahshur are a match for the brightest two stars in the open cluster Hyades, two more pyramids near Giza are bright stars of Orion, and the pyramids of Abusir are exactly where the head of Orion should be."

Most ancient pyramids throughout the world were placed on geo- mantic or energetic points on the Earth, and their layout almost always corresponds with star systems, illustrating the "as above, so below" principle that was prominently outlined by the Egyptian god Thoth, who was reputed to be the master builder of the pyramids. He is also said to have brought writing to the Egyptians after the great flood, among many other cultural achievements.

Thoth is the author of *The Emerald Tablets,* in which he says, "That which is below is as that which is above, and that which is above is as that which is below, to perform the miracles of the one thing. And as all things were from the one, by means of the meditation of the one, thus all things were born from the one, by means of adaptation." This means in essence that there is an origi-

nating force permeating all of creation and naturally inducing corresponding relations within all-that-is. When we honor this principle and use our free will to align with it, as the ancients did when they built the pyramids, this consequently advances harmony and coherence in our lives. Thoth or Hermes, as the Greeks would call him, was, in my memories, an early incarnation of the soul the world now knows as Jesus. I was in this lifetime with him and in many other lives, as I'll relate in future chapters and books in this series.

Beneath the Giza Plateau is a vast megalithic metropolis, a complete city with waterways, lakes with islands, chambers of enormous size that are the equals of the largest cathedrals on the surface of the Earth, and also enormous statues carved into the rock. High-level initiates that had knowledge of sound keys allowing access to these chambers accessed them over vast periods of time. Most, if not all of the ancient pyramids throughout the world, have similar-sized structures beneath them, quite literally "as above, so below." Today these chambers beneath the Giza Plateau are being mapped out and explored, but disclosure is kept from the general public.

The largest known pyramid complex in the world is currently being uncovered twenty miles north of Sarajevo in Bosnia near the town of Visoko. Bosnian American archaeologist Dr. Semir Osmanagic is heading the project to uncover the pyramids, the largest of which reaches 720 feet high, one and a half times as high as the Great Pyramid of Giza. Underground tunnels have also been found that are believed to connect the five pyramids of the complex. Carbon dating of the soil, clay, and humus that are entirely covering the pyramids indicates an age of around 25,000 years.

It was only after people began to dig on and around these pyramid-shaped hills that the remnants of the pyramids started to be uncovered in 2006. In a 2012 press release, it was announced that different professionals, among them a physicist, an electrical engineer, and a sound engineer independently confirmed the existence of an energy beam that is thirteen feet in radius and transmits an unexplainable electromagnetic signal measuring twenty-eight kilohertz coming from the center of the Pyramid of the Sun, the largest one in the complex. The Bosnian pyramids currently stand at 767 meters or 2,516 feet above sea level, so the fact that a thick layer of soil covers them should give you an idea of how high at a minimum the water rose at least in this area of

Europe. Not surprisingly, mysterious underground tunnels and chambers are being discovered underneath the Bosnian pyramids.

Recurring changes in sea level silted over many of the ancient pyramids of the world. Graham Hancock, one of my favorite authors in the field of "alternative history," also believes that advanced civilizations existed before the great worldwide flood event that is mentioned by many ancient cultures. In his highly successful book *Fingerprints of the Gods,* he uses a combination of astronomy, archaeology, geology, and folk myth to come to the inevitable conclusion that civilizations rose at least 17,000 years ago and vanished beneath a rising sea level. Their traces are to be found in flood myths in Sumerian and Vedic texts, in ancient maps, and in still-submerged ruins.

Some of the most impressive underwater monuments are near Yonaguni, the southwestern-most inhabited island of Japan. Pictures from the ruins as well as from other underwater cities that existed on previous coastlines before the great deluge are featured in his book *Underworld.* Graham has personally examined a large number of these places on his diving sessions all over the world. The book is visually stimulating, and, once you see the pictures, you will be convinced that they are indeed ancient cities now submerged.

Excavation work from volunteer groups is still ongoing around and on the Bosnian pyramids, and more mysteries are being discovered almost daily. They are not officially acknowledged as the pyramids that they are, because human history would need to be entirely rewritten. This is also why the stone structure called Adam's Calendar in South Africa, which has been analyzed in detail by Michael Tellinger, is not acknowledged by the mainstream as a legitimate, consciously created structure.

Adam's Calendar is apparently a 75,000-year-old celestial map, the existence of which jeopardizes the coherence of the mainstream narrative of history and adds more credence to the idea that there has been an advanced species present on Earth in the very ancient past. In his book *Slave Species of god,* Michael argues that humanity was actually created by an extraterrestrial species, just like many of the ancient cultures believe. The lowercase gin the title of Michael's book is meant to indicate that he doesn't refer to the source of all-that-is, or what some people may call God, but to extraterrestrial beings that have demanded to be worshipped as gods or that were simply deified by the people.

Currently, ancient pyramid structures are found all over the world in various sizes and shapes, and fields of energy have been measured radiating out from many of them. My intuitions and memories are that these structures have been used as power sources, which is corroborated by Christopher Dunn's excellent book *The Giza Power Plant*. Pyramid shapes were also used for healing, spiritual ceremonies, local weather modification, and as communication devices to name but a few of the many possible applications.

Recognized by academia as the starting point of the first civilization, the valley between the Tigris and Euphrates in present-day Iraq is where the ancient cities of Ur, Nineveh, and Babylon are located. The Sumerian civilization that is credited with the start of this empire sprang up from the fertile valley between the rivers virtually overnight with advanced capabilities. Surrounded by nomadic tribes that lived in tents, this area developed the architectural ability to erect multistoried buildings and ziggurats. The Sumerians were advanced in metallurgy, agriculture, animal husbandry, writing, sciences, art, government, and much more with little indication of slow and gradual progression. History cannot sufficiently explain where the Sumerians came from.

It would appear as if the Sumerians had a helping hand. This could have come from an extraterrestrial species, as the Sumerian myth of the Annunaki suggests, but maybe also from survivors of the great flood, who had stashed away the necessary information, seeds, animals, and other apparatuses needed to restart a civilization. There are stories in over one hundred cultures all over the world of boats that carried survivors, who then brought the necessary plants and animals to many different shores and helped rekindle the fires of civilization that had been dowsed by the flood. The story of Noah's Ark in the Bible is but one of many similar stories told throughout the world. The Sumerians had their own flood story, but in their accounts it lasted only seven days and nights versus the forty days and nights in the Bible story.

One of the Sumerians' important contributions to history would be their support in the establishment of the Phoenician civilization. The Phoenicians were gifted seamen and have been found to have traveled all over the world in their ships, but there doesn't seem to be a centralized place that you could say they were originally from other than springing forth from the Sumerians. Pharaoh Menes's family has also been said to be among those that were the precursors of the Phoenicians.

Menes was the son of the Sumerian king Sargon, and the first pharaoh to unify Upper and Lower Egypt into one kingdom, which made him the founder of the First Dynasty. He established his new capital city of Memphis on the banks of the Nile by diverting the river with dikes and thus creating a more defensible island. As I remember him, he was very light skinned and with reddish-blond hair. After unifying Egypt, we would travel by ships to many faraway lands and create settlements. Menes was a great seafarer, who repeatedly sailed the long three-thousand-mile voyage from the Persian Gulf and the Indus Valley to Egypt by way of the Arabian and Red Seas.

I want to note that while I feel very certain about the connection between Menes and Sargon, this is not accepted as a fact in mainstream history. Interestingly, Lieutenant Colonel Laurence Austine Waddell, who lived in the nineteenth and twentieth centuries and who was a British army surgeon, historian, and explorer, presented a whole range of revolutionary historical perspectives that are still not accepted by most scholars, but that concur with my assessment. I have found much of the copious amounts of historical work he authored to be so accurate and detailed that it seems to me that he must have been tapping into past life memories himself. In his book *Makers of Civilization in Race and History,* he described much of Menes's life in detail and has provided significant supporting evidence to corroborate many of my own past life memories.

Waddell also agrees that it was Menes and not the Greek mythological figure of Minos who started the first colony on the island of Crete where the palace of Knossos would be built in a later day. Minos would come much later as I will relate in a future chapter. The island of Sicily and mainland Italy would also see colonies started by Menes. After his Mediterranean journeys, he sailed through the Straits of Gibraltar to the British Islands where an Egyptian colony was located near the tin mines of Cornwall.

I had fought side by side with this amazing king for many years; we had galloped into many battles with our gleaming chariots and war- horses bedecked in gold. Just the sight of our armies and the rumor of our abilities had made many large cities and empires capitulate and allow themselves to be absorbed into our growing kingdom. I had protected this wise king throughout many lands from the swords and spears of uncountable brave warriors. I could not protect him, however, from nature. While exploring, the first pharaoh of Egypt would meet his match from a reaction to a hornet's sting. At over eighty years of age, the great sea king would then be laid to rest in a tomb in Ireland near the Newgrange area.

In the year 1901, Sir F. Petrie explored what was considered to be King Menes's prepared tomb at Abydos in Upper Egypt, but Menes's remnants were nowhere to be found. A long record inscribed in the Sumerian Egyptian transition script on the great ebony label that was found instead narrates in graphic and circumstantial detail how this great admiral and "world emperor" in his old age on "a voyage of exploration with his fleet" made the complete course to "the farthest west sunset land in the western ocean," where he met his tragic death. It also states that what was considered to be his tomb in Abydos was merely a cenotaph and therefore remained empty. A cenotaph is a monument erected in honor of a person whose remains are buried elsewhere, in this case on this particular island in the "western ocean," which appears to read "Urani," suggesting that the place of his death and the real tomb are in "Erin," or Ireland as it is known today.

To give you an idea of how far and for how long Pharaoh Menes's influence has stretched, let's take a closer look at just one item that has come down to us through more than five thousand years of history. The "kilt," which as you may know is a knee-length garment with pleats at the rear, is an unusual garment worn historically only in two places, Egypt and the isles of northwestern Europe. The kilt is still worn to this day by Scottish highlanders, in parts of Ireland, and in other Celtic regions such as Wales or Cornwall. The pharaohs depicted in traditional royal dress, from Pharaoh Menes all the way to Cleopatra VII, are all wearing kilts. The kilt is but one of many links that Egypt has over time with "the farthest west sunset land in the western ocean."

The ties between the two lands and cultures also have one of my favorite links, and that is a well-crafted beer. Two different beer-brewing companies recently used hieroglyphic evidence to craft ancient Egyptian beer. In 1996 CE, thanks to the work done by the Egyptian Exploration Society and the British brewer Scottish & Newcastle, a limited edition batch was made. In 2002 CE, Japan's Kirin Brewery produced what it claims is a brew fit for the pharaohs. It has no froth, is the color of dark tea, and carries an alcohol content of 10 percent, about double that of most contemporary beers. Sakuji Yoshimura, an Egyptologist at Waseda University in Tokyo, helped transcribe the recipe from

Egyptian wall paintings. Kirin spokesman Takaomi Ishii said, "It has a taste very different from today's beer. It tastes a little like white wine."

The principles of sacred warfare that I learned and practiced in that lifetime would be something for me to draw from in many lives including my current, as I will continue to relate in the following chapters. Having shared my memories from an incarnation as a black African person, I want to note that incarnating within different races is a common theme for many of us. Understanding this can help you tremendously in overcoming prejudices against another race, culture, gender, or religion.

Having a life with the first dynasty pharaoh would prepare me for my own future life as a pharaoh. We don't just jump into positions of leadership and influence. They take lifetimes of preparation. Although I'm outlining lives with or as historical figures, keep in mind that I have also had countless obscure incarnations. These lifetimes as poets, writers, philosophers, scribes, warriors, chariot drivers, and so on help develop key aspects that will be important to the overall aspects required of leadership of vast soul groups. Many of us have worked together in several different capacities in numerous lifetimes.

Ebony plaque of Menes in his tomb of Abydos. According to Manetho, Menes reigned for 62 years and was killed by a hippopotamus.

The Narmer Palette contains some of the earliest hieroglyphic inscriptions ever found. The tablet is thought by some to depict the unification of Upper and Lower Egypt under the king Narmer.

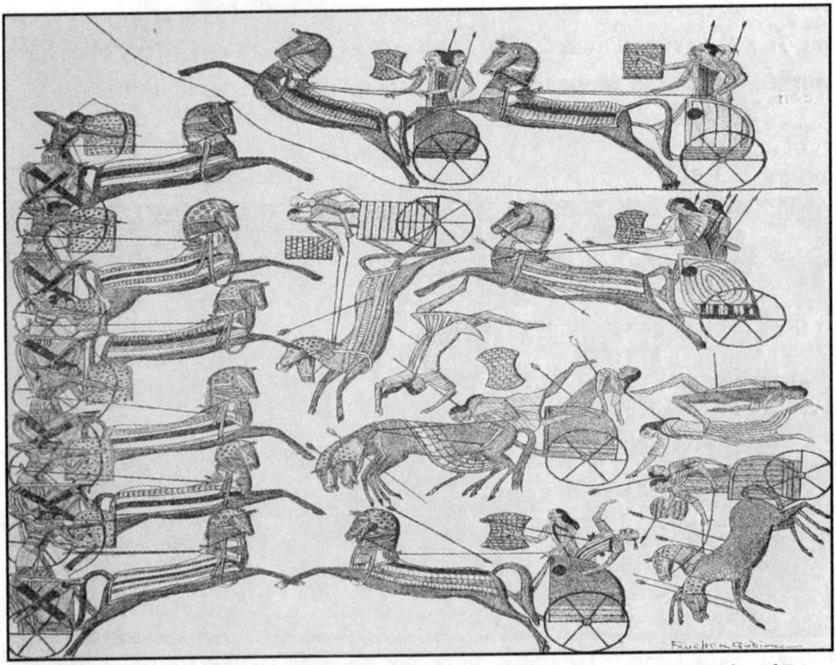

Ancient Egyptian war chariots were superior to many of its enemies. The geography of Egypt served to isolate the country and allowed it to thrive. This circumstance set the stage for many of Egypt's military conquests. They enfeebled their enemies by using small projectile weapons, like bows and arrows. They also had chariots which they used to charge at the enemy.

It is presumed the 30,000-year-old Bosnian Pyramids were built with human-made cement.

Façade of the Temple of Seti I in Abydos, built circa 1300 BCE. The pharaohs of the First Dynasty were buried in Abydos, including Narmer, who is regarded as the founder of the First Dynasty and Pharaoh Menes.

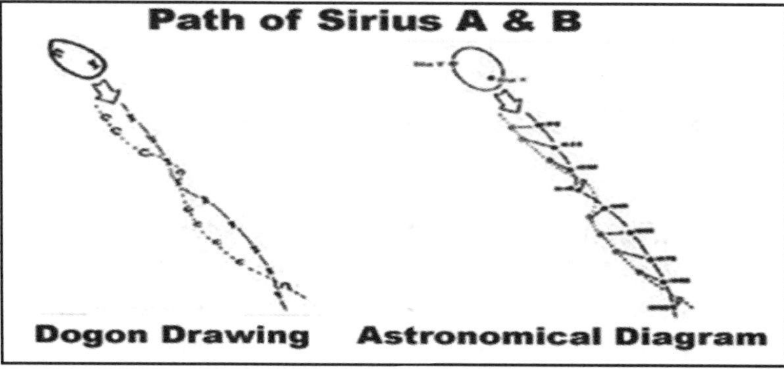

Together, Sirius A and B is the brightest star in our night sky. It should be noted that Sirius B was only "discovered" in 1862 and only analysed in 2005. However, the Dogon are a West African tribe who have known about, and worshipped, Sirius A and its twin the invisible star Sirius B, for the past 5,000 years.

"HE IS A LORD OF MERCY, FULL OF KINDNESS. HE HAS CONQUERED BY LOVE, AND HIS CITIZENS LOVE HIM MORE THAN THEMSELVES."

◊ *Tale of Sinuhe* ◊

CHAPTER 4

EGYPTIAN PHARAOH SENUSRET I, RULED FROM 1971-1926 BCE

Senusret I was the second pharaoh of the Twelfth Dynasty of Egypt, which was considered the start of the Middle Kingdom and a golden age of Egyptian history. Senusret's reign is recognized as the most powerful and influential of this particular dynasty. He was the son of Amenemhat I and his wife, Nefertitanen.

The exact circumstances under which Amenemhat came into power and started the Twelfth Dynasty are not known to history. What is known is that he was not related to his predecessors in the Eleventh Dynasty. Amenemhat's father was a priest in Thebes also named Senusret. His mother was named Nefret and, according to the *Prophecy of Neferti,* came from Elephantine in the south of Egypt.

My thoughts are that Amenemhat was the vizier of Mentuhotep IV, the last king of the Eleventh Dynasty. A stone plate found at el-Lisht, bearing both the names of Mentuhotep IV and of Amenemhat, indicates that Amenemhat was a co-regent during the later years of Mentuhotep's reign. This would suggest that Mentuhotep IV had intended or anticipated Amenemhat to be his successor.

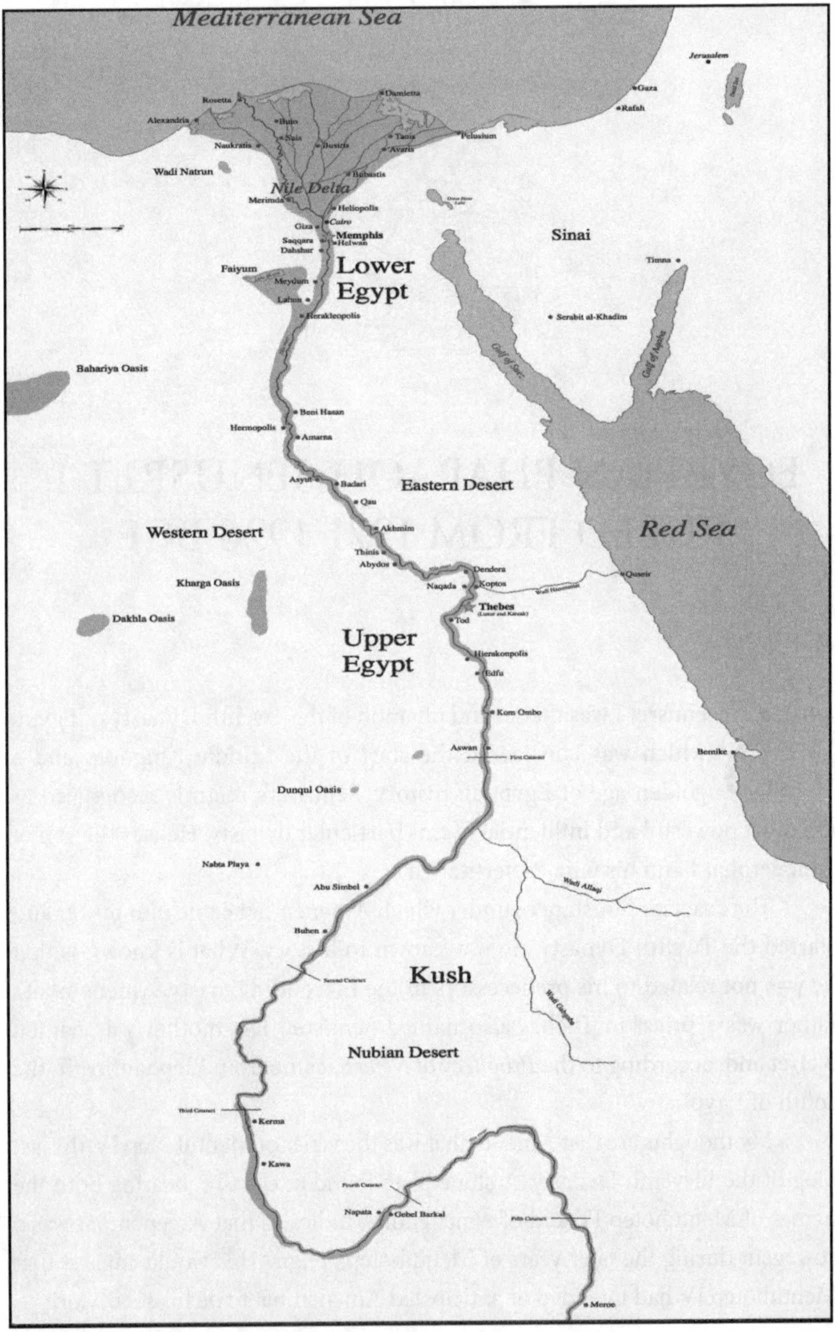

Mediterranean Sea
Jerusalem
Rosetta
Damietta
Gaza
Rafah
Alexandria
Buto
Sais
Tanis
Pelusium
Naukratis
Busiris
Avaris
Wadi Natrun
Bubastis
Nile Delta
Merimda
Heliopolis
Cairo
Giza
Memphis
Saqqara
Helwan
Dahshur
Sinai
Faiyum
Lower Egypt
Timna
Meydum
Lahun
Herakleopolis
Serabit al-Khadim
Gulf of Suez
Gulf of Aqaba
Bahariya Oasis
Beni Hasan
Hermopolis
Amarna
Asyut
Badari
Eastern Desert
Qau
Western Desert
Akhmim
Red Sea
Thinis
Abydos
Dendera
Quseir
Kharga Oasis
Naqada
Koptos
Thebes
Dakhla Oasis
Tod
Upper Egypt
Hierakonpolis
Edfu
Kom Ombo
Aswan
Bernike
Dunqul Oasis
Nabta Playa
Abu Simbel
Wadi Allaqi
Buhen
Kush
Nubian Desert
Kerma
Kawa
Napata
Gebel Barkal
Meroe

It is clear that Amenemhat established Egypt's first co-regency with his son, Senusret I, in about the twentieth year of the older king's rule. He was not only seeking to assure the succession of his proper heir, but also providing the young prince valuable training under his tutelage. Senusret was given several active roles in Amenemhat's government, specifically including those related to military matters. Neferti, a prophet in the Old Kingdom, who said that the pharaoh would be the harbinger of a new golden age, foretold Amenemhat's reign.

Amenemhat set about rapidly consolidating the country in a very purposeful manner. He moved his capital north to establish Amenemhat-itj-tawy, which means "Amenemhat—the seizer of the two lands." This is reminiscent of Pharaoh Menes who was the first pharaoh to combine both Upper and Lower Egypt. The new capital was located south of the former capital Memphis on the edge of the Faiyum Oasis. This gave Amenemhat a more central control of Egypt, as well as a more direct access to problem areas in the Nile Delta. It also marked the end of an old era and the beginning of a new one.

The new pharaoh of the Middle Dynasty reorganized the administration of the country, keeping the provincial governors, or nomarchs, who had supported him, while weakening the regional governors by appointing new officials. An inscription records that he also divided the provinces, or nomes, into different sets of towns and redistributed the territories by reference to the Nile flood. During Amenemhat's rule, we see a steady march back to a more centralized government, together with an increase in bureaucracy. This might seem counterintuitive from a contemporary point of view, as an increasing number of people rightfully seek self-empowerment and the preservation of a small state apparatus like our Founding Fathers envisioned it, but under the societal conditions of the early Second Dynasty right after the disarray of the First Intermediate Period, this was a necessary move, both to dilute the army's power and to raise personnel for coming conflicts, as Amenemhat also reintroduced general conscription.

One of Amenemhat's earliest campaigns was against the Asiatics, who were described in the *Prophecy of Neferti* as the people causing trouble on Egypt's eastern frontier. While also finding the time to crush a few unrepentant local governors, he drove the Asiatics back and built the "Walls-of-the-Ruler," a series of fortifications along Egypt's northeastern frontier. However,

even as late as his twenty-fourth year of rule, we still find inscriptions recording expeditions in that region.

By year twenty-nine of his rule, Amenemhat appears to have no longer been happy with the loose trading and quarrying network with Nubia, so he pushed his army southward to Elephantine where he consolidated his rule. The new policy was one of conquest and colonization with the principal aim of obtaining raw materials, especially gold. An inscription at the site of Korosko about halfway between the first and second cataracts of the Nile states that the people of Wawat in northern Nubia were defeated in his twenty-ninth year, and that he apparently drove his army as far south as the second cataract.

In order to protect Egypt and fortify captured territory in Nubia, he founded a fortress in the region of the second Nile cataract, which would begin a string of future Twelfth Dynasty fortresses. Along with protecting his newly acquired territory and gold mines, he also got a greater control over the economic relations with northern and southern Nubia. From a foreign relations standpoint, diplomatic and commercial relations were renewed, after a long absence, with Byblos in present-day Lebanon and the Aegean world in the area of Greece and southwestern Turkey.

Besides his efforts to construct fortresses, Amenemhat also initiated a number of building projects at temple complexes and undertook important building works at Karnak, from which a few statues and granite shrines, called *naoi,* survive to this day. He may have even established the original temple of the mother goddess Mut south of the Temple of Amun in Karnak. He worked at Gebtu, where he partly decorated the Temple of Min; at Abydos, where he dedicated a granite altar to Osiris; at Dendera, where he built a granite gateway to Hathor; and at Memphis, where he built a temple for Ptah.

Beginning with Amenemhat and throughout the Twelfth Dynasty, there was an increase in the mineral wealth of the royal family, which is confirmed by the jewelry caches that have been found in several Twelfth Dynasty royal burial sites. It is obvious from several sources that the standard of living for the average Egyptian was on the increase in proportion to the individual's status in society. Amenemhat was a very wise leader, setting about to correct the problems that commenced with the end of the Old Kingdom during the First Intermediate Period in Egypt's history that is often described as a dark age. He again

protected Egypt's borders from invasion and assured a legitimate succession.

But the head of a royal family has a constant source of those who would conspire to steal that powerful position by intrigue or force. My father in this lifetime was assassinated while I, his co-regent, was leading a campaign in Libya. There are two literary works, the *Tale of Sinuhe* and the *Instructions of Amenemhat,* reflecting the pharaoh's tragic end. The latter presents the account of Amenemhat's murder, dictated to a scribe by the pharaoh himself before he succumbed to his wounds:

"It was after supper, when night had fallen, and I had spent an hour of happiness. I was asleep upon my bed, having become weary, and my heart had begun to follow sleep. When weapons of my counsel were wielded, I had become like a snake of the necropolis. As I came to, I awoke to fighting, and found that it was an attack of the bodyguard. If I had quickly taken weapons in my hand, I would have made the wretches retreat with a charge! But there is none mighty in the night, none who can fight alone; no success will come without a helper. Look, my injury happened while I was without you, when the entourage had not yet heard that I would hand over to you when I had not yet sat with you, that I might make counsels for you; for I did not plan it, I did not foresee it, and my heart had not taken thought of the negligence of servants."

There are several more lines where much sage advice is given, one of which was to trust few and constantly check that those you trust are absolutely worthy of it. It's invaluable advice that is still worthy of adhering to today for those in positions of power, authority, and wealth.

The other work is the *Tale of Sinuhe,* attributed to Senusret. I have memories of working on it in collaboration with other talented writers of the time. Today this work is considered one of the finest works of ancient Egyptian literature, set in the aftermath of the death of Pharaoh Amenemhat. The tale is based on actual events involving an individual named Sinuhe, but it is mostly a work of fiction meant to inspire its readers and lift them up to a higher level of understanding. Due to the universal nature of the themes explored in Sinuhe, including divine providence and mercy, contemporary scholars have described it as being the work of the "Egyptian Shakespeare." The story, whose ideas have parallels in biblical texts, is a work written in verse, and it was also performed.

Amenemhat's foresight in creating the co-regency with Senusret proved successful, for I quickly returned, quelled the uprising, and succeeded my father, whose body was then honorably buried in his pyramid at el-Lisht, near the Faiyum Oasis. There was almost no disruption in the administration of the country. As the second pharaoh of the Twelfth Dynasty of Egypt, I would rule for a total of almost forty-six years, including ten years of co-regency with my son, the same son that I have in this life I was told. I continued my father's aggressive expansionist policies against Nubia by initiating two expeditions into this region, eventually establishing Egypt's formal southern border near the second cataract where I placed a garrison and a victory stela.

While I was doing research for a past life as the Spartan general Pausanias, I came across the Greek historian Herodotus's account of Senusret. I had memories of being a pharaoh, but I could not quite recall the time frame. Reading this account stirred a flood of memories for me. When I asked Ahtun Re, he confirmed that the lifetime as Pharaoh Senusret had been one of my past lives. He also informed me that he went on expeditions meant to establish trade as he strengthened the diplomatic relations with rulers of towns in Syria and Canaan. The warriors that joined him on the expeditions were made up mostly of warrior priests, so comparatively few battles were fought. The trading that resulted from his expeditions was what fueled much of the peace, economic success, and the golden age of the Twelfth Dynasty. In Egypt, Senusret continued to centralize the country's political structure by supporting nomarchs who were loyal to him.

Herodotus also cited a story told by Egyptian priests about Senusret, where he subdued the Arabian Gulf and defeated every nation in his way in a massive land campaign. Herodotus refers to a number of stelas recording Senusret's deeds that were still in existence during his time frame of 485-425 BCE or more than 1,500 years later, which the pharaoh had placed at the limits of his empire. The pharaoh allegedly subdued the Scythians near the Black Sea and the Thracians in what is today northern Greece, Bulgaria, Romania, eastern Serbia, and Macedonia. He also left a band of warriors at the river Phasis who settled and formed the people of Colchis that were the guardians of the Golden Fleece known from the Greek myth of Jason and the Argonauts.

According to Greek historians Diodorus Siculus and Strabo, he con-

quered the whole world, even Scythia and Ethiopia, divided Egypt into administrative districts or nomes, was a great lawgiver, and introduced a caste system into Egypt and the worship of Osiris, whom they called Serapis at that time. But the figure of Serapis was an amalgamation of Osiris and the bull god Apis mixed with Greek elements. Ptolemy Lagides, a general under Alexander the Great who from 323-283 BCE was the ruler of Egypt although born in Macedonia, devised it. Ptolemy hoped that Serapis would win the reverence of both the Egyptians and the many Greeks who then lived in Egypt, so that he could further consolidate his rule.

Senusret is also attested to be the builder of a number of major temples and shrines in ancient Egypt and Nubia, including the Temple of Min at Koptos, the Satet-Temple on Elephantine, and the Temple of Monthu at Armant and at El-Tod, where a long inscription of Senusret is preserved. Senusret rebuilt the important temple of Atum in Heliopolis, which was the center of the sun cult, and he also erected two red granite obelisks there to celebrate the Heb Sed festival marking his thirty- year jubilee.

One of the obelisks still remains and is the oldest standing obelisk in Egypt today in the Al-Masalla area of Al-Matariyyah district near the Ain Shams district where ancient Heliopolis is located. The obelisk is sixty-seven feet tall and weighs 120 tons or 240,000 pounds. The so- called White Chapel, a shrine made of alabaster with fine, high-quality reliefs of Senusret, was also built at Karnak for the Heb Seb festival. It has subsequently been successfully reconstructed from various stone blocks discovered by Henri Chevrier in 1926.

Senusret is credited with building the first temple complex at Karnak, which virtually every following pharaoh added to over the next two thousand years. Today, the religious complex of Karnak in Luxor is the largest ancient religious site in the world. The word "amen" is at the end of many prayers, yet few people are aware that the word itself is a direct reference to the Egyptian god Amen, or Amun, the chief deity of Karnak. The area of the sacred enclosure of Amun alone—there are three other sacred enclosures at Karnak not open to the public—is sixty- one acres in size and would hold ten average European cathedrals.

The great temple at the heart of Karnak is so big that St. Peter's, Milan's, and Paris's Notre Dame cathedrals could be lost within its walls. It literally dwarfs everything else. Measuring 54,000 square feet with 134 columns, the

Hypostyle Hall at Karnak is still the largest room of any religious building in the world. In addition to the main sanctuary, there are several smaller temples and a giant sacred lake, compelling respect for the vastness of Karnak and showing the raw power, wealth, and prestige this temple possessed. Among his other major building projects, Senusret also remodeled the temple of Khenti-Amenti-Osiris at Abydos.

The focus on Osiris reflects in every pharaoh of the Twelfth Dynasty, and Senusret was no exception to that rule. Osiris was usually identified as the god of the afterlife, the underworld, and the dead. He was classically depicted as a green-skinned man with a pharaoh's beard, partially mummy-wrapped in linen at the legs, wearing a distinctive crown with two large ostrich feathers at either side, and holding a symbolic crook and flail.

Osiris is considered the oldest son of the Earth god Geb and the sky goddess Nut, as well as being brother and husband of Isis, with Horus being considered his posthumously begotten son. Osiris's other siblings were Nephthys and Set, both of whom are considered to personify the darker nature of mankind as opposed to the light of Isis and Osiris.

One of the central spiritual teachings of Egypt is connected to the resurrection of Osiris, which reveals the process of attaining enlightenment, or imperishability, as it is called in Egyptian texts. The concept of resurrection can be found in many cultures and is associated with many historical or mythological figures like Jesus, Tammuz, Dionysus, Attis, Mithras, the maize god Hun Hunahpu of the Mayans, and many more, who all resurrected at the time of the spring equinox. There are more parallels between Jesus and Osiris: both were betrayed and killed before they were brought back to life to live eternally. In the life of Jesus, Joseph of Arimathea wraps the body of the crucified Jesus in linen before he places it in a tomb, while in the life of Osiris, Anubis conceals Osiris's body in a tomb. The two Marys bring spices and perfumes to anoint the body of Jesus, just as Isis and Nephthys would do to Osiris.

Resurrection is always preceded by death, but this death doesn't have to be a physical one. It can be an inner one, which takes place as part of a spiritual maturing process involving the death of all that is evil, inferior, and dark within oneself, such as hatred, anger, jealousy, lust, and so on in a process of psychological and energetic purification. In Egypt this turned into a religious

belief, as it has happened in many other cultures, but it was misinterpreted by later generations of people who had lost the ability to understand the esoteric meaning of Egypt's sacred texts.

Pharaohs believed that their physical death would lead to physical resurrection in the afterlife, which prompted them to surround themselves with jewels and spells that would apparently assure them safe passage in their journey to reach immortality. However, the esoteric death is inner, and its resurrection is achieved in life through spiritual and alchemical work. While Osiris was indeed killed physically, he could still have resurrected on a higher level.

Also associated with mummification and the afterlife in ancient Egyptian culture is Anubis, whose skin is often seen as very dark black or with a tinge of red. His flesh is a representation of the earthy energies with which he is connected; the color of his flesh is similar to that of the dark soil along the Nile. This rich, fertile soil was highly prized and gave the ancient kingdom the name Khem, which means the "black land." The color of Anubis could be an identifying link to Osiris, whose green flesh represents the fertile fields.

As the mother of Anubis, Nephthys can be seen depicted with him in the *Book of the Dead* most often. She is usually seen as a goddess of nighttime and darkness, which could be the reason for the dark color of his skin. Being a goddess of darkness, she is in opposition to her sister Isis, but maintains a friendly nature with her and Osiris. Nephthys and Isis worked together to find Osiris and bring him back from the dead, eventually standing behind him in the Hall of Truth to give eternal life to the deceased. Often Nephthys's husband and Osiris's brother Set is depicted as the father of Anubis, but it is also said that Nephthys longed for the relationship and love that Osiris shared with Isis, so she disguised herself as Isis and seduced him, which led to the birth of Anubis.

As guide of the underworld, Anubis takes the soul of the deceased before the gods to give the negative confession. In the underworld, Anubis also took care that the dreaded Ammit—a beast made up of the head of a crocodile, front of a lioness, and the hindquarters of a hippopotamus—could not devour the heart of the deceased, causing the soul to be restless for all eternity. Some of the tools of Anubis were the Was Scepter and the Ankh.

The Was Scepter appears as a stylized animal head or phoenix head at the top of a long, straight staff with a forked end. It was a symbol of health, happiness, and divine prosperity but also of power and dominion, while its green color was based on the understanding that green is connected to fertility, life, and resurrection. The Was Scepter was also associated with the qualities of divine rulership and carried exclusively by gods and goddesses until late in Egyptian civilization, when the pharaohs took on this attribute in funeral works.

When the journey through the underworld was nearly complete, the deceased was taken to the Hall of Ma'at to be judged. There the heart would be weighed against the feather of Ma'at that stands for truth, balance, and justice. If the heart is light and the deceased is found to be true of voice through his trials and negative confessions, Anubis brings him before Osiris to join him in immortality. Many halls related to the Hall of Ma'at in the spirit world are secretly located in symbolic form under major temple sites.

Some chambers in the pyramids that are considered tombs were rather like wombs in a spiritual sense, as they were never designed for actual deceased bodies. Many chambers and sarcophagi were used for initiatory rites to symbolize the process of the inner death and resurrection, which is why the stone sarcophagi in the chambers of the Great Pyramids were found empty. What was found, however, was a white powder that accumulated at the end of the sarcophagus where the head of the person would have rested. This powder was taken to the British Museum and later found to be a natural secretion from the pineal gland, indicating that the pineal gland of the person inside the sarcophagus was highly active. It actually seems that the whole pyramid with all its structural elements related to sacred geometrical patterns was specifically built for the purpose of being an amplifier for psychic energies. For the experience of utilizing the power of the Great Pyramid in such a way, it took the initiate decades of training in the Egyptian mystery schools, according to Drunvalo Melchizedek, who laid out the details in his book *The Flower of Life*.

The Great Sphinx and the rest of the Giza complex, which includes the Great Pyramids, were built using the sacred principles that underlie creation and enlightenment.

A place unparalleled anywhere else on Earth, the Giza complex was not built as a cemetery, nor primarily as an astronomical observatory, nor as a mathematical timepiece, although it is all these things. By uncovering the esoteric principles underlying the Great Pyramids and the Sphinx, it's possible to

reveal their purpose—as a place of sacred knowledge and initiatory rites that facilitate the individual attainment of enlightenment, once the great goal of life and the focal point of ancient Egypt.

If we look carefully at the head of the Sphinx, we will notice it is out of proportion. The head is much too small for its body, and is far less weathered than the rest of the body and surrounding enclosure. It has obviously been recarved, and its body has been covered with restoration stones dating from thousands of years right up until today, giving the Sphinx its leonine shape.

When I asked Ahtun Re about the carving of the Sphinx human head, he said it was only meant to be a representation of a perfect form. The interesting thing that he told me was that a face of gold was cast with the likeness of the current pharaoh and placed over the head of the Sphinx and this is why it is smaller than the rest of the Sphinx. In King Tutankhamun's burial chamber was found a golden faceplate, and this is similar to what would have been on the Sphinx but on a grander scale.

Breastplates with jewels were also placed over the body of the Sphinx. These jeweled plates were aligned with the energy of the current pharaoh. Many princes of Egypt including Moses had breastplates that were bejeweled. Each precious stone had a certain energy vibration that heightened and projected the particular noble's energy focus and abilities. When these breastplates and mask were placed on the Sphinx, the energy would be spread throughout Egypt. If you think this is grandiose, think of Mount Rushmore with presidents' heads and Stone Mountain in Georgia with the largest bas-relief sculpture in the world featuring southern Civil War heroes carved in a huge granite mountainside.

Today there are many statues, sculptures, and monuments throughout the world that far surpass the Sphinx in size and grandeur. Many of these monuments like the Sphinx are located in geographical locations that are or were considered sacred. The energy and intent of the statues or monuments were positioned so that they would be magnified by their locations. By adding precious metals and jewels to a monument you would increase its power and purpose. When we adorn our bodies with precious metals and jewels we can do the same thing.

The pharaohs' job, after they were awakened themselves, was to awaken as many people as they could. Moses's admonition to king Ramses to "let my people go" was because Ramses was not an initiate and was not awakening people but enslaving them. Moses left Egypt not with just Jews but also with Libyans, Egyptians, Nubians, and many others. Moses would become the equivalent of a pharaoh for many years until he started training priests and delegating authority down to representatives from the different tribes.

Jesus, who had lived in Egypt with his family for several years as a young boy, had started the initiations and later returned to go through the final ceremonies along the Nile River. He went through the same process as the princes and princesses of Egypt had for thousands of years. The underground chambers were important because the locations and designs themselves would react with the physical and psychic energies of the initiates. Rediscovering and integrating the chambers for initiations again would be an important process in reigniting the positive processes that will accelerate humanity's evolution.

The greatest leaders throughout history not only provided an environment for peace and prosperity but also for spiritual enlightenment. The Twelfth Dynasty was focused on providing the means for all citizens to more easily reach the immortal spiritual status that had been previously reserved for only the pharaoh. The environment around many Egyptian cities reflected this ideal in the temples, statues, and ceremonies above *and* below ground.

As I've pointed out, the Egyptians built underground temples and halls that were as large and in some cases significantly larger than the ones above ground. These complexes were initiatory cathedrals that allowed the initiate to progress significantly on the path to enlightenment. They were secret only to keep the uninitiated away from advanced information that they would not understand and were not ready to accept. It was a goal of the people to rise in consciousness so that they could participate in ceremonies they knew were happening. The initiations were not a secret and many people strived to obtain the necessary level to participate. It was also open to all peoples, not just Egyptians.

In the fifth century BCE, Herodotus, who is considered the father of history, describes a labyrinth complex in Egypt "near the place called the City of Crocodiles" that he considered surpassing the pyramids in grandeur.

The labyrinth Herodotus spoke of was situated in the current day Faiyum Oasis district, which today is a depression or basin in the desert immediately to the west of the Nile south of Cairo. It was in that lush, fertile valley that pharaohs calling themselves the "masters of the royal hunts" fished and hunted with the boo-

merang. Lake Moeris once bordered the Faiyum Oasis, and on its shores was the famous labyrinth, described by Herodotus as "an endless wonder." I have memories of these underground cities and temples. The lake has receded over time and is now about six times smaller than it had been over three thousand years ago.

Senusret I built a large pyramid complex near this site, very reminiscent of the Giza complex in form but on a smaller scale. The complex is located near the present city of Lisht located sixty-five kilometers south of Cairo. The labyrinth that will be spoken of in detail in the rest of the chapter was at this location. The Metropolitan Museum of Art in New York City did some of the most extensive and scientific excavation work ever performed in Egypt at this pyramid site. Statuary and small temples from this site were transported in great abundance to the New York museum's Egyptian antiquities display.

The labyrinth contained 1,500 rooms and an equal number of underground chambers that Herodotus was not permitted to inspect. According to labyrinth priests, "the passages were baffling and intricate," designed to provide safety for the numerous scrolls they said were hidden in subterranean apartments. That massive complex particularly impressed Herodotus, and, in *Book II* of his Histories series, he spoke in awe of the structure:

> *There I saw twelve palaces regularly disposed, which had communication with each other, interspersed with terraces and arranged around twelve halls. It is hard to believe they are the work of men. The walls are covered with carved figures, and each court is exquisitely built of white marble and surrounded by a colonnade. Near the corner where the labyrinth ends, there is a pyramid, 240 feet in height, with great, carved figures of animals on it and an underground passage by which it can be entered. I was told very credibly that underground chambers and passages connected this pyramid with the pyramids at Memphis.*
>
> *It has twelve courts covered in, with gates facing one another, six upon the north side and six upon the south, joining on one to another, and the same wall surrounds them all outside; and there are in it two kinds of chambers, the one kind below the ground and the other above upon these, three thousand in number, of each kind fifteen hundred. The upper set of chambers we ourselves saw, going through them, and we tell of them having looked*

upon them with our own eyes; but the chambers underground we heard about only; for the Egyptians who had charge of them were not willing on any account to show them, saying that here were the sepulchers of the kings who had first built this labyrinth and of the sacred crocodiles.

Accordingly we speak of the chambers below by what we received from hearsay, while those above we saw ourselves and found them to be works of more than human greatness. For the passages through the chambers, and the goings this way and that way through the courts, which were admirably adorned, afforded endless matter for marvel, as we went through from a court to the chambers beyond it, and from the chambers to colonnades, and from the colonnades to other rooms, and then from the chambers again to other courts.

Over the whole of these is a roof made of stone like the walls; and the walls are covered with figures carved upon them, each court being surrounded with pillars of white stone fitted together most perfectly; and at the end of the labyrinth, by the corner of it, there is a pyramid of forty fathoms, upon which large figures are carved, and to this there is a way made underground. Such is this labyrinth, but the lake, which is called the Lake of Moeris, along the side of which this labyrinth is built, affords a cause for marvel even greater than this. The measure of its circuit is 3,600 furlongs, and this is the same number of furlongs as the extent of Egypt itself along the sea. The lake lies extended lengthwise from north to south, and in depth where it is deepest it is fifty fathoms.

That this lake is artificial and formed by digging is self-evident, for about in the middle of the lake stand two pyramids, each rising above the water to a height of fifty fathoms [three hundred feet], the part which is built below the water being of just the same height, and upon each is placed a colossal statue of stone sitting upon a chair. Thus the pyramids are a hundred fathoms high; and these hundred fathoms are equal to a furlong of six hundred feet, the fathom being measured as six feet or four cubits, the feet being four palms each, and the cubits six.

The water in the lake does not come from the place where it is, for the country there is very deficient in water, but it has been brought thither

from the Nile by a canal. And for six months the water flows into the lake, and for six months out into the Nile again. And whenever it flows out, then for the six months it brings into the royal treasury a talent of silver a day from the fish which are caught, and twenty pounds when the water comes in. The natives of the place moreover said that this lake had an outlet underground to the Syrtis, which is in Libya, turning toward the interior of the continent upon the western side and running along by the mountain, which is above Memphis. Now since I did not see anywhere existing the earth dug out of this excavation.

This I saw myself, and I found it greater than words can say. For if one should put together and reckon up all the buildings and all the great works produced by Hellenes, they would prove to be inferior in labor and expense to this labyrinth, though it is true that both the temple at Ephesos and that at Samos are works worthy of note. The pyramids also were greater than words can say, and each one of them is equal to many works of the Hellenes, great as they may be, but the labyrinth surpasses even the pyramids."

The first century BCE Greek geographer Strabo is the only other ancient eyewitness of the Egyptian labyrinth whose account has survived. Strabo said of it that it was "a great palace composed of many palaces" and marveled at the enormity of the stone slabs that made up its roof and walls. He wrote that it had many great courts, each with its own entrance, but that "in front of the entrances are crypts, as it were, which are long and numerous and have winding passages communicating with one another, so that no stranger can find his way either into any court or out of it without a guide."

Diodorus, also in the first century BCE, wrote in the *Library of History:*

For selecting a site at the entrance to Lake Moeris in Libya they constructed their tomb of the finest stone, and they made it in form a square but in magnitude a stade in length [six hundred seven feet] on each side; and in the carvings and, indeed, in all the workmanship they left nothing wherein succeeding rulers could excel them. For, as a man passed through the enclosing wall, he found himself in a court surrounded by columns, forty on each side, and the roof of the court consisted of a single

> *stone, which was worked into coffers and adorned with excellent paintings. This court also contained memorials of the native district of each king and of the temples and sacrificial rites therein, artistically portrayed in most beautiful paintings. And in general, the kings are said to have made the plan of their tomb on such an expensive and enormous scale that, had they not died before the execution of their purpose, they would have left no possibility for others to surpass them, so far as the construction of monuments is concerned.*

Pliny the Elder, who was a Roman scholar and military commander, described the labyrinth in the first century AD in his work *Natural History:*

> *We must mention also the labyrinths, quite the most abnormal achievement on which man has spent his resources, but by no means a fictitious one, as might well be supposed.*

The labyrinth obviously existed and was of immense proportions. It was used in extensive initiatory ceremonies. The Twelfth Dynasty's vast wealth built through trade that Senusret painstakingly expanded over time was instrumental in the refurbishment of and start of many complexes throughout Egypt, many of which are still visible. Unfortunately, over time the massive labyrinth complex and Twelfth Dynasty pyramids' covering limestone was looted to build other buildings. Now only foundation stones and mounds exist where amazing structures once graced the landscape.

The brilliant Twelfth Dynasty of Egypt eventually came to an end in the eighteenth century BCE with the death of Egypt's first female pharaoh named Sobekneferu. Apparently, she had no heirs, causing the Twelfth Dynasty and the Golden Age of the Middle Kingdom it represented to come to a sudden end. The chronology of the Twelfth Dynasty is the most stable of any period before the New Kingdom; the Ramses Papyrus Canon in Turin gives the length of this dynasty as 213 years. The Second Intermediate Period in Egyptian history was followed by five rather unstable dynasties that ensued in only one hundred years after the Twelfth Dynasty.

Senusret's trade between nations brought great wealth, peace, art, sacred building programs, and spiritual development to the masses. Today Egypt has the potential of again creating this environment and expanding a rebuilding campaign to restore its amazing heritage. Blooming the desert once again as

was done in the past by creatively using the waters of the Nile to supply Lake Moeris would bring in vast amounts of revenue.

Expanding tourism could also help bring in the wealth needed to restore and rediscover the vast temple complexes throughout Egypt. Not only would this new wealth be beneficial to Egypt and its people, but also all of humanity could profit by rediscovering the deeper ways of connecting with higher consciousness that was and still is available in the temple complexes. It was done in the past by a king with vision and the will of his people, and it can easily be done again.

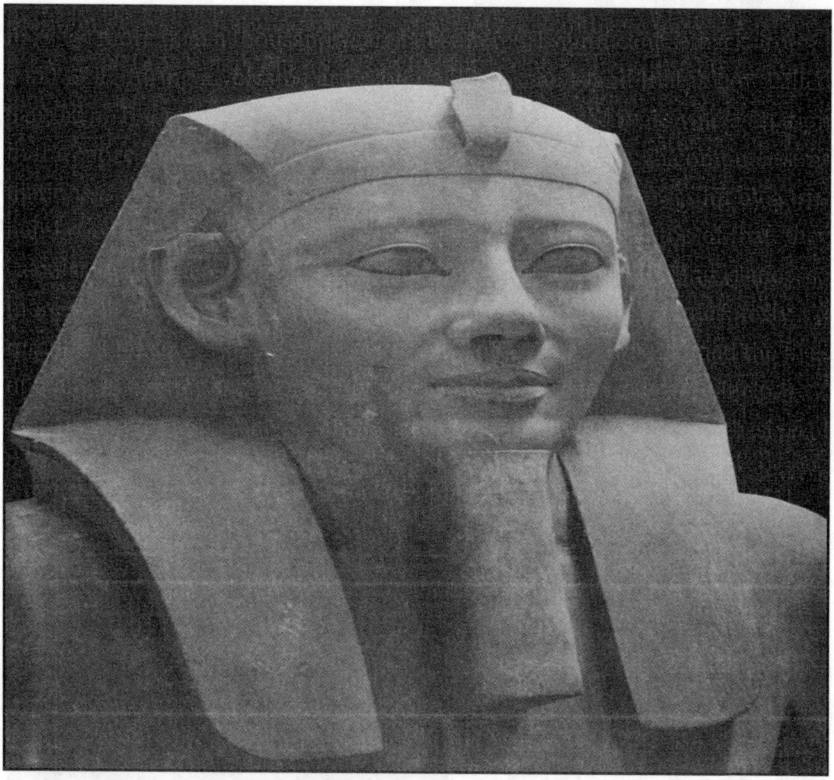

Senurset I was the second pharaoh of the Twelfth Dynasty of Egypt. He ruled from 1971 BCE to 1926 BCE, and was one of the most powerful kings of this Dynasty.

Osiris is the god of fertility, agriculture, the afterlife, the dead, resurrection, life, and vegetation in ancient Egyptian religion. He was classically depicted as a green-skinned deity with a pharaoh's beard, partially mummy-wrapped at the legs, wearing a distinctive atef crown, and holding a symbolic crook and flail.

Anubis is the god of death, mummification, embalming, the afterlife, cemeteries, tombs, and the Underworld, in ancient Egyptian religion, usually depicted as a canine or a man with a canine head.

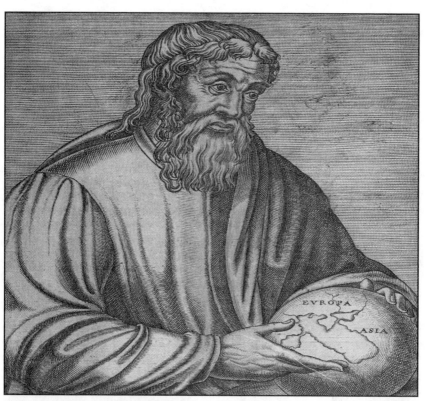

Strabo was a Greek geographer, philosopher, and historian who lived in Asia Minor during the transitional period of the Roman Republic into the Roman Empire.

Herodotus was an ancient Greek historian and geographer from the Greek city of Halicarnassus. He is known for having written the *Histories* – a detailed account of the Greco-Persian Wars. Herodotus was the first writer to perform systematic investigation of historical events. He is referred to as "The Father of History," a title conferred on him by the ancient Roman orator Cicero.

“WHENEVER I AM BORN IN EVERY LIFE TO COME, MAY I MEET AGAIN MY GUARDIAN ANGEL OF THIS LIFE! SPEAKING AND UNDERSTANDING THE MOMENT I AM BORN, MAY I ... REMEMBER MY FORMER LIVES!”

◊ *The Tibetan Book of the Dead* ◊

CHAPTER 5

WITH PATRIARCH ABRAHAM AS KING ABIMELECH OF GERAR, 1800 BCE

I initially found out about my incarnation with Abraham while doing research for a lifetime during the time frame of Jesus. I was told that I was one of seven tribal kings that Abraham integrated into one group, whose purpose was aligned with the same principles of sacred warfare that I touched upon in the third chapter. I discovered through my own memories, which were confirmed by Ahtun Re, that I was King Abimelech of Gerar mentioned in Genesis of the Bible. I participated in the campaign to rescue Abraham's nephew Lot in the aftermath of the Battle of Siddim, which you may also reference in the Book of Genesis. But before I relate the details of my personal memories, let me first give you a little background on Abraham.

Abraham was born in the city of Ur in Babylonia as the son of Terach, a wealthy idol merchant. His name was originally Abram, meaning high father, but was changed later in his life to Abraham, meaning the father of many. In the Hebrew Torah, he is also described as Ivri, which comes from the word *ever*, meaning "the other side." This could pertain to the fact that Abraham was born east of the Jordan River or to the fact that he was in opposition to the pa-

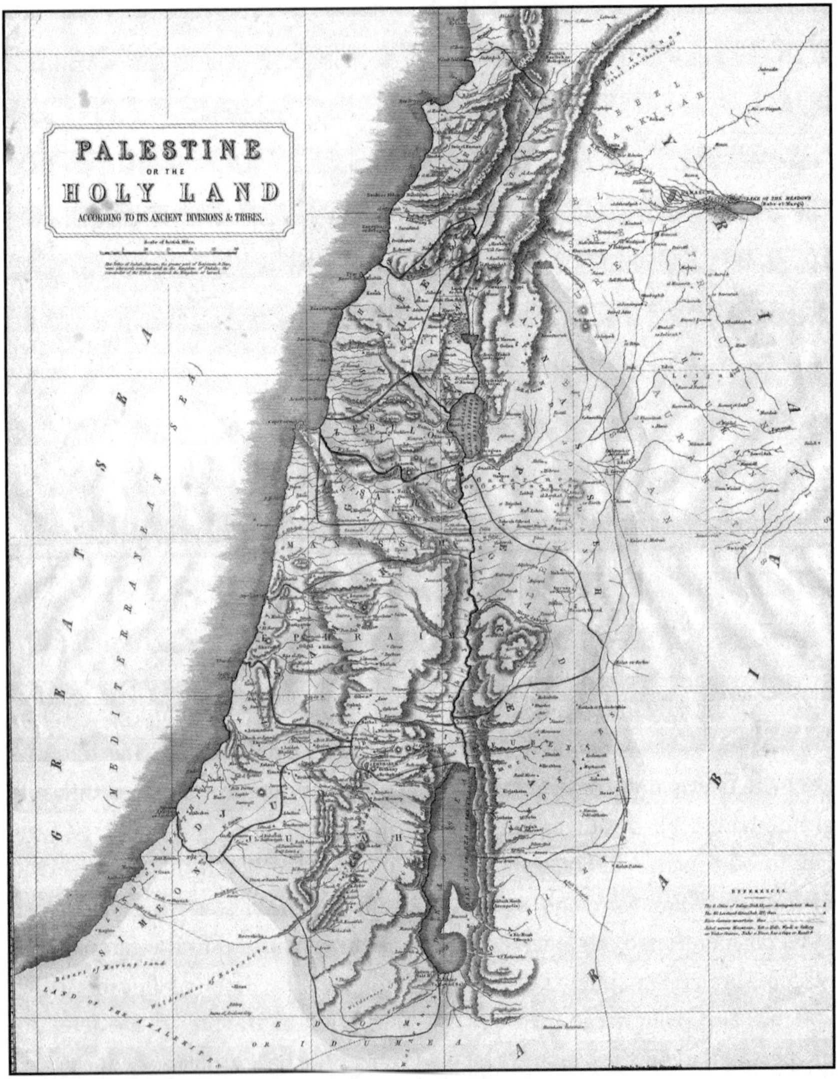

PALESTINE
OR THE
HOLY LAND
ACCORDING TO ITS ANCIENT DIVISIONS & TRIBES.

gan ideals of his time. Another possibility is that Ivri refers to Abraham being the descendant of Ever, the great- grandson of Noah's son Shem.

As was the custom for sons of wealthy families during that time, Abraham studied in many different locations as a boy and young man. He would gather much knowledge in Egypt and become an advanced initiate in the wisdom schools. During his studies he came to believe that the entire universe emanates

from one single Creator, which is a core tenet of Judaism, Christianity, and Islam. They all trace their origins back to Abraham, which is why they are called the three Abrahamic religions. His progressive stance in regard to monotheism, the belief in one God, demanded a high amount of determination and integrity as he rejected the worldview handed down to him by his father.

It was surely not by coincidence that Abraham was born as the son of a man who made a living by being loyal to a superstitious belief; it rather seems that this fact served as a catalyst on his path. There is an interesting anecdote that illustrates the creative and awakened mind of Abraham who just wouldn't acquiesce in growing up as another idol merchant. One day, when Abraham was left alone to mind the store, he took a hammer and smashed all of the idols except the largest one. He then placed the hammer in the hand of the largest idol, and when his father Terach returned and asked what happened, Abraham replied, "The idols got into a fight, and the big one smashed all the other ones." Terach said, "Don't be ridiculous. These idols have no life or power. They can't do anything." This is what Abraham wanted to demonstrate all along, so he concluded this scene trenchantly by asking, "Then why do you worship them?"

Being the son of a merchant, Abraham would carry on with the family business and become wealthy in his own right. He would travel to the British Isles for trading and on one of these visits would marry a local princess named Sarai or Sarah. It would be during his trading adventures that he would travel to Egypt with his new young wife.

On this trip to Egypt, Abraham impressed the pharaoh so much that he gave him his daughter Hagar as a wife. There are many variations to this story on record, but my memories are that Abraham eventually had several wives over the course of his life. As with most households with multiple wives, one wife is in charge of the household, and in Abraham's case it was his wife Sarah.

But Hagar, having grown up a princess and used to having her way, was very strong willed, opinionated, and vocal about the way she thought things should be run, and so she and Sarah would often argue. Another reason why the queen of the household and the princess from Egypt did not get along was that Sarah was dissatisfied with the fact that Hagar gave birth to Abraham's first son, Ishmael. This occurrence was during a time when Sarah thought of herself as being past childbearing age. But nevertheless, several years later, at an advanced age, Sarah would give birth to Isaac, whose son Jacob was later renamed Israel, and that is what the land of Canaan would eventually be called. Israel would also be considered one of the three patriarchs of the Jewish religion, the other two being Isaac and Abraham.

After Sarah's death, Abraham would eventually have another wife named Keturah, who would bear him six sons named Zimran, Jokshan, Medan, Midian, Ishbak, and Shuah. All of these children would later have their own tribes and move eastward, spreading the same monotheistic thought that Abraham propagated.

Having multiple wives for a wealthy and influential man was common but not standard in that time and is still practiced in several Middle Eastern countries to this day. Social norms can vary heavily over time and within different cultures, so when I recount my memories of past lives I try not to use a harsh judgment toward norms that are not aligned with how I live my life now. Even today when looking at other cultures and lifestyles that may be different from yours, be aware that it is quite possible that during the course of your own incarnations you have lived in numerous cultural environments with various different lifestyles yourself.

Abraham was a very loving and devoted husband as well as a great leader and consolidated the power of several kingdoms through agreement. I know that the Bible has a story in which God commands Abraham to take his son Isaac and sacrifice him to prove his loyalty and devotion. Many of the surrounding tribes worshiped the god Baal, who demanded sacrifice. Often these sacrifices involved the firstborn son or the son of the main wife, which was Sarah's son Isaac. Sacrifice of humans and animals in the name of gods is a common thread throughout history that is regrettably still practiced today.

The story is related that as they are climbing Mount Moriah, Isaac is collecting wood for the sacrifice and carrying it up the mountain when he asks his father where the animal is that they are going to sacrifice. Abraham replies that God will provide one, but then takes his son and ties him over the wood that he had just collected. Just before he is going to slit Isaac's throat, an angel stops him and tells Abraham that he has proven himself to God, after which he suddenly finds a ram caught in brambles that is then sacrificed instead of Isaac.

This event is claimed by Muslims to have taken place on the Temple Mound

in Jerusalem and that Ishmael was the one that was going to be sacrificed, not Isaac. The submission of Abraham is commemorated and celebrated by Muslims on the days of the Eid al-Adha festival that takes place during the annual Hajj pilgrimage. Those who can afford it sacrifice a ram, cow, sheep, or a camel, which is then split into three parts with one part of the meat eaten by the household and the remaining two parts distributed to the neighbors and the needy.

However, because of my understanding of God and religion during the time of Abraham and because I knew him and his family well, I must say that this story is a fabrication made at a later time. The loving God that we knew would never ask this of one of his devoted followers, and Abraham would have never followed a God that would request such a horrific act. In my opinion, this story is a later addition to make people fear a God whose nature is actually one of inspiring love, not fear. I say this in no disrespect to anyone's idea of this event and hope that the truth will eventually come to light to validate my claim.

The actual event in my memories was one of a symbolic gesture. A sacred knife was used to cut away the bonds that restrain a boy from becoming a man. By running the knife over a prostrate boy and asking that his cords to boyhood be released so that he could become a man, we were conducting a rite of passage into manhood. Sacrifice was still conducted by many barbaric religions and tribes in the area, but our faith was a way out of barbarism and into higher levels of consciousness.

Raised as a city-dweller, Abraham would eventually adopt a nomadic lifestyle traveling all over the Middle East, but especially through Canaan, which encompasses present-day Israel, Palestine, Lebanon, and parts of Syria. On one occasion while traveling on his trade route to the Desert of Paran or what is today called Mecca, Sarah, Hagar, Ishmael, and several other families accompanied Abraham. His plan was to set up a trading base in this area, and for that purpose he had many families and warriors with him from Canaan that would stay in this area and establish contacts. It was there that Hagar decided to stay with Ishmael and become the matriarch of Abraham's new trading base to which he would return many times over the years while Hagar and Ishmael would maintain it as their home. Only occasionally Hagar would return to her homeland of Egypt helping to establish another trading route and eventually finding an Egyptian wife for Ishmael.

While setting up the camp area and building permanent foundations, the thirteen-year-old Ishmael was gathering stones for foundation work and came across black stones that were milky white on the inside. Further inspection of these stones by Abraham and others revealed what would eventually be the most sacred object in Islam. A huge meteorite that was black on the outside and milky white on the inside was found to be the source of the other smaller black stones that were scattered around the site. They had been flung from the main body of the meteorite after it slammed into Earth.

This large stone was left in place and made into a cornerstone of the original camp. Abraham, who was well versed in the art of divining Earth's sacred areas or power centers, chose the area of present- day Mecca for its high energy and crystalline structure underneath the sands of the desert. This is the way that Islam got its essential pilgrimage site and the reason why Muslims honor the memory of Abraham and Ishmael as the founders of their religion.

It is a symptom of the patriarchal paradigm that has been prevalent throughout most of human history that the contributions and leadership of Abraham's wives are not that prominently remembered, but I can attest to the fact that this is not doing them justice. I have a very clear memory of what happened in that life when my queen of that time, who is incidentally my wife in my current life, and I sat next to each other in awe as the beautiful Sarah allowed God to speak through her. Interestingly, my memories of Sarah's physical appearances are that she was petite and fair skinned, with long blond hair and blue eyes.

Sarah would always attract a lot of attention from people seeing her for the first time. We were sitting on large cushions laid out on carpets on the ground in Abraham's tent after we had finished a meal together when Sarah started to speak of how the tribes of Abraham would multiply tremendously and that we would all be favored with peace and prosperity. Sarah had also been trained as an advanced initiate in the mystery schools of Egypt, and Abraham would rely on her channeled messages several times throughout their lifetimes when he made important decisions.

Abraham's second wife, Hagar, is still a prominent part of a beautiful ceremony in Islam that honors the divine feminine in all women. After Hagar settled in Paran, there had been a severe drought in that area. She was wandering desperately in search of water for her son and her people who were nearly

dying of thirst. She wandered between two hills and is reputed to have made seven counterclockwise searches before being divinely guided to the spring of Zamzam, which is to this day a well in the area of Mecca. When Muslim pilgrims go on the annual Hajj, they travel between the same two hills and make seven counterclockwise turns around the cube of the meteorite, the Kaaba.

They also drink from the waters of Zamzam, which is said to have healing powers. Throughout my many years of travel in the Middle East during this lifetime, I have seen many people returning from the Hajj carrying large plastic jugs full of water from Zamzam. I can easily imagine how the positive focus of millions of pilgrims charges the water in Zamzam tremendously, not least considering that it has been scientifically proven by Dr. Masaru Emoto and others that directing thoughts, emotions, or sound toward water changes its physical structure. This discovery by Dr. Emoto is actually a rediscovery hinting at the significance of what I described in the third chapter in regard to the shaping of matter through thoughts and sound harmonics during my incarnation in Egypt. We now live in a time where we pull together the loose ends of history, merging science and ancient spiritual knowledge.

Abraham had been an advanced initiate in many different spiritual practices in Egypt. He would eventually be referred by Egyptian priests in Heliopolis to the priest king Melchizedek in the city of Salem, centrally located in the land of Canaan. Salem, also known as the city of peace, would later become the city of Jerusalem. Inspired by the teachings of the priests in the different initiatory temples along the Nile and the teachings and guidance from Melchizedek, Abraham later instituted these teachings among his growing tribe as well.

Who Melchizedek really was has been shrouded in mystery for almost four millennia now. If you read the Book of Enoch, you will find that many of the sayings and ideas bear a huge resemblance to the later teachings of Melchizedek and Yeshua. Interestingly, the famous psychic Edgar Cayce, when looking at the akashic records, would tell us that Yeshua in previous incarnations was both Enoch, the city builder, and Melchizedek, the mystical high priest and king of Salem. Melchizedek's teachings would be adopted by Abraham and spread far and wide through the children and descendants of his tribe.

When Ahtun Re questioned me about my thoughts on the time frame with Yeshua, I said that I felt that at one time I was an Essene. I was then actually told of two previous incarnations involving the Essenes, a Jewish religious tribe that Yeshua and his family belonged to. They traced their lineage back to Enoch, who was also the founder of the city of Ur, as I was told as well. Although I have been to Babylon twice in this lifetime on security missions for the US Department of State in 2004,1 have not visited Ur because it was unfortunately unsafe to travel to the area 160 miles southeast of Babylon where Ur was located. I was told that was too bad as Ur was a place I surely would have enjoyed visiting, because I had been there in a past life with Enoch.

Enoch appears briefly in the Old and New Testaments and is considered a prophet in Islam. Muslims identify the prophets of Islam as those humans chosen by God to teach mankind. Enoch is also represented in the Book of Enoch, which is a constituent of the Dead Sea Scrolls collection and reportedly written by Enoch himself. The Dead Sea Scrolls were found in the ancient Essene city of Qumran, fifteen miles east of Jerusalem on the northwestern banks of the Dead Sea. Qumran contained libraries of ancient scrolls and was used as a place of deep spiritual study with most of the inhabitants being celibate men, although several families coexisted there as well. Many of the Essenes who were on a deeply spiritual path like Yeshua and John the Baptist would visit Qumran and sometimes stay there for years to study and attend lectures. The city was destroyed by the Romans during the same time frame they destroyed Jerusalem around 70 CE, but an attempt at the last minute to conceal some of the vast library's scrolls that had not already been safely removed or destroyed was successful in that they were found unharmed almost two thousand years later in multiple caves, another indicator of how the puzzle pieces are falling together in this day and age.

Enoch was the father of Methuselah, who is reputed in the Bible as having lived 969 years. This was due to the fact that Methuselah and many others of Enoch's lineage were initiates in the Egyptian art of attaining longevity. Masters of this process would reformulate their bodies after reaching an advanced age and return their bodies to an age of around thirty to thirty-five years old. This process entailed placing the body into a state very similar to what you see Egyptian mummies on display today. The body was wrapped in specially prepared oiled linen strips of cloth and laid to rest while other initiates would stand by day and night. The spirit then left the physical body and reconstituted

itself over time before it returned to renew the physical body. Through diet, regular fasting, proper nutrition, meditation, and visualization practices, the process of aging was greatly reduced while in the physical realm until the process of renewing the body was repeated.

In the Book of Enoch, it is written that Enoch had foreknowledge of the Great Flood of the Bible, as it was revealed to him in a vision upon the birth of Methuselah, who would be the father of Noah. My thoughts are that the Great Flood mentioned in the Bible is not the worldwide devastating flood that happened over twelve thousand years ago and destroyed the large island of Atlantis in the Atlantic Ocean. This worldwide, Earth-changing event, which is mentioned in over one hundred cultures throughout the world, caused mass migrations from Atlantis through much of Europe, particularly Greece, but also to Egypt and the Americas. The flood event mentioned in the Bible was also very devastating, but confined to a smaller geographical area in what is now western Russia and much of the Middle East, several thousand years after the other great cataclysmic deluge.

According to Old Testament tradition, Enoch is also noted as the only human besides Elijah who ascended into heaven. The New Testament then has Jesus ascending and the Qur'an has Mohammad ascending at the same location as the current Dome of the Rock at Temple Mount, Jerusalem.

The concept of ascension or entering heaven alive is a belief held by multiple religions and traditions, described in various terms over time such as assumption, rapture, or translation. Since death is generally considered the normal end to an individual's life on Earth, transcending physical existence without dying first is considered exceptional. The ascension process is important to reincarnation because it is a process that occurs over many lifetimes; you can liken it to climbing a staircase. As we unveil, develop, and expand our spiritual awareness through the rebirth process, we climb the steps, so to speak, toward ascension.

In each incarnation you usually learn important lessons and advance up the staircase a step or two. In some lives you may advance many steps while in others you may actually take a step backward or not advance at all depending on your life purpose and whether or not it was fulfilled. This is one of the reasons why suicide is such a tragedy, because it prevents you from working

through the challenges you set out for yourself, meaning that you will have to return to the same type of situation until you master it.

In some lives, however, we just come to take a break. Especially after very stressful or traumatic experiences, it can be helpful to learn to enjoy life on Earth again in order to heal and prepare for future lives. I also believe that we all have the choice to decide whether we work on hard issues or challenges in our current lives, which most of us do, or whether we postpone some lessons for future lives, which could be considered procrastination in the reincarnation progression.

Eventually, after many life lessons and advancement up the many stairs, we will reach a higher realm of consciousness where we are no longer compelled to incarnate the way we do now. In the bigger picture, this is not just a possibility but also everyone's destiny, as our lessons simply won't fade away until we really learn them. This means that the ascension process always requires our conscious freewill decisions and creative actions. The possibility of ascension is one of the things that is so interesting about studying the reincarnation process. But no matter where we are on that road, we are never really separated from the one true God, the one true love.

This is exactly what Abraham taught and what is also expressed within the fourth and youngest proclaimed Abrahamic religion, the Baha'i faith founded by Baha'u'llah *in the nineteenth century in Persia.* It is Baha'u'llah's understanding that religion is simply a means to inspire us to honor the fact that "all men have been created to *carry forward an ever-advancing civilization.*" Baha'i writings describe God as an imperishable and uncreated being, who is the source of all existence, "a personal God that is unknowable in the physical sense, the source of all revelation, eternal, omniscient, omnipresent, and all powerful." This concept of God in the Baha'i faith is expanded upon by religious scholar Peter Smith, who writes, "Though transcendent and inaccessible directly, his image is reflected in his creation, which is everything in existence, and the purpose of creation is for the created to have the capacity to know and love its creator."

In Abraham's time, when the worship of multiple gods through idol worship was quite prolific throughout the known world, these ideas were truly revolutionary. The general attraction toward Abraham's effort to gather and refine the focus and energy that had formerly been scattered in hundreds of different idols was one of the main reasons why he has been successful in ex-

panding his tribal base so rapidly. Another reason was that he allowed the former kings of the different tribes to remain in their leadership roles. This encouraged the already loosely existing confederation of tribes to more consciously work together to create a tighter bond with each other.

My tribe was already endorsing the ideas of Melchizedek when Abraham arrived in the area, so I was sympathetic to Abraham's ideas right away. Associating early on with him and becoming part of his immediate family set an example for the other tribes. A nomadic tribal group usually had a unique culture and traits, but, with Abraham, all the diverse ideas were assembled under one central authority figure or king with authority in religion, trade, law, education, and so on. Simply put, he was bringing the ideas that had worked in the cities such as Ur where he grew up and integrated them into the nomadic lifestyle. This had not been effectively done before, but it was a model that would prove to be very effective.

Abraham also had the idea to establish seven cities along the Jordan River similar to the seven temples that Menes had built along the Nile. Accordingly, Abraham's seven kings would correspond to the chakra system of the body that he had learned about during his studies in Egypt. A system of training was initiated that would educate the tribal warriors not only in the art of war but also in the art of awakening within themselves the kundalini energy. Kundalini can be "awakened" or "aroused" from its "slumber" at the base of your spine by intense meditation or intense breath control practices. An aroused kundalini within an individual can exert tremendous energy and thus increase the potency of meditation and other spiritual practices. Horses were also part of this training; it was taught to establish a connection between the rider and his horse using this internal energy.

Every male from a young age onward until senectitude or old age was expected to be a warrior to protect the tribe and its belongings. Use of the staff, which could quickly be turned into a spear by lashing on an edged weapon, was part of every person's training, including the women. I have very vivid memories of training Abraham's wife Sarah in the use of the staff. I have personally worked with a staff in my current life, but when I connected with these past life memories an additional flood of very effective techniques came into my awareness. Many of the men carried edged weapons of various sizes from small daggers to large curved swords, all of which were part of the men's periodic training for battle. Dances with fighting instruments were common in our tribes and often performed during celebrations.

This eminent significance of martial preparedness should not be confused with a bellicose attitude; our goal has always been to preserve peace. Exercising our ability to engage an aggressor was simply essential for the prosperity of our tribes.

Abraham was a wise and peaceful leader, as he incorporated the sacred warfare information that had been part of his teachings in Egypt into use within our rapidly expanding tribal system. The city of Salem had long been recognized far and wide for its mysterious abilities to hold an energy that effectively kept the peace, so that warring tribes were ineffective around this area. Abraham's intent was to make Salem the center of his growing kingdom.

Peace did not always reign, however, when four allied kings from Mesopotamia led by King Chedorlaomer waged war against the five cities in the Vale of Siddim, south of the Dead Sea. These five cities, also known as the Pentapolis or cities of the plain, had been made to pay tribute for twelve years by this powerful king and his coalition after having lost an earlier battle. But they rebelled in the thirteenth year of tribute.

The following year Chedorlaomer led his coalition back into the region, defeating and subduing many of the surrounding kingdoms. An allied force from the five cities of Sodom, Gomorrah, Adma, Zeboyim, and Bela went out to meet Chedorlaomer's force, but in the ensuing battle Chedorlaomer was victorious and plundered Sodom and Gomorrah. Among the many survivors taken into captivity to serve as slaves was Abraham's nephew, Lot, along with the rest of his family.

Upon hearing this, Abraham assembled the tribal elders, and a large force of several thousand warriors was made ready for a quick pursuit on horseback and chariots. The biblical account has only 318 men listed, but we were going to ride with over three thousand men, which still meant that we would be clearly outnumbered by the force of well over ten thousand that we were going to face. Our advantage would have to be surprise, the number of horses we had, and our training in the art of war as well as the internal training we had been practicing for many years.

Another factor that we had in our favor was the size of many of our men. We were already far larger than many of the tribesmen outside our domain, but we also had real giants among us that sometimes stood ten to fifteen feet tall. These men were rare, but they were part of our fighting force and would often strike terror into the enemy when they saw them. Our growing ability at sacred warfare and their awe-inspiring presence were important factors for our relatively peaceful existence. The Old Testament accounts of a future warrior named David who would defeat a giant with a rock and sling are reminiscent of these giants that still were in existence.

We pursued Chedorlaomer's forces, finally engaging them in battle near present-day Damascus, Syria. Even during that time there was a small city established. I remember skirting the mountains and sending up scouts to view the movement of the forces we tracked in the distance. Their main body would encircle at night and set up a defensive perimeter. During the day the baggage and prisoners would trail behind the main body that would often be strung out for over a mile.

We made a plan to attack them early in the morning, after they had broken camp and spread out. The larger part of our forces would approach them from the rear while another part would come down from the mountains on their left flank. The weather had been hot and dry for several weeks, so any movement along the parched earth easily kicked up dust. Because of this, we kept our main force well back from theirs and our movements down until night, relying on our scouts to keep us informed of their movements.

We were fortunate that they had not yet detected us as we had watched them the previous day. After a signal from our scouts in the mountains, we began a slow trot of our horses from behind their position. They were encamped on a rise from the main trail, and we were able to slowly come up from behind them from an area that was shielded from their view.

Soon after they started for the day, we attacked, riding two abreast up from their rear. Abraham and I were positioned with our best men in the rear attack group where we both had chariots with drivers so that we would be free to direct our men and fight with our lances and bows. The left flank position was ordered to hold until a preordained signal, because we needed to position close enough to quickly attack their rear to effect maximum surprise and confusion within their ranks. The formation of our left flank consisted simply of two lines that were spread out very far with a gap of two or three horse lengths in between. The idea was that by galloping as hard as they could, they would raise a huge dust cloud and create the illusion of a large army attacking.

Chedorlaomer's forces thought they were out of danger and had let their guard down, which enabled us to trot right up to the rear of their column without being detected when eventually the alarm was given by their rear guard. As the lead group drew their swords and attacked the rear guard, the entire column behind began to gallop and split. The left column led by Abraham drove down the left side of the baggage train striking down guards while I did the same at the head of the right column. We quickly penetrated far up their lines, passing the long baggage train as the troops on our left flank along the mountains received their signal and began their gallop, raising a large dust cloud in the distance.

Chedorlaomer's powerful force could have easily defeated ours if we had clashed man to man on the open battlefield. But by determinedly utilizing all the stratagems available to us we stacked the odds in our favor. Just moments prior to our attack, Chedorlaomer's soldiers were already quietly pondering how they were home free and just marking time until they finally returned to the comfort of their homes with their war treasures. Mentally they were not prepared for a fight for their lives, and they were completely caught off guard.

We had practiced sacred warfare for years and always did our best to avoid physical confrontations, but, on this day, the field would be littered with thousands of dead as Chedorlaomer's forces began to run in panic. The dreadful screams from dying men and prisoners, who did not yet know that we were their liberating force, began to strike terror and confusion into Chedorlaomer's entire army.

Fleeing men rarely put up a fight, as their only thought is escaping as fast as possible from the terror of dying. Spears, shields, and swords were tossed aside as Chedorlaomer's completely panicked army now fled in their direction of travel to the northeast. Our men who had practically lived their entire lives on horseback and who could strike a man down with a sword, spear, or bow at full gallop quickly eradicated any resistance that was formed while they decimated the fleeing force.

Even the advance guard of the four kings that was on horseback fled from the field as fast as their horses would take them. They had no idea that they were being attacked by a much smaller force thanks to the dust that was being raised by our men from the left flank and rear. We knew that we had to inflict heavy casualties quickly or they would regroup and return to kill and enslave us. After we spent almost half the day pursuing and destroying the remnants of Chedorlaomer's dwindling army, we pulled up and returned to the baggage train. It was a great victory with only a few lost and wounded on our side. The Mesopotamians would not threaten us for many generations after their defeat at Abraham's hands.

After the battle we gathered up the arms of the fallen, and Abraham and Lot had a joyous reunion. He and his family joined our baggage train as we made our way back to the lands around the city of Salem.

Upon our return, Melchizedek expressed his gratitude for our victory and confided that he had prayed for our return the entire time we were gone. He then blessed Abraham, and together they blessed bread and wine before they ate and drank in a spirit of communion. The king of Sodom offered the recovered goods in reward for the rescue of his people, but Abraham refused to take them so that he would not be beholden to the king in any way. He did offer 10 percent of the recovered goods to Melchizedek, however, as was customary, because Abraham considered Melchizedek the rightful ruler of the lands we occupied. Eventually Melchizedek would pass his order and lands to Abraham, who had been a loyal follower of the order since settling in these lands long ago.

There is another event that I would like to shed a light on before I close this chapter. I remember when I was very old in that lifetime that I heard a deep rumbling like an earthquake in the direction of the Pentapolis one night. Many days later we learned that the area where it once stood was completely flooded. In the wake of this event, the entire area was avoided for many years because of a mysterious sickness that would overcome and eventually kill any living creature that went close to this contaminated area.

This event was the destruction of Sodom and Gomorrah, which I think needs clarification because the Bible misrepresents a lot of what happened there. In this time frame, it was not uncommon for the gods, as they were known then, or off-planet beings, as we know them now, to become openly involved in the affairs of men. And in this instance they brought about the destruction of Sodom and Gomorrah with a nuclear device. The two cities were situated below the level of the Dead Sea, so they used the nuclear device to destroy an area of land between the Dead Sea and the Pentapolis which allowed water to rush in and flood the cities. Even today the area where these cities were located still has high levels of radiation. The story of Lot having angels enter his home prior to the event and the people of the city wanting him to bring them out so that they could see the angels physically is a story pertaining to these off-planet beings, who were able to blind the people outside Lot's home with a flash of light and make their escape.

It is true that they told Lot before they departed that they were going to destroy Sodom and Gomorrah, which is why Lot fled with his family into the mountains and entered deep into a cave to avoid the destructive wave and radiation from the nuclear blast. The family was told to stay in the cave for several weeks until the radiation dissipated enough so that they could travel farther away. Lot's wife, however, became impatient, and, despite Lot's pleadings not to go outside as they were instructed by the beings, she went out anyway to see what was going on. Subsequently, she was hit by the radiation blast and thus turned to salt or rather burned to ashes just like Sodom and Gomorrah.

Abraham was a splendid example of a man with true merits and with a genuine devotion to God, seeking to strengthen the same in everyone around him. During my lifetime with him, I was fortunate to participate in establishing a spiritual legacy for mankind that would help further humanity's development in many ways. I was also able to work with Melchizedek, who would later incarnate as Jesus. We would meet again as part of a greater soul group that would incarnate together over many lifetimes to support each other and help guide mankind toward ascension. Conversely, the experiences in that lifetime were very conducive to my personal soul development, helping me tremendously to further prepare for what was yet to come.

Abraham is the common Hebrew patriarch of the Abrahamic religions, including Judaism, Christianity, and Islam. In Judaism, he is the founding father of the special relationship between the Jews and God; in Christianity, he is the spiritual progenitor of all believers, whether Jewish or non-Jewish; and in Islam, he is a link in the chain of Islamic prophets that begins with Adam and culminates in Muhammad.

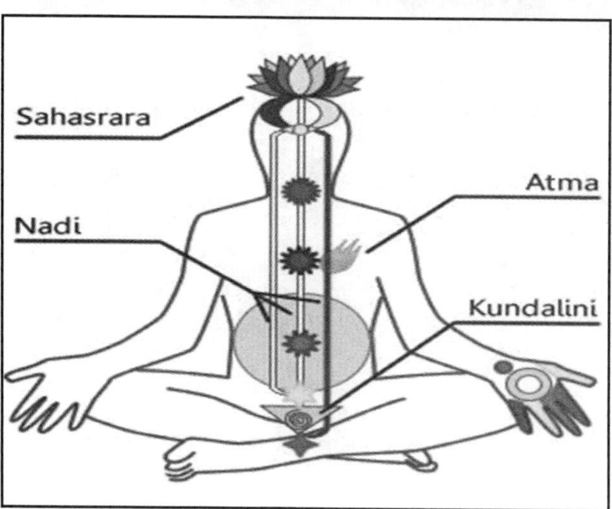

Kundalini is a form of divine feminine energy (or *Shakti*) believed to be located at the base of the spine, in the *muladhara*. It is an important concept in Śhaiva Tantra, where it is believed to be a force or power associated with the divine feminine or the formless aspect of the Goddess. This energy in the body, when cultivated and awakened through tantric practice, is believed to lead to spiritual liberation.

Jesus is portrayed as "The Christ Pantocrator" in the Saint Catherine's Monastery at Mount Sinai, in a 6th century CE painting.

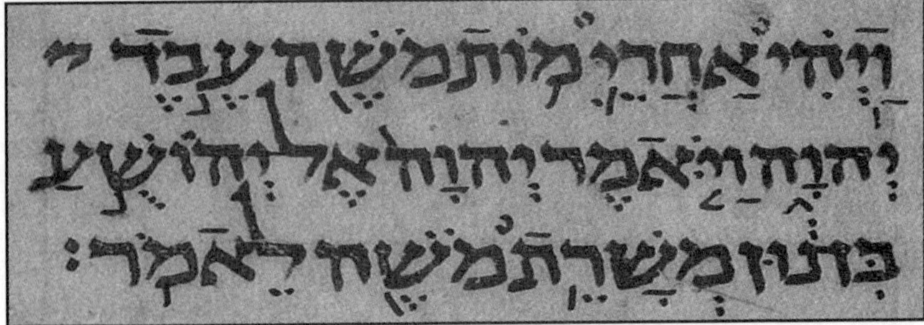

The Book of Genesis is the first book of the Hebrew Bible and the Christian Old Testament. Its Hebrew name is the same as its first word, *Bereshit* "In the beginning." Genesis is an account of the creation of the world, the early history of humanity, and of Israel's ancestors and the origins of the Jewish people.

God took Enoch, as in Genesis 5:24: "And Enoch walked with God: and he was not; for God took him." (KJV) illustration from the 1728 *Figures de la Bible*; illustrated by Gerard Hoet (1648–1733) and others, and published by P. de Hondt in The Hague; image courtesy Bizzell Bible Collection, University of Oklahoma Libraries.

"HEAR YE, ALL PERSONS! YE PEOPLE AS MANY AS YE ARE, I HAVE DONE THIS ACCORDING TO THE DESIGN OF MY HEART ... I HAVE RESTORED THAT WHICH WAS IN RUINS; I HAVE RISEN UP THAT WHICH WAS UNFINISHED."

◊ *Queen Hatshepsut* ◊

CHAPTER 6

WARRIOR SAGE FOR PHARAOH QUEEN HATSHEPSUT TO TRADITIONAL WARRIOR FOR PHARAOH THUTMOSE III, 1480 BCE

I would have many incarnations as an Egyptian over the centuries from well before the time of Pharaoh Menes to many incarnations after his long reign. When you examine a particular incarnation, you have to determine where you want to focus your attention. Just as it can take a lot of concentration to remember what you had for a meal three weeks ago, it also takes time and substantial mental effort to pull out pieces of past life memories from thousands of years ago.

Once you make a connection, be aware not to be carried away by your memories to the point where you become absorbed to the exclusion of your current life. Some memories can become quite intoxicating. Find ways to integrate and apply what you learn from past lives in your current incarnation. Your current life is the main focal point where all the aspects of these many lives are focused into the now. As the advancement to spiritual enlightenment unfolds within your current life, you will intuitively begin to connect more and more with the different past lives that have the greatest impact on your current life.

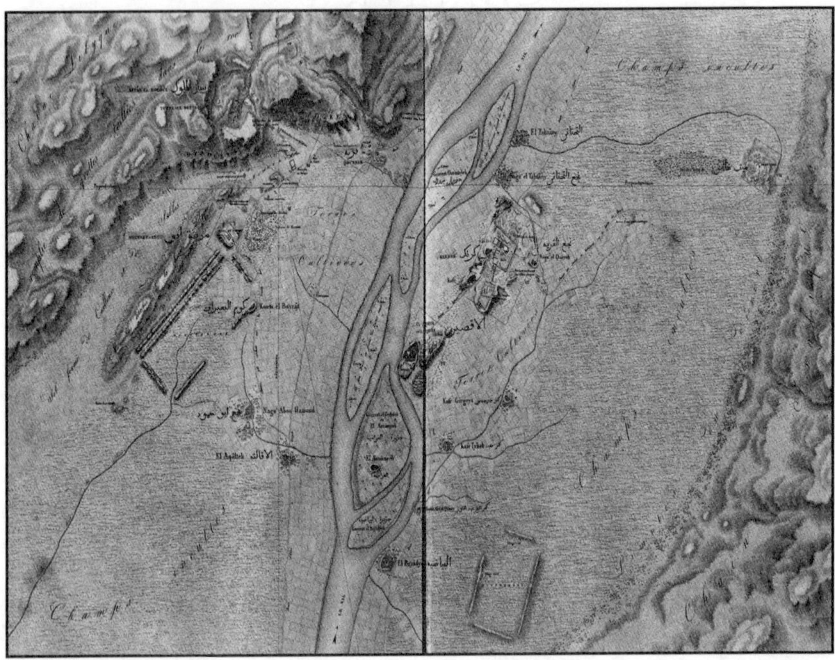

This particular incarnation during the reign of Hatshepsut and Thutmose III would advance my current skills in sacred warfare to a higher degree. The skills that I would master in this past life would become important in preparing my soul for future lifetimes and especially my current life. As I'm learning to reconnect with my past life abilities, I am now able to instantly access more and more of the information that took me many lifetimes to master.

You can liken this to studying a particular skill or acquiring specific knowledge in your current life as a child or young adult. It may even happen that over time you have drifted away from the development of a particular skill as you desired to develop other skills instead, but, at a later time, you may reconnect to that skill again. Sometimes you may not like a particular experience or you don't see the purpose of it, until you find yourself in a situation where what you had learned during that experience would be of great benefit to you. These experiences are mapped out by the higher self, which sees the whole fabric of life in its entirety and can therefore lead us most gracefully if we listen to its advice.

Let's say you develop a particular expertise in mathematics, and as a budding architect you will need this particular skill or knowledge often dur-

ing the course of studying in a university for several years. You will also study the sciences and other electives that are perhaps not specific to becoming an architect, but, as you begin your career as an architect, you may remember that information as you build a home near a particularly unusual rock formation with a stream and a waterfall running next to it. You remember how this rock formation is very solid and perhaps use it as a foundation for a part of your building, very similar, perhaps, to what Frank Lloyd Wright would have done when building his famous house called Fallingwater in Pennsylvania.

Throughout your life, there will be occasions where you tap into your prior knowledge of a particular physical or mental skill to enrich, enjoy, or develop new interests or abilities, whether you do that consciously or unconsciously and whether it is related to capabilities developed in this lifetime or in previous lives. Can there be any doubt in even the most severe skeptics' minds that the child prodigy incarnations of Wolfgang Amadeus Mozart or Ludwig van Beethoven, who were playing and composing orchestral works from a very early age, were anything other than the reincarnations of gifted musicians?

How else can we account for the extraordinary capability of these amazingly gifted musicians at such an early age? They were clearly demonstrating the ability to access skills that made it very easy for them to intuitively grasp and apply a profound knowledge of musical harmonies that must have come from somewhere. It would be far easier to comprehend how child prodigies of today in many different fields are capable of displaying their amazing gifts if we were to accept the fact that they are often tapping into skills developed in previous lifetimes.

If you search for it, you can actually find many children who have past life memories and tap into them. A very prominent case is that of Patrick Flanagan, who was born the year after Nikola Tesla, the great scientist and inventor, had died. From a very early age Patrick had been aware of his past life memories, and his prolific inventiveness indeed supports his claim, as he built a Tesla coil at eight years old and many other things that he either reproduced or newly invented in his current lifetime.

Many of us have marveled at the beautiful scenes of wild lions in their natural habitat. Perhaps we have been awed at the circus when witnessing lions performing under the direction of their trainers. Several documentaries and

movies have been produced that show humans taking wild lion cubs, raising them to adulthood, letting them go into the wild, and coming back years later to find the lions joyously returning to them like they were still family. They would even bring their new wild mates and have a reunion with them as well. It is a demonstration of how man and nature can coexist in harmony.

The animal kingdom is highly evolved to a great degree in some species, but all species are on the path of spiritual progression and evolution just as we are. By recognizing this, we could empower them and ourselves far more than we do now on average. It is very common for us humans to think that everything we encounter outside of us should be made subservient to our needs and whims. But I believe you can communicate with nature on any level, whether you look at a mineral, a plant, or an animal; there is life in each of them. The knowledge that they hold can greatly benefit us; it is up to us to go ahead and reach out. When was the last time you've been hugging a tree or saying a few nice words to the environment around you? Don't feel awkward about it; we have forgotten our ability to interact with the environment on a higher level. Having the courage to once again utilize this talent and seek this connection is something that will make you a true pioneer.

The animal kingdom is very aware of the negative aspects of consciousness in mankind and has been bearing the brunt of this ever- creeping and growing cruelty from humans for many thousands of years. There was a time when we truly respected and revered animals. Our interactions had once been on a much higher level, as I've alluded to before. The role that the animal kingdom can play to help us stop this cruel creep of negative consciousness has been largely underestimated in modern society for a long time, but fortunately there are many indicators showing that this is about to change. In recent fantasy films we can see this idea represented in the popular movies *The Chronicles of Narnia* and *Avatar.* In these popular films, large groups of different species of animals team up with positive-minded humans who are trying to stop the negative aspects of mankind and protect all life before things get out of control. The negative aspects of human consciousness can be called back to a higher consciousness even by the animal kingdom.

I would once again profit from my abilities to intimately connect with the animal kingdom during the lifetime I'm covering in this chapter as a Nu-

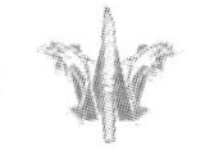

bian warrior in ancient Egypt, where I expanded upon what I had done before in the same region. Reincarnating into a particular culture that we have made experiences in can make it easier to focus on developing a particularly difficult aspect of ourselves. The timing and circumstances are often appropriate in a familiar culture to continue a particular lesson. By reincarnating into familiar territory, we don't have to work on learning a new culture; it's already ingrained on a deeper level. Although I would not limit myself to being a Nubian warrior, it worked quite well in Egypt over many of my lifetimes as it helped me advance in the art of sacred warfare.

As I have described before, the Nubian warrior priests could commune with the animal kingdom and enlist their help in battles. One particularly strong memory I have is of a group of us warriors that would sit and meditate close to a known pride of wild lions that we had worked with in the past. We would build a relationship with this particular pride and had adopted them as brothers and sisters, just as they had adopted us. We would sit or lie with them for many days on end, becoming one with them just like family. The young cubs would run and play, and we would play right along with them. We would often go on hunts together and share our food with them, and in return they would share theirs with us. Our communication with them happened on a telepathic level, which strengthened this ability among us as well. Often when spending time with a pride of lions, nothing would be said among us for days until we returned to the city.

It was Hatshepsut, as she became pharaoh of Egypt, who would help our group to further cultivate and utilize these abilities by initiating a project to foster the art of sacred warfare in her kingdom. Hatshepsut was the elder daughter of the Eighteenth Dynasty Pharaoh Thutmose. His consort Ahmose was married to her half-brother Thutmose II, son of the Mutnofret, Thutmose I's second wife. Since three of Mutnofret's older sons had died prematurely, Thutmose II inherited his father's throne in about 1492 BCE with Hatshepsut as his consort or royal wife. Hatshepsut bore one daughter, Neferure, but no son. When her husband, Thutmose II, died about 1479 BCE, the throne passed to his son, Thutmose III, born to a lesser harem queen named Isis.

What is interesting and shows the expansiveness and mystery of the world of spirit and soul development is the fact that Hatshepsut was the incarnation of my twin soul. I will give the best description of a twin soul as described by Shirley MacLaine in her book *The Camino*: "Twin souls have been together many times and serve each other's journey back to the Divine, as you have just realized. Twin souls often wait for reunion, so that one or the other can serve others."

This reunion of twin souls is sought after but not always necessary for ongoing soul development. Twin souls are part of the same soul energy and have the same ideals for evolving the soul as a whole. In different incarnations they can be teachers, parents, siblings, or partners in everything from relationships to business. They help each other advance, and in the best circumstances like I describe, in this lifetime they help an entire civilization advance. This advancement in civilization can have positive consequences throughout history.

Queen Hatshepsut was an incarnation of my soul energy who I supported with my own incarnation as a Nubian warrior. She was pulling on our combined incarnations for information. For instance, my previous incarnational memories as Pharaoh Sesostris would have affected her abilities and decision as Pharaoh Hatshepsut. My twin soul who I have met in this lifetime—both of us recognize each other as such—is happily married to another man as I am happily married to my soul mate. She is the part of my soul that balances out my feminine side and I her masculine side. We have played this role for our entirety of existence here on Earth. I will thread several of our parallel lives throughout this book and upcoming books on my past lives throughout history.

My current wife in the lifetime I describe here and my wife in my current lifetime is and has been my soul mate for many lifetimes. Here is a description of soul mates from Shirley's book *The Camino:*

"The soul mate reflects the identical oscillations of frequency as its mate. The pair of soul mates was created at the beginning of time. They are meant to be together and continually search for a reunion."

My current wife is in virtually every lifetime that has been of historical note, and she will feature strongly in many of my lifetimes.

When Thutmose III was an infant, Hatshepsut acted as regent in his place for several years until he was old enough and able to handle the responsibility himself. In general, a regent is someone who reigns in a kingdom in the minority, absence, or disability of the sovereign. Hatshepsut's regency lasted for fifteen years during which she eventually attained unprecedented power

for a woman, adopting the full titles and regalia of a pharaoh. When studying the Egyptian kings and queens, realize that they often have Greek names that are different from their Egyptian ones. For instance, Thutmose III can be also found as Amenhotep III in Greek. Sometimes you will find more or less information when jumping back and forth between the names.

Queen Hatshepsut was very knowledgeable in the intuitive arts that were taught to every royal family. She was particularly gifted and had reached very advanced levels in the mystery schools of the goddess Isis and wanted to take the idea of sacred warfare to one of the highest levels ever achieved in known history. Based on that premise, the head of the army recommended a small group of less than one hundred of us who had exhibited advanced skills in sacred warfare, whereupon we intensified our training with specifically selected members of the priesthood.

This training took several years in which elements of all aspects of the ancient wisdom, science, magical arts, and sacred warfare skills available to the priesthood were taught to us. We would learn how to project a calming spirit of peace to armies that were massing on our borders for war, and they would stop before entering our lands. The queen's best negotiators would then be sent, and treaties and alliances would be built without any bloodshed.

Our group would also learn the art of using precious and semiprecious stones to amplify our personal energy and extend our thought vibrations. Lapis lazuli, pearls, onyx, turquoise, emeralds, garnets of various colors, crystals, and many other stones were interchangeably set in our ceremonial breastplates, helmets, and faceplates made of gold and silver. As we meditated to calm potential foreign invaders, we would connect with the vibrations of our particular stones. Each of us had his own stones that we would learn to connect with. We were instructed on how to build a rapport with these stones similar to the connection we had developed with the wild animals, accepting the stones as our brothers and sisters.

Everything is made out of consciousness; it's the substance of all creation, whether it assembles in the form of a biological human, animal, plant, or in the form of a mineral. By realizing that everything is consciousness, we were able to connect with the thoughts of peace within the memories of these stones. Then we amplified them together with our own intention to the point where it would raise the vibrations of our surroundings, including the vibrations of the warriors outside our borders. We had thus moved the art of sacred warfare to a higher level by learning to raise vibrations and not weapons. As Nubian warrior priests, we strove to experience our original divine state of being, the sacred center of creation.

During our long training, our select group had performed many sacred initiations over the years. Our path had not been easy, as we were required to overcome many fears and learn a vast amount of information in a relatively short period of time. Several members of our initial group had not continued on for various reasons. Some had failed the initiations. Other initiates had decided for themselves that the tests were too difficult. For a few it had been decided for them that they would not continue. Our ranks had eventually been thinned from several dozen to just twelve. We had been refined into a cohesive working unit that could effectively focus thoughts and create a sacred space throughout vast regions of Egypt.

Before entering the temple complex at Karnak for our sacred work, we would go through a cleansing and purification process, both physically and mentally, to prepare ourselves for the sacred art we were about to perform. The first temple we would enter was the Temple of Ptah, in which a statue of Sekhmet was located. As you entered the dimly lit outer chambers of the chapel, you would encounter rows of the fierce warrior statues of Sekhmet. While walking through these corridors, you would release your troubles or thoughts of violent physical warfare into her ebony granite, which would absorb your negative thoughts and troubles. This way you were making sure you did not bring them into the peaceful and serene inner chamber of the chapel.

There were seven doorways or gateways within the chapel that represented the seven major chakras of the body. All of the major religious temples along the Nile contained seven representative doorways. The base chakra at the bottom of the spine was represented by the first door and so on till the last doorway that represented the crown chakra at the top of the head. The crossing of a doorway was like entering a portal or vortex to another aspect of ourselves that is contained within the different chakras of the body. Within the seventh or last inner chamber stood an exquisite life-size statue of Sekhmet.

Placed on her lion head was the peaceful sun disk crown of the god-

dess Isis, while in her left hand, at the heart level, she held a lotus blossom representing purity, as the lotus grows in muddy waters but rises above it to unfold in its pure splendor. The lotus being held next to the heart indicated a connection with the pure divine love that is within each of us. In this last room of the chapel you would receive your lion heart, a symbol of fearlessness that you would then carry into the outer world where your warrior calm would overcome your enemies through powerful but peaceful means.

It was fitting that the statue of Sekhmet would be in the temple of her husband Ptah. The name Ptah means "opener," and, by opening his mouth, he spoke the world into being, having dreamed creation in his heart and speaking it. It was believed that he fashioned the universe through the love harmonics of the heart and creative thought, as I have described in an earlier chapter. It was also thought that Ptah could manifest himself as Apis the bull, who was held sacred during the time of Pharaoh Menes in the age of Taurus.

In art, Ptah is portrayed as a bearded mummified man, often wearing a skullcap, with his hands holding an Ankh, Was, and Djed, the symbols of life, power, and stability, respectively. I have already written about the Ankh and the Was; the Djed is depicted as a column with a broad base and capital. At the top of the column, the capital is divided by four parallel bars. The Djed column is also called the backbone of Osiris that was considered necessary to aid in the transformation of the physical body into its spiritual form of consciousness and light.

After purifying ourselves in the Temple of Ptah, we would continue with a short journey to an inner chapel that Queen Hatshepsut had built within the great Karnak temple complex for the purpose of holding a further cleansing ceremony. The theme and layout of the chapel was a botanical garden with ornate carvings of nature scenes throughout. Lush tropical foliage in large pots held palm trees, ferns, and iridescent flowering plants. Tropical birds in ornate cages were placed around the chapel, and the sweet chirps and whistles mingled with several softly flowing water fountains. Large standing metal and stone pots held slowly smoldering incense that further calmed and settled our minds.

Muted oil lamps that cast soft flickering light dancing shadows around the walls lighted the high-ceilinged stone chapel. Everything in this environment was designed to bring our brain-wave states to a level that would make our work possible. We would calm and connect our energies with nature and go into a meditation in which we would vanquish the base desires of the ego, putting it in its proper place as a servant and allowing our higher self to rise to the forefront of our awareness. Stone benches were set up within this temple for us to sit on and meditate while wearing our sacred armor. After spending up to an hour in this temple, we would head toward our final destination. Before moving we would form into two lines abreast of each other and start out in step. Drums within the temple were beat in a slow rhythm that we would march in cadence to, while our golden armor, encrusted with jewels and crystals, glimmered and sparkled with flashes of light from the oil lamps within the vast temple. Our leather sandals made quiet scrapes in unison against the stone floor of the temple as we progressed in step and were assisted by Hathor priestesses to our final temple.

My wife, Tracy, in that life was a priestess of the goddess Hathor, whom Hatshepsut brought back into focus during her reign. The Hathors were a group of interdimensional, intergalactic beings that actually predate Egypt by millennia. But when they started working in Egypt, they did so through the Hathor priestesses. The Hathor goddess became associated with fertility, the sacred sexual union, ecstasy, and bliss. What they were working with was the balancing of the masculine and feminine principles within each of us, archetypally represented by the sun and the moon.

When these two aspects within us are brought into harmony within our bodies, we are balancing the electric male principle and the magnetic female principle. This is light years ahead of the crude approach to sex that pervades modern society. What the Hathors would teach about the principle of gender or polarity had to do with balancing subtle energies on every level of existence—first and foremost within ourselves, so that we can radiate this balance out into the outer world.

In the Hathor temples, the priestesses were trained in the art and use of sacred dance to align with sacred geometric forms through their movements, thus creating a very pure and uplifting space. They chanted and shook rattles, which created waveforms, and they used these waveforms to move energy. The Hathor priestesses were masters of sound, which is the primordial basis of all manifest creation. We look solid, but, from another perspective, our physical bodies are comparatively dense wave patterns of energy, complex harmonics

pervaded and surrounded by a luminous egg, a shining orb with filaments of light often referred to as the auric field.

The aura of humans can also be perceived or encoded as sounds, and the Hathor priestesses could discern this sound. The priestesses would then emote sounds to heal or increase the energetic field of the people that would visit them as well as use traditional methods of herbal remedies. Being aware of the cycles of the stars, Earth, and moon, they would gather herbs at specific times to facilitate the maximum effect of energetic healing and auric rejuvenation.

As we walked toward our final destination, we were surrounded by a group of barefooted Hathor priestesses wearing tight, form-fitting, sheer white linen *kalasiris* with golden threads interwoven into the material. Their light brown skin glistened with perfumed oils. The priestesses played symbols and hand drums as they danced sinuously and writhed their lithe bodies around us to create sacred harmonics and balance our masculine and feminine energies. This ceremonial dance was important in that it ignited energies at the base of our spines that, similar to a DNA spiral, would coil up our spines like the caduceus that you see as a symbol for the medical profession. This would allow us to harness powerful kundalini energies that we would then use when projecting out thought forms.

Between two of the largest obelisks ever created in Egypt stood a chapel of red granite. It was within this third and final temple that we would gather and send out the sacred harmonics of love. A large golden chest would be rowed up the Nile from Heliopolis where it was normally located in a secret temple near the Mediterranean Sea. The golden chest was carried on wooden poles on the shoulders of four priests who brought it quietly into the chapel. The priests would place it in the center of the chapel and then depart while we meditated.

All the lighting in the inner temples was from a source that glowed softly but was not lit. This lighting was from a battery source, which was located in many ancient temples. Ancient advanced technology from a past golden age still existed during this time frame. The amazing *Agastya Samhita* from the times of the Vedic Age in India gives the precise directions for constructing electrical batteries: Place a well-cleaned copper plate in an earthenware vessel. Cover it first by copper sulfate and then moist sawdust. After that, put a mercury-amalgamated-zinc sheet on top known by the twin name of Mitra-

Varuna (or cathode- anode as we know it today). This current will split water into oxygen and hydrogen molecules. A chain of one hundred jars was said to give a very active and effective force.

We were admonished to never touch or look into the golden chest, or ark as it was called, because it was so very powerful and sacred that to touch it would result in death. The energy in the red granite temple would become very great at this point, and if it hadn't been for the fact that we were of exceptional fitness and trained in controlling and focusing energy, we would not have been able to remain conscious, aware, or even stay alive under the influence of this intense energy. After the ark was brought in, we would begin to meditate and focus on building up our refined chakra energy and then commence to spiral it up from our base chakra, which matched the red granite of the temple we were in, up and around our spinal columns—or Djed/Jedi columns—and from there out of the chapel.

Creation, we were taught, begins as a source of sound, light, and color emanating from a pulsating orb of consciousness. We were twelve spiraling cones of harmonic energy as our conscious thought burst forth, forming a circle around the source consciousness expressed through the ark. We connected with this and each other to create a grid following a geometric blueprint aligned with sacred geometry. There were always six of us on each side of the ark for a total of twelve warrior priests. The cross total of twelve is three, which in sacred numerology throughout time is a reference to our three-dimensional physical reality. We were taught that we are spiritual beings brought forth in a biogenetic experience based in linear time to experience emotions. The most intense emotion is love, and we were sending this emotional thought form out. We were shaping and transforming our environment with the energy of love, creating peace, abundance, and a sacred connection with nature and all life.

To support us in our work, Queen Hatshepsut had commissioned the construction of two massive pink granite obelisks at the red granite chapel. In fact, the queen was on a massive building campaign during the almost twenty-two years of her reign. Her desire and aim was to create structures that would resonate to the sacred harmonics that we were creating. By creating these peaceful harmonics, the citizenry was also becoming more reasoned and enlightened. One of the granite obelisks still stands at the entrance to the Temple

of Karnak; the other one would be toppled in an upcoming cataclysmic event. Senenmut, who had been Queen Hatshepsut's architect, had supervised the quarrying, transport, and erection of the twin obelisks, at the time the tallest in the world. The red granite chapel between the once powerful and impressive twin obelisks would later be moved to another location.

The color vibration of pink has a peaceful, calming effect, and the crystalline structure of the granite would vibrate with the energies we would send into them. The knowledge of this vibratory ability of crystal is utilized in today's watches and computer chips that have piezoelectric crystalline structures. An example of the unseen power of crystals to hold and vibrate a specific rhythm can be noticed in watches, which keep accurate time through their consistent vibratory pattern. Another example would be in the use of silicon or crystalline computer chips, which absorb and store vast amounts of information relative to their size.

The pink granite of the obelisks held a crystalline structure that resonated with our own peaceful thought patterns and would then transmit them like giant antennas to vast regions, further refining the energies that we were sending out mixed in conjunction with the ark's powerful force. On top of the obelisks were capstones made out of gold and silver to amplify the energies being transmitted. These energies would burst out and connect with hundreds of other obelisks up and down the Nile and further strengthen and hold the energies we were sending out.

At one time there were hundreds of obelisks throughout Egypt that were used for ceremonial purposes, as markers of victories, and for honoring previous rulers. Their main function, however, was for transmitting the positive energies that helped create the longest continuous reign of any civilization in modern history. The Egyptian obelisks were toppled and removed to different countries over the centuries. As they were removed, the power and beauty of Egypt slowly crumbled and faded away. The real purpose and use of the obelisks has been largely forgotten and suppressed, so that today only a few consciously benefit from their use.

To this day a massive unfinished obelisk lies at the Aswan quarry along the lower Nile. This obelisk had been intended to be utilized in our work but was eventually abandoned after Hatshepsut's death. The unfinished obelisk would later crack in a massive earthquake during the exodus of Moses.

During Hatshepsut's reign, an amazing period of peace, prosperity, and construction work in alignment with sacred geometrical patterns took place. Our meditative practices were also having an effect on our neighbors in that they opened themselves up for a very productive and beneficial economical exchange to unfold between Egypt and the surrounding empires near and far. Counting in the years of Hatshepsut's co-regency with her husband, a golden era of almost forty years would settle over Egypt.

Her personal architect, Senenmut, made major contributions to this golden era. Inspired by a funerary temple of the Middle Kingdom built by Pharaoh Mentuhotep, Senenmut built Djeser-Djeseru, one of the most beautiful monuments of ancient Egypt. It is built into a cliff face that rises sharply above it and consists of a succession of terraces, that were once graced with gardens, whose supporting walls are masked by long colonnades divided in the center by monumental access ramps. Together with the other buildings of the Deir el-Bahari complex, Djeser-Djeseru is considered to be among the greatest buildings of the ancient world. On the second terrace, a portico gives entry to a peristyle courtyard leading to the sanctuary, which is cut out of the cliff. The work of Senenmut is, in the strictness of its composition, architecturally very successful and a fine example of the integration of architecture and a natural site.

It was widely believed that Senenmut was the queen's concubine or lover. But because Senenmut was a common man and Hatshepsut needed to depict herself as a man so that she could rule, it must have been a challenging life for both of them to be with each other discreetly.

I have read that several psychics had placed the reincarnation of Senenmut as the architect Frank Lloyd Wright, who lived from 1867 until 1959. I asked Ahtun Re if this was accurate, and he also confirmed it. The American Institute of Architects billed Wright in 1991 as "the greatest American architect of all time," even though he never attended an architecture school. Despite his lack of formal training, he designed more than one thousand projects and completed over five hundred works in his lifetime, varying from single-family homes, churches, schools, hotels, and offices to skyscrapers and museums like the Guggenheim in New York.

This seems to be another fine example of pulling past life abilities forward into a current life. I have seen much of the surviving work of Frank Lloyd Wright, from Fallingwater in Pennsylvania to Taliesin East and West in Wisconsin and Arizona, respectively, and I greatly admire his ability to integrate the natural world with architecture, just as Senenmut did many thousands of years ago.

For the first few years of her stepson's reign, Hatshepsut was an entirely conventional regent. But by the end of his seventh year, she had persuaded the royal house that she was meant to be queen and adopted the full royal titulary, the full royal protocol for Egyptian sovereigns. Hitherto Hatshepsut had been depicted as a typical queen, with a female body and appropriately feminine garments. But after a brief period of experimentation that involved combining a female body with the regalia designed for a male king, her formal portraits began to show Hatshepsut with a male body, wearing the traditional regalia of kilt, crown or headcloth, and false beard. The Egyptian artistic convention of the time showed things not as they were but as a stylization of what they determined they should be.

During the co-regency between Hatshepsut and Thutmose III, an understanding was reached between the two. Thutmose III was happy to be the head of the army and allowed Hatshepsut to focus on developing specific priestly classes and conducting the normal routines of a pharaoh. In a future chapter, I will talk of Thutmose Ill's reincarnation as King Leonidas of the Spartans.

Hatshepsut would eventually disappear, and many believed that she was murdered along with her female vizier and Senenmut. Thutmose III would quickly assume the throne after his stepmother's mysterious disappearance.

It would not be long before Thutmose III was convinced and manipulated by the priests outside of Hatshepsut's focus and that aggressive wars became necessary to protect Egypt's borders. So within ten days of the queen's announced death, the former head of the army and now pharaoh would march to war. The work that my group had been doing was abandoned and we were commissioned into different military units. I was given the position of head of the pharaoh's chariots, because I had exhibited an unusual ability with the lions. It was clear that I was telepathic with animals, as I could also direct my horse- drawn chariot without using my hands on the reins, which freed me to use multiple weapons simultaneously for combat.

Our group's intuitive skills were utilized in determining where the enemy was located in strength, so that our army would maneuver around them. By coming up on the enemy's exposed flanks, we would easily defeat them with little loss of life. We would have many great victories over the coming years through the use of our intuition. Today Thutmose III is recognized as one of the greatest conquerors in the history of Egypt. Ahtun Re told me that many of the great military leaders throughout time would be incarnate during this time, including the future incarnation of Napoleon the Great.

In this past life, I would shift from the high spiritualizing aspects of the sage warrior to the traditional aspects of the warrior after Queen Hatshepsut's death, while at all times protecting my country as I was tasked to do. After having had this experience, Ahtun Re told me that I had planned my current life to start out as the traditional warrior and progress to the spiritual warrior sage, so that I could help to empower people and teach intuition to the world through my example.

My ability in my current life to practice sacred warfare has reached an even greater level of capability. I have come into large cities that were ridden with violence and helped transform them into peaceful enclaves by projecting the thought of love. I have also progressed my skills to moving or calming violent weather systems and dissipating the energies of earthquakes and tsunamis. I feel that in the future these abilities will become increasingly prevalent and more pronounced, as I can see that there is a rapidly growing number of people connecting with these abilities. And I want to emphasize that everyone is capable of these things that I do and much more.

Today we are presented with the transformation of a humanity that is becoming aware of the sacred aspect of everything in our world. The higher aspects of life that Queen Hatshepsut focused on during her reign are now being remembered, as humanity awakens to its true potential. We can again have the kind of peace and prosperity that existed over 3,500 years ago. Actually what happened in this bygone time was but a foretaste of what is possible through the power of the sacred aspect of creation.

By opening our hearts we can once again connect with this ideal of the sacredness in all things. By regarding all things with reverence and humility in our minds and heart, we can once again transform our world into one of

peace. As a collective I believe we are at a point where we can manifest a new golden age that can be more profound and longer lasting than anything humanity has experienced before.

Hatshepsut came to the throne of Egypt in 1478 BCE. As the principal wife of Thutmose II, Hatshepsut initially ruled as regent to Thutmose III, a son of Thutmose II by another wife and the first male heir. While Thutmose III had inherited the throne at about two years old, Hatshepsut continued to rule by asserting her lineage as the daughter and only child of Thutmose I and his primary wife, Ahmose.

Fallingwater at Mill Run, Pennsylvania is a house designed by the architect Frank Lloyd Wright in 1935.

The Dendera light is a motif in the Hathor temple at Dendera in Egypt. It depicts the Egyptian creation myth, and the text surrounding the pieces confirm this. The motif became famous when the History Channel claimed it depicts an ancient light bulb, something that the text around the motif disproves.

It is believed the Karnak Temple Complex to be the second most visited historical site in Egypt; only the Giza pyramid complex near Cairo receives more visits. It consists of four main parts, of which only the largest is currently open to the general public. The term Karnak often is understood as being the Precinct of Amun-Re only, because this is the only part most visitors see. The three other parts, the Precinct of Mut, the Precinct of Montu, and the dismantled Temple of Amenhotep IV, are closed to the public. Photograph of the temple complex taken in 1914, Cornell University Library.

The High Priest of Ptah was sometimes referred to as "the Greatest of the Directors of Craftsmanship." This title refers to Ptah as the patron god of the craftsmen. Reconstruction of the temple of Ptah in Memphis during the 19th Dynasty.

"THERE IS THE HEAT OF LOVE, THE PULSING RUSH OF LONGING, THE LOVER'S WHISPER, IRRESISTIBLE— MAGIC TO MAKE THE SANEST MAN GO MAD."

◊ *Homer, Iliad* ◊

CHAPTER 7

KING IDOMENEUS OF CRETE WITH HERACLES, CREW OF THE ARGO, AND THE TROJAN WAR, 1520-1470 BCE

Now I need to introduce you to more advanced aspects of reincarnation. I know that there are likely some of you who are pushing your boundaries of credibility in regard to past lives, so, given the subject matter, I will keep the information I'm about to present as logical and scientific as possible. I discovered through my own work and the work of Dr. Michael Newton that 5 to 7 percent of the population of Earth could be having multiple incarnations simultaneously. This means that you are multitasking your lifetimes so that you can accomplish more in a given period of time. It also means, as I will relate in future chapters, that you can help sway a major event of historical importance for humanity in the most beneficial direction.

You may begin to notice that I have overlapping lifetimes from this point on. Michael Newton's book *Journey of Souls: Case Studies of Lives Between Lives* is an excellent reference for understanding this concept. Imagine you are cooking a meal, talking on the phone, and watching television all at the same time. Many of you would think this no big deal, and those of you that have a full understanding of reincarnation are beginning to perceive that this is possible in multiple simultaneous incarnations. For those of you still trying to grasp this information, hang in there because you will achieve insight through exposure to this idea as you continue through the chapters.

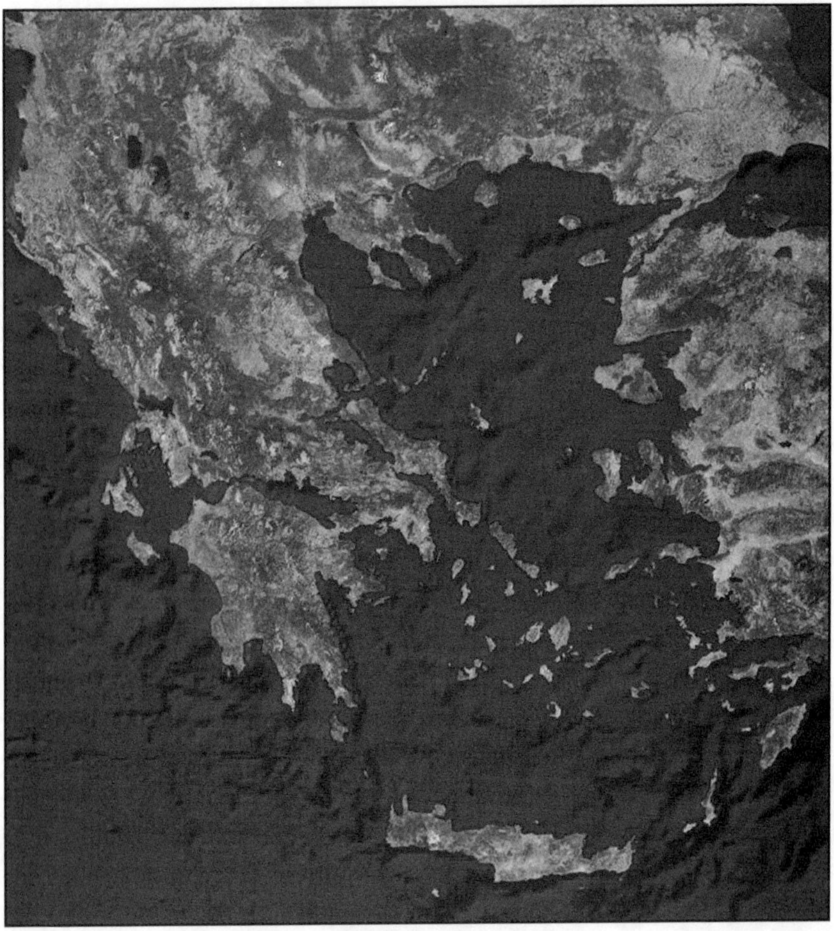

The culture that Pharaoh Menes had started on Crete two thousand years earlier had flourished and had become one of the most successful cultures in the Mediterranean. The feminine aspect would become the leading influence in the Minoan culture. A goddess culture or priestess-hood would rule the island. This goddess culture would influence the entire Mediterranean region and be attributed as the first advanced European civilization to emerge.

They had cultivated the art of sacred warfare brought from Pharaoh

Menes and his son Hor-Aha to an unusually high degree. No walls were erected around Minoan cities and no standing army existed. Their ships' sailors were trained in warfare to protect from pirates, but never did they initiate armed conflict with another nation. Because of Crete's location as a remote island, the people would enjoy the ability to develop one of the most peaceful and prosperous nations that has existed at any time in history.

The palaces and villas that were spread throughout the island were all luxuriously laid out. These sophisticated structures were made with large cypress-shaped pillars; multiple stories with vaulted ceilings; large, open floor plans; light, airy, dividable rooms; and winding staircases, while nearby springs provided water for the first indoor tubs and flushing toilets. Even in the more compact cities, where houses were close together, people had multistory homes that were well laid out, indicating that wealth was well distributed. The Minoans had the first known paved streets of the ancient world. Boulevards lined with cypress trees stretched out into the countryside and made movement into the cities for festivals, plays, museums, art displays, and restaurants available to many.

Crete was very fertile and a virtual Garden of Eden. The Cretans were skilled agriculturalists and had large tracts of fruit- and nut-bearing trees, verdant fields of cereal grains, vegetables of every description, and a unique hybrid of the valuable spice saffron. Wild cattle, pigs, horses, sheep, and goats were also plentiful throughout the island. The Cretans had exported their highly regarded and sought-after wines and olive oil, ceramics, saffron, and bronze all over the Mediterranean. They had well-established trade relations with the Egyptians, Phoenicians, Mycenaeans, and many city-states such as Troy.

In this process of transporting very desirable items, they had a positive social influence on the Mediterranean coastal areas that they traded with. In essence, the most valuable commodity that this matriarchal society exported throughout the region was peace and goodwill. They were able to balance the scales of power, because their ships alone supplied key resources that were deemed indispensable throughout the whole Mediterranean. An overly aggressive or warlike state could be returned to consciousness by withdrawing trade. The power of trade is what has been one of the driving forces throughout humanity's existence on Earth.

Because of the early influence from Pharaoh Menes, who would build a palace in Knossos, the Cretans fostered a spirit of cooperation with all of the nations surrounding the Mediterranean Sea and even beyond. Just as Pharaoh Menes had united Upper and Lower Egypt, Menes united all of Crete in a spirit of communion. This mutual fellowship contributed to a non-martial society that had embraced the concepts of sacred warfare, laying the foundation for a cohesive and successful economy and social equality that was enjoyed by all Cretans.

Pharaoh Menes and his son had also set up trading colonies on the west coast of Britain. The tin mines close to the areas now known as Glastonbury and Cadbury Hill were used as trading hubs for thousands of years. The British tin ore was smelted with high-grade copper ore from the island of Cyprus to form bronze. Crete was the main manufacturer of this highly coveted metal during the early Bronze Age. The expertly skilled Cretan fleets that had been initially trained and led by Pharaoh Menes initiated all of this trade.

An interesting artifact that links Crete with Britain is the Phaistos Disc, which was discovered in 1908 by the Italian archaeologist Luigi Pernier. The disk is named after the Minoan palace of Phaistos on Crete, where it was found. On the disk are features of 241 tokens, comprising forty-five unique signs, which were made by pressing preformed hieroglyphic seals in a clockwise sequence spiraling toward the center into a disc of soft clay, which was then fired. The disc connects Crete with megalithic artifacts found throughout Britain and France that contain the same astronomical, geometrical, and mathematical information.

Beautiful frescoes adorned the walls of Crete's homes, villas, and palaces. Statuary, terra-cotta, and ceramic pottery, gardens, parks, and fountains from the many natural springs all abounded throughout Crete. The arts were common and theater was very popular with many plays performed by wandering groups of actors. Musical performances with various musical instruments were also popular to the enjoyment of many.

After Pharaoh Menes had introduced the worship of the bull during the age of Taurus, the Cretans had taken this worship and transformed it into an entertainment event called bull leaping. At these events, specially trained and conditioned acrobats would enter an arena with bulls. As the bulls charged with their heads down to gore their challengers, the acrobats would deftly grab

the bull by the horns and as the bull flipped its head back to free itself of the man or woman, they would use the momentum to leap over the bull's back.

The athletes would gracefully tuck, somersault, and land on their feet behind the bull. Another athlete would quickly appear and distract the bull until it charged and then repeat the process of grabbing the horns and flipping over the bull's back until the bull became tired. This event is still performed in present times by Spanish *recortadores,* who continue a bull-leaping tradition that they claim goes back to the legendary King Minos from Crete's Minoan civilization.

These events were conducted not as a mere sporting event but as a spiritual transformational rite. The underlying idea was that of overcoming one's fear and working with the energy of a determined being of nature. The bull in the arena is focused to assert its perceived domination. His energy is representative of misguided aspects of our own ego. So the challenge was to counter this egoic energy from the bull, turning this energy into grace and beauty by dodging and leaping over and around the bull unscathed. This ideal of a spiritual basis for sports is something that has widely been forgotten during the course of the centuries.

The modern-day goring, spearing, and using of swords in bullfights is a sad distortion of bull leaping. It's symptomatic for the descent into the lower aspects of mankind and a reflection of the desire to dominate and conquer on the material plane. Bulls were considered sacred and revered in ancient times and were treated with respect and honor, never with such disregard.

The Minoan goddess culture and civilization of Crete were extraordinary for more than a thousand years but suffered a significant setback around 1450 BCE during a volcanic eruption on Thera, the island that is now called Santorini. The resulting earthquakes and tsunami caused massive devastation to the entire island. Scientists have recently calculated through computer simulations that the northern side of Crete facing toward Thera was hit by a tsunami over sixty-five feet high from one end to the other. On top of that, they calculated that there were waves rebounding off other surrounding islands, so more walls of water were coming in approximately thirty minutes, forty-six minutes, and seventy-three minutes apart. These later waves claimed the lives of many struggling survivors and those who had rushed in to try to help.

But although many of the coastal communities on the north side of

Crete facing Thera were virtually wiped off the face of the Earth, many others survived farther inland. They endured the earthquakes but still had major damage. Fortunately, Crete had been saving food in vast storage containers in the prosperous period preceding the event, so survivors were able to continue on initially. But the rebuilding efforts were further complicated as a drop in temperatures caused by the massive amounts of sulfur dioxide spouted into the atmosphere led to several years of cold, wet summers in the region, ruining harvests. With the inability to grow decent crops and many of the surrounding communities of the Mediterranean also affected and unable to provide sufficient support, many survivors perished.

When some of the ship crews that had been far away from port returned to Crete, they were in shock at the devastation. But these sailors quickly recovered and began tirelessly plying distant lands for basic essentials like food. Much of the bronze trade and manufacturing was slowly restored over many years but would never again reach its full potential. The massive destruction, loss of life, starvation of survivors, and loss of income from trade devastated the economy. This once dominant civilization in the Mediterranean crumbled as a result of the eruption, leaving a power vacuum in the political landscape of the ancient world.

Today many geologists believe that the eruption on Thera was the single most powerful explosive event ever witnessed. It has been scientifically compared to the detailed records available from other volcanic eruptions, such as the famous eruption of Krakatoa, Indonesia, in 1883. That fiery explosion killed upward of forty thousand people in just a few hours, produced colossal tsunamis forty feet tall, spewed volcanic ash far across Asia, caused a drop in global temperatures, created strangely colored sunsets for three years, and was heard up to three thousand miles away. But geologists believe that the Minoan eruption was four or five times more powerful, exploding with the energy of several hundred atomic bombs in a fraction of a second.

The effects of the eruption were more easily absorbed on the mainland where the destruction from collapsing buildings was not as great, because most of the architecture on the mainland at that time was rather primitive. The mountain ranges on the mainland also blocked most of the devastating effects of the eruption, and prevailing winds carried much of the crop-smothering ash south and east.

In the wake of this event, any help from the Mycenaeans in mainland Greece was very welcome. The two cultures had never been at odds, and the youth from the mainland was routinely trained at the universities in Crete. But the dynamics and cultural influence shifted, and over time the Mycenaeans would easily and inevitably begin to dominate militarily. The survivors of Crete would be transformed from a peaceful goddess culture into a patriarchal warrior culture.

In just a short time, their peaceful, efficient bureaucracy made way for the warring city-state system of the Mycenaeans. Initially offering help to the survivors, the Mycenaeans took advantage of the weakened Minoan culture and would begin to dominate the Mediterranean for their own belligerent interests.

Most of Crete had self-governed for centuries with no taxation and no monetary unit or fiat currency ever widely used within Crete, only in foreign trade. When the Mycenaeans came in they set up local governmental bodies and introduced taxation, demanding gold and silver coins for payments. This would hinder and eventually crush the regrowth of Minoan culture. The Mycenaeans also seized the opportunity to take over the once prosperous trading routes of the Minoans. Unfortunately, the formerly powerful and pervasive goddess culture and its peaceful ideas of trade were not also held by the patriarchal warrior culture of the Mycenaeans, so conflicts ensued. One of these skirmishes was one of the first battles of the Argonauts, whom I would also belong to as a teenager in my lifetime as Idomeneus. It involved the city-state of Troy and would eventually stir up into one of the paramount clashes in all of recorded history, the Trojan War, in which I would then command the Cretan army as King Idomeneus.

I remember reading Homer's *Iliad* for the first time at the age of twelve in my current lifetime. I had heard much about the ancient text in references in other books and in school and felt a strong draw to its story and was eager to read about it. I was mesmerized by the story of the Trojan War as told by Homer, and I remember identifying with the characters and felt absorbed into the story, as if I was really there. All of these earnest desires to learn about historical places and times are indicators of a potential past life memory, as I would learn as I matured.

Homer was a poet and storyteller who lived several hundred years after the actual events. It seems obvious to me that Homer was very gifted in picking up and relaying stories passed down through time. In fact, this form of passing on information about past and current events was the preferred and sometimes only way that information was conveyed in cultures without a written language or where most of the population could neither read nor write. Information, knowledge, and entertainment were brought from cities and countries throughout much of history by wandering bards who told stories and passed on news from far away—like today's newspapers and Internet, only at a far slower rate.

These wandering bards would have been paid for their services, and popular ones were making a very good living from that. Imagine a famous actor like Brad Pitt wandering from city to city, pulling in large audiences for his performances, earning substantial income, and being revered by the common folk and nobles alike.

After feverishly reading the *Iliad,* I had to find out how the sequel of the story ended and read the *Odyssey* as if nothing else in life existed. But I still felt unsatisfied after I had finished reading about Odysseus's journey home, so I searched for more books that were similar and possibly held other nuggets of information. For many hundreds, if not thousands of years, the Trojan War was thought to be a myth, but it has actually been proven that much of what Homer has compiled about the Trojan War is indeed factual.

The rediscovery of Troy would begin as early as 1822, when Scottish journalist and geologist Charles Maclaren identified a site near present-day Hisarlik, Turkey, as the possible site of Homeric Troy. In 1865, English archaeologist Frank Calvert excavated test trenches in a field he had bought from a local farmer at Hisarlik. Then, in 1868, a wealthy German businessman named Heinrich Schliemann would arrive on the scene and help reintroduce academia to the long lost city of Troy.

Schliemann, who at one time was proclaimed as the father of modern archaeology, also began excavating in the area after a chance meeting with Calvert in Qanakkale, Turkey. These excavations revealed several cities built in succession. Schliemann was, at first, skeptical about the identification of Hisarlik with Troy, but was persuaded by Calvert and took over Calvert's excavations on the eastern half of the Hisarlik site, which was on Calvert's property.

Schliemann's vision, passion, open mind, and strong belief in Homer made his discovery of Troy at Hisarlik in Turkey possible. He was not just a

greedy, ignorant amateur as many have postulated; he had studied the classics at the Sorbonne in Paris, earned his PhD in Rostock, Germany, became an honorable member of the Society of Antiquaries of London, and was also an honorable professor of the University of Oxford and the Queen's College of London.

The rediscovery of Troy is a wonderful reminder of the fact that myths almost always have some kind of factual basis, as I've learned from experience. But they usually earn that moniker, because at some point in distant history the people no longer understood or knew of the ancient technology or the former locations and events; they had become lost in time. What also happened quite often is that people would add extravagant feats into the story line that would obviously twist a once factual story into a concocted fantasy. Sometimes this was done innocently, but fabrication was also used to mask deeper insights and hide them from those uninitiated into deeper mysteries.

As a young boy in my lifetime as Idomeneus growing up in the royal family, I was always fascinated by the soldiers' armaments and watched enthralled as they drilled with their swords and spears. I was slight of build and skinny, so I never thought that I could live up to my dream of being a warrior and instead focused my natural abilities in the study of everything scientific. Crete was a very learned society with many universities and was a place where the nobility of foreign lands would send their children for study. We had also supported many children from the primitive mainland of Greece and regularly allocated spots in our universities in the hope that education would help counter the more aggressive and violent tendencies that were showing up in that area. It was in these universities that a young Heracles would study for several years.

Because I was a brainy lad without a very athletic physique, it was fitting that I would practice a trade that was one of Crete's most famous, technologically advanced, and profitable—the building of ships. I was a nephew and apprentice of Argus, the man that built the ship named after him. Jason, the captain of this unique ship, later conscripted me at the recommendation of my uncle to sail on the ship. I was ordered to help ensure that it performed correctly, because the *Argo* was a highly advanced but experimental vessel.

We used a unique multiple sail system that, in addition, to the traditional square sail also included an adaption from the Egyptian felucca sail. The felucca sail was a triangular sail, set on a long yard, mounted at an angle on

the mast, and running in a fore and aft direction. This type of sail offers a high level of maneuverability but can easily be taken down during stormy weather. The tiller and oar system all had aqua- dynamic shapes with the oars having a slightly curved structure to get more thrust in the water. My uncle, Argus, was also knowledgeable about magnetics and designed a rudimentary form of compass featuring a lodestone that was developed from a primitive form of iron alloy. Suspended pieces of lodestone were the first magnetic compasses used for navigational purposes while at sea. I was in charge of recording the new device's workings.

Another useful and innovative design that was included in the *Argo* was the ability to attach large wooden wheels so that the *Argo* could be hauled overland. The wheels were attached by screwing the axle through the center of the wheel and into a keel support system similar to what is used while a ship is docked or being built on land. Turning was accomplished by several men helping the wheels turn more on one side or putting wedges in front of the wheels on one side to make sharper turns. Lamb's wool was used to further cushion and protect the hull on the keel supports.

The ship was hauled by attaching rope systems to the rear or front keel supports, or both. These rope systems could also be attached to harnesses so that horses could be used. The onboard horses from our support ships in the *Argo* fleet had multiple functions, such as pulling chariots, being part of a scouting force, providing a small cavalry unit, and hauling the *Argo* overland for special missions. We could even use the ship as a movable fighting platform on land. The *Argo* would be considered a special operations boat today because of its unusual capabilities.

I was thrilled to be going on the *Argo.* It was like a dream that had come true. I was to be in the company of the most famous warriors of that time assembled in one place. Several of the more rough and seasoned members of the Argonauts were not particularly wild about being accountable to such a youth as I, however. Today I can understand this type of mentality after having been a warrior and leader in SEAL Team Six. We would also initially frown upon anyone joining our tight-knit group from the outside and would often grumble when we had to work with someone who was unproven. I was not even a warrior when I joined the crew of the *Argo,* but I had always dreamed of being one.

During sea trials for the Argo in the crystal blue waters off the coast of Crete, I was routinely harassed and bullied by the more dashing warrior crew of the *Argo.* I was very fortunate when Heracles eventually took me under his wing and began training me in various means of self- defense. Heracles taught me the skills of grappling and, because of my slight build, leveraging. By using leveraging techniques together with proper body mechanics, I was able to generate more power than by using muscular strength alone.

Under the tutelage of Heracles, I also earned a good knowledge of the circulatory and nervous systems of the human body. I say "earned" because Heracles made me work very hard while the *Argo* was in port for adjustments after initial sea trials. Heracles helped me tremendously to develop my body, and through his own studies of advanced scientific knowledge of the human body he taught me how to use my skeletal, vascular, and muscular systems to full advantage. I would use this knowledge to eventually become the greatest spearman of my era, which is also mentioned in Homer's *Iliad.* In a past life, Heracles was my brother Bhima that I mentioned in Chapter 1. We would reincarnate many times together in our soul group. In the most recent life that we worked together, he was the American tank commander Patton.

To the classical Greek wrestling techniques, I also added some of my own innovations, like applying pressure to the jugular vein. And I had developed a technique for taking a bow ora staff and sweeping it behind the knees of an opponent to take him off his feet. I was more interested in using, for instance, the pressure on the jugular and sweeping techniques, because they were designed as defensive techniques that could be successfully applied in a conflict where I would be unable to match the brute force of many of my opponents. After training with Heracles and winning several wrestling matches, I eventually earned the respect of my fellow Argonauts. Interestingly, I have quickly relearned many of these techniques in my present life and also taught them to others.

Even in my time with Heracles, he was already considered a legend. It was said that he was the son of Zeus and Alcmene, but his terrestrial mentor and stepfather was Amphitryon. Although it was rather uncommon for gods or demigods to walk among us openly in those days, many people were firmly convinced that the offspring of off-world beings or gods more or less discretely walked among us. Many also believed that gifted individuals could openly see and communicate

with the gods and goddesses, who would interact in our affairs at times. Some would mate with the men and women of our royal families and occasionally with a rare beauty or robust masculine type outside the royal families.

Heracles was a very introverted man but observant of everything around him. He could see through to the heart of a difficult situation and become a very focused and determined man of action once he had made up his mind to accomplish something. He was highly intelligent, and his training in the universities of Crete had honed his mental and intuitive faculties to a very high level. I believe that this was the reason he was capable of accomplishing his earlier twelve labors.

It was rumored at the time that Heracles, who was also known for his occasional ill temper, had killed his wife and children during a drunken rage one night. As a sentence for this crime, his cousin Eurystheus, the king of Tiryns and Mycenae, gave him twelve impossible tasks. It was thought that Heracles would never accomplish even one of them in his lifetime and would suffer till the end of his days or more probably would be killed in the performance of his tasks.

The first of these responsibilities was the killing of a mountain lion without traditional weapons. In the mountains around the Greek city of Thebes, where Heracles was born, was a mountain lion that had been terrorizing and carrying off several individuals of the local population for many years. Heracles tracked it down and killed it inside a cave with a long, stout wooden club. This same club was with him for much of his life after his twelve labors. He carried the lion back down the mountains across his shoulders so that everyone could see that he had accomplished his task. He then skinned the giant lion and wore its hide in many battles and duels thereafter. The present-day depictions of a very large and muscular Heracles wearing a lion skin and carrying a knotty club are also part of my memories.

Some details about the fifth of these labors, the task to clean the stables of King Augeas, were relayed to me by Ahtun Re. Augeas was very rich and had many herds of cows, bulls, goats, sheep, and horses, which rendered the stables where they were kept filthy. The stables had been designed in a far distant time by ancient engineers and had become not only filthy but also fossilized by bat guano. These stables were similar to the ones that were actively in use in Crete at the time.

Heracles cleansed the stables of King Augeas by diverting two nearby rivers through them, adroitly using his intelligence and intuition—not just his physical strength. When the combined power of the rivers water came through the stables, it cut through and washed away the fossilized guano as well as the more recent animal dung. The cleansing effect of the water also revealed and restored the original water system of this ancient facility. The stables were originally engineered so that animal husbandry could be conducted more efficiently, providing a constant water supply for self-cleaning, drinking water, and cleansing the animals.

Each of Heracles's labors was actually based in fact, but over time the story of Heracles became bigger and bigger in the telling. At one time in Athens several hundred years after Heracles's time, dramatic actor troupes were in competition to come up with the most elaborate dramas and plays of the popular stories of Heracles's life. The stories were stretched from the actual truth to appeal to the audience even more. Several hundred years later, the Romans would rename Heracles to Hercules and further elaborate on the tales. During the Renaissance times, the tales were romanticized with even more flourish until today the tales of Heracles are discounted as mere myths and dismissed as having no basis in truth.

Just like with the story of Heracles, mainstream historians do not generally acknowledge the actual historicity of the *Argo*. Of course, it's hard to come up with irrefutable tangible evidence that would convince the narrow-minded academia of today, but I can assure you that the *Argo* indeed existed. When it finally set sail after all the sea trials and after provisions were gathered and stored below decks, we had nonstop adventures punctuated by periods at sea during which we would sail the vessel to our next adventure.

One of the journeys was later called "Jason and the Argonauts in search of the Golden Fleece." Our destination had been the region of Colchis, east of the Black Sea and south of the Caucasus Mountains in present-day Georgia. In Colchis it had been a local practice to use fleeces of ram skin to sift gold dust from rivers. The fleeces were hung out to dry in the sun and sometimes combed so that they would produce a static charge that would attract fine, loose gold particles. They were then used like a filter and secured to the bottom of streams that were known to be downstream from where gold was being mined. By an electrolytic

process, the very fine gold would cling to the ram's fur, which would eventually take on the sheen of a golden fleece when rehung out to dry in the sunlight.

The existence of these skins would eventually evolve into the mythical idea of the search for the one Golden Fleece. The gold was so refined on these skins that it held healing properties when ingested, just like the alluvial silver that was captured using the same technique. Both of these alluvial precious metals had the ability to fight bacterial and viral infections.

One of the early battles the Argonauts would wage would be against a king of the Trojans, as I mentioned earlier. Most of these campaigns and adventures were little more than pirating raids in which we would sack a city, take their valuables, and leave. Heracles grew tired of these conquests after a bit, and after a particularly heavy night of drinking, he argued with the other Argonauts about the validity of what they were doing. In response, the Argonauts decided to abandon Heracles and myself on an island beach, where we waited for several weeks until another ship passed through the area. After this, Heracles would begin his own campaigns and would always chose the hardest and virtually unconquerable kingdoms to raid.

I believe that Heracles had been trained in an advanced level of priesthood at some point in Crete. The stories of the goddess Hera being at odds with him and causing many of his hardships are false. Hera was actually the patron goddess that he worshipped.

Heracles was his own worst enemy at times and fighting hard with his inner demons. I believe that toward the later part of his life, Heracles was feeling a pull toward more altruistic devotions of serving people—rather than subjugating them through force. Ahtun Re told me that Heracles was a very high-level initiate and actually held the gods accountable to man. He demanded that they honor the same standards they had imposed on mankind, and they eventually agreed to these demands.

I would later take all the knowledge I had garnered from Heracles and train the Cretan army into one of the finest in the world. In a few decades, Crete would go from virtually no standing army to one of the best in the Mediterranean, an army I would lead into the Trojan War alongside many other Greek armies.

In the *Iliad,* twenty-nine contingents under forty-six captains or kings are listed, accounting for a total of 1,186 ships. The area of ancient Greece

called Boeotia used the figure of 120 men per ship, which would result in a total of 142,320 men transported to the shores of Troy. My memories are actually closer to a little over 120,000 men at the peak, as some of the supply ships had only around fifty men.

Take into account that not all of these men were active combat soldiers. There were, of course, many warriors, who would stow their armaments under their benches as they rowed the combat ships, but many rowers were also ordinary sailors. Also along for the war were farmers to grow crops to feed the army, animal caretakers for the horses that pulled the chariots and for the livestock that also fed the army, armorers, woodworkers, and so on. In the most pampered armies, the number of support personnel can be as high as a quarter or even half of the army force. When I was at SEAL Team Six as an assault team operator, at one time the support personnel far exceeded our numbers.

Throughout the Trojan War, support forces varied for us as we began to raid the cities surrounding Troy up and down the coastline. As prisoners were taken for ransom and highly desirable educated Troad slaves were taken to be sold, the total number of Greeks involved in the campaign would wax and wane sometimes by as much as fifty thousand. Troad, also known as Troas, is the historical name of the Biga peninsula where Troy was located in the northwestern part of present-day Anatolia, Turkey.

During the fiercest battles, there were actually anywhere from fifty to seventy-five thousand warriors on the battlefield on either side. The largest number of ships brought into battle was by King Agamemnon of the Mycenaeans at one hundred ships. The second largest group of ships at ninety would be brought forth from the great King Nestor of Pylos, and the third greatest number of ships brought to battle was tied by the Argive commander Diomedes and King Idomeneus of Crete, each of whom had eighty ships in his fleet.

In the *Iliad* it is stated that Idomeneus is found among the first rank of the Greek generals, leading troops as well as engaging the enemy head-on. As one of Agamemnon's trusted advisers, Idomeneus was the eldest warrior chieftain of the entire Greek coalition. He was one of the primary defenders when most of the other Achaean heroes were injured, and he even fought Hector briefly and repulsed one of his major Trojan-led attacks.

I was also one of the Achaeans to enter the famous Trojan horse, which

was built with the same design concept as the wicker man that the priestly class or druids in Britain used for symbolic ceremonies. The wicker man took on negative connotations in later history through the negative propaganda that Julius Caesar would initiate to garner support for his war on Britain, as he discredited the druids after suffering one of his few defeats at their hands.

So this is where part of the inspiration for the Trojan horse came from. The transfer of information and trade between Crete and the British Isles had been ongoing for hundreds of years. In my mind's eye, I can still look down and see that my chariot was designed with wicker. I remember riding it to battle on the vast plain before Troy. I also remember the chariots in Egypt that I drove and rode in; their design was also fashioned after the chariots from the tribes of the British Isles, which should be new information for historians. I only found this out through accessing my past life memories.

The wicker material was sturdy, lightweight, easily repaired and maintained, economical, and perfect for storing on ships where space and weight of materials were closely controlled. Even shields and body armor were fashioned of wicker by the majority of soldiers who could not afford the price of metal.

This scarcity of quality battle weaponry has been a problem for battle commanders in almost every battle fought throughout history. In order to loot the battlefield for better arms from the bodies of the fallen, troops would, at times, refrain from immediately pursuing the combatant army after a victory, which would be very frustrating for generals. Quality battlefield gear on soldiers prevents them from losing focus at key points in battles, and not surprisingly the wealthiest nations that invested in high-technology gear and distributed it among their men were often the ones that won battles.

Also factors, of course, were fortifications and siege engines. Troy had seen massive building efforts following the decades after Heracles and the other Argonauts had sacked Troy several decades earlier. I had been present at this earlier sacking of Troy with the Argonauts as a young lad. The city had been much smaller back then, and we were astonished to find that they had worked on their city walls to the point where they were virtually impregnable. But as the Spartan lawgiver and reformer Lycurgus would say several hundred years later in reply to the question of whether or not it would be prudent to build a wall around Sparta, "A city is well-fortified which has a wall of men instead of brick."

We would eventually conquer the city of Troy, but only after we had fought the Trojan War for several years and sacked many of the cities around Troy, gathering huge amounts of wealth. Conquering other cities and countries by force to seize the fruits of their labors has almost always been part of warfare, but that wasn't the main purpose of our campaigns against the cities surrounding Troy. We determined that we could not initially breach Troy's walls, so the piecemeal destruction of the surrounding infrastructure was undertaken. This was considered a strategy to weaken Troy enough to bring about its eventual collapse, also demonstrating Troy's inability to protect its coalition of cities throughout the region. We were sending a clear message that we were in control, and that we would now be the ones charging a tax on goods that were gathered from the distant lands through the straits. Troy had tried to tax the ships of the *Argo* fleet many years before and had been defeated over it. We were now embroiled in this long war so that the Greeks would be the ones to control these rich trading zones.

But the subterfuge of this war had been to rescue Helen of Sparta. All wars need a motivated citizenry, and honor is one of the greatest drivers for initiating a population to fight for a cause. King Menelaus of Sparta had married into great wealth when he married Helen, who had been courted by many suitors. Helen was extremely wealthy and the rightful heir to the lands of Sparta when she abandoned Menelaus for Prince Paris of Troy. So in rescuing Helen we also sought after her wealth and the rights over the lands of Sparta, making sure that Troy didn't get a foothold in Greece. But the most coveted prize and main reason for this war with Troy was to gain the complete control of the trading routes from the Aegean Sea through the Hellespont and the Bosporus to the Black Sea.

It was these possessions that were actually sought after and not so much the honor and beauty of Helen. The face that had launched a thousand ships was indeed enchanting, but they had not been launched for it. Helen's beautiful image was used as a point of honor to commit the nobles of Greece because one of the laws of ancient Greece was that all noble suitors of a woman that would be shamed were liable to help extract revenge and honor for her family name. At that time, many of the kings throughout Greece had at one time wooed Helen. Wealth, lands, and power are often the driving forces for marriage among the elite classes, and Helen had all of these in enormous quantities. Many men had sought this wealth for themselves and were now committed to retrieving it for Menelaus at the command of his brother Agamemnon, king of Mycenae.

I was one of the first to join with the coalition out of respect and gratitude for the Mycenaeans who had come to the aid of Crete after the devastation from the Santorini eruption many years earlier, even though their influence turned out to be ambiguous over time. One concession I sought, however, and was honored with, was to be the second- in-command of all forces after Agamemnon. As the eldest noble warrior still actively engaged in combat in the group of kings, and one who had been with the crew of the *Argo* when they had sacked Troy many decades ago, I felt I was uniquely positioned to help provide success for the mission. Further committing me was the fact that, like most of the other aristocrats in the expedition, I was also a former suitor of Helen.

In one of my sessions with Ahtun Re, I would relate to him that I remembered Achilles fighting during the final sack of Troy. Some accounts had described Achilles being killed during a raid that had taken the irascible warrior into the city itself. Paris was reputed with shooting him from behind with an arrow from the walls of the citadel of Troy. Achilles had been pursuing the Trojans who were fleeing from his wrath, after he learned that his second-in-command and lifelong friend Patroclus had been killed. He and his band of warriors had slipped through the gates of Troy before they could close them with many of their warriors caught outside the city.

Achilles was hit in the exposed unarmored heel, hence the term Achilles's heel or tendon, as he recklessly chased the fleeing Trojans through the city to the inner gates of the citadel. I believe he was hit with a tainted or poisoned arrow shot by Paris that became an infected wound, which caused a systemic shock to his system. Paris held a deep grudge against Achilles for killing his brother Hector in an earlier duel and would find his revenge on this day.

Ahtun Re relayed to me that my thoughts were accurate about Achilles. He also told me that the family of Achilles—like the island of Crete—had traded with the tribes located on the British Isles. This trade had resulted in many secrets being shared, among them the art of resurrection or the literal coming back to life. He told me of a vessel that exists today called the Gundestrup Cauldron that was similar to the one used in the process of bringing Achilles back to life again.

The Gundestrup Cauldron is made of silver and some gold. You will remember the healing properties of silver and gold from the story of the Golden Fleece. It is interesting to note here that Achilles's father, Peleus, had been one of the heroes of the *Argo* that sailed in search of the Golden Fleece. On the Gundestrup Cauldron is the image of a green man in a cross-legged lotus position. The green man was the symbol of resurrection or rejuvenation and is often depicted today as a nature spirit. The druid priests made images of the green man in wicker and used to burn them in a sacred ceremony similar to the one in ancient Egypt featuring the phoenix.

Originally, the Egyptians identified the phoenix as a stork or heron-like bird, known from the *Book of the Dead* and other Egyptian texts as one of the sacred symbols of worship at Heliopolis, closely associated with the rising sun and the Egyptian sun god Ra. These ancient ceremonies were all mostly symbolic, but the actual regeneration of tissue was real when a body was placed in a particular solution within the silver cauldron.

On one of the panels of the cauldron, you can see the depiction of a warrior being dipped into the vat by a deity initiating the resurrection process. The panel also shows other soldiers either waiting in line to be rejuvenated or already healed and returning to battle.

This process of rejuvenation brought Achilles back to life. I remember having been with him in the Trojan horse along with many others, including King Odysseus of Ithaca and King Diomedes of Argos, who had been the fiercest warrior after Achilles. Another famous Greek noble inside the wicker horse was Philoctetes, king of Methone, who had killed Paris with the bow and arrows of Heracles given to him by his father Poias. Poias had also been an Argonaut who had received the famous weaponry by Heracles before he died and then passed them on to his son.

My memories of the Trojan horse had us all seated in a specially designed planking system a quarter way up from the bottom of the horse's belly. This protected us from being seen from below if any of the wicker material would have been displaced. It also gave us protection from spears if the Trojans would have decided to probe for secreted warriors by thrusting their spears up into the belly of the horse.

The wicker material had been soaked in seawater for several days prior to the construction, making it more pliable to bending and shaping. The wood was thus waterlogged and hardly flammable, so we felt somewhat safe from the threat of being burned alive. The planking led to the neck of the horse and a ladder system that we used to go up into the neck where a secret trapdoor was installed. To minimize weight and better enable us to move rapidly, we wore light clothing with no body armor and carried light wicker shields and short swords, although some of us had spears or bows and arrows.

The plan, which would work out perfectly, was for us to be pulled into the city inside the gift horse after the deception from a supposed Greek defector. This man's name was Sinon, and, before the war, he had been a famous Greek actor. The ruse was that he was left behind with his arms tied and his clothes torn to shreds. He pretended to be enraged with the Greeks, stating that he had escaped being sacrificed to Athena, who had become angry with the Greeks for stealing the Palladium.

The Palladium was a wooden statue of Athena that had earlier been stolen by Odysseus and Diomedes in a bold night raid. He assured the Trojans that the wooden horse would appease the goddess and would bring victory to the Trojans. Some of the Trojans argued vehemently that the horse should be burned, but the ruse eventually worked, and we were wheeled into the city.

We would sneak out that night after the Trojans had celebrated all day, thinking that we had abandoned the long war and returned home. First we came out through the trapdoor in the back of the neck and then onto the back of the horse, which had been reinforced for that purpose. From there we lowered ourselves down with ropes attached to special anchor points concealed on top of the horse. We then overcame the guards at the gate, removed their attire, put it on as a disguise, and climbed to the walls to give a signal to our fleet that was hidden behind an island in the distant Aegean Sea.

We gave the signal with the shield of Achilles, who had been the only one in the group to bring a metal shield. His armor was made of a special metal that would later be called Damascus steel; it also had a thin coating of bronze over it. A light focused in the concave area of the shield magnified its intensity many times, making it the perfect tool to be used as a signaling device.

After we gave our signal, it took our Greek comrades longer than ex-

pected to beach the ships. The troops then tried their best to quietly close the distance from the shore to the walls of Troy, but, just before they reached the gates, a change of the guard was supposed to take place. In the struggle to quietly overpower the new guards a cry went out, and people close to the gate began to stir, but even more cries went out throughout the city as we opened the gates for our warriors dressed in full battle gear.

They were breathless as they entered the city from their dash to help us and immediately began to fight Trojans. Because of the delay in arrival of our troops, the Trojans unfortunately had time to sleep off some of their drunkenness. Combined with the realization that they were fighting for their lives, the lives of their families, and their city, they became the fiercest of adversaries.

House to house fighting ensued, and fires began to break out. People were running everywhere with whatever valuables and family members they could keep together. Groups of fully armored Greeks and Trojans formed into battle phalanxes in the streets and clashed violently. Together, with the warriors from the fleet, we then began to make our way to the citadel of Troy. It was on this foray through the streets that earthquakes began to strike.

Our shaman priests had predicted the start of cataclysmic events starting that night, after we had already observed many anomalies over the past few months, including light earth tremors. Even the sun had actually seemed to stop in the heavens for a relatively long period of time while we were fighting a battle on the plains a few days earlier. The rivers had raged with water during a clear day with no rain having fallen for over a week. Fog had filtered into the battlefield during the peak of a hot day. Our seers had interpreted these events as omens of good fortune for the Greeks, and we intended to capitalize on that prophecy tonight. These events were also recorded in the *Iliad:*

"The mountain shook, the rapid stream stood still. Above, the sire of gods his thunder rolls, and peals on peals redoubled rend the poles. Beneath, stern Neptune shakes the solid ground; the forests wave, the mountains nod around; through all their summits tremble Ida's woods, and from their sources boil her hundred floods. Troy's turrets totter on the rocking plain."

The Old Testament of the Bible relates how Joshua dropped the walls of Jericho during this same time frame and how the sun also stood in the heavens while a battle raged:

"Then spoke Joshua to the Lord in the day when the Lord gave the Amorites over to the men of Israel; and he said in the sight of Israel, 'Sun, stand thou still at Gibeon, and thou Moon in the valley of Aijalon.' And the sun stood still, and the moon stayed, until the nation took vengeance on their enemies. Is this not written in the Book of Jashar? The sun stayed in the midst of heaven, and did not hasten to go down for about a whole day. There has been no day like it before or since, when the Lord hearkened to the voice of a man; for the Lord fought for Israel."

This could be brushed aside as only another Biblical myth or literary dramatization, but similar occurrences have been reported from various places around the globe. Legends in America tell of a period when, for a whole day's time, the sun did not rise. Cold fell upon the land, and the people lived in great fear, gazing in all directions, speculating on where the "new sun" would rise. Finally, after the passage of some hours, the sun rose again, but in a different direction from where it had risen before.

Another instance of the sun standing still, according to Roman historian Plutarch, occurred in the reign of Romulus. Also in Egypt there are legends that at one time the sun rose in the west and set in the east. A mural discovered in the tomb of Senmut shows the constellations in a different relationship to the rising and setting of the sun than they are today.

There is a very controversial book that describes historical accounts of cataclysmic events during this time frame called *Worlds in Collision.* In the book, author Dr. Immanuel Velikovsky's work crosses so many of the boundaries that few experts could grasp its scope. The main body of evidence in *Worlds in Collision* consists of literal interpretations of historical texts. You should think that this is how these texts should have been analyzed in the first place, but, in fact, Velikovsky was able to present many perspectives that have been greatly overlooked by researchers before him. Other sources that he draws from are the Old Testament, the Talmud, the Egyptian papyri, and the historical texts, traditions, and legends of Rome, Greece, Babylonia, Arabia, Persia, India, Tibet, Finland, Iceland, West Africa, Siberia, China, Japan, the Pacific islands, Mexico, and Peru. Dr. Velikovsky describes the area of his investigations as "anthropology in the broadest sense," concerning itself with "the nature of the cosmos and its history."

On the night of our final battle in Troy, the ground shook so viciously that some of the outer walls that we had been trying to burrow under before began to collapse. This was fortuitous because the gate where our forces were entering was now a bottleneck. The press of Trojan civilians trying to escape, Greek warriors battling to get into the city, and Trojan defenders battling to stop the flood of Greeks was jeopardizing our capture of the city. The massed Greek soldiers waiting impatiently outside the gate were quick to seize upon the opportunity new entrances to the city would hold and began to flood in through the breach points in the wall.

The streets of Troy were lined with houses and shops. From the roofs, arrows, stones, pots, and spears rained down on us as we navigated our way through the winding streets up to the highest point in Troy. It was during this brutal march that Achilles would be lost. The last that anyone knew after the battle was that Achilles, being his usual impulsive self, had chased after Trojan combatants into a building that had collapsed during a particularly aggressive earthquake. Because of the mayhem in the streets, no one was able to mark or remember the location.

We eventually reached the citadel and entered through the gate that was wide open because of people flooding out to escape. This was where the most intense fighting was enjoined, because the best and most loyal fighters were kept here to guard the royal family. It was here that many noble Trojans perished.

It was not long after we captured the citadel of Troy that the sun began to come up into red skies. The flames of the city mixed with violent upheavals in the atmosphere dampened our victory. What treasure could be scavenged was quickly taken out of the city, as many of us were concerned that we could lose more men to collapsing buildings from continuing earthquakes.

It was during the battle at the citadel that I sustained a serious injury to my heel. The Trojans in desperation had resorted to ignoble fighting practices in the last weeks of the war and had found a weakness in our armor at the back of the leg. This part was usually not armored to conserve weight and provide more mobility. Achilles was one of the first to receive an injury in this vulnerable location and had apparently died, but he was later revived, as I recounted earlier. My tendon was nearly severed by a spear as I passed by a doorway that concealed a Trojan fighter. I was already short of armor because I had been in the Trojan horse, so some of my men had met up with me and had helped provide security as we went through the streets. Because the fighting in the citadel was extremely fierce, I had then been separated from my loyal band of men and left vulnerable, but like most of the other leaders of the Greeks, I would still be alive as the battle came to an end.

As we made our way back, the spoils of war were loaded onto our ships, and I was carried to our fleet wounded and unable to walk on my own. The other fleets of the Greek kings were also loaded, and we all pushed out into the seas that were beginning to churn. They soon became increasingly violent seas as we fought to return to our respective cities.

It was during this time that stories arose of the odyssey of King Odysseus from Ithaca. In the Homer's *Odyssey*, it is said to have taken Odysseus ten years to find his way home, which is the same amount of years that was given for the Trojan War in the *Iliad*. But, in both cases, the number of ten years is not literally accurate; it should be translated as many years. Imagine being gone from home for twenty years and how different everything would be. It's manipulations of truths and false translations like these that cause a story to lose credibility as a real account of ancient history and be thrown into the myth category.

Various accounts in different works relate that all the kings had serious trouble getting home. King Menelaus with his reunited wife Helen was stranded along the shores of Egypt with their fleet for many years in one account. The leader of the Greek armies, King Agamemnon, was also lost at sea for a long period of time. What could cause these gross miscalculations from some of the most seasoned and accomplished seafarers of their day?

The Earth may have been pushed about by a passing body strong enough to disrupt the orbit and rearrange the position of the poles, as has been discussed by Immanuel Velikovsky, whom I had mentioned before. I think that this indeed contributed to the disorientation that we experienced after the Trojan War. The stars in the heavens were now in different locations and the sun rose in a new part of the sky. The old landmarks in the sky that we had used to navigate for thousands of years had become useless, and the only way you could navigate now was by locating familiar coastlines and islands or using dead reckoning. This required us to use a known landmark or position from where we would set the course and advance, calculating our future posi-

tions based on our speed while visually keeping track of a forward landmark if possible. The frequent and unrelenting storms also made celestial navigation virtually impossible.

My own Cretan fleet was lost at sea for a long period of time, and one story recounts how I was lost overboard close to the coast of Crete. As I was tossed about in the waves nearly drowning, the story goes, I swore to Poseidon, the god of the seas, that I would sacrifice the first living thing that I came across if he would let me live. The first living thing I encountered after I was safely washed ashore was my son, who was wandering at the shore looking for me. So I was obligated to sacrifice my own son to Poseidon in this story. But I have no memories of this and believed strongly that it was a fabrication. I asked Ahtun Re about this and told him my thoughts.

The story that he told me was an amazing revelation that transcended many lifetimes. Ahtun Re told me of a relative of Agamemnon who had been in a high command position during the Trojan War and afterward, and it was on his behalf that the true historical record of the Trojan War has been altered. Scribes were ordered to change certain aspects of the story to fit his twisted version of events, and unfortunately these alterations were later picked up by Homer, who incorporated some of it into the *Iliad,* and by Euripides, who would write *Iphigenia in Aulis.*

In the latter, the Greek fleet is stranded and cannot leave the port of Aulis for Troy, because the goddess Artemis has punished Agamemnon after he killed a deer in a sacred grove and boasted that he was the better hunter. Artemis was the Greek goddess of the hunt, wild animals, wilderness, childbirth, virginity, and young girls, bringing and relieving disease in women. She was often depicted as a huntress carrying a bow and arrows, and the deer and the cypress were sacred to her. On their way to Troy to participate in the Trojan War, Agamemnon's ships were suddenly motionless as Artemis stopped the wind in Aulis. Euripides then went on to say that Agamemnon had sent for his eldest daughter Iphigenia to come to Aulis on the pretense that she would be married to Achilles. But when she arrived she was sacrificed to Artemis, whereupon the winds picked up again and the fleet sailed to Troy. A goddess that was the protector of virginity and young girls wanted a virgin sacrifice to be appeased? I think not.

The other account of sacrifice whereby I would sacrifice my son Idamante to Poseidon is another manipulation initially fabricated by the same person, who I would also come across in my current lifetime, as I will describe later. What actually happened during my lifetime as Idomeneus was that I had made a living sacrifice similar to what Abraham had done in the Old Testament of the Bible. In a living sacrifice, you don't literally kill a living being, but ceremonially cut away the old self.

Another way to look at this ceremony is the right of passage into manhood. The cords of the youth are cut away so that they can flourish into adulthood, like trimming a tree or bush so it grows healthier and more directly.

This is what Abraham had done with Isaac in a ceremony marking Isaac's transition to adulthood. Abraham had passed a blade over his son to cut away the bonds, or cords, of his youth. I was told that I had done the same thing with my son Idamante and—like Abraham—had, in fact, forbidden ritual sacrifice on Crete.

In one lifetime I would help to create a different account of the story of Idomeneus and the alleged sacrifice of his son, so that this lie would eventually be corrected, even though at that time when I contributed to the creation of an alternative version of this story, I had not fully realized the true implications of why I felt the urge to do so. One day I told Ahtun Re I believed I was Charles Theodore, prince-elector of Bavaria, which he confirmed. In the eighteenth century, Charles Theodore had commissioned an up-and-coming musician named Wolfgang Amadeus Mozart to write what would be Mozart's first mature opera, called *Idomeneo.*

In this operatic account Idomeneo, the king of Crete, is returning from the Trojan War. To gain a safe return to shore during a violent storm at sea, Idomeneo vows to sacrifice to Poseidon the first living being he sees on land. Unfortunately, it's his son Idamante, so Idomeneo flees instead of greeting him, leaving him dumbfounded. Meanwhile, Idamante falls in love with Ilia, the captured daughter of King Priam of Troy, but, on the advice of his confidant Arbace, Idomeneo decides to send his son away with another woman. But this plan gets thwarted by Poseidon, who, enraged over having been cheated out of his sacrifice, sends a sea monster destroying the entire Cretan fleet. Idomeneo presents himself as a sacrifice to appease Poseidon but to no avail. Idamante and Ilia then confess their love to each other, and Idamante sets out to slay

the monster. Meanwhile, the high priest of Crete recounts all the horrors the monster had brought upon the Cretans and asks the king to present and kill whoever Poseidon wanted as a sacrifice. Idomeneo eventually gives in and everything gets prepared for Idamante's sacrifice. But right when Idomeneo is about to strike the fatal blow, Ilia jumps before the blade to save Idamante, who had just slain the monster, and the voice of the oracle says Poseidon will be propitiated if Idomeneo will pass his crown on to Idamante with Ilia as his queen, to which Idomeneo agrees.

The opera is still famous to this day with several excellent recordings, and it is regularly performed. Mozart quoted Charles Theodore as saying, "No music has ever made such an impression on me. It is magnificent." Mozart himself claimed that *Idomeneo* was his favorite operatic work. Charles Theodore liked to present himself as a prince of peace, in contrast to other princes like his chief political opponent, the great warrior Frederick II of Prussia. In an interesting note, I was also the simultaneous parallel incarnation of Frederick the Great.

Ahtun Re told me that anywhere between 3 to 5 percent of a given population will have simultaneous incarnations. He gave the example of today, where there are seven billion humans currently incarnated on the planet. This would mean that 210 million to 350 million people are having multiple, simultaneous incarnations right now. Doesn't sound so special or exceptionally advanced when you put it into perspective like that, does it? Dr. Michael Newton, a certified hypnotherapist, details in his book *Journey of Souls* how and why the soul incarnates in multiple incarnations. I highly recommend this book to anyone with an interest in lives between lives, as it gives an excellent account of life in the spirit realm.

My lives as Charles Theodore and Frederick the Great were part of a greater pattern of incarnate lives to bring in a greater connection to who we are as souls having a human experience. I have strived to bring a greater cohesion and richer experience to the human condition, even when presented with conflict. It is relatively easy to live a life of peace and prosperity for yourself, but try to bring that to others and you will encounter great resistance and ridicule. There are those who believe that you have to keep humanity in a small box and under control. I don't agree with that sentiment, and although I have strayed at times—even in the best of lives—I have always come full circle in serving humanity and helping to create a greater harmony.

To demonstrate to you how current life experiences are linked in a timeless thread throughout your lives, let me relate some examples. The same person who manipulated the story with the alleged sacrifice of my son Idamante had a similar experience himself in Sedona, Arizona. While conducting a sweat lodge ritual during a motivational seminar, several of his attendees died and several more were hospitalized. Thus, his still existing belief in the value of human sacrifice would cost the lives of several trusting individuals. Several others had died previous to this incident over the years, but it wasn't until multiple lives were lost that his operations were halted. This individual is now serving time in prison to reflect on his misdirected thinking.

As a former Navy SEAL, I have endured the hardships and pain of disciplined physical training. But safety was always of extreme importance in our training and even in combat when it was demanded and allowed to push the envelope to the maximum. I have witnessed people transform without harsh physical sacrifice and have personally designed and taught several courses outside of the military establishment that have accomplished this transformation while still being completely safe. I believe this is possible because I have done the work, paid the price, and have constantly strived to achieve a transition point with as little time and effort as possible. I bring the essence of that knowledge to humanity in a way that is heart-centered or done out of love for humanity. Most military training in modern times has been fear-based and therefore sets a poor foundation for advanced intuitive training.

In another life during the Middle Ages, this same individual and I were Knights Templars. King Philip IV of France, who was already heavily in debt to the Knights Templars, requested a further loan, but the Knights Templars refused his request. Philip's subsequent order to arrest all Knights Templars in France was sent out several weeks before the planned arrests and got through to us, giving us time to hide our wealth. The greatest wealth of the Templars, however, did not consist of gold and silver, but knowledge. Vast libraries were quickly shipped to safe locations. I remember being a part of the group that protected this valuable treasure. Meanwhile, this other gentleman followed the gold and silver. I will talk much more about the Templars in my next book.

In his current life, the gentleman in question was again overly focused on the material aspect by charging exorbitant sums for his motivational semi-

nars. Interestingly, I had followed this fellow's work and had been intrigued by his message but was concerned about his focus on money. He had even said in a motivational speech one day that he fully believed that he would be a billionaire someday. It is now obvious how the obsessions that he carried through many lifetimes culminated in the events that manifested in his current life. Human sacrifice and money had been obstacles to his advancement as a soul and presented themselves once again as a challenge for him. He failed in overcoming these trials of the spirit and now has time to reflect on them in an environment that is similar to what a monk would subject himself to.

I have balanced my soul evolution with lives as warriors and as sages; many lifetimes were even a combination of both archetypes. Often a disciple seeking knowledge and enlightenment will also need extreme physical and mental discipline, which can come from militaristic training but also other sources as well. The soul knows the path it has chosen before incarnating, and one need only still the mind and look quietly within to find one's path in life. You will intuitively know what is right for you and what is not, and take comfort in the fact that we often learn the most from the hard lessons in life.

Having taken a closer look at my own past life experiences as well as my path in this life, I know that I was attracted to Sedona, Arizona, for multiple reasons. One of the main attractions to living in Sedona is the amazing energy of the telluric currents, also called Earth currents, that are exceptionally strong in certain areas on the planet, as in the breathtakingly beautiful red rock mountain area surrounding Sedona. This natural electric current flows on and beneath the surface of the Earth and generally follows a direction parallel to the Earth's surface. Telluric currents arise from charges moving to attain equilibrium between regions of differing electric potentials. In certain key locations, these energies spiral out in what are called vortices of energy.

This powerful telluric energy appears in many sites around the world including Machu Picchu, Stonehenge, Chartres Cathedral, Glastonbury Tor, and many more. These energies are available to anyone and can be used creatively and responsibly or can be misused as the case of the fellow with the obsession for money and human sacrifice has shown. Once these energies are misused, they have to be re-sacralized or cleansed. This is one of the things that I have come to Sedona to do. I use the energies in a positive way to teach people to become more intuitive. Using the energies in a positive way revitalizes the telluric forces and transforms them into a beneficial sacred force. In effect, I'm helping to clean up the mess this fellow has created in time once again along with some others who over time have misused the energies here in a similar way. Fortunately, I'm now in the company of many people who were drawn to Sedona for the same reason—to revitalize the currents in this highly charged area.

My wife, Tracy Jo, is very intuitive and has linked with the energies of Sedona in a powerful way. She was traveling to a vortex she was drawn to recently when she suddenly found herself at a place where she had a vivid dream that she was driven off the cliff. She slowed the car down, not knowing whether or not she was in potential danger, when a deer moved out into the road. She then stopped the car fully and made eye contact with the deer for several seconds before it traveled off toward the spot where my wife was heading. When powerful coincidences like this happen, you take notice and pay particular attention.

It was not long after this encounter that Tracy Jo was stopped by another peculiar synchronicity on a side road above our house. Her initial motivation to take that road was the mundane idea to get better cell phone coverage. At the same time, my son was also driving on that road when one of his passengers who was clowning around in the front seat bumped into him, causing the wheel to veer to the left. His truck swerved up onto the median and ran into a road sign. At that point, my son immediately regained control over the truck, thus avoiding a collision with oncoming traffic. My wife saw the truck in her rearview mirror and was close enough to hear the truck hit the sign.

To give you some more background, the truck my son was driving was a truck that I'd had for ten years and recently had given to him. I had actually been drawn to name the truck, Poseidon. I found all this to be an interesting connection with the Trojan War, which was supposed to have lasted for ten years, and after which I would allegedly sacrifice my son to Poseidon. When my son was in this situation in the truck, my wife synchronistically was close to the scene, which was also close to the place where she had seen the deer before. Remember, the deer is an animal sacred to the goddess Artemis, who supposedly wanted a human sacrifice to allow the ships of the Greek fleet to sail. But like I explained before, this was a manipulation of the truth, and, here in this instance, it could be seen that she is indeed a protecting influence. It is obvious to me that my wife

was there close to the scene where she had also seen the deer in order to hold a positive energy so that my son would not be a human sacrifice.

I later asked Ahtun Re about the past life connection to this event in Sedona. He gave me even deeper insights into a lifetime where my son had been a young prince in Egypt. Just before he went through his manhood ceremonies, he had taken one of the war chariots out for a game of chicken with his friends. This game of chicken, where two highly skilled war chariot drivers would charge each other and veer off at the predetermined last second, was an actual training tactic to build courage and fortitude. There was drinking of wine involved, and our son was flipping the war chariot right when my wife arrived on scene; it was out of respect to her royalty that both of the young men stopped their game. As a punishment, they then had their manhood ceremony delayed, as they were required to attend remedial ceremonies before they could go through the manhood ceremony.

Both of these episodes have very similar characteristics carrying over through time. My son, who got into a lot of trouble in this lifetime and had to go through remedial training, had the same thing happen in a lifetime in Egypt. We repeat patterns throughout time until we learn our lessons. Many of us know people who seem to attract the same type of person in abusive relationships over and over. It's obvious to us that the same type of behavior is attracting the same types of partners, but, to the person having the difficulty, it seems that life is giving them a raw deal. My son, Michelangelo, later said that this recent incident in Sedona matured him considerably. Hopefully, the lesson has been learned, but the temptation will present itself again until it is irrefutably incorporated into his experience.

My daughter in this life, Ashley, was also present as one of my offspring in the life as King Idomeneus. In that life she was an expert at weaving fine threads of gold and other precious metals as well as jewels into clothing to have a certain effect on the consciousness of the wearer. When I returned to Crete as Idomeneus, my wife in this life, who was a temple priestess in a powerful healing monastery, would heal me, and she would heal my injuries, which were considered incurable at the time. Her technique of healing damaged tendons, ligaments, and nerves would inspire me to open a hospital with her as the lead. Everyone was offered treatments in this new healing center, whether they were

Greek or Trojan or rich or poor. The horrors of warfare were a great shock to the people of Crete. It sounds almost too good to be true, but eventually all of the people that had been captured by the armies of Crete were freed.

Prince Aeneas from Troy, who had escaped during the sack of Troy with a large group of Trojans, was allowed to settle on a portion of Crete. The times were very unstable after the cataclysmic events of the time period, and growing food on the once highly fertile Cretan soil was now difficult. The survivors of the once mighty Troy would later band together with Prince Aeneas and depart on a long journey through the Mediterranean Sea and eventually settle in what would later be called Rome.

It would be a very long time before humanity would rebuild the greatness of the Mediterranean cultures. For instance, the Palace of Minos at Knossos was bigger than Buckingham Palace in England with its 775 rooms that were built more than three thousand years later. The Palace of Minos with 1,400 rooms on several floors was one of the greatest architectural accomplishments of the Cretan society and rivals anything in existence today.

A balanced goddess culture had made Crete the dominant power in the Mediterranean Sea. Peace and prosperity ruled throughout the coastal communities because of its positive influence. It was after the eruption of the super-volcano on Thera that the balance of power throughout the Mediterranean shifted. The unbalanced, patriarchal warrior culture that sprang up from the mainland of Greece in the wake of the devastation would forever change the region. The seafaring civilizations of the Mediterranean would lose their focus on oneness, harmony, and success for all and transition into a period of endless wars and unbalanced materialism that carried through and reverberates to this day. It is now up to us to overcome this pattern.

Trojan horse statue from the movie "Troy" on display in a plaza at Çanakkale, Turkey.

The story of Jason and the Argonauts endured for centuries, mainly because its heroes' exploits exemplified resilience and took them on adventures to new lands. The Argonauts, named for the ship they sailed on, the *Argo*, were gathered by legendary hero Jason in search of the Golden Fleece.

Heracles, also known as Hercules in Greek texts, is one of the most recognized and famous of the divine heroes in Greek mythology. The son of Zeus and the mortal woman Alcmene, he was considered the greatest of the heroes, a symbol of masculinity, sire of a long line of royal clans and the champion of the Olympian order against terrible monsters.

Homer is the legendary author to whom the authorship of the *Iliad* and the *Odyssey* is attributed. The two epic poems are considered foundational works of ancient Greek literature. He is regarded as one of the greatest and most influential authors of all time. In Dante Alighieri's *Divine Comedy*, Virgil refers to him as "Poet sovereign," king of all poets; in the preface to his translation of the *Iliad*, Alexander Pope acknowledges that Homer has always been considered the "greatest of poets."

As the tale goes, the Trojan prince Paris falls in love with the Spartan queen Helen, who is married to King Menelaus. The couple steal away to Troy, where they are cautiously welcomed by Troy's ruler, Priam. As the plot unfolds, Helen remains an elusive presence at Troy, as the different Greek kingdoms come to demand her return to Menelaus. The outcome of her adulterous relationship with Paris hardly needs to be repeated here: a ten-year war and the annihilation of the city of Troy.

"BE UPRIGHT IN THY WHOLE LIFE, BE CONTENT IN ALL ITS CHANGES. SO SHALT THOU MAKE THY PROFIT OUT OF ALL OCCURRENCES, SO SHALL EVERYTHING THAT HAPPENETH UNTO THEE BE THE SOURCE OF PRAISE."

◊ *Pharaoh Akhenaten* ◊

CHAPTER 8

PHARAOH AKHENATEN'S WARRIOR PRIEST, HEIR TO THE THRONE AS PRINCE NAKHTMIN, AND EXODUS WITH MOSES, 1400–1350 BCE

In my lifetime during Queen Hatshepsut's reign, I had reached a very high level of mastery in the art of sacred warfare while I was part of a specifically trained group. I would assume a similar role in my lifetime as Nakhtmin.

I would be born into the large royal family as a Nubian prince and cousin of the later Pharaoh Akhenaten, one of the greatest reformers that Egypt has ever seen. His seventeen-year-long reign would be one of the most defining eras in the history of ancient Egypt, as he would introduce, for example, the worship of one supreme force called Aten, portrayed as the sun disc and standing above all the other gods and idols that had been worshipped in Egypt before that.

After the resurrection of Osiris, the code of moving from one level of consciousness into another had been imprinted in his chromosomes. This knowledge was passed on through a pantheon of gods, or *neters*. Each *neter* would guide the adept through the process of unlocking the codes in a particular chromosome within himself. But over time the true meaning of the gods was lost, and it got even more complicated when the attributes of the gods would be slightly altered in Upper and Lower Egypt, so that it eventually seemed as if they were different gods. When Pharaoh Menes unified both regions, he unfortunately didn't merge the understanding of these *neters* again, but instead adopted all of them, thus officially doubling the initial number of *neters*. This further obscured the true purpose of the *neters* and also led to fights among the Egyptians as to which gods would be more authentic or powerful.

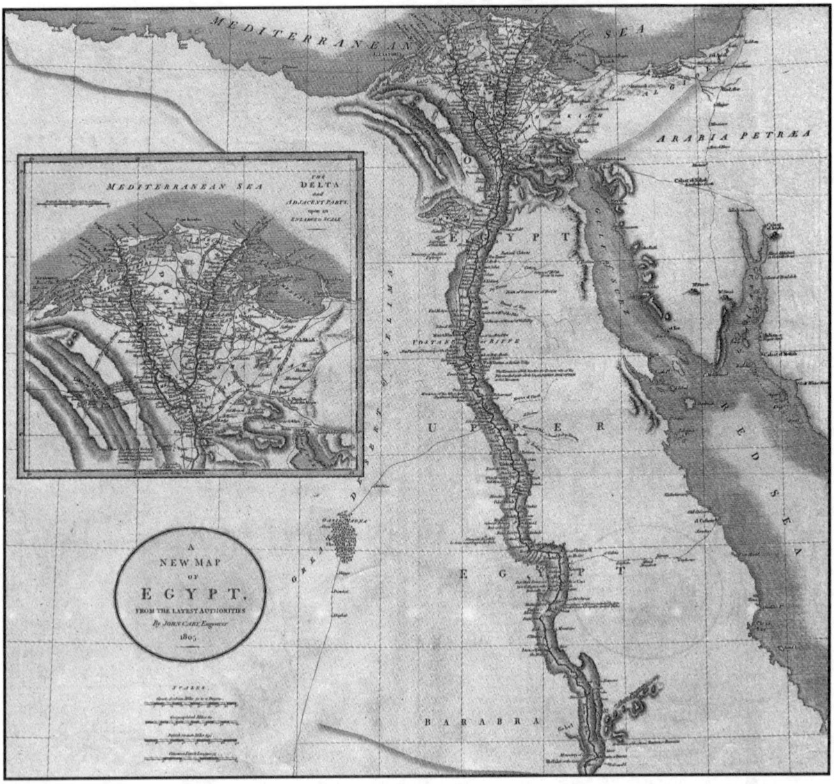

Akhenaten intended to solve this dilemma by getting people to focus on a whole new idea that all of creation emanates from one God, Aten. Although Aten was depicted as a sun, it did not refer to the sun in the center of our solar system. Aten was a symbol of the source from which all things come and from which the life-giving and life-sustaining influence emanates symbolized by rays of the sun. These rays have human hands at their ends, illustrating how Aten is a creative and supportive force that pervades all of

existence. Akhenaten's name had first been Amenhotep IV, but he changed it to Akhenaten, which meant "living spirit of Aten." Interestingly, Aten had first been described as the divine source in the *Tale of Sinuhe,* which I had written about in my lifetime as Senusret.

As Nakhtmin, I would once again prove to be a telepathic communicator with animals, which was still highly regarded. The lions would be my friends, and I could once again run with them into battle. I was also highly skilled as a chariot driver, steering my horses telepathically. I quickly and easily displayed all the necessary skills that were closely watched for by Horemheb, the leading general of the pharaoh's army.

My wife was again the same twin soul that had been my partner in many previous lives, this time incarnated as a beautiful Nubian princess. She would once again enter the temples as a royal priestess, because this gave Egyptian women the most freedom and access to knowledge and wisdom. At that time, temple priestesses were often the most educated and respected women in Egypt. They held positions of power and prestige in many of the temples in which their feminine energies were seen as a balance for the often dominant, masculine energies.

This balance was critically important to effectively keep the focus on the sacred aspect of life that much of Egyptian life revolved around. When Egypt lost this connection, as it would at the end of this lifetime, it began a long decline from a world power to a lower level patriarchy devoid of the sacred feminine.

This decline began when certain elements within the Egyptian military and priesthood decided to conspire against Akhenaten, because they were just not willing to adapt to the radical reforms that Akhenaten launched. Akhenaten grew up as the son of Amenhotep III and Queen Tiye. My personal thoughts, intuitions, and information from many different sources are that Queen Tiye was part Hebrew and also part of the Nubian royal family. She was the daughter of Joseph, who was mentioned in the Old Testament of the Bible. His jealous brothers sold Joseph into slavery, but he would eventually rise to the position of a vizier of the pharaohs.

The biblical account of Joseph being sold into slavery is an accurate depiction, just like the stories of a famine that brought many of the Hebrew tribes from the Levant area on the east coast of the Mediterranean to Egypt. But the time frame and length of time that the Hebrews allegedly stayed in Egypt are inaccurate due to misinterpretations and differences in calculating time from one culture to another. The Egyptian scholar and author Ahmed Osman has a well-researched book that I believe very accurately depicts the events in this time frame. In *The Hebrew Pharaohs of Egypt: The Secret Lineage of Patriarch Joseph,* he also explores the possibility that the biblical Joseph and Yuya, a vizier of the Eighteenth Dynasty Pharaoh Thutmose IV, were one and the same person.

This also helps to shed a light on the sudden rise of monotheism in Egypt as spread by Queen Tiye and her son Akhenaten, as it connects them to the monotheistic ideas that Abraham had been exposed to in the mystery schools of the ancient Egyptian city of Heliopolis several hundred years earlier. Abraham in turn introduced these ideas to the Hebrew tribes, and Joseph would bring that same belief back to the forefront of Egyptian life when he became a vizier to several pharaohs, which was the highest official position in ancient Egypt, subordinate only to the pharaoh and active in virtually every area of responsibility.

The story goes that one day Joseph interpreted a dream of the pharaoh's in which he said that there would be seven years of bountiful harvests and seven years of famine. The pharaoh then planned ahead for these events by storing grain, which would later be of great benefit internally. There was enough food for the Egyptians, but there was more that could be exported. These food exports brought incredible wealth to Egypt and saved many kingdoms that would become loyal friends afterward.

Joseph, or Yuya, was held in such high regard after this that he and his wife would eventually have their own tomb in the Valley of the Kings. This burial privilege was given to only one vizier, Yuya, and to no one else besides the pharaohs throughout the history of Egypt.

Together with Pharaoh Amenhotep III, Yuya's daughter Tiye raised four daughters and two sons, of which Akhenaten's brother Djhutmose was the first. He was appointed the high priest of Memphis and also the crown prince, but his untimely death caused Akhenaten to later become pharaoh.

It is interesting to note that during his adolescence, Akhenaten seemed to be ignored by the rest of his family. He never appeared in any portraits and was never taken to public events. He received no honors. The royal family for some mysterious reason rejected the young Akhenaten. He was never shown

with his family nor mentioned on monuments, yet his mother favored him, because Akhenaten's conception was very unusual, which also accounts for his extraordinary characteristics.

Queen Tiye had been trained in the art of immaculate conception, the same process that Mother Mary would go through more than thousand years later. Claire Heartsong described how Mary would be prepared and guided through this process in her book *Anna, Grandmother of Jesus,* which gives an account of the woman that the Catholic Church would later sanctify and call Saint Anna. Anna, the mother of Josef of Arimathea, was a Briton from a royal family who would come to Egypt and learn the ancient mystical preparations for immaculate conception. She would later end up in the sacred Mount Moriah area and assist Mary Anna, who would eventually give birth to Yeshua.

Queen Tiye, like some advanced adepts of the time, was also able to conceive the children of gods or extraterrestrials. By opening her womb to interdimensional insemination, she could fuse her genetics with those from off-world entities. This was one of the reasons why the people of Egypt considered and treated the pharaohs as gods; they were in distant times the descendants of extraterrestrial races. Queen Tiye also had several children with Amenhotep III, but Akhenaten was not of his loins, which was probably why the pharaoh rejected Akhenaten. Although these divine births had been happening periodically within the royal family for thousands of years, this would be the last time that such a birth would happen in Egypt's long history.

Akhenaten eventually succeeded Amenhotep III after his death at the end of his thirty-eight-year reign, possibly after a brief co-regency lasting between one to two years. When Akhenaten ascended the throne he was just a teenager, but it was the desire of Queen Tiye that he would rule. At that time Egypt had never been richer, more powerful, or more secure. It was the peak of Egypt's imperial glory. Up and down the Nile, workers built hundreds of temples to pay homage to the gods. The Egyptians believed that if the gods were pleased, Egypt would prosper. And so it did.

Akhenaten and his family initially lived in the great religious center of Thebes, the city of the god Amun where thousands of priests would serve the gods. These gods that were worshiped throughout Egypt had not been entirely abolished by Akhenaten as he spread his monotheism. He simply asserted that there was one God that he was focused on, and no other god was above this God whose force permeates all-that-is. This concept incensed the priestly class because they were in competition to attract pilgrims to their respective god and goddess temples. This was how the priests made money and stayed in power. Religion was a business.

But Akhenaten encouraged the Egyptians to directly seek God within themselves, which was seen by the priests as an erosion of their power base, because up until this point they were seen as the intermediates between the populace and the higher spiritual realms. Akhenaten also implemented a policy that nepotism within the priestly ranks was to stop. Priests would be in top positions only by their proven service to the people, which further angered the priestly class.

Another thing that created a rift was the construction of a completely new capital. It was said that one day Akhenaten had a vision wherein he saw God as a sun disc between two mountains. He felt that God was guiding him to make a change, to build a city between two mountains. It was a virgin site, not previously dedicated to any other god or goddess, and he named it Akhetaten, meaning "Horizon of the Aten." Today the site is known as el-Amarna.

To sanctify and commemorate this new land, he wrote a poem titled "Great Hymn to the Aten":

How manifold it is, what thou hast made!
They are hidden from the face (of man).
O sole God, like whom there is no other!
Thou didst create the world according to thy desire,
Whilst thou wert alone: All men, cattle, and wild beasts,
Whatever is on Earth, going upon (its) feet,
And what is on high, flying with its wings.
The countries of Syria and Nubia, the land of Egypt,
Thou settest every man in his place,
Thou suppliest their necessities:
Everyone has his food, and his time of life is reckoned.
Their tongues are separate in speech,
And their natures as well;
Their skins are distinguished,
As thou distinguishest the foreign peoples.

Thou makest a Nile in the underworld,
Thou bringest forth as thou desirest To maintain the people (of Egypt)
According as thou madest them for thyself,
The Lord of all of them, wearying (himself) with them,
The Lord of every land, rising for them,
The Aton of the day, great of majesty!

This hymn portrays the Aten, or Aton, as the giver of all life, just like the warmth and light of the sun provides sustenance to the pastures, plants, humans, and animals. There is great emphasis on the diversity and holiness of all living things, which praise the Aten through the very act of living. It has been noted by scholars that this hymn has a remarkable similarity to Psalm 104. In fact, several of the psalms in the Bible are the work of Pharaoh Akhenaten.

The relocation of the capital 180 miles north of Thebes has been a clear break with the oppressive controlling powers of the priesthood. The city of Akhetaten was established precisely at the center of Egypt as measured from its four corners. My friend Ahtun Re, who would be incarnate at that time for his last lifetime before ascending, would architecturally design the city and also be the city's head priest. Everything about Akhetaten was to be constructed in a sacred format, from the layout of the streets, to the artwork and clothing, to the palace and temple complexes.

As you approached Akhetaten, you would first notice the elaborate Temple of Aten. This temple was constructed with the traditional long corridor and seven gateways leading up to the inner chamber with a statue of Aten in the last chamber. The temple was covered with various depictions of Aten, the sun disc with its rays shining down, ending in hands holding ankhs, the hieroglyph for life.

In its finished state, the city of Akhetaten offered a theatrical setting for celebrating Akhenaten's kingship. The city sprawled for miles over the plain. There were elegant palaces, statues of the pharaoh, good housing throughout the city, and a royal road that ran through the center of town. It was probably the widest street in the ancient world, designed for chariot processions with Akhenaten leading the way. Spanning the road, a bridge connected the palace with the temple area. Akhenaten and Nefertiti would appear before the people on the balcony known as the "window of appearances," tossing down gold ornaments and other gifts.

Pharaoh Akhenaten would move to this new city after only a few years as the new ruler of Egypt with his wife Nefertiti. No record of Nefertiti's lineage can be found in Egyptian records, because she was a royal princess from Crete who had survived the devastation from Mount Thera.

Remember that Pharaoh Menes had founded the first settlements on Crete and that the Minoan culture had flourished from the earlier Egyptian influence. Crete had become a peaceful and profitable trading partner with Egypt and the rest of the Mediterranean region.

Akhenaten gave sanctuary to the survivors of the Minoan civilization in the area called Goshen located in the Nile Delta. It was in this location that the royal survivors would build a small palace. The artwork of Crete that was used in this palace would influence the Egyptian artists and transform their twenty-one-grid system of measurement into the Cretan eighteen-grid system, used to create more curved and fluid art forms. The visual arts would also change to depict humans, animals, and plants in a much more realistic way, not stylized like before. This gave the artists of Akhetaten new freedom to show scenes of the real life in a very detailed and accurate fashion, something that had never been done before. Akhenaten changed thousands of years of art in Egypt by adopting these new forms of art.

When Akhenaten built his monuments with images of the pharaoh, he also moved away from the traditions of a strong and muscular pharaoh. Images of pharaohs with idealized bodies were gone. Mainstream historians would argue that the exact opposite is the case, because the royal family would be depicted in a very unusual way with elongated heads, faces, fingers, toes, wide hips, swollen lower abdominal region, and misshapen legs. But all of these physical anomalies were in fact real and signs of their Sirian extraterrestrial heritage.

Also today there are many star seeds present on Earth, meaning people whose souls came here from other star systems. But because the star seeds of today were usually conceived physically, you don't see the remarkable physical features that, for instance, Akhenaten, Nefertiti, and their offspring would display. Still, the purpose of today's star seeds is the same as it had been for Akhenaten—raising the consciousness of humanity and the planet.

Drunvalo Melchizedek states in his book *The Flower of Life* that an essential contribution Akhenaten made in his life had been done secretly. It is

said that Akhenaten founded a mystery school, the Tat Brotherhood, where he would teach three hundred disciples how to reach immortality. These disciples would 850 years later move to Masada in Israel and become the Essenes, among whom Yeshua would later grow up.

Because Akhenaten intended to let the Egyptians learn and utilize the principles of sacred warfare, he would eventually call me to his new city of Akhetaten on the recommendation of his head general Horemheb. When I arrived, I was initially surprised to see that the city had no defensive system, because it was an unusual sight in Egypt at that time. With the help of Cretan survivors, the city of Akhetaten was purposefully laid out without fortifications, just like Knossos on the island of Crete. There were no walls, no fortifications, nothing visible to protect the city. Accordingly, I was to keep the city secure with sacred warfare techniques that I would call upon easily after I had developed them over many previous lifetimes.

I would also again be trained in the art of projecting a peaceful influence. Much of our training would be in Heliopolis, where I would study together with a fellow warrior priest named Moses, who was a royal prince from the Hebrew line of Joseph. He was very skilled in the art of sacred warfare and would rise to prominence as the man who led the Hebrews out of Egypt upon the country's decline when a faction of the military had taken over power in Egypt.

Akhenaten first used the army to dismantle the old powerful priesthood and spread his new monotheistic ideas throughout Egypt. But he angered many generals of this militarily superior empire when he ordered them to refrain from wars of aggression. Many of the leading generals were also still attached to the old beliefs, and as their resentment against Akhenaten had grown substantially, they organized a rebellion in his seventeenth year as pharaoh.

It had been clear to Ay, the brother of the former Queen Tiye, that the balance of power shifted in a way where Akhenaten's progressive reforms could not withstand the upcoming pressure. Ay was also the leader of the supreme chariot division of the army, but even with my help he was in no position to crush the rebellion, so he began negotiations with the defiant generals to convince them to allow for the abdication of Akhenaten and the appointment of his son Tutankhamun as his successor. But these negotiations were only in part successful, as Akhenaten and Nefertiti were secretly disposed of.

According to Drunvalo Melchizedek, it was impossible to physically kill Akhenaten, because he had become an immortal. So three black magicians from Nubia were hired to mix a potion that would be added to one of Akhenaten's public meals. This potion would temporarily stop his vital signs, so that he could publicly be declared dead. He was then placed in a sarcophagus that was magically sealed. This seal would only be broken after two thousand years, whereupon Akhenaten would enter the Halls of Amenti, an interdimensional location mentioned by Thoth in his *Emerald Tablets:*

> *In the great city of Keor on the island of Undal, in a time far past, I began this incarnation. Not as the little men of the present age did the mighty ones of Atlantis live and die, but rather from aeon to aeon did they renew their life in the Halls of Amend where the river of life flows eternally onward.*

After the royal couple disappeared, their young son Tutankhamun became pharaoh. He would then leave his father's capital of Akhetaten for Memphis in his fourth year, when a compromise was reached in which all ancient temples were reopened and worship restored. Nevertheless, Aten remained holding its supreme position, at least as far as Tutankhamun was concerned.

Although it first seemed that Tutankhamun could be controlled, he eventually embraced the same monotheistic truths that his father had propagated. Subsequently, the same plotters who had been able to take away power from his father would also conspire against Tutankhamun. They then found an opportunity to dispose of the young pharaoh after he would break his leg in a chariot accident hunting lions. Tutankhamun was surreptitiously denied treatment until an infection set in, and by the time the treatment was started it was too late and he died of his wound. A quick burial ensued after a hasty tomb was completed; the tomb was then sealed and forgotten.

His successor would be Ay, who had been Tutankhamun's vizier before his death and who was already very old when he became pharaoh. Ay had no son, but his daughter Mutnedjmet was my wife, making me his son-in-law and heir to the throne, but unfortunately General Horemheb would usurp us both when he married Akhenaten's eldest daughter.

These were very volatile times, characterized by radical reforms and then a deliberate falsification of history by Horemheb and his coconspirators.

Their intention was that no one associated with the Amarna period at the end of the Eighteenth Dynasty would be remembered. They destroyed records and created false accounts to cover up their perfidious plot and legitimize the royal succession that was to come. If you research what the scientific consensus says, especially on the events toward the end of the Amarna period, you will find that it does not match with my account. Historians are mostly groping in the dark there, because very few records from that period are available today, and many of them give false or misleading information.

All of this intrigue was engineered because Akhenaten disempowered the priesthood and the military. Powerful individuals within these groups had plotted for years without even making an attempt to understand or apply the sacred warfare techniques. These groups had decided not to adapt to the new ideals and had schemed to remove all traces of the Amarna revolution and its ideas.

Under Pharaoh Horemheb, virtually all of the monotheistic ideals and reforms were finally abandoned. Ahtun Re relayed to me that it was only because of our previous service together that Horemheb would partially give in to my arguments to not completely wipe out all the reforms that had been started by Akhenaten. But the overall direction clearly and drastically changed as Horemheb reinstated the old temples and selected their priests from the military, enabling the new pharaohs to keep tighter controls over the religious orders.

Never again would the royal families of old lead Egypt. All of the future pharaohs would have a military background and the Egyptian society would be carefully controlled by the military. Horemheb's new vizier would be Ramses, a former general under Horemheb and now also a high priest of the old religion that Akhenaten had abandoned. A systematic destruction of Akhetaten would ensue after Ramses succeeded Horemheb as pharaoh.

Ramses would be the first pharaoh of the Nineteenth Dynasty in ancient Egyptian history. In his short reign he enslaved the once esteemed and welcomed Hebrews and Cretans who had settled in Egypt in the Goshen region and considered it their home. The newly enslaved Hebrews were then ordered to build a new city for Ramses near present-day Alexandria. For the construction they would not make new bricks from straw but use the bricks and building stones from the beautiful city of Akhetaten that they had helped to build when they had still been free. This disparaging treatment under Pharaoh Ramses eventually caused the Hebrew people to revolt and escape from Egypt. Their leader during this revolt would be Moses, who returned to Egypt after he conquered a far-off kingdom in Africa and became a virtual king in this isolated land.

My wife and I would leave Egypt with Moses along with many other Hebrews and Egyptians who had adopted monotheism. The story of our escape during this time of upheaval would only later be written down during the many years spent in the wilderness after the actual event. The book called *The Kolbrin Bible* contains ancient accounts from this period that were recently compiled by Marshall Masters. This book also mentions the passage of a rogue planet that periodically returns to our galaxy and causes great destruction with violent storms and fire raining down from heaven during its close pass to Earth.

The Sumerians also talk about this planet, which they called Nibiru. *The Twelfth Planet* by Zecharia Sitchin describes how this planet passes Earth approximately every 3,600 years in an extremely elliptical orbit, meaning that unlike the other known planets in our solar system, its distance to the sun greatly varies. On this planet is a race of beings that had colonized Earth and set themselves up as the controlling elite of the world, successfully infiltrating and dominating almost every culture on the planet.

There is, of course, a great controversy in mainstream academia as to whether or not Nibiru even exists. A very plausible explanation in that regard comes from Andy Lloyd, the thought-provoking researcher and author of the book *The Dark Star.* He suggests that there is actually a brown dwarf traveling on this elliptical orbit around the sun and that Nibiru itself is in turn closely orbiting this dark star. Many researchers use the terms Planet X and Nibiru synonymously, but Andy clearly distinguishes between the brown dwarf as Planet X and Nibiru as the planet that is orbiting it. When describing the events that have occurred in my lifetime as Nakhtmin, I will just stick to the term Planet X, also to give credit to the fact that what it precisely is has yet to be understood.

The last time that Planet X came close to Earth it had caused intense flooding in Babylonia, and during a previous passage it played a role when Atlantis was destroyed and sank beneath the Atlantic Ocean. Immanuel Velikovsky wrote several books outlining catastrophic events, including *Ages in Chaos* and *Worlds in Collision* in which he describes what he thought was the planet Venus as a former comet causing destruction when it came into our galaxy until it was even-

tually captured in an orbit around the sun. He described how ancient cultures throughout the world described Planet X as a red fire-breathing dragon with a tail of debris being dragged behind it, similar to the appearance of a comet.

There is also the allegory of a witch riding a broom with her hair flowing behind her. The Hopi describe how the Earth has been destroyed several times intermittently by fire and water, and there are many tales from ancient cultures that reportedly survived by going into inner Earth until the cataclysmic events had settled down. Regardless of how the ancients interpreted Planet X, it has always caused cataclysmic destruction over the entire Earth.

Immanuel Velikovsky describes how calendars and astrological megaliths all over the world were thrown completely off-kilter. He spoke of how at one point in Earth's history a year was measured as precisely 360 days. But the last time the Earth was affected by the passage of Planet X, our planet was knocked into a new orbit that created the 365.25-day cycle. Because of this increase in days it was not until the Julian calendar was created over a thousand years later that the new time was accurately calculated.

The information of Planet X's arrival and what it will do has been a closely guarded and suppressed secret for thousands of years, because those who control this information can position themselves in well- stocked underground shelters to ride out the devastations on the surface. After several years they then come back to quickly regain and consolidate their power, as many of those who remained on the surface would be struggling to survive. I believe this has happened countless times throughout history. But not only negative factions position themselves to gain power and control. There are also positive groups that would use their foreknowledge and abilities to help humanity during and after the cataclysmic events.

Moses, for instance, was trained in astrology in Heliopolis and knew that Planet X had affected the Earth in the past and was due to return. The priesthood of Heliopolis had related to him in exacting detail what had happened in ancient history, so when Moses returned to Egypt at the behest of Ahtun Re to lead the Hebrew people, he shared his knowledge of what was coming and thus created a following that quickly grew as his predictions continued to come true.

Prior to the near pass of Planet X, Earth experiences major cataclysmic events as a prelude to the final crescendo and eventually a gradual calming

over many years. Some of these events are recounted in the Old Testament in which the Nile turns red, fire rains down from above, and so on. The event that we would use to begin the Exodus was the eruption of Mount Thera, where a previous eruption many decades earlier had nearly wiped out the Minoan civilization. The ash from this new eruption would drift over Egypt, and some places would be entirely buried in ash and not be uncovered until the present. The darkness, chaos, and lightning storms that raged over several days were utilized as a literal smoke screen as we made our escape.

The devastation caused by the passage of Planet X are most intense during a period of approximately one hundred years when it's closest to Earth. In this period during Planet X's 3,600-year orbit, many of the civilizations on Earth have been devastated and then rebuilt over time. The eruption of Thera that I described in the previous chapter happened at the beginning of such a one-hundred-year period. Planet X's close encounter with Earth was also responsible for the ten plagues of Egypt mentioned in the Book of Exodus.

Planet X is also called the red planet because of its accompanying massive red dust cloud full of foreign microbes and bacteria. Because of the vast magnetic field of this planet that is larger than Jupiter, it has also picked up several moons and other debris. This red dust is what covered the Nile River and made the water turn red like blood. The lightning storms that erupted were also caused by the proximity between Planet X and the Earth, which caused magnetic arcs to pass between the planets. The reason why Planet X has such a strong magnetic pull is because it is a brown dwarf star. This also accounts for its ability to bend light with its strong magnetic field, and because of this it is usually only seen for several weeks when it's closest to Earth.

But despite all the havoc that has been caused by the passage of Planet X in the past, I believe that the negative effects of its next passage can be mitigated through the power of our collective consciousness. As things are developing right now, we will ascend together with Planet X and our solar system into a five-dimensional existence. But this doesn't mean that we just have to sit back and wait, because just like in any other dimension, the actualities are being created through a conscious choice. You might already experience an awakening of your higher abilities, and maybe you notice how things in your life that you focus on manifest with increasing ease and speed. These are signs of the

dimensional shift that is occurring. So ride with it, be bold, and be assured that any action that focuses on creating a peaceful and enlightened environment will be favored by the energies that are influencing our solar system right now.

To better explain the nature of this shift, maybe it would be more appropriate to call it a shift in density. When we raise our vibrations, we literally become less dense as our energetic frequency increases. For instance, if you learn to perceive auras, you can observe the increase in luminosity and vibrancy in the aura of someone who is truly advancing on the spiritual path. But you can also feel it, so make full use of your intuitive senses. In fact, nobody is completely oblivious to this aspect of reality, even though some people have been programmed or program themselves to disregard these things. But to disregard them only gives power to those who will then use their influence on these higher dimensions to enslave us. To keep humanity down they have to keep us in ignorance of our true power and the truth of what we really are—infinite consciousness.

As we make the shift, our responsibility increases. We will not just enter a world of eternal bliss where we will live happily ever after. Our process will depend on our actions; that will be as true for living in five dimensions as it is for living in three. Many basic themes that are important today will continue to be so, for example duality. But the difference is that the fifth dimension is the most stable of the dimensions in which duality still exists, meaning that we will understand and deal with it on a higher level. Experiencing duality can actually be very enjoyable as it is only the imbalance between the polar opposites that creates an unpleasant experience. Now as we move toward higher dimensions, this will only be possible if we can bring these opposites into greater harmony within ourselves.

During my lifetime as Nakhtmin, Pharaoh Akhenaten worked hard to balance out the disharmonious influences that were affecting Egypt, as he tried to inspire people to see the common source of everything, the all-pervading force of Aten. But unfortunately he was removed, and the Egyptian civilization experienced a spiritual downfall.

During the next two dynasties the god Seth became the most worshipped deity in Egypt. Seth was the god of the desert. He was viewed as an immensely powerful god of strength and violent force. He is said to have murdered his brother Osiris and then battled with his nephew Horus to be the ruler of the human race.

In a way, the struggle between Horus and Seth could also be seen in the struggle between Upper Egypt and Lower Egypt, associated with Horus and Seth, respectively. During the Early Dynastic Period it was the desire of the ruler of each region to control all of Egypt, until Pharaoh Menes would be the first to unite Upper and Lower Egypt. Once the two lands were united, Seth and Horus were often shown together crowning the new pharaohs, symbolizing the pharaoh's control over the energies of both Upper and Lower Egypt.

Seth was the companion and flip side of Horus; he embodied the principle of adversity that can potentially threaten or overrule harmony on any given level. The struggle between Seth and Horus was also representative of the inner struggle between base desires and the divine self. As long as we live in duality, this ambivalence will always be present. To move forward in our evolution it's necessary to balance both aspects instead of taking sides.

But this was not what happened after Ramses had become pharaoh. The proclivity of him and his successors for Seth together with Ramses's abuse of the Hebrews led them to demonize Seth. The very word "Satan" is derived from Seth. Its original meaning in Hebrew was "adversary," but it would eventually be used to describe the force that kept the Hebrews in bondage and slavery. This even caused Moses to classify the pig as an unclean animal in the Torah, because it was a sacred animal in Seth's cult. But in duality, one side should never to be abolished or demonized, because this only perpetuates imbalance in the bigger picture. We need to be aware that whenever we condemn or demonize the lower aspects within ourselves, we actually strengthen them, because condemnation is an impulse directly emerging from these lower potentials. We all have the higher and the lower aspects within ourselves, so only through the understanding and appreciation of both sides can we manifest a harmonious whole.

I'm sure everybody could think of an example in his or her life that shows how it can be helpful to demonize something for a while in order to start the process of releasing a negative attachment. But eventually, only moving beyond demonization and reaching a higher level of understanding will truly liberate you from this attachment. Because whether you are pulled toward something or repelled, either way the object sways you. Only by understanding both forces and finding the divine spark and a balance within yourself will you truly become free.

When we began our escape from Egypt, we realized that the pharaoh did not use his power in a balanced way, and so we decided to remove the ark that was previously used in sacred warfare to broadcast thoughts of harmony and peace. In the right hands this ark could be used for good, but in the wrong hands it could cause chaos and destruction. We determined that the hijacked Egyptian royal family would no longer use it for good, and so we took it. We would use it successfully to keep both the ark and ourselves safe and to use it for positive purposes in the future.

I would carry the ark together with several other priests and Moses in the lead. During our departure I remember wondering if we would make it, because we could not see clearly in front of us. It was dark and at the same time lightning storms ignited the atmosphere as we moved eastward away from the city of Heliopolis where the ark had been stored. We allowed the force of the ark to direct us; after all, we had no other choice. It seemed to me that we were heading toward an area above the Red Sea, which was usually swampy. I didn't believe we could quickly make passage through this area with so many people and animals, but we trusted the invisible force that was pulling us to our destination.

Much to our astonishment, the ark was indeed directing us straight toward a point close to the top of the Red Sea. This was not the route that we had expected, but because Moses was a high-level initiate and knowledgeable in the use of the ark and his intuitive abilities, we felt confident that we were being guided correctly. When we eventually came to the point where the Red Sea should have been, we realized that it was gone. We would later learn that the reason for this temporary anomaly was the effect of the gravitational pull during the passage of Planet X. On the other side of the Red Sea was a short rise of hills where we set up the ark, which was glowing at that time and acting like a beacon.

Then shouts were coming up from the long line of refugees that the Egyptian army was approaching with Ramses at the lead in his chariot. We could see the chariots approaching at full gallop while the last of us were passing through the dry seabed. Ramses wanted the ark back, because even though he didn't honor the principles of sacred warfare, he definitely realized that much of his dominance would be in jeopardy if he would lose the ark. We all knew that he would stop at nothing to have it back; this was even more important to him than capturing the Hebrews and the Egyptians that had also fled. So after a short hesitation, the chariots of Ramses's army began crossing

the seabed after us. A great cry of fear sprang up from our people at this point, and I had serious doubts that we could survive the onslaught of this force. It seemed ironic to me that here I stood as the last rightful heir to the throne of Egypt, and that the very chariot force that was baring down on us to bring certain destruction was the one that I was once in charge of.

But then a colossal event saved us. When the waters in the Red Sea were due to return as the effects of Planet X on the Earth were continuing to unfold, Moses connected his intentions with the power of the ark to further stimulate and focus the powerful forces that were hitting the Earth at that point. This happened right in time and brought a wall of water flooding back into the original basin of the Red Sea. Ramses was drowned along with the entire elite chariot force and many of my former noble friends and subordinates.

We would then spend many years in survival mode in the deserts and the wilderness, because it was still unsafe to build structures. The Earth was still very unsettled and earthquakes constantly rumbled throughout the land, and darkness and storms would also last for a long period of time. Manna was our main carbohydrate source that was gathered every morning. It was like dew, but sticky and full of substance. It was believed that the intense storms during the passage of Planet X had created it in some way, that it was a by-product of this energy that was still in the atmosphere.

During that time I would train Joshua in the art of sacred warfare, and at a future date Joshua would use these skills together with the power of the ark that Moses introduced him to in the Battle of Jericho.

Many sacred warfare principles that I had mastered in the past would be used in this battle. First the city was surrounded while one gate was left open for people to leave. Trumpets, drums, chants, and sacred songs were sung around the city and thought was sent into it to release the people from their spell and bring them out. Thus the old negative selves of the men, women, and children could die as they came back to consciousness.

Many soldiers and ordinary people left the city liberated from the tyranny of the negative rulers. Only a few stayed and were subsequently tried, like the Nuremberg trials that were held after World War II. The rest of the city was taken apart brick by brick and refashioned into a new city. Thus the walls came tumbling down literally and figuratively. It was important to deconstruct the bricks

from the old city and sanctify them, because they also held a negative vibration.

The ark would be used for many centuries after the Hebrew tribes resettled in their homeland. At one time the Philistines captured the ark for a seven-month period but returned it, because as they tried to utilize it in different cities it would always cause boils and tumors to erupt on people. The power source of the ark was misunderstood and thus many people were afflicted with radiation poisoning. Accounts of people falling dead upon touching the ark also attest to its intense force.

We had always used the ark in a positive way. Misuse of the ark's energetic forces could easily have disastrous consequences for anyone involved. I will speak more about the ark in my next book, because I experienced a pivotal point in the history of the Ark of the Covenant in my lifetime as a priest during King Solomon's reign. The events that manifested in that lifetime were the reason why the ark had been secreted away for more than two thousand years now.

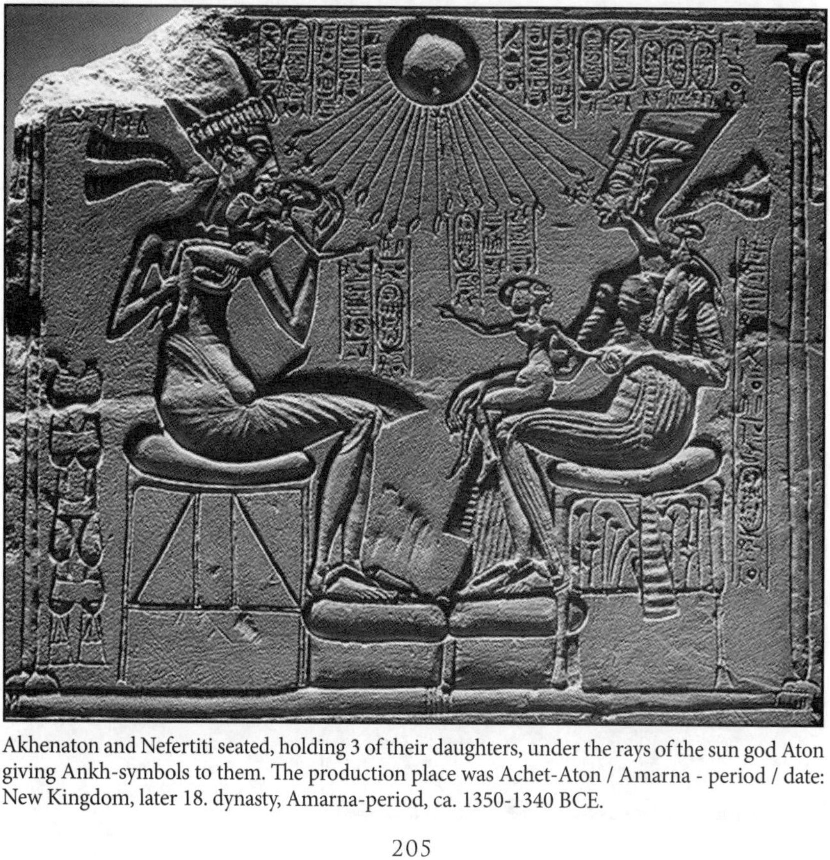

Akhenaton and Nefertiti seated, holding 3 of their daughters, under the rays of the sun god Aton giving Ankh-symbols to them. The production place was Achet-Aton / Amarna - period / date: New Kingdom, later 18. dynasty, Amarna-period, ca. 1350-1340 BCE.

Akhenaten and the his family worshipping the sun rays. Nefertiti, the queen is depicted in realistic size. Or were they giants?

Scene from gilded shrine of Tutankhamen showing him and his wife Queen Ankhesenamun offering a lotus to the seated King.

Bust of queen Nefertiti in the old Berlin museum.

Ramses II is said to be the instigator of the first peace treaty in history.

During his reign, Ramses II embarked on an extensive building program throughout Egypt and Nubia, which Egypt controlled. Nubia was very important to the Egyptians because it was a source of gold and many other precious trade goods. He, therefore, built several grand temples there in order to impress upon the Nubians Egypt's might and Egyptianize the people of Nubia. The most prominent temples are the rock-cut temples near the modern village of Abu Simbel, at the Second Nile Cataract, the border between Lower Nubia and Upper Nubia. There are two temples, the Great Temple, dedicated to Ramesses II himself, and the Small Temple, dedicated to his chief wife Queen Nefertari.

"HATRED STIRS UP CONFLICT, BUT LOVE COVERS OVER ALL WRONGS."

◊ *King Solomon* ◊

CHAPTER 9

BENAIAH, SON OF URIAH, DURING KING DAVID'S AND KING SOLOMON'S REIGN, TENTH CENTURY BCE

After the Ark of the Covenant had been brought to the land that would later be called the United Kingdom of Israel and Judah, I also chose to incarnate into this society in a role similar to that in my life as Nakhtmin. I would again be focused on both the spiritual and warrior aspects in order to assist a very wise and powerful king—in fact, two of them.

The first would be King David, who had been the second king of Israel and an ancestor of Yeshua, as mentioned in the New Testament Gospels of Matthew and Luke. David is depicted as a righteous king, though not without faults, as well as an acclaimed warrior, musician, and poet, traditionally credited for composing many of the psalms contained in the Book of Psalms.

One particular story of David for which he is famous is the one where he defeated the giant Goliath. When the Israelites under King Saul faced the Philistines near the Valley of Elah, the Philistine giant Goliath challenged the Israelites to send their own champion to decide the outcome in single combat. But neither the soldiers nor King Saul himself had the courage to stand up to the giant. Only David, a young warrior famed for his bravery and for his skill

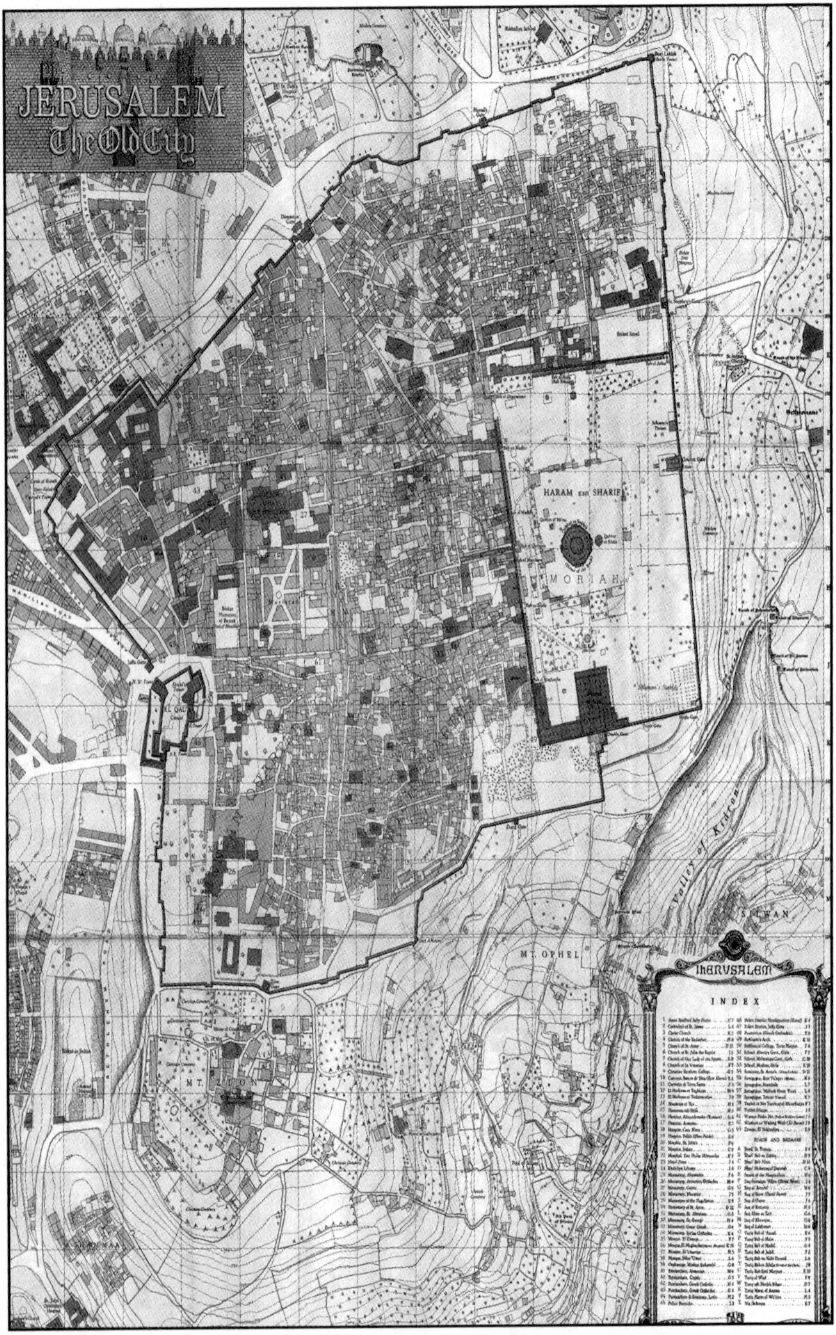

JERUSALEM
The Old City

with the harp, told Saul that he was prepared to face Goliath alone. Saul tried to fit him with a suit of armor, but none was small enough, so David went into the fight unarmored. He just picked five smooth stones from a nearby brook, and with a shot from his sling he struck Goliath in the forehead, killing the giant on the spot. David then took the sword of his adversary and beheaded him, at which point the Philistines fled in terror.

After this victory, Saul made David a commander over his armies and offered him his daughter Michal in marriage. David would engage successfully in many battles, but over time his growing popularity awakened Saul's fears. The jealous king would seek David's death by various stratagems, but David's resilience would only endear him more to the people and especially to Saul's son Jonathan. Warned by Jonathan, David fled into the wilderness, where he gathered a band of followers and became the champion of the oppressed while evading the pursuit of Saul. He accepted the town of Ziklag from the Philistine king Achish of Gath, but continued secretly to champion the Israelites. When Achish marched against Saul, David was excused from the war on the accusation of the Philistine nobles that his loyalty to their cause could not be trusted.

After both Jonathan and Saul were killed in the battle against the Philistines, David went to Hebron and was anointed the new king over Judah. In the north, Saul's son Ish-bosheth became king of the tribes of Israel. A war ensued between the two in which Ish-bosheth was assassinated by two of his own men. They were hoping that David would reward them, but instead he had them both executed for high treason. With the death of the son of Saul, the elders of Israel came to Hebron and anointed David king over Israel and Judah, which he would be for another thirty-three years.

It was during this time that I would be born as the son of Uriah and Bathsheba. My name in this life was Benaiah and I was partially raised and made responsible to the head temple priest, Jehoiada. The Bible says that he was my father in this lifetime, but this is a misconception because he spent more time tutoring me than my father. Jehoiada descended from the Aaronic line and was the leader of 3,700 priests who joined David at Hebron at the commencement of his reign.

My father, Uriah the Hittite, was one of David's "mighty men." They were a group of the king's best thirty-seven fighters, but later it expanded to around eighty. Many of these warriors had already been loyal followers who stayed with David when he was fleeing King Saul. They all used to fight side-by-side with David, as in the battle against Ish-bosheth, and they lived in close proximity to his palace.

My mother, Bathsheba, was a daughter of Eliam, who was also among these mighty warriors. According to the biblical Second Book of Samuel, King David was tempted upon seeing Bathsheba bathe in her courtyard from the roof of his palace. He had her brought to his chambers, where he seduced her and had sex with her, resulting in a pregnancy. Informed that her husband was Uriah and in an effort to conceal his sin, David summoned Uriah from battle to meet him, suggesting that he go home and "wash his feet," meaning to spend time at home and attend to his wife, so that he would later think that the child was his.

But Uriah refused, claiming a code of honor with his fellow warriors while they were in battle. It was common for warriors in preparation for war and even more so during the battle to abstain from sex, as a practice of discipline. After repeatedly refusing to see his wife Bathsheba, David allegedly sent Uriah to his commanding officer Joab with a letter ordering Joab to place Uriah at the front of the battle lines and have the soldiers move away from him so that he would be killed.

My thoughts and memories are that this is a false account that was circulated to discredit King David. If you read other accounts from this era, you see that brothers were betraying and killing brothers, cousins, uncles, wives, husbands, and so on in an internecine struggle for power and revenge. Already during that lifetime, I was under the belief that my father had met an honorable death in battle and King David took in my mother out of generosity and respect for my fallen father. I was given preferential treatment and schooling until I was mature enough to follow in the footsteps of my father. My loyalty to David and his family in response to what I perceived as his good will had been unwavering.

Another reason David married Bathsheba was his intent to consolidate his bond to the Hittites. My mother had been a Gilonite, who were Hittites that had settled in Gilon. Her grandfather Ahitophel had actually been a counselor of David, but later betrayed him and conspired against him with David's son, Absalom. To assert his claim to be the new king, Absalom had sexual inter-

course in public with ten of his father's concubines and led an insurrection that plunged the kingdom into civil war. Absalom's army would eventually be defeated, and Joab, David's commanding general, would kill Absalom to the regret and grief of the king.

But the Hittites, who had lived in and around the region of Canaan since before the time of Abraham, also helped David rise to power in the first place. So David was now hoping to again strengthen this alliance. Marriage was often a way of gaining trust and loyalty from different tribes or peoples. After Bathsheba and David married, I was accepted into King David's court as one of his sons. My mother and David would also have a child together, Solomon, who would later succeed David as king of Israel.

It was under the instruction of Jehoiada that my brother Solomon and I would learn many secrets and be prepared to lead the country into a very prosperous period. Still under David's rule, I would be appointed as the king's bodyguard and general of the army because of my extraordinary courage and courtesy. At one time, I would kill a wounded lion in a snowy pit to deliver him from his pain while nobody else dared to enter the pit. I also defeated two Moabite heroes, described as "lionlike men," and an Egyptian giant by grabbing his spear and killing him with it because I was only equipped with a staff.

In David's old age, his eldest son, Adonijah, conspired against him and proclaimed himself the new king of Israel. He did not invite me to join the conspiracy because he knew that I was loyal to David and Solomon. However, two of David's closest advisers, Joab and the priest Abiathar, would side with Adonijah. Bathsheba, after she discovered this plot, relayed the information to David and thus secured the succession to the throne of her son Solomon. At her intercession, David ordered his servants to bring Solomon to the Gihon Spring where he was anointed while David was still alive.

Adonijah's coconspirators abandoned him and he outwardly acknowledged his brother as king, but, when he came to Solomon and requested the king's servant as a wife, Solomon saw that as a veiled threat to take over his kingdom. He lost all his trust in Adonijah and had me execute him as well as Shimei and Joab, who had been involved in Adonijah's conspiracy against David. Solomon thus followed his father's last instructions in which David had ordered him to kill both Shimei and Joab. He also banished Abiathar to the city of Anathoth.

After Solomon overcame the last potential threats to his kingdom, he appointed his confidants to key military, governmental, and religious posts. In the period following these events, Solomon created a peaceful and prosperous nation. His kingdom extended from the Euphrates River in the northeast to Egypt in the south. He had peace on his borders and established Israelite colonies to look after military, administrative, and commercial matters. The empire was divided into twelve districts, with Judah constituting its own political unit and enjoying certain privileges. He had a large share in the trade between northern and southern countries and strengthened his kingdom through marital alliances. The First Book of Kings records that he had seven hundred wives and three hundred concubines.

King Solomon was renowned for his wisdom, his wealth, and his writings. He composed 3,000 proverbs and 1,005 songs. He wrote the Song of Songs, the Book of Proverbs, and Ecclesiastes. In Solomon's understanding, wisdom is the judicious application of knowledge. It is a deep understanding and realization of people, things, events, and situations, resulting in the ability to apply judgments and actions in keeping with this understanding. It often requires control of one's emotional reactions or passions, so that universal principles, reason, and knowledge prevail to determine one's actions. Wisdom is the comprehension of what is true, coupled with optimum judgment as to action.

The first and most famous incident of his cleverness as a judge was when two women came to his court with a baby whom both women claimed as their own. Solomon threatened to split the baby in half, literally dividing it up between the two. One woman was prepared to accept the decision, but the other begged the king to give the baby to the other woman instead. Solomon then knew the second woman was the mother, as she cared more about the life of the baby than about having it being given to her.

On a more material level, Solomon was renowned for various building projects in which he also used slave labor from the Hittites, Amorites, Perizzites, Hivites, and Jebusites. He spent thirteen years building his own palace and also built a city wall, a citadel called the Millo, a palace for the pharaoh's daughter, who was one of his wives, and facilities for foreign traders. He erected cities for chariots and horsemen and created storage cities. He extended Jerusalem to the north and fortified cities near the mountains of Hebron and Jerusalem.

There are also many legends and tales of mystery and magic that have come down to us from the time frame of Solomon. One is a well- known story in the collection *One Thousand and One Nights,* which describes a genie who had displeased King Solomon and was punished by being locked in a bottle and thrown into the sea. Since the bottle was sealed with Solomon's seal, the genie was helpless to free himself and was only released many centuries later by a fisherman who discovered the bottle.

The Seal of Solomon is now better known as the Star of David, but in some legends it was known as the Ring of Aandaleeb. It was a highly sought-after symbol of power, and different groups or individuals attempted to steal it or attain it in some manner. It was relayed by the classical rabbis that Asmodeus, a king of demons, was one day captured by Benaiah using the ring and subsequently forced to remain in Solomon's service.

According to the Rabbinical literature, on account of his modest request for wisdom only in his prayers to God, Solomon was rewarded with riches and an unprecedentedly glorious realm, which extended over the upper world inhabited by the angels and over the whole of the terrestrial globe with all its inhabitants, including all the beasts, fowl, and reptiles, as well as the demons and spirits. His control over the demons, spirits, and animals augmented his splendor, the demons bringing him precious stones, besides water from distant countries to irrigate his exotic plants. The beasts and fowl of their own accord entered the kitchen of Solomon's palace, so that they might be used as food for him, and extravagant meals were prepared for him daily.

In other stories from *One Thousand and One Nights,* protagonists who had to leave their homeland and travel to unknown places of the world saw signs that proved that Solomon had already been there. Sometimes protagonists discovered Solomon's words, aiming to help those who were lost in deserted places.

There are also legends that describe Solomon as having had a flying carpet that could travel so fast that it could take him from Damascus to Medina—a distance of 660 miles—within a day. Early adherents of the Kabbalah portray Solomon as having sailed through the air on a throne of light placed on an eagle, which brought him near the heavenly gates as well as to the dark mountains behind which the fallen angels Uzza and Azazel were chained. The eagle would rest on the chains, and Solomon, using the magic ring, would compel the two angels

to reveal every mystery he desired to know. Solomon is also portrayed as forcing demons to take his friends, including Hiram, on one-day trips to hell and back.

The Kabbalah is an esoteric method, discipline, and school of thought. Esoteric ideas are those that are either of rare or unusual interest, or preserved and understood only by a small group whose members are often specially initiated. The Kabbalah seeks to define the nature of the universe and the human being, the nature and purpose of existence, and addresses various other philosophical questions. It also presents methods to aid understanding of these concepts and to thereby attain spiritual realization.

According to traditional belief, early Kabbalistic knowledge was transmitted orally by the patriarchs, prophets, sages, and eventually to be interwoven into Jewish religious writings and culture. Around the time frame of Solomon, Kabbalistic knowledge was studied by probably over a million people. This involved white-magical acts as well, but these were only taught to those who were considered to be completely pure of intent.

Angels and magic were also thought to be part of Solomon's building of the Temple. The edifice was, according to rabbinical legend, miraculously constructed throughout, the large megalithic stones rising and settling in their respective places without being touched physically. The general opinion of the rabbis is that Solomon hewed the stones by means of a Shamir, a mythical substance that had the power to cut through or disintegrate stone or iron and whose mere touch cleaved rocks. These methods are all reminiscent of ancient building techniques like those employed in the construction of the Great Pyramid in Egypt.

The Holy Temple in Jerusalem would be Solomon's crowning achievement, in which he also received help from King Hiram of Tyre after he sent out a formal request for workers and materials. King Hiram would send wood and a man called Hiram Abiff, a master mason and part of the lore of Masons to this day. I spoke with Ahtun Re about my memories of this man, and he told me that he was also incarnate during Queen Hatshepsut's reign as her lover and architect. If we were to go back farther in time, we would also find him choreographing the layout of Stonehenge, Ahtun Re said.

Hiram Abiff's workers built the structure of the Temple, its decorations, and its vessels. The Temple would take seven years to complete. It was built of

stone and cedar, carved within, and overlaid with pure gold.

Two pillars named Boaz and Jachin stood in the porch on the left and right side of the Temple. The Bible records their measurements in cubits, which can be converted to a height of twenty-seven feet and a width of six feet with a hollow of four fingers thick. Their eight-foot- high capitals were each decorated with rows of two hundred carved pomegranates, wreathed with seven chains, and topped with lilies. According to most translations, these two pillars were cast of brass, though some believe the original Hebrew word used to describe their material, *nehosheth,* is actually either bronze or copper, because the Hebrews were unfamiliar with zinc, which is a required component to create brass, the other being copper.

Jachin and Boaz were really isolated columns and not, as some have supposed, a part of the ornamentation of the building. Their tops were crowned with ornamentation as if they were lamps. There is another word translated either as "pillar" or "idol" whenever some covenant or submission is implied, which would apply to a phallic pillar, but this word was not used for Jachin and Boaz. After Moses, this type of pillar or idol became unacceptable within the religion. The Bible text therefore calls for different explanations than the archaeologists' phallic pillar suggestion.

The north-south alignment ascribed to Jachin and Boaz allows for a number of practical astronomical observations without further equipment. Assuming that they were open to the sky at midday, these observed events were also widely visible in the city:

> *When the shadow of Jachin aligns with Boaz it marks midday, so it could be used to divide the morning and afternoon temple rituals.*
>
> *The last rays of the sun on the tips of the pillars mark sunset, and the end of the day and dawn is shown similarly. Both events have ritual relevance.*
>
> *The longest noon shadow of Jachin onto Boaz marks the day of the winter solstice. From there, the days to the vernal equinox could be counted in a standardized form, for example, thirteen sevens plus a day—analogous to the count of Pentecost.*
>
> *At midnight during the first full moon after the vernal equinox, the shadow of Jachin cast by the moon aligns with Boaz, marking the begin of Passover.*

In a fledgling state in the process of establishing a formal administration, these key observations made centrally were of practical administrative importance. In that sense, Jachin and Boaz were like church clocks and bells, telling the time to worship without being objects of worship themselves.

The pillars also represented the two main supports of the largely theocratic state, namely the priesthood and the king. Jachin was the name of the head of one of the families of priests, and Boaz was the name of King David's great-grandfather.

Another very important aspect of the Temple was that it housed the Ark of the Covenant in a special inner room called the Holy of Holies. It was located on the westernmost end of the Temple building, being a perfect cube that measured thirty feet in each dimension. Other chambers were also built on the southern, western, and northern sides of the Temple. Ahtun Re informed me that many of these chambers were secret chambers holding special artifacts that the priests would use in special ceremonies.

The Babylonian king Nebuchadnezzar II in 587 BCE would eventually destroy the Temple, but by that time the ark had already been removed from it. According to Abune Paulos, who had been patriarch of the Ethiopian Orthodox Tewahedo Church and one of the seven presidents of the World Council of Churches before he passed away in 2012, this removal had to do with the visit of the queen of Sheba to Solomon.

Her empire included large portions of modern-day Yemen and Ethiopia, an area that was rich in gold and other precious stones, spices, frankincense, and myrrh. Solomon needed her products and trade routes, and the queen of Sheba needed Solomon's cooperation in marketing her country's goods. When she asked Solomon questions and riddles, she was amazed at his wisdom. She would give herself to Solomon, and on her way home bear his son, Menelik.

Upon reaching adulthood, Menelik went to visit his father in Jerusalem. It was during this visit that the ark was stolen by the firstborn sons of some of the Israelite nobles, who carried it with them to Sheba as they accompanied Menelik on his way back. When Menelik learned of the theft, he reasoned that since the ark's frightful powers hadn't destroyed his retinue, it must have been God's will that the ark remain with him.

The Ethiopians now claim that the ark rests in a chapel in the small town

of Aksum, in their country's northern highlands. It arrived nearly three thousand years ago, they say, and has been guarded by a succession of virgin monks who—once anointed—are forbidden to set foot outside the chapel grounds until they die. Graham Hancock, who wrote about the ark in his book *The Sign and the Seal*, says he met three of these guardians in only two years. They were very short-lived, because their assignment took a heavy toll on their health. When Hancock met the third guardian, who by that time had already developed cataracts over his eyes, he was told that this is because "the ark is a thing of fire," alluding to the ark's enormous power.

The removal of the ark from the Holy Temple can be seen as a symptom for the fact that Solomon lost the ideals of his youth and became restless and unsatisfied. His writings in Ecclesiastes, proclaiming that "all is vanity," support the view that the world's wisest man had become cynical in his advanced years. I also asked Ahtun Re about the spiritual aspect of Solomon's reign, because I have memories of being involved with the priesthood at that time. I was told that Solomon had gone recklessly into magic and the angelic realm to include demons. I had frowned on the careless pursuit of this type of knowledge by Solomon.

But Solomon wanted to explore and study various philosophies and meditations almost indiscriminately, like mind-altering herbalism and alchemy, astrology and divination, and various forms of ritual magic. The constant influx of wives and concubines in Solomon's court also contributed significantly to his downfall. Solomon broke the Mosaic Law and violated the warning not to stray from the path of his father, David. This law was created so that many wives would not distract rulers and thus allow them to focus on the needs of the people.

Solomon had taken many foreign wives, whom he allowed to worship other gods. He even built shrines for the sacrifices they were performing. The result was that Jerusalem and even its Holy Temple became the scene of pagan practices and idol worship. Solomon's own faith was weakened. He approved of these idolatrous acts and eventually even participated in them. The example he set for the rest of the nation was demoralizing. This unfortunate error was a severe blow to the security of Solomon's throne and to the nation he had built.

In his early years he was both noble and humble and therefore one of the best rulers of his day, if not one of the best rulers in all of history. Although he was surrounded by wealth and luxury as a young man, he seemed to be a person

of honor and integrity. He was the first king of the United Kingdom of Israel and Judah who was the son of a king. The glory of his empire was a reflection of his own royal tastes, which he satisfied through shrewd and successful policies.

Unfortunately, Solomon was not strong enough to completely withstand the temptations that go along with a long life of luxury. On one hand, he made Jerusalem one of the most beautiful cities of the ancient world, and he will always be remembered as a great builder. The Temple of Solomon is iconic to this day, as is his wisdom. But on the other hand, he did not heed his own advice that can be found in Proverbs 25, "It is not good to eat too much honey, nor is it honorable to search out matters that are too deep." The tragedy is that after Solomon made his great contributions in his younger years, he did very little to further promote the religious life of his people. His example of frivolous and reckless exploration of the mysteries was the downfall of his life and his nation.

Within his kingdom, Solomon placed heavy taxation on the people, who became bitter. He also had an increasing number of people work as soldiers, chief officers, and commanders of his chariots and cavalry. He granted special privileges to the tribes of Judah, which alienated the northern tribes. The prophet Ahijah of Shiloh then prophesied that Jeroboam, son of Nebat, would become king over ten of the twelve tribes, instead of one of Solomon's sons.

Years before Solomon's death, his heavy taxation of the people eventually brought unrest and rebellion. Surrounding nations began to marshal their forces to free themselves of Israel's tyranny, but the most serious uprising came from within the nation itself. Ahijah's prophecy would come true when Jeroboam, a young leader who had the support of Egypt, led ten of the twelve tribes out of Israel. When Solomon's son Rehoboam ascended the throne after his father, Jeroboam returned to lead a successful civil war against him. The result was a division of the United Kingdom into two separate nations, the Kingdom of Judah and the Kingdom of Israel. What had been unified under David's reign and consolidated through Solomon's prudent policies in his earlier years was separated shortly after Solomon's death, as his lack of focus toward the end of his life caused the United Kingdom of Israel and Judah to disintegrate from the inside.

The lesson that Solomon's reign brings to us is that prosperity and wealth are the natural consequence of wisdom and peace. Wisdom is the foundation of prosperity, just as folly is the foundation of poverty. Through a wise practice

of prosperous trade and alliances, King Solomon was able to have one of the most successful and peaceful examples of government in all of history, but he did not have the discipline to expand from this foundation.

Every achievement brings new challenges, so we must never cease to be vigilant. As the Greek philosopher Aristotle would say several hundred years later, "Excellence is an art won by training and habituation. We do not act rightly because we have virtue or excellence, but rather we have those because we have acted rightly. We are what we repeatedly do. Excellence, then, is not an act but a habit."

I have long believed that a life that is lived humbly, honestly, and with hard work will have just rewards. Accordingly, a decadent lifestyle will inevitably pave the road for one's demise.

"Solomon Dedicates the Temple" illustration from Henry Davenport Northrop's *Treasures of the Bible*, 1894.

Solomon's Temple was the first temple built in Jerusalem.

David as he fights Goliath.

The Ark of the Covenant, as depicted by French artist James Jacques Joseph Tissot (1836-1902).

The Queen of Sheba is a figure first mentioned in the Hebrew Bible. In the original story, she brings a caravan of valuable gifts for the Israelite King Solomon. Her legend has become the subject of one of the most widespread and fertile cycles of stories in the Middle East.

"NOBLE BIRTH, SO ADMIRED OF THE MULTITUDE, AND OUR BEING DESCENDED FROM HERACLES DOES NOT BESTOW ANY ADVANTAGE, UNLESS WE DO THE SORT OF THINGS FOR WHICH HE WAS MANIFESTLY THE MOST GLORIOUS AND MOST NOBLE OF ALL MANKIND, AND UNLESS WE PRACTICE AND LEARN WHAT IS GOOD OUR WHOLE LIFE LONG."

◊ *Lycurgus* ◊

CHAPTER 10

LYCURGUS OF SPARTA, REGENT, LAWGIVER, AND CREATOR OF THE COMMONWEALTH OF SPARTA, 820-730 BCE

Lessons and ideas gathered from recent lifetimes are often assimilated into current incarnations, and a number of motives that were important in my lifetime with Solomon would present themselves again in my life as Lycurgus. This incarnation and my next parallel incarnation as Numa Pompilius are also interesting because the Greek historian Plutarch compared both of them many centuries later. My feeling is that Plutarch was incarnate during some of the lifetimes he wrote about, which enabled him to more easily pick up on what had happened then. For many years, he was also one of the two priests of Apollo at the Temple of Delphi responsible for interpreting the oracles. You could say he had special access to inside information on several different levels.

Plutarch writes in his comparison of Numa with Lycurgus that their "points of likeness are obvious; their moderation, their religion, their capacity of government and discipline, both derived their laws and constitutions from the gods." But while the underlying principles were very similar in both lives, their courses of action were in some ways almost polar opposites. While

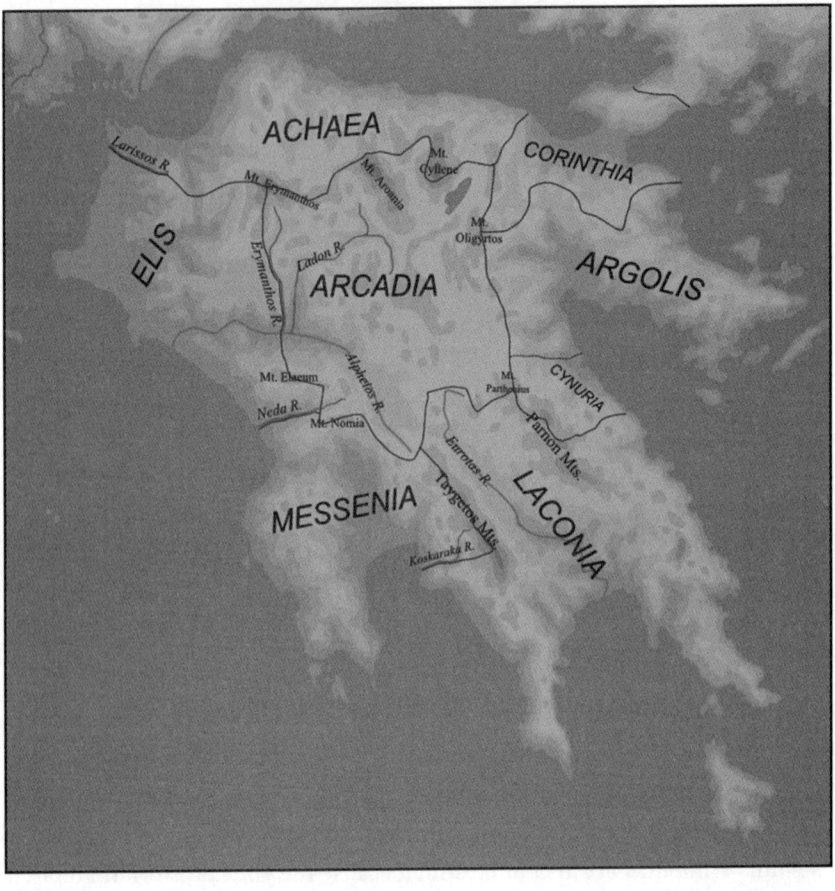

Lycurgus is heavily responsible for the fact that the very word "Spartan" is now used synonymously with disciplined or frugal, often with a martial undertone, Numa was "bringing the hard and iron Roman temper to somewhat more of gentleness and equity," as Plutarch noted.

This is exemplary for how we strive to find a balance over many lifetimes and try different approaches to work on an issue. My focus has always been on assisting the evolution of humanity, so in order to become more efficient I ventured to experiment with a variety of methods to grow and inspire others to unfold their full potential. Considering the great diversity of mentalities that may exist even within just one person, it is generally very useful to be open to different approaches when interacting with others. Be very sure and certain of

your main focus, but at the same time also flexible in how you reach out. Even if it may seem awkward on some level or go against what you would normally do, sometimes doing or saying a particular thing can serve as a major catalyst in the life of someone else. When your focus to work for the highest and best good of all is firmly established and you feel a nudge to do something out of the ordinary that you cannot rationally understand, then this is often a sign that your higher self is guiding you.

Looking at this life I very much appreciate the experiences that I would undergo both as Lycurgus and as Numa because I think the experiments they initiated were valuable contributions to the collective evolution of humanity. As Lycurgus I would be born into a royal family and even be king for a short period of time after my older brother had died. As was common for many thousands of years in such cases, the surviving brother would often take up the responsibility for his brother's wife and any children. Accordingly, Lycurgus would agree to marry his brother's wife when he ascended the throne.

It may seem imposing that I incarnated in royal families in so many lifetimes, but remember that we all incorporate life lessons from many lifetimes as common people as well. I'm obviously not a king in my current incarnation, but as I reflect on the amazing lessons from previous lifetimes I'm incredibly enriched on many different levels. You will be as well when you begin to consciously connect with your own past lifetimes and with the thread that you are weaving into the giant fabric of existence.

After all, I don't see how it would be necessary for every soul to become a king in the traditional sense at some point. The need for kings and rulers as we know them is part of a paradigm in which the majority of humanity is not sufficiently empowered to live truly self-responsible lives. We currently are moving toward societies in which everybody is his or her own master. The ideal is that you don't need someone to rule your life.

When Lycurgus became king, his new wife was already carrying the child of his deceased brother. She was aware of this and of the fact that this child—if it would be a boy—would immediately become the new king. The queen told me that she would abort the child so that we could stay on the throne, but I was horrified by the idea of killing the unborn child. I told her that it would be unsafe for her health and suggested that I would kill the child

after its birth in case it would be a boy. However, at no point did I really intend to do this. This lie was only meant to prevent her from aborting the child. When she was close to labor, I told her maids to bring me the baby if it was a boy. If it was a girl they were to keep her with themselves.

The baby did turn out to be a boy, and, when brought to me, I was at court. I immediately held him up and announced to all those assembled that Sparta had a new king, Charilaus. I didn't think that growing up without his real father would be negative for the boy, quite probably because the memories of my own experiences when I was in a similar situation were ingrained in my subconscious memories.

Remember that in my life as Benaiah, the head priest Johoiada and King David mostly raised me. In a later incarnation as William the Conqueror, I was also known as William the Bastard. Even in my current life my mother would never marry my biological father. In fact, I have never met my real father in this lifetime, believing that it is not essential that I do. The circumstances under which we are born are always unique, and it's sometimes not necessary at all in the bigger picture to be in a lifelong relationship with your biological parents. We will naturally attract to us the circumstances we need to progress and mature in the human experience.

Charilaus's mother was incensed that I had fooled her with my supposed intention to kill the boy. We would remain regents at first until Charilaus was of age to begin his kingship, but already with my announcement of who he was she would no longer enjoy being queen of Sparta. Her relatives then began spreading vicious rumors that I was going to kill Charilaus so that I could remain in power. This intrigue against me was just a natural consequence of the fact that she had not properly processed her initial intent to kill the child to gain more personal power and status. In this dangerous environment I wisely decided to leave Sparta and put the future king in the custody of men of honor that would ensure he would be protected.

I had decided to explore the kingdoms and laws of all the major nations of the time. My idea was to return after finding the best system for Sparta, so that the current corrupt system of kingship, which many of the people and I despised, could be replaced with something better for the commonwealth. Sparta had a dual kingship, descended from the lines of

Heracles's twin sons, but I still felt it would be appropriate to involve more individuals in running the state.

Although at times there have been great monarchs who tremendously helped their countries, I think it's much more desirable to come to the point where the population seeks knowledge and education itself, acting self-responsibly. If you strive to develop yourself to the highest degree you are capable of, you will naturally also be of best service to the community, much more so than someone who is merely following the rules and guidelines of an external authority. Of course we can always learn from individuals who are ahead of us in knowledge and skills, but the focus on the empowerment of the individual is of paramount importance and should be encouraged in any free society. This is humanity's purpose and destiny, but fulfilling it requires prudent decisions on the way. It has to be considered what beneficial steps can realistically be taken at any given time, because if there is a power vacuum at a time when the population is not ready to take the step into self-responsibility, negative leaders would likely emerge and mislead the population.

On my quest for the perfect governing system for Sparta I traveled to Crete, Egypt, Babylon, India, and the British Isles, where I had lifetimes before or would have in the future. I don't believe this was apparent to me in that lifetime, but it is interesting that I would be attracted to these places. When you are drawn to particular places, there is always a reason. Maybe you've had lifetimes there before, maybe you will incarnate there in the future, and most probably you have something important to do at this place right now.

I would also train in new martial skills and share some of my knowledge and expertise with selected others during my travels. I was an accomplished warrior and carried my shield and weapons with me wherever I went. As part of the elite of the time, I would often be housed as a guest of the rulers of the different countries that I visited. I made it known early on in conversations that I was interested in creating a new form of government derived from the best information I could gather in my travels. It is amazing how accommodating people can be when they are trying to flatter you with what they consider their best qualities. The ruling elites of the time, intrigued with my idea, were also eager to know what my discoveries amounted to. In return they provided for my comfort while educating me in their finest merits.

From these different countries I would pick and choose the best examples, discard the worst, and with this knowledge create a constitution that would propel Sparta's rise to the greatest of the Greek states. In every great age in history we find a sort of portal or window of opportunity where an environment can be created that lays the foundation for the advancement of humanity's development on various levels. After I had spent many years compiling information for this new commonwealth, I eventually returned to Sparta.

One of the ideas that would be transformative was to separate the military from the citizenry. Most armies of the time did not consist of professional soldiers. The citizens trained together on occasion and picked up arms as needed, sort of like a militia is described in current times. The idea for the transition of the military into a professionally recruited and trained army came from my visit to Egypt. There is one caveat, though, because the more powerful any group becomes, the more important it is to deal responsibly with that power. We can see throughout history—and I had seen it clearly in my life as Nakhtmin—how powerful armies would at times use their force to overthrow the countries they were supposed to protect. There must be an ethical foundation to prevent this from happening. Just like with any other particularly powerful tool or ability, it takes a lot of integrity to refrain from handling it abusively. I would hence create various laws meant to inspire a sense of humility and sobriety among the Spartans that would ground our military and help it stick to the path of reason.

We often think that warriors are not evolved and that a culture focused on developing its martial aspects can't become truly great. But as part of the process of spiritual development, we must transition through the warrior archetype. Sparta had a very spiritual culture during my time when I helped to create an environment in which the Spartans could safely evolve through the warrior archetype. The laws that I helped to create were instrumental in keeping small groups from obtaining too much power over others, and they also inspired the population to develop a genuine sense of appreciation for one another. Thus transitions to higher states of awareness beyond the warrior archetype while still being a warrior were possible, endorsed, and highly celebrated.

In war, there were laws as well. A retreating enemy was only pursued until victory was assured. Often when an enemy army saw the disciplined and

well-outfitted army of Spartan soldiers, it would retreat with very little battle or none at all. During my time there was mostly peace, and war was never carried out for long against an enemy lest they observe and learn our tactics and begin to use them against us.

The strength and discipline of our army had its foundation in the system of education that I devised called the *agoge.* It was very pragmatic and focused on developing fortitude and vitality as well as grace and unpretentiousness. I actually got the idea to train young boys from the age of seven from Babylon. Although the *agoge* training evolved into very severe and austere indoctrination over time, it was initially a very subtle training methodology. The boys were trained in discipline, sports, basic to advanced martial skills, teamwork, survival, and artistic expression through dancing, singing, and playing musical instruments. This type of training was something that I think would be beneficial in any era, including today.

Implementing any new governmental structure is difficult even under the best of circumstances and must first have the backing of a critical mass of influential people. I was fortunate to have the necessary support, but the new laws would still need to be integrated over time. For the new commonwealth to be successful, it was essential to build a proper foundation, and having the children grow up in this system was a major step to anchor it in Spartan society.

The system of the *agoge* on the other hand was meant to rear the children as strong and self-responsible individuals able to stand up for themselves and determine the right course of action on their own. Lycurgus would crystallize this idea by saying, "Those who are trained and disciplined in the proper discipline can determine what will best serve the occasion."

Not only the boys were trained in athletics, wrestling, martial skills, dancing, and singing, but the young girls as well. The women were the bearers of the men and thus were held in high regard and respect. It was believed and still holds true that the more fit women were, the better their offspring and their raising would be. When the men were involved in war, the women took over their responsibilities at home and were treated with even more dignity. Inspired by what I knew about the Minoan civilization, the women in Sparta were held in much higher esteem than in the surrounding Greek states.

Among the customs that were to instill a sense of groundedness and respect, young women and men would often train and compete in the nude. Nudity was also common when they danced in the processions of festivals. This was to teach modesty, simplicity, and a focus on good health. Today, nudity is often immediately sexualized or seen as offensive, but if it is as common as it was during my time in Sparta and combined with a sober attitude, nudity helps to create a serene atmosphere with less tension.

The more superficialities you give importance to in life, the more complicated everything becomes. This is true for your outward appearance as well as your inner state of being. More than two thousand years after my lifetime as Lycurgus, the great Italian Renaissance polymath Leonardo da Vinci encapsulated this sentiment by stating, "Simplicity is the ultimate sophistication." We were striving for the highest clarity in our words and actions, and for that reason we also cultivated the habit of speaking very concisely and to the point. This way of communicating is known today as laconic, which refers to the area of Laconia where Sparta was located.

Socrates, who lived in Athens in the fifth century BCE, commented on the Spartans' ability to seemingly effortlessly throw off pithy comments, saying that "they conceal their wisdom and pretend to be blockheads, so that they may seem to be superior only because of their prowess in battle." Actually, our overall attitude toward battles has been very similar to our style of communication. Just as we were focused on keeping military campaigns as short as possible, we preferred to engage in short conversations that were straight and efficient. Socrates concluded, "This is how you may know that I am speaking the truth and that the Spartans are the best educated in philosophy and speaking: if you talk to any ordinary Spartan, he seems to be stupid, but eventually, like an expert marksman, he shoots in some brief remark that proves you to be only a child."

Another very keen move to promote humility among Spartans was the abolition of gold and silver as a currency. Looking at it from today, having a currency backed by physical assets would surely be preferable over using fiat currencies backed by nothing and created out of thin air by a private central banking cartel, but during my time in Sparta we had none of these problems. The features of the newly created Spartan iron currency may seem impractical from today's point of view, but at that time the Spartan iron ingots served their purpose very well.

Even a great weight and quantity of these ingots, which were not accepted anywhere outside Sparta, were worth very little, so it required a pretty large closet to store them. To remove them took nothing less than a yoke of oxen. As a consequence, extensive wealth accumulation disappeared and a more consistent equality reigned throughout the country. Litigation and the court system virtually disappeared overnight. This kind of money was hard to rob, because it was hard to carry and hide. This also made financial bribery almost impossible.

All these rules and regulations would never be formally reduced into writing, because for any law to be upheld it is most important that it is alive in the hearts and minds of the populace. As for things that were considered to be of lesser importance, as pecuniary contracts and such, I had also realized that the forms of their regulations had to be changed as occasion required. I determined that it would be most appropriate to prescribe no positive rule or inviolable usage in such cases, so that their manner and form could be altered according to the circumstances of time and determinations of men of sound judgment.

For that purpose, I would create a senate in which the two kings would be counterbalanced by twenty-eight of the most highly regarded men over sixty years of age. These wise men would have the responsibility of making sure that the laws were observed. Most men would remain in military service until the age of sixty when they would transition into a life of debate and observing the young men in their training. Often these older men would watch, question, and give guidance to the young boys during their early training. The goal was to genuinely empower every individual for the state to be strong.

All of Spartan society would be completely revamped. Once the laws were implemented and firmly established, I traveled to the Oracle of Delphi as I did before I had implemented the laws. I was told previously that Sparta would be greatly served by the laws, and now I was told that since they were implemented Sparta would rise to greatness and thrive as long as these laws were observed. I carried this information back to Sparta and told the people to swear to follow my laws until I returned once again. They promised they would observe them, whereupon I departed for good. I was advanced in age and traveled to Crete where I fasted until my death. My friends cremated my body and, according to my instructions, scattered the ashes on the crystal blue waters of the Mediterranean.

Spartan society would continue in greatness under the observance of the laws I had implemented, but as you might suspect, the laws would be changed eventually, which led to the downfall of Sparta. One major turning point would be the advent of the Ephors a little more than hundred years after my time. The Ephors were a group of five men specifically chosen to observe all of Spartan society and answer to the kings. But in fact, they would become increasingly tyrannical as they began to assume unchecked power. I would have several encounters with the Ephors in future lifetimes in Sparta that I will speak about later.

The laws that I would pass as Lycurgus have inspired people ever since; there is even a bas-relief of Lycurgus in the chamber of the US House of Representatives as one example of twenty-three great lawgivers. Similar to my reforms in Sparta, the US Constitution was the reason that our country rose to greatness. It is based on some of the principles and examples that Lycurgus and others throughout time had proven were sound, but again a self-serving political elite undermined it while a large part of the population looked the other way.

The reason why such tragedies occur has been the same throughout time. The Irish politician John Philpot Curran made it very clear in the year 1790, "It is the common fate of the indolent to see their rights become a prey to the active. The condition upon which God hath given liberty to man is eternal vigilance; which condition if he break, servitude is at once the consequence of his crime and the punishment of his guilt."

Where we are headed today is essentially up to us as individuals. Either by our actions or by our negligence, we determine our own and also the future of mankind. Learning the lessons of history not only allows us to not repeat mistakes but also to better inform us of how to shape our future.

Apollo has been recognized as a god of archery, music and dance, truth and prophecy, healing and diseases, the Sun and light, poetry, and more. One of the most important and complex of the Greek gods, he is the son of Zeus and Leto, and the twin brother of Artemis, goddess of the hunt. Seen as the most beautiful god and the ideal of the *kouros* (beardless, & athletic youth), Apollo is considered to be the most Greek of all the gods.

The north side view of the Temple of Apollo in Corinth, ca 540 BCE.

Lycurgus was the legendary law-giver of Sparta who established the military-oriented reformation of Spartan society in accordance with the Oracle of Apollo at Delphi. All his reforms promoted the three Spartan virtues: equality (among citizens), military fitness, and austerity.

Lycurgus of Sparta is depicting the transfer of the kingship to the child when it was born.

Naked Spartan youths engage in various exercises, designed to both increase bodily strength and to strengthen their will. To toughen them up even more, Spartan boys were compelled to go barefoot and seldom bathed or used ointments, so that their skin became hard and dry, Plutarch wrote. For clothing, they were given just one cloak to wear year-round, to make them learn to endure heat and cold, and made their own beds from plants that they had to rip out of the ground with their bare hands from river banks.

"THE VERY POINTS OF MY CHARACTER THAT ARE MOST COMMENDED MARK ME AS UNFIT TO REIGN, LOVE OF RETIREMENT AND OF STUDIES INCONSISTENT WITH BUSINESS, A PASSION THAT HAS BECOME INVETERATE IN ME FOR PEACE."

◊ *Numa Pompilius* ◊

CHAPTER 11

NUMA POMPILIUS, SECOND KING OF ROME, 753-673 BCE

After my very first psychic reading, I had often contemplated my role as a Roman centurion whose life path crossed with that of Yeshua and his disciples. While I meditated on that lifetime, further memories started flooding in and I started to connect with many historically significant lifetimes as Romans. This will happen for many of you as you begin to unlock the convoluted layers of interconnectedness that have largely remained unexamined in the human experience for many thousands of years. Shining a light on our evolution as souls takes the focus of an investigative detective, the discipline of a warrior, the analytical research of a scientist, and the intuition of a spiritual scholar. We all can develop these abilities and support each other in this quest, as I hope this book is doing for you.

You will often have many lifetimes in a particular area to learn at a soul level what is happening in a certain social environment. Depending on your soul level, this is to prepare you to advance to more complicated roles such as leading and influencing vast groups of people in a positive direction. You will also adapt your experiences lived in other cultures and races to fit your chosen life

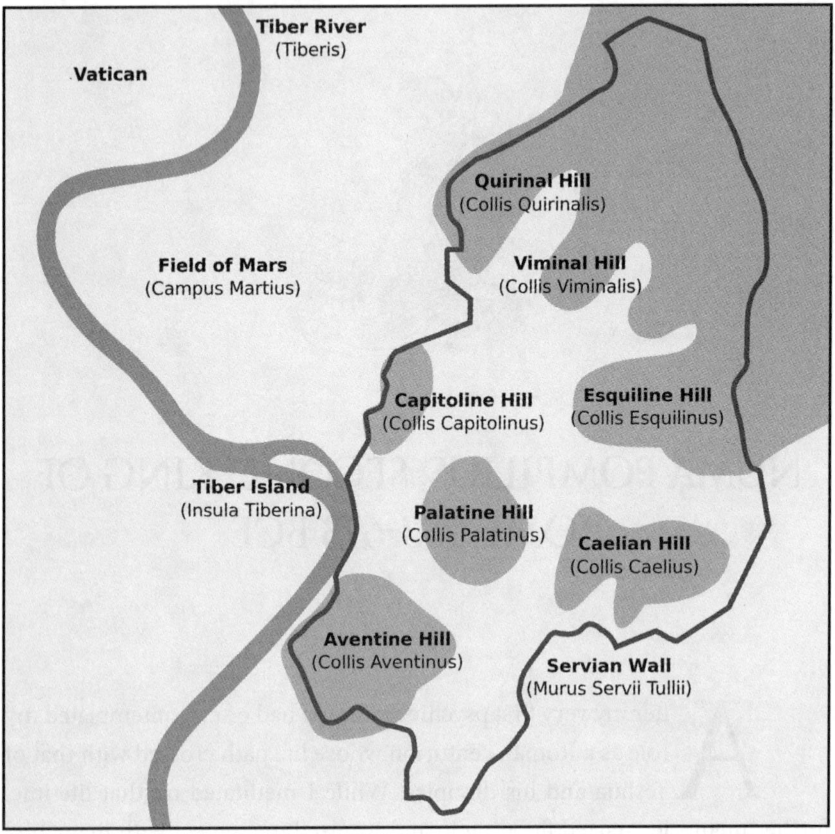

Tiber River
(Tiberis)
Vatican
Quirinal Hill
(Collis Quirinalis)
Field of Mars
(Campus Martius)
Viminal Hill
(Collis Viminalis)
Capitoline Hill
(Collis Capitolinus)
Esquiline Hill
(Collis Esquilinus)
Tiber Island
(Insula Tiberina)
Palatine Hill
(Collis Palatinus)
Caelian Hill
(Collis Caelius)
Aventine Hill
(Collis Aventinus)
Servian Wall
(Murus Servii Tullii)

path. Once you have gained a feel of what you can contribute to awakening and guiding a particular group, you will continue your work at an even higher level.

I had long felt very strongly that I must have experienced several incarnations in the area that is now Italy. Looking at it now, the motivation to create a more perfect human experience after many lifetimes at the pinnacles of the Egyptian and Greek eras would naturally lead me to key lifetimes in Roman history as well, because in many ways Rome's foundation was built on the accomplishments of these other cultures. I would again insert myself to make a positive impact on the greater human evolution in Italy. As happened previously, my efforts combined with other awakened souls would not bring about the ultimate change for humanity. There have been many great leaders throughout history who had a beneficent and inspiring influence on humanity for periods of time,

but more often than not the majority of the population would lose their focus and return to a rather unconscious lifestyle. Of course there are also elements in society that deliberately manipulate the population into this direction.

In hindsight, I can say that bringing about positive change seems to be among the most demanding activities you could get involved in, but it is also very rewarding. I can see now how all these lifetimes of dedicated work for the greater good really helped to prepare the ground for the monumental awakening that is unfolding on Earth in this day and age. In fact, I feel absolutely certain that every little deed in history that was genuinely focused on lifting up the human experience made it possible that today more people than ever have an interest and motivation to learn more about our true nature and to create an environment in which humanity can truly unfold its potential in peace, just as I had envisioned it as Numa Pompilius.

Numa was the second in a line of seven kings that would last approximately 250 years. The succeeding Roman Republic began with the overthrow of the monarchy, traditionally dated around 509 BCE, and replaced it with a governing body headed by two high government officials or consuls who were elected annually by the citizens and advised by a senate. The Roman Senate existed throughout its history, beginning since the founding of Rome by Romulus on April 21,753 BCE, which was also reputed to be the day of Numa's birth.

Before this founding date, Aeneas and the survivors of the Trojan War I mentioned in an earlier chapter settled in what would eventually be called Rome. The Roman poet Virgil (October 15, 70 BCE—September 21, 19 BCE) wrote of Aeneas's legendary exploits in the classic book *Aeneid*.

Numa was descended from the Sabines, who considered themselves a colony of the Spartans. He was born and lived in the famous Sabine city of Cures where their king, Titus Tatius, had his palace close to the Tiber River twenty-six miles northeast of Rome. The Sabines are best known for an episode in Roman history that took place in 750 BCE, when the first generation of Roman men acquired wives for themselves from the neighboring Sabine families. This event has become known as "the rape of the Sabine women." It should be noted here that the English word "rape" is the conventional translation of the Latin *raptio*, which in the original context refers to abduction or bride kidnapping rather than sexual violation.

This event took place in the early history of Rome, shortly after its founding by Romulus and his mostly male followers. Seeking wives for their predominantly male population, the Romans negotiated unsuccessfully with the Sabines, who populated the surrounding area. Because they didn't want to support the emergence of a potentially rival society, the Sabines refused to allow their women to marry the Romans.

Consequently, the Romans planned to abduct Sabine women during a festival that they would host and where they would invite all their neighbors. According to the first century CE Roman historian Livy, many neighboring tribes attended, including the Sabines. At the festival, Romulus would give a signal at which time the Romans grabbed the Sabine women and fought off the Sabine men. The indignant abductees were soon implored by Romulus to accept Roman husbands.

Livy is clear that no sexual assault took place. On the contrary, Romulus offered them free choice of their husbands and promised civic and property rights to women. According to Livy, Romulus spoke to each of them in person "and pointed out to them that it was all owing to the pride of their parents in denying the right of intermarriage to their neighbors. They would live in honorable wedlock, and share all their property and civil rights, and—dearest of all to human nature—would be the mothers of free men."

The men of all the tribes were outraged and went to war separately with the Romans, who defeated and occupied all tribes except the Sabines. It was said that the Sabines almost succeeded in capturing the city of Rome because of the treason of Tarpeia, the daughter of the governor of the citadel on the Capitoline Hill, one of the seven hills of Rome. Later versions of the story claimed that Tarpeia opened the city gates for the Sabines in return for "what they bore on their arms." She allegedly believed that she would receive their golden bracelets, but the Sabines would just take them off and toss them at Tarpeia along with their shields until she was crushed from the weight. So instead of enriching Tarpeia, the Sabines crushed her to death with their shields and threw her from a rock that has since borne her name, the Tarpeian Rock.

About 250 years after the rape of the Sabines, the seventh and last king of Rome leveled the Capitoline Hill. He went by the name of Lucius Tarquinius Superbus and was so corrupt that the people of Rome swore off the monarchi-

cal system forever. By leveling the Capitoline Hill he destroyed all the shrines built by the Sabines in an effort to wipe out their memory. The Tarpeian Rock, which is located on the Capitoline Hill, survived this remodeling and continued to be used for executions. To be hurled off the Tarpeian Rock was considered a particularly grim fate because of the stigma it carried.

The story of Tarpeia illustrates how history is often changed to vilify a certain group or elevate another. The Sabines had come to liberate their women, so why would they ruthlessly kill a woman who was helping them? Would they toss aside their shields right before a battle with the Romans? After they supposedly piled their shields on her, would they then bother to dig her out from under all those shields to throw her over the cliff for good measure? Who revealed the story of how she was killed and why? Who had an interest in denigrating her memory as well as that of the Sabines? Dead people tell no tales and murderers rarely tell theirs either. Always use your discernment with everything you read, hear, and see. If it doesn't ring true for you, then do the research to try and find the actual evidence.

Mettus Curtius led the Sabines who came to rescue their women. They gained control over the citadel and managed to kill Hostus Hostilius, who had led the Roman counterattack. When Hostus fell, the Roman line gave way and retreated to the Palatine Hill. There the semiconscious Romulus, who had been carried to the rear, regained consciousness and led the Romans back into battle, which continued in great fierceness with mounting loss of life and many wounded as each side struggled to prevail. Livy writes that at this point the women intervened in the battle to reconcile the warring parties:

"They went boldly into the midst of the flying missiles with disheveled hair and rent garments. Running across the space between the two armies they tried to stop any further fighting and calm the excited passions by appealing to their fathers in the one army and their husbands in the other not to bring upon themselves a curse by staining their hands with the blood of a father-in-law or a son-in-law, nor upon their posterity the taint of parricide. 'If,' they cried, 'you are weary of these ties of kindred, these marriage-bonds, then turn your anger upon us. It is we who are the cause of the war, it is we who have wounded and slain our husbands and fathers. Better for us to perish rather than live without one or the other of you, as widows or as orphans.'"

Following the reconciliation, the Sabines agreed to form one nation with the Romans and settled on the Capitoline Hill. Titus Tatius, who would be my father-in-law in that lifetime, jointly ruled Rome with Romulus until Tatius's murder five years later. Many believed that the Laurentes killed Tatius. The blood feud started when members of the Laurentes family claimed Tatius's relatives mistreated them. They were dissatisfied that Tatius didn't try them for their crimes so had him killed.

Romulus, the first king of Rome and the one after whom the city had been named, supposedly ascended to heaven some thirty-three years later in 715 BCE after prophetically proclaiming that Rome would one day be the ruler of the world. After Romulus's departure there was almost a yearlong deliberation on who should be crowned the new king, and eventually Numa was asked to be the new leader.

Up until that point, Numa had been a priest and a scholar living a very quiet, secluded life of study and devotion with no desire or ambition to be king. At first it was said that he refused the offer saying, "I should but be, methinks, a laughingstock, while I should go about to inculcate the worship of the gods and give lessons in the love of justice and the abhorrence of violence and war to a city whose needs are rather for a captain than for a king." If I were to point to the role model of a leader in history that should be emulated in current times, it would be Numa.

Because of his reluctance, Numa's father and Sabine kinsmen, especially Marcus, who was his teacher and the father-in-law of Numa's own daughter, banded together with the Roman envoys to persuade him to accept. Plutarch and Livy recount how Numa, after being summoned by the Senate from Cures, requested that prior to his acceptance a divination should reveal the opinion of the gods on the prospect of his kingship. Jupiter was consulted and the omens were favorable. Thus placated by the Roman and Sabine people and anointed by the heavens, he took up his position as king of Rome.

Numa's very first act as king was to disband the personal guard of three hundred Celeres, the "quick-stepped," which Romulus had surrounded himself with permanently. According to Plutarch, Numa said that "he would not distrust those who put confidence in him, nor rule over a people that distrusted him." It was also rumored that the Celeres in Rome were involved in

the death of Romulus and Titus Tatius, which might have been another reason why they were disbanded. In any case, this move by Numa had been a signal of peace and moderation for all to see and emulate.

When Numa became king, people still thought of themselves first as Romans or Sabines rather than citizens of Rome. To overcome this tendency, Numa organized the people into guilds based on the occupation of the members, whatever their origin. He also made sure that every group was adequately represented. Plutarch notes, "The frame of government which Numa formed was democratic and popular to the last extreme, goldsmiths and flute-players and shoemakers constituting his promiscuous, many-colored commonalty." Hoping that an agricultural way of life would make the Romans more peaceful, Numa then distributed the land conquered by Romulus to poor citizens. He used to inspect the farms himself, promoting those whose farms looked well cared for and as if hard work had been put into them, and admonishing those whose farms showed signs of laziness. Numa's thinking was that "agriculture would be a sort of charm to captivate the affections of his people to peace," as Plutarch says, "viewing it rather as a means to moral than to economical profit."

The Romans celebrated Numa for his natural, practical wisdom and piety. His mental serenity would also open him up to receive special guidance from higher planes of existence. In addition to the endorsement by Jupiter, he is supposed to have had a direct and personal relationship with a number of deities, most famously the nymph Egeria, who taught him to be a wise legislator. According to Livy, Numa claimed that he held nightly consultations with Egeria on the proper manner of instituting sacred rites for the city.

Having a conscious personal relationship with discarnate entities is not unusual, especially if you leave behind any preconceptions that would obstruct your connection to this aspect of life. As I have described in my previous book. *The Intuitive Warrior*, during my first mission in Iraq I had a personal interaction with Archangel Michael that tremendously helped me to awaken to my life purpose in this lifetime. This happened unexpectedly for me as a result of my longing to expand my awareness and help others grow as well. Many people all over the world experience similar encounters and relations with a great variety of entities, whether they have always been spirit beings or souls that had lifetimes as humans but chose to guide humanity from the other side.

Egeria was a minor goddess of the Roman religious system. She is often associated with the goddess Diana, whose cult was celebrated at sacred groves. Both Diana and Egeria are also associated with water bearing and wondrous religious or medical properties. Numa would regularly meet with Egeria in a grove close to Rome with a spring dedicated to the exclusive use of the Vestal Virgins, for whom Numa would build a temple in Rome.

Egeria helped to awaken Numa's gifts of wisdom and prophecy. She had been his counselor and guide in the establishment of the framework of laws and rituals of Rome. It is my observation that when a masculine and feminine balance occurs in any organization, the result is a higher level of achievement in all aspects of human endeavor. We can also individually achieve this male and female balance internally, a task in which Egeria would greatly support Numa in that lifetime. Her teachings were written down and buried with Numa at his request. They were allegedly brought back to light some four hundred years later but deemed inappropriate for disclosure to the people by the Senate and destroyed.

According to Dionysius of Halicarnassus, a Greek historian at the turn of the eras, they were actually kept as a very close secret by the pontiffs, the chief priests of Rome. Perhaps these writings still exist and their disclosure would help in the awakening of humanity. I strongly believe that many sacred works have been held in abeyance until the right time for disclosure, because in historic times it was often too dangerous to come forward with such knowledge. Currently, we are beginning to see many of these ancient secrets uncovered, and as more of these truths are being revealed the unveiling will accelerate even more. After all, I think the knowledge contained in all of these ancient sacred writings did never really cease to exist. Just as we can access our past lives and revive their memory, with the right focus and discipline we can also tap into everything that had been written down at any time.

Having been a very spiritual man, Numa would also found the Roman religious system in an effort to promote humility, harmony, and simplicity among the Romans. Plutarch says of this early religion of the Romans that it was imageless and genuinely spiritual. He says Numa "forbade the Romans to represent the deity in the form either of man or of beast. Nor was there among them formerly any image or statue of the divine being. During the first one hundred and seventy years they built temples, indeed, and other sacred domes, but placed in them no figure of

any kind, persuaded that it is impious to represent things divine by what is perishable, and that we can have no conception of God but by the understanding."

Numa was of the opinion that people should make worship and gratitude a part of their daily lives and respect the gods that were believed to exert their influence in human affairs. He would initiate the Collegium Pontificum, the College of Pontiffs, which was the most important body of the Roman priesthood. He would also lay out the laws of this institution, like the appointment of the high priest, the Pontifex Maximus, who would usually hold this office for life. The word "Pontifex" is Sabine and means "member of a college of five," according to the original number of pontiffs in the Pontificum. The title was later adopted for the pope by the Roman Catholic Church and is often mistranslated as "bridge builder." Although it is not included in the pope's official titles, it appears on buildings, monuments, and coins.

Close to the Regia, which Numa built as the king's residence and that later served as the office of the Pontifex Maximus, he originally built the Temple of Vesta as one of the earliest structures located in the Roman Forum. Vesta was the goddess of the hearth, home, and family. All temples to Vesta were round and had entrances facing east to symbolize the connection between Vesta's fire and the sun as sources of life. Instead of a statue in the center of the building, there was a hearth holding a sacred flame. The temple would be the storehouse for the legal wills and documents of Roman senators and cult objects such as the Palladium, a wooden statue of great antiquity on which the safety of the city was said to depend. Reputedly carved by the Greek goddess Athena, it was stolen by Odysseus and Diomedes from the citadel of Troy and later taken to Rome by Aeneas, who survived the Trojan War and found refuge on Crete before establishing a colony in Rome.

Numa also reformed the calendar by adjusting solar and lunar years. After the year had been segmented into ten months during Romulus's reign, Numa introduced Januarius and Februarius as the first two months of the year. The month of Januarius is associated with the god Janus, for whom Numa had also built a temple very soon after he became king. This temple served as an indicator for war and peace, as its gates were left open in times of war and closed in times of peace. During the entire forty-three years of Numa's kingship, the Gates of Janus remained closed, which would be unparalleled in Roman history.

After all these great accomplishments, Numa finally perished of old age after living roughly eighty-three years. Livy wrote, "When Numa died, Rome by the twin disciplines of peace and war was as eminent for self-mastery as for military power." Even Niccolo Machiavelli, the Italian Renaissance politician known for canonizing deceptive and manipulative political tactics in his book *The Prince,* admitted that Numa's legacy very much contributed to the prosperity of the Roman people: "All things considered, therefore, I conclude that the religion introduced by Numa was among the primary causes of Rome's success, for this entailed good institutions. Good institutions lead to good fortune, and from good fortune arose the happy results of undertakings." The people were successfully diverted from military conquest, and their belief that the gods took part in human affairs caused great alarm against breaking the law. Machiavelli explains, "Marveling, therefore, at Numa's goodness and prudence, the Roman people accepted all his decisions." Machiavelli even goes so far as to say that the Roman people were more indebted to Numa than to Romulus.

Many have said that Numa was one of the most if not the most influential of all the Roman leaders throughout history. Can we as humanity have this type of leadership once again? I think the time is now upon us where in this case it would be fortunate for history to repeat itself I don't mean to say that we should rebuild Roman institutions, but to draw inspiration from Numa's general approach toward life and living. The pattern for success is not complicated, as Numa impressively showed us more than 2,700 years ago by living a life of pious simplicity.

I would have many lifetimes as Romans or rulers of Rome with the attribute "the Great" after their names. But the emperors Constantine the Great, Theodosius the Great, and Charlemagne the Great all had that moniker because of the force of their arms, not because of their contributions to peace. I would also have many lives in Rome as famous generals, dictators, and consuls who would gain great public support and prestige through force of arms. Of all these lifetimes, in my opinion, the one as Numa Pompilius was the most noteworthy. Yet how many people today even know of Numa? I personally only found out about him through past life research. From my current point of view, I think "the Great" should be attached after Numa's name to draw more attention to his rare accomplishments in peacemaking.

Is peace something that we want as humanity? It is time to make conscious decisions in our everyday life. Just as Numa would lead by example, each person returning to a conscious lifestyle that is focused on creating peace and harmony increases the speed of the shift that is taking place on a global scale right now. Each one of us has "the Great" waiting inside us. The way I see it, realizing the divine purpose that is waiting to unfold within us and devotedly allowing that objective to evolve once discovered is the most fulfilling aspect in life we can ever experience. This very book would have never seen the light of day if I hadn't recognized its higher purpose to encourage you to let your own divine light shine through. Allowing your higher self to guide you through your life will not only dramatically boost your own development at a soul level, it will also greatly inspire everybody around you.

The image of a she-wolf suckling the twins in their infancy has been a symbol of the city of Rome and the ancient Romans since at least the 3rd century BCE. Although the tale takes place before the founding of Rome around 750 BCE, the earliest known written account of the myth is from the late 3rd century BCE. Possible historical bases for the story, and interpretations of its various local variants, are subjects of ongoing debate.

A stone relief of gladiators fighting in the Roman Colosseum.

Machiavelli was an Italian diplomat, author, philosopher and historian who lived during the Renaissance. He is best known for his political treatise *The Prince*, written in about 1513 but not published until 1532. He has often been called the father of modern political philosophy and political science.

Numa Pompilius was the legendary second king of Rome, succeeding Romulus after a one-year interregnum He was of Sabine origin, and many of Rome's most important religious and political institutions are attributed to him, such as the Roman calendar, Vestal Virgins, the cult of Mars, the cult of Jupiter, the cult of Romulus, and the office of pontifex maximus.

In Roman mythology, Romulus and Remus are twin brothers whose story tells of the events that led to the founding of the city of Rome and the Roman Kingdom by Romulus, following his fratricide of Remus.

According to Plutarch, Numa was the youngest of Pomponius's four sons, born on the day of Rome's founding (traditionally, 21 April 753 BCE). He lived a severe life of discipline and banished all luxury from his home. Titus Tatius, king of the Sabines and a colleague of Romulus, gave in marriage his only daughter, Tatia, to Numa. Plutarch is depicted here in in the Nuremberg Chronicle.

"NOTHING IS MORE ACTIVE THAN THOUGHT, FOR IT TRAVELS OVER THE UNIVERSE."

◊ *Thales* ◊

CHAPTER 12

THALES OF MILETUS, PRE-SOCRATIC GREEK PHILOSOPHER, 624-546 BCE

We all incarnate with a definite goal in mind in each of our lives that we set according to our greater soul journey. In my lifetime as Thales, one of my main objectives would be the search for an explanation of the fundamental force of life in a concise way that is easily understood by many, a task that has been a challenge for mankind from time immemorial.

Thales was from a Greek coastal colony called Miletus, whose ruins are located near the modern town of Balat in Turkey. Before the Persian invasion in the middle of the sixth century BCE, Miletus was considered the greatest and wealthiest of all Greek cities. To study geometry and astronomy, Thales traveled to Egypt and Babylon, where he would also be influenced by the monotheistic ideas that have their roots in these regions.

After his return, Thales surprised his contemporaries with his unusual mathematical abilities. For example, he calculated the distance of a ship at sea from observations taken on two points on land, and he knew how to determine the height of a pyramid with a staff, its shadow, and the length of the

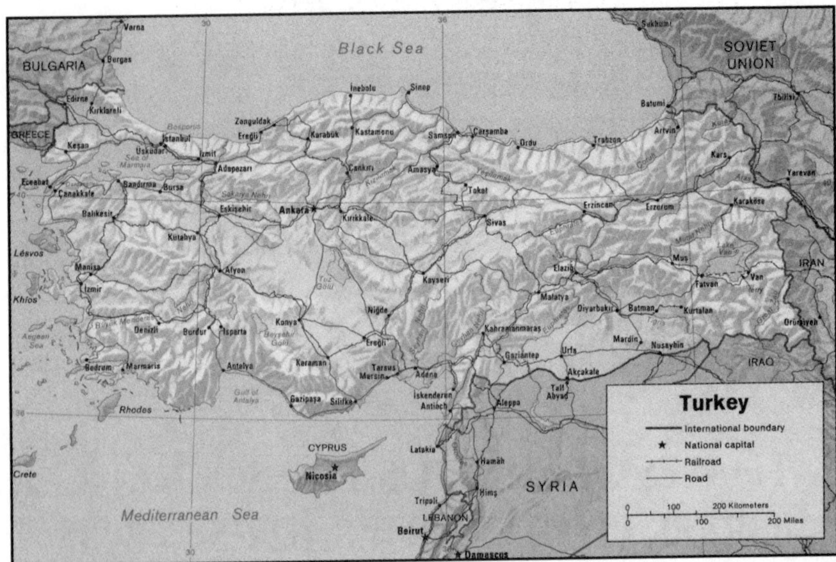

pyramid's shadow. He also predicted the full eclipse of the sun in May 28, 585 BCE, and discovered that any triangle that has the diameter of a circle as its base will have a right angle at its opposite corner when it's also positioned on the circle. This discovery is known today as Thales's theorem.

The ancient Greeks would later count Thales to the Seven Sages, a group of seven early sixth century BCE philosophers, statesmen, and lawgivers who were renowned in the following centuries for their wisdom. These early philosophers were deeply spiritual people. They often received their information and guidance after going into seclusion and connecting with divine entities. This practice of meditating and sleeping in a sacred area with the intention of experiencing divinely inspired insights was called incubation. According to Peter Kingsley, it is part of a shamanistic tradition that has its roots in Central Asia and heavily influenced the pre-Socratic philosophers, the *iatromanteis,* which literally means "physician-seers."

Later Greek philosophers would often focus more on the cerebral aspect of philosophy instead of the inner spiritual work necessary to cultivate your entire being in order to find answers to deeper questions about life, maybe assuming that they could achieve greater objectivity when they avoid getting into the more mysterious realms of consciousness. But in order to understand the

mystery you have to experience it; you cannot fully comprehend it by looking at it from the outside and much less by refraining from looking at it altogether.

History is replete with examples of individuals going into incubation periods where they would experience great revelations. Moses on Mount Sinai, Buddha underneath the Bodhi tree, Yeshua in the wilderness, Mohammad in the cave, the priestess known as the Oracle of Delphi—all used the process of incubation to get into higher states of consciousness. In *The Intuitive Warrior* I also described my personal experiences on a vision quest in my current lifetime. Vision quests are periods of incubation as practiced by Native Americans. On a vision quest, you go into seclusion in nature and fast for three days while you meditate and open yourself up to receive higher guidance or a vision for your life. All of us are capable of experiencing incubation revelations, and given the right focus and insight into the techniques, it can become something that's being done at will.

Another fascinating incubation experience is that of Frank Chester, who has discovered a scientific way of connecting the spiritual world and the world of form. Frank is an artist, sculptor, and geometrician with more than thirty years of experience in teaching art in high schools and colleges. After having explored the relation between form and spirit for most of his life, an incubation event in January 2000 revealed to Frank a new geometric form never seen before.

While past experimentation on geometric forms was founded on the principles of contraction and gravity, Frank created a new path to geometry based on expansion and levity. Instead of utilizing truncations, which refer to the cutting or flattening of existing corners in order to change a form, Frank was transforming the Platonic solids internally by expansion.

In his lectures, Frank presents his discoveries and how architecture and form can visually and scientifically describe the interrelationship between the spiritual and physical world through our hearts. When you place and spin one of the five Platonic solid shapes, a tetrahedron or pyramid form, inside a larger tetrahedron that is twice its size, it produces what Frank calls the chestahedron, its name being derived from both his own last name and the chest as the room of the heart.

The chestahedron can show an internal transformation moving in two opposite directions at the same time. These motions, when related to physiol-

ogy, provide a picture of how the human heart is formed out of two opposite moving vortexes; one is pumping and the other is drawing blood. In the greater human experience, these opposite vortexes can be likened to the archetypal male and female energies that also represent the materialistic and the spiritual worldview. It is our task to bring these energies and viewpoints into a balance so that a new understanding can be born that integrates both aspects fully.

Thales had been instrumental in pushing this evolution of thought and understanding by his efforts to explain phenomena that were hitherto believed to be the workings of anthropomorphic gods. He believed that things such as earthquakes, storms, and other natural events could be explained by the intrinsic properties of the elements themselves, which gave way to the scientific revolution. For this reason, Thales is also called the "Father of Science."

Thales's belief is described today as material monism, which provides an explanation of the physical world by saying that all of the world's objects are composed of a single element. Thales believed that everything was composed of water. His student Anaximander believed it must be something limitless, and his student Anaximenes believed it was air.

Many modern scientists continued this search for a unifying theory of everything that explains all phenomena as the product of a single substance or force. Max Planck, the originator of the quantum theory, concluded that this fundamental force must be conscious. He said, "As a man who has devoted his whole life to the most clear headed science, to the study of matter, I can tell you as a result of my research about atoms this much: There is no matter as such. All matter originates and exists only by virtue of a force, which brings the particle of an atom to vibration and holds this most minute solar system of the atom together. We must assume behind this force the existence of a conscious and intelligent mind." In 1922, the British mystic Alice Bailey, a contemporary of Planck, published an excellent book called *The Consciousness of the Atom* in which she also explains how atoms are conscious and aware. I found it fascinating that atoms also have a level of achievement much like our own souls. They start out as the atoms of minerals and progress over time in consciousness to atoms of human form.

I have come to believe that there is an inherent intelligence within everything and that "all things are full of gods," as Thales said, meaning that every-

thing is alive and indwelled by a sentient divine spirit. There are also numerous accounts of people who during past life regressions remembered, for instance, being an animal, a plant, a rock, or part of the air or the water. It's very likely that you have experienced these existences at some point in the past as well before you came to have this incarnation in a human body right now.

There seems to be no unconscious aspect of existence, and therefore it appears wise to me to make an effort to listen and communicate, just like, for example, shamans around the world would listen to plants to discover their medicinal properties. Listening to the consciousness within everything can help us understand how to apply and integrate everything we find around and inside of us most harmoniously. This act of tapping into the inherent knowledge of all-that-is can be done through our direct perception, especially if we open up our intuitive potentials. I believe that most of you reading this have already had some positive experiences with these abilities. I can see an exponentially growing number of people from all walks of life that are now actively developing their higher awareness, catalyzing the human evolution on every level.

Initially getting an inkling of these intuitive abilities in this lifetime can be quite easy for many, especially if they already developed them to some degree during their soul journey, but to really refine and integrate them it takes a sustained effort. You can liken this evolutionary process to the development of Thales's concept of a primordial substance of which everything else consists, the fundamental building block of matter. His idea that there is such a thing was quite right, but you can observe how his initial description was being gradually refined to the point where many scientists and researchers today have found strong evidence that it's not water but an ethereal field or tapestry that is the canvas on which everything is but a holographic projection. Very interesting books explaining this in more detail are *The Holographic Universe* by Michael Talbot and *The Source Field Investigations* by David Wilcock, both of whom are essentially following in the footsteps of a long succession of pioneering thinkers such as Thales.

In another example of souls working together throughout time, we have David Wilcock, who looks like Edgar Cayce did when he was young. David also has similar prophetic abilities while in dream states that are amazingly like Cayce's. My lovely wife, Tracy Jo, and I have been with David on one of his seminars in beautiful Hawaii, and I had strong feelings of having been associated with him in past lives. I asked Ahtun Re if David was the reincarnation of Cayce, and he said that he was the reincarnation of the biographical author of Edgar Cayce named Thomas Sugrue who wrote the book. *The Story of Edgar Cayce: There Is a River.* Ahtun Re said that a strong connection and identification with another soul in a previous incarnation could bring many different traits of that entity into focus. Ahtun Re went on to tell me that Edgar Cayce had incarnated again. Cayce's own readings said that he would incarnate again in 1998.

During a reading, Cayce identified Thomas Sugrue as having been a priest with him when Cayce was the high priest Ra Ta during the building of the Great Pyramid. The time frame for this was around 10,500 BCE. Levitation of stones is mentioned in the readings. I have memories of having the abihties to levitate blocks without help. I also have memories of levitating stones at Stonehenge, although the process was different there. I also believe the pyramid may have been built by the top down, meaning we that levitated the whole pyramid and then added stone beneath it until we finished another level. We then levitated the whole pyramid and added another level and so on. Recent dating of the pyramid lends credibility to this possibility.

In spite of his wisdom, Thales was a poor man. Aristotle wrote in his *Politics* that Thales was reproached for his poverty, which was supposed to show that his philosophy was of no use. To prove that his knowledge was indeed useful, Thales would on one occasion give deposits for the use of all the olive presses in Chios and Miletus at a time when the harvest was still far away and he could hire them at a low price because no one bid against him. Observing the weather patterns, he foresaw a great harvest of olives in the coming year during which the olive-presses now owned by him were in great demand and he could rent them out for a higher price, thereby making a huge profit. "Thus he showed the world that philosophers can easily be rich if they like, *but that their ambition is of another sort,*" wrote Aristotle.

The philosopher Pythagoras would be a student of Thales. Pythagoras was influential in philosophy and religious teaching in the late sixth century BCE and is today revered as a great mathematician, mystic, scientist, and a strong proponent of reincarnation. Edgar Cayce, the "Sleeping Prophet" who was famous for giving spiritual readings for over forty years to thousands of people, was an

incarnation of Pythagoras. We have had numerous lifetimes together in a larger soul group helping and supporting each other and humanity throughout time.

Many of the philosophers before the Athenian philosophers that most of the Western world is familiar with were also prominent political figures in their city-states. Thales served as an adviser to Croesus, the king of Lydia, and was instrumental in the defense against the growing power of the Persians under Cyrus. Croesus had pursued a very aggressive policy and conquered most of the states of coastal Anatolia, including the cities of the lonians. He was considered the richest king in the entire Greek world at the time. To contain the growing influence of the Persians, Croesus sided with the Medes.

Before Croesus marched together with the Medes against the Persians, he had sent an envoy to ask the Oracle of Delphi what his prospects might be if he went to war. The ambiguous reply was that a great kingdom would be destroyed if he went to fight, which Croesus believed to foretell the defeat of the Persians. Croesus was certain of victory as he set out with an army that was much smaller than necessary. The army was stopped on its way by the Halys River because it was in flood stage and not fordable. Thales came up with the idea to get the army across by digging a diversion upstream so as to reduce the flow of the river, making it possible to ford it.

The ensuing battle at Pteria in Cappadocia was indecisive but paralyzing to both sides, so Croesus marched home, dismissed his mercenaries, and sent emissaries to his dependents and allies to ask them to dispatch fresh troops to his capital at Sardis. Meanwhile, Cyrus moved so swiftly that help from allies such as Sparta had not even prepared to leave before word came that Croesus was defeated and captured before the city of Sardis. He was then placed upon a great pyre of wood by Cyrus's orders, who wanted to see if any of the heavenly powers would appear to save Croesus from being burned alive.

After the pile was set ablaze, Cyrus heard Croesus call out "Solon" three times and asked his interpreters to find out why Croesus said this word with such resignation and agony. The interpreters answered that one of the Seven Sages named Solon had warned Croesus of the fickleness of good fortune. This touched Cyrus, who was suddenly overcome by the realization that he and Croesus were much the same man, so he bade the servants to quench the blazing fire as quickly as they could.

They tried to follow his order, but the flames were not to be mastered. Then the story goes that soon after Croesus called out and prayed to the god Apollo, dark clouds gathered and a violent rainstorm speedily extinguished the flames. Up until then, the sky had been clear and the day without a breath of wind. Cyrus was so impressed by Croesus's charisma and his connection to the sages and the gods that he would spare his life and later take his council on various matters of importance.

When Cyrus was vexed at conquering Babylon, Croesus suggested that to overcome the impenetrable walls of the city he should divert the Euphrates River that ran into the city through an iron bar gate. When the water had drained low enough, Cyrus's army walked under the gate and easily defeated the unaware Babylonian army. As Thales, I had directed Croesus to divert the waters of the Halys, and now this same technique would be passed on to my parallel incarnation as Cyrus.

This incident shows how past life endeavors will often overlap to help you in your next incarnation. Standing on both sides of a conflict as Thales and Cyrus also shows how we are often literally battling with ourselves. In the bigger picture, our perceived enemies are also part of the divine energy that connects all of us; hence we should treat everyone as divinity incarnate. One person doing this cannot end all wars and conflicts overnight, but each person looking at life from this higher perspective and making wiser decisions certainly helps to pave the way toward a world of peace.

THALES OF MILETUS, PRE-SOCRATIC GREEK PHILOSOPHER, 624-546 BCE

Thales of Miletus was a Greek mathematician, astronomer, statesman, and pre-Socratic philosopher from Miletus in Ionia, Asia Minor. He was one of the Seven Sages of Greece. Many, most notably Aristotle, regarded him as the first philosopher in the Greek tradition, and he is otherwise historically recognized as the first individual known to have entertained and engaged in scientific philosophy. He is often referred to as the Father of Science.

Pythia was the name of the high priestess of the Temple of Apollo at Delphi. She specifically served as its oracle and was known as the Oracle of Delphi. Her title was also historically glossed in English as the Pythoness.

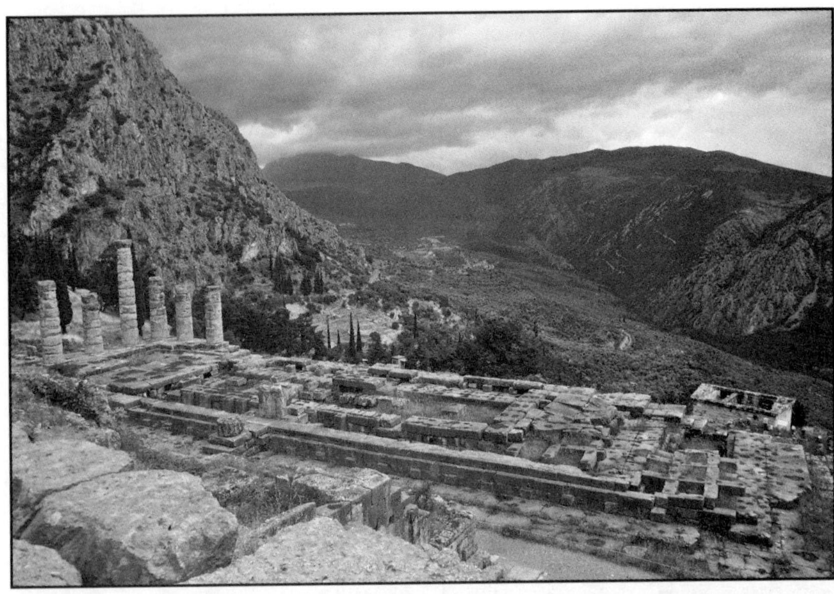

The Temple of Apollo, god of music, harmony, light, healing, and oracles occupied the most important and prominent position in the Delphic Panhellenic Sanctuary. The famous oracle, the Pythia, operated inside the temple, the location chosen, according to one tradition, due to a sacred chasm beneath the site emitting vapors, which were inhaled by the Pythia.

Pythagoras was an ancient Ionian Greek philosopher and the eponymous founder of Pythagoreanism. His political and religious teachings were well-known in *Magna Graecia* and influenced the philosophies of Plato, Aristotle, and, through them, the West in general.

THALES OF MILETUS, PRE-SOCRATIC GREEK PHILOSOPHER, 624-546 BCE

Apollo is one of the Olympian deities in classical Greek and Roman religion and Greek and Roman mythology. The national divinity of the Greeks, Apollo has been recognized as a god of archery, music and dance, truth and prophecy, healing and diseases, the Sun and light, poetry, and more. One of the most important and complex of the Greek gods, he is the son of Zeus and Leto, and the twin brother of Artemis, goddess of the hunt. Seen as the most beautiful god and the ideal of the *kouros* (*ephebe*, or a beardless, athletic youth), Apollo is considered to be the most Greek of all the gods.

"BY THE RIVERS OF BABYLON WE SAT AND WEPT WHEN WE REMEMBERED ZION."

◊ *Psalm 137:1* ◊

CHAPTER 13

A JEWISH GENERAL IN CAPTIVITY IN BABYLON, 587 BCE

I first became aware of my connection to the Essenes after I had extensively studied the history of the Essenes at the Edgar Cayce Institutes' library in Virginia Beach, Virginia. This realization was several years before my first past life reading with Mary Roach. I felt strongly that at some point I belonged to their tribe, and when Mary told me that I had been with Yeshua, I instantly connected with that lifetime with the Essenes. If you do the research you will find that Jesus, his family, and many of his disciples were from the Essene sect or tribe. Even more knowledge of this life surfaced after I queried Ahtun Re about a possible past life as an Essene.

When you first receive past life information, you will initially go through a deep soul evaluation. For me, it made no difference that I was virtually convinced that reincarnation was real. It didn't matter that I had eagerly anticipated my first past life reading with a reputable psychic after searching for more than a decade. I had also read dozens of excellent books on reincarnation that were very enlightening, but nothing prepared me for the shock of learning about all the different lives that I had lived. It was especially difficult for me

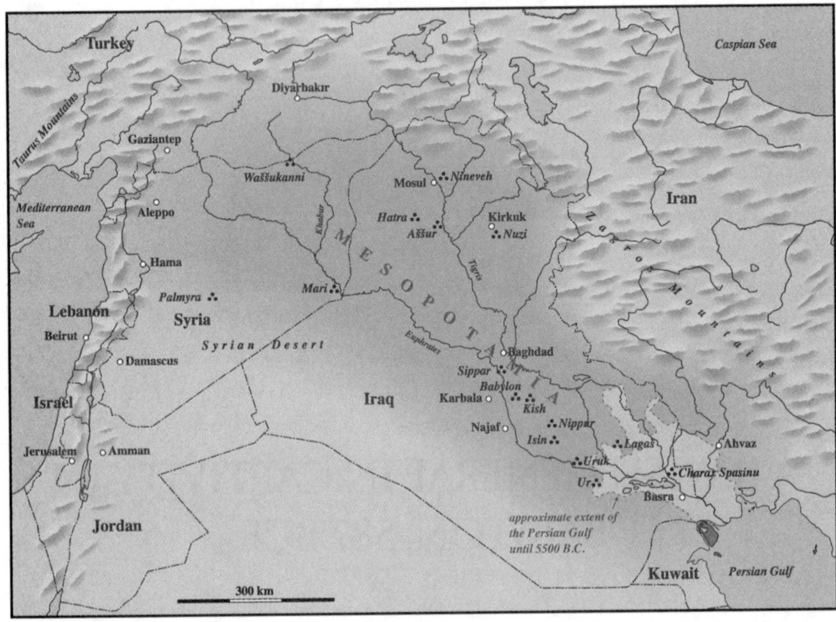

to accept that I had been with Yeshua, and that I as a humble person with an average life could have stood next to this great being.

Later through many more readings, past life regressions, and my own meditations, I would learn that I had been with many masters throughout time. I would even help some of them on their path, sometimes when they were still considered average men or women. Many were so different in their day that they were ostracized or ignored by their contemporaries. It often took a long period of time before humanity caught up with their great ideas and visions and recognized them as advanced beings.

More than ten years have now passed since my first past life reading. After the first, it took me three years to have a second one, because I needed this time to get comfortable and digest the information that I had obtained. The next readings followed two and three years after second one, and eventually I got to the point where I finally found a past life regressionist with whom I felt entirely comfortable. The work with him added greatly to my maturation in dealing with past lives and also helped me develop my own intuitive powers to a greater extent over the course of several past life regressions. In hindsight, I believe that a personal reflection upon past lives is a key component of one's spiritual development.

Before Ahtun Re told me anything about my past life as an Essene, he wanted me to tell him what I knew of the Essenes and what scholars generally think of the group. By that time I knew that the Roman historian Pliny the Elder stated that the Essenes were members of a small Jewish religious order originating in the second century BCE, but that later the Essenes were thought to be one of the three orders of Jews that formed after the destruction of the during the Second Temple Period Temple and the time frame Fm speaking of in this chapter. Only later I found out that their roots probably go back much farther in time.

When the Dead Sea Scrolls were discovered in the Essene city of Qumran between 1947 and 1956, it was initially thought that the sect consisted of only adult males and that celibacy was encouraged. The Essenes seemed to have lived as a highly organized community that held possessions in common. Ceremonial purity entailed scrupulous cleanliness, the wearing of only white garments, and the strict observance of the Sabbath.

There is also evidence of Persian and Greek influences in the sect's thought. The Essenes subsisted by pastoral and agricultural activities and handicrafts; they avoided the manufacture of weapons. They embraced a frugal lifestyle, abhorred untruthfulness, and forbade oaths with the one exception that a new member would swear an oath after two years of probation. In this oath, the member pledged piety toward God, justice toward men, honesty with fellow Essenes, preservation of the sect's secrets, and proper transmission of its teachings. The belief in the immortality of the soul was a core tenet among the Essenes.

I found over time that Edgar Cayce's readings very well confirm my personal intuitions about the Essenes. In a reading about Mount Carmel, where an Essene community existed, he said, "The movement was not an Egyptian one, though adopted by those in another period, or an earlier period, and made a part of the whole movement. They took Jews and Gentiles alike as members. The Essenes were a group of individuals sincere in their purpose and yet not orthodox as to the rabbis of that particular period. They were students of what ye would call astrology, numerology, phrenology, and those phases of study of the return of individuals—or reincarnation."

In addition to all the above, many Essenes were also prophets or had the ability to see into the future. Having this ability was encouraged along with many other esoteric ideas. I also told Ahtun Re that I knew that Yeshua, Mary and Joseph, John the Baptist, Yeshua's uncle Joseph of Arimathea, and Mary Magdalene, along with many other family members of Yeshua and several of the disciples, were all of the Essene community.

Ahtun Re then began to relay to me how the Essenes became the keepers of the library and the scribes of the Judaic people after the fall of Jerusalem. When Nebuchadnezzar II of Babylon finally sacked the city of Jerusalem and destroyed Solomon's Temple in 587 BCE, he also enslaved virtually all of the people. All copies of the Torah that had been hidden within secret chambers in the walls of the Temple were destroyed. During this time period, it would be the Essenes who would rewrite the Torah and include other chapters.

Prior to his destruction of the Temple, Nebuchadnezzar II unsuccessfully attempted to invade Egypt in 601 BCE but was repulsed with heavy losses. This failure led to numerous rebellions among the states of the Levant, most of which owed allegiance to Babylon, including Judah. The king of Judah stopped paying tribute to Nebuchadnezzar and took a pro-Egyptian position. I have often wondered who these wicked leaders are throughout time and if they have a corresponding incarnation in current times.

The Iraqi dictator Saddam Hussein who would be toppled out of power by coalition forces led by the United States was the reincarnation of Nebuchadnezzar II. He even stated himself that he was the reincarnation of that former king. I stated in my book *The Intuitive Warrior* that when I first landed in Iraq in this lifetime, Hussein was ignominiously pulled out of a secret hiding place in the ground by US forces. I visited Babylon again in this life, and Saddam was actually in the process of rebuilding the ancient site. A massive new palace had been built on the site and new bricks were being made to rebuild the ancient walls. It's fascinating how the threads of long-ago times are interconnected with the present.

My reflections as a general in the army of Judah were that the king was making a poor deal with the Egyptian nobility by taking this stance. The agreement was that they would come to our defense if the mighty army of Babylon decided to rise against us for aligning ourselves with Egypt. But I and the other generals believed that the Egyptians were setting us up and would gladly desert us and avoid the confrontation with Nebuchadnezzar's army should he decide to attack us.

As it would turn out, Nebuchadnezzar would very quickly deal with our rebellion. Only two years later he assembled his army, invaded our lands, and laid siege to the city of Jerusalem. After he took the city the king was made a prisoner along with his court and other prominent citizens and craftsmen. Also taken was a sizable portion of the Jewish population of Judah, numbering about ten thousand. Among them was the prophet Ezekiel who would during his captivity become the author of the Book of Daniel. Ezekiel would prophesize the complete destruction of Judah, the enslavement of its people, but also its eventual freedom and return to prosperity. The Essene scholars would help him write his book in secret while in captivity.

Following the siege, Nebuchadnezzar installed Zedekiah, the king's uncle, as king of Judah. But against the strong recommendations of his generals and the prophet Jeremiah, Zedekiah decided to revolt against Babylon several years later in alliance with Pharaoh Hophra. The royal family of Judah had become arrogant and prone to foolish decision making against the advice of the nobles and prophets who advised them. They had become unconscious of their duties to serve the people and had let their egos cloud their decision making.

The people of Judah would pay a tremendous price for the haughty decisions of their monarchs when Nebuchadnezzar responded to this new insurrection in 589 BCE by invading and besieging Jerusalem once again. During the first siege, we had lasted only three months and were told that this was insufficient time for the armies of Egypt to respond. Consequently, we had built our defenses much stronger, dug plenty of new wells, and had crops and animals inside the walls that could sustain us indefinitely.

We were thus able to resist ten times longer as during the previous siege, but we were fighting a losing battle as the expected relief forces never arrived despite our repeated pleas and the promise from the Egyptians to send their army. During this new siege, "every worst woe befell the city, which drank the cup of God's fury to the dregs," as the Bible illustratively states. Eventually the empire that had built mighty palaces all along the Tigris and Euphrates rivers and the famous hanging gardens of Babylon was able to defeat us through an extensive tunneling system. Both our armies had fought several raging battles deep under the earth. We dug our own tunnels through which we had been able to collapse many of their tunnels, but they had finally surpassed us with one particular tunnel that collapsed a huge section of our once impregnable wall.

After Nebuchadnezzar broke through Jerusalem's walls, Zedekiah and his followers escaped through one of our secret tunnels that we had used as a supply route and for night raids. They would eventually be captured on the plains of Jericho and taken to Riblah on the northern frontier of Israel where Nebuchadnezzar had his headquarters during the campaign against Jerusalem. There, after witnessing his sons put to the sword one at a time, Zedekiah was blinded, bound, and taken captive to Babylon where he remained a prisoner until his death.

After the fall of Jerusalem, when Babylonian general Nebuzaraddan was sent to complete its destruction, Jerusalem was plundered and Solomon's Temple was completely destroyed. Most of the remaining members of the royal family as well as the priesthood, scholars, and scribes were taken into captivity as slaves in Babylon. The entire city was razed to the ground and its treasures taken to Babylon, including the furnishings of the Temple such as the golden vessels dedicated by King Solomon.

Gedaliah, who was not part of the royal family, would be installed as the new puppet ruler of the remnant of Judah. This smaller portion of Judah called the Yehud Province would also have a Babylonian garrison stationed at Mizpah, the new capital. On hearing this news, many of the Jews in Moab, Ammon, Edom, and in other countries returned to Judah believing that the worst was over.

But as if the royal family had not done enough already to destroy Judah, merely two months later a member of the imperial family assassinated Gedaliah and launched an attack that wiped out the Babylonian garrison. Most of the population that had remained and those who had returned started fleeing to Egypt knowing full well that a vicious reprisal would be forthcoming. Although the Egyptians had not helped us militarily before, they did provide refuge and settlements within their lands for the exiles of Judah.

The Babylonian army then made a third and final sweep through the reduced lands of Judah and killed or enslaved virtually all of the people who had not escaped. Only a small number of people were permitted to remain to tend to the land. A biblical text written around that time reports that "none remained except the poorest people of the land."

Right after the fall of the walled city of Jerusalem and our final military

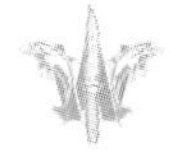

defeat, I was captured and taken to Babylon. As it has been for any military professional in the same position throughout time, as a general of the army I felt very frustrated and humiliated to see my people conquered and enslaved. The feelings of guilt that I experienced almost depressed me to the point of being completely useless. But I eventually shook off my melancholy and made the commitment to work behind the scenes to the best of my ability to help my people in any way that I possibly could. If there was even the slightest contribution I could make, I was determined to make it. For the first few years in Babylon, we suffered from severe oppression and mistreatment, but this gradually changed as more Jewish exiles arrived. With each new wave of exiles, the process of adapting to the demands and the culture of the Babylonians was getting easier, because those who had already arrived earlier assisted the succeeding exiles. The new groups would thus overcome psychological stresses much faster than those who had arrived before them.

Babylon from my past life memories was an architectural marvel for its day. The walls around the main city were wide enough that two chariots could ride on them side by side, and the waters of the Euphrates River were used to create a paradise of exotic vegetation throughout the city. Archimedean screw pumps were fashioned to rotate with the water current to pull water up to the top of the hanging gardens. There it would nourish the plants, create waterfalls and fountains, and feed the aqueducts and piping systems that traversed the city.

The hanging gardens that seemed to be floating far above ground consisted of many platforms on multiple stories that had hanging plants growing down the walls so that the walls were completely hidden. On the terraces were different fruit-bearing trees, palm and date trees, flowering trees and bushes, and many varieties of flowering plants. Stairways that were covered with different colored grasses and hidden from view from the ground by vegetation connected the terraces, enabling people to stroll on the pathways and rest in the seating areas.

Vast quantities of food and wine gathered from the fertile irrigated lands up and down the valleys of the Tigris and Euphrates rivers were stored in massive storage vats inside the city. The many gates of the city were adorned and covered in brilliant blue tiles with skillfully designed exotic creatures on them. Roads made of bitumen ran through the inner city and outside the city in long thoroughfares, making it easy for carts and chariots to move quickly within the city and its environs.

Even compared to our modern world, the wealth of Babylon was staggering with ornate gold and silver doors and statuary in many parks and along the avenues and squares. Precious jewels encrusted the inner walls of many homes of the nobility, in which costly rugs and richly embroidered pillows were available for large numbers of guests. Exquisite woods were used to make furniture of every description carved in ornate and artistic designs. The clothing of most of the people was of fine linens richly embroidered, and the women wore exotic jewelry from the far ends of the vast kingdom.

Some of the prisoners from Judah adapted well to this new environment and even became well respected, rising to high positions within the Babylonian nobility. One of these Jewish exiles was the prophet Daniel, who had been among the young Jewish nobility initially carried off to Babylon. He and his friends Shadrach, Meshach, and Abednego were chosen for their intellect and beauty to be trained as advisers to the Babylonian court.

Since their ancient origins, the Essenes had trained many prophets throughout time. The training was intensive and took many years of study and practice. Not just members who were born into the sect but anyone who showed a genuine desire and proclivity to the deeper mysteries of life was eligible to be trained in the wisdom, knowledge, and arts of the Essenes.

During their lifetimes, not all of these prophets were regarded in a positive light. The prophet Jeremiah, for example, was called the "weeping prophet" because he was ridiculed, humiliated, and mistreated for years by his own people. After he had prophesied that the royal family would cause much of the hardships that would befall Judah, he was attacked by his own brothers, imprisoned, threatened with death, and thrown into a cistern by Judah's officials. When Nebuchadnezzar seized Jerusalem in 587 BCE, he freed Jeremiah from prison and ordered that he be treated well.

Many of the prophets who had been trained by the Essenes were highly regarded, sought after, and often rewarded by leaders of other countries. Remember the prophet Yuya who had interpreted the Egyptian pharaoh's dreams and predicted that seven years of plenty would be followed by seven years of famine? Yuya would eventually become the right-hand man of the pharaoh, but like Jeremiah he was mistreated and ended up in slavery after being betrayed by his own brothers.

It was this kind of treatment that would drive the Essenes into deeper secrecy for the protection of their wisdom. But even Yeshua, their later and most famous member, would eventually die at the hands of an oppressive regime and a society that didn't realize the significance of his mission. John Wesley, cofounder of the Methodist Church, commented on this saying, "No prophet is acceptable in his own country—that is, in his own neighborhood. It generally holds that a teacher sent from God is not so acceptable to his neighbors as he is to strangers. The meanness of his family or lowness of his circumstances bring his office into contempt: nor can they suffer that he, who was before equal with or below themselves, should now bear a superior character."

In the biblical Book of Daniel it is recorded that in the second year of the reign of Nebuchadnezzar II, the king has a disturbing dream and asks his wise men to interpret it, but he refuses to divulge its content. When they protest he sentences all of them, including Daniel and his friends, to death. Daniel, then requests from Arioch, the captain of the guard, that his execution might be postponed so that he can petition his God for a solution.

After having prayed to God to receive a revelation about the king's dream, God's messenger, Archangel Gabriel, reveals the dream's mystery to Daniel in a vision that night. Daniel then praises God for enabling these intuitive insights, which was in alignment with Daniel's education where sincere gratitude is considered a key in activating and developing intuitive abilities.

When he meets with Arioch again, Daniel is granted access to the king and relays to him the description of the dream as well as its interpretation. Nebuchadnezzar had dreamed of an enormous idol made of four metals and feet of mixed iron and clay, which gets destroyed completely by a rock that turns into a huge mountain. The idol's composition of metals is interpreted as a series of successive kingdoms, starting with Nebuchadnezzar's. Finally, all of these dominions are crushed by God's kingdom, a kingdom that will "endure forever."

With Daniel's successful interpretation, the king expresses homage and praises the power of Daniel's God as he revealed to him the mystery of his dream. Daniel is then promoted as chief governor over the whole province of Babylon. At Daniel's request, his companions are also promoted, and thus they remain at the king's court.

Nebuchadnezzar later recounts another dream of a huge tree, which is suddenly cut down at the command of a heavenly messenger. Daniel, who was summoned to interpret the dream, says that the tree is Nebuchadnezzar himself, who for seven years will lose his mind restored when Nebuchadnezzar eventually acknowledges that "heaven rules."

In Daniel's later years, he would also be an assistant to the Babylonian king Belshazzar. After defeating the Persian army of Cyrus the Great outside the city's walls and routing them, Belshazzar held a great feast for all his nobles. In a drunken state, the king calls for the sacred vessels that had been captured from Solomon's Temple and blasphemously drinks from them, when suddenly the fingers of a man's hand appear before the king and write on the wall of the palace.

None of his wise men were able to interpret the message, so at the suggestion of his wife, Nitocris, he summoned Daniel and asked that he interpret the message for him. Daniel deciphers its meaning, saying that Belshazzar is about to lose his kingdom to the Medes and the Persians. For successfully reading the cryptic handwriting, Daniel was rewarded with a purple robe and elevated to the rank of "third ruler" of the kingdom.

In the very same night and while they were still drinking, Cyrus's army, led by General Gobryas, infiltrated Babylon. By diverting the flow of the Euphrates River into irrigation channels, Gobryas was able to lower the level of the river that was flowing into the city so that his armies could storm the city from the riverbank by wading through an opening under the city's walls and enter Babylon without opposition. The Babylonian citizens actually welcomed the invading army, because they detested Belshazzar, who was soon after slain by the Persians.

Many years later after the Persian conquest of Babylon, Daniel became one of three senior administrators of the empire during the reign of Darius the Mede. But when Darius decided to grant unprecedented powers to Daniel, the other officials plotted against Daniel. Unable to uncover any corruption, they used his religious devotion to defeat Daniel, as they tricked the king into issuing an irrevocable decree that for a thirty-day period no god was to be worshiped.

When Daniel continued to pray three times a day toward Jerusalem, he was thrown into a den of lions, much to the distress of Darius. But surprisingly,

the lions' mouths didn't even open and the animals showed no aggression in any way. Daniel was then delivered and his opponents thrown into the den where they were devoured instantly.

Remember that part of the training of the ancient Egyptians was to be able to be at one with the animal kingdom. After Moses had conducted the Exodus and I had trained Joshua and others in the secrets of sacred warfare, this information was carried forward in the secret training of the Essenes. The secret training that Daniel had continued throughout the exile of the Jews allowed him to integrate the deeper mysteries of calling the animals to conscious alignment through his heartfelt energies of love. Of course Darius's priests, as could be determined by their actions, were in no way able to step into this alignment and were thus eaten.

Another demonstration of the amazing capabilities that the secret teachings from the Essenes were providing for the Babylonians was the furnace story of the three friends of Daniel. Shadrach, Meshach, and Abednego had ignored a proclamation demanded by the citizens to bow before a new golden idol when a horn was sounded. The idol was nine stories tall and located in what is present-day Karbala, Iraq, where coincidentally today there is a sacred mosque with a golden dome that pilgrims come to bow before.

During the dedication ceremony of the golden image, certain officials noticed Shadrach, Meshach, and Abednego not bowing down to the idol upon hearing the cue of instruments, for which the known punishment was execution in a fiery furnace. Burning as a form of execution was a typical practice of Babylonian rulers. In the Code of Hammurabi, the Babylonian system of law set forth in the eighteenth century BCE, burning appears twice as a penalty for certain crimes. In an earlier period of the exile, Nebuchadnezzar had already burned to death two men named Zedekiah and Ahab.

Nebuchadnezzar was enraged about the disobedience to the golden idol and demanded that these three men who dared to act in such a way come before him. He then immediately recognized them, because it wasn't too long ago when Daniel had petitioned the king to assign Shadrach, Meshach, and Abednego as advisers to the Babylonian court. Because of Daniel's merits and his close connection to them, Nebuchadnezzar offered them another chance to show their patriotism to Babylon.

In their defense they said, "O Nebuchadnezzar, we do not need to defend ourselves before you in this matter. If we are thrown into the blazing furnace, the God we serve is able to save us from it, and He will rescue us from your hand, oh king. But even if He does not, we want you to know, oh king, that we will not serve your gods or worship the image of gold you have set up."

Nebuchadnezzar demanded that the execution furnace should be heated seven times hotter than usual, and valiant soldiers of the king's army were ordered to firmly bind the fully clothed Shadrach, Meshach, and Abednego and cast them in the blazing furnace. Already upon approaching the mouth of the furnace, the fire was so hot that the soldiers perished while attempting to throw in the three tightly bound friends.

Mastery over the elements was one of the secret training rituals that the three men had undergone, and so the fire from the furnace released them from their ties but did not harm them. When the king saw the men unbound and walking about, he ordered them to come out. He then acknowledged the power of their God, even going as far as to make a decree whereby any contemptuous remark by any nation against the God of the Jews would be viewed as an act of war. Shadrach, Meshach, and Abednego were then reinstated in their positions and even promoted.

The amazing spiritual training by the Essenes that many of the prophets underwent was setting impressive examples for the Babylonians. The prophets had warned the people in general as well as the royal family and priesthood in particular that they were deviating from their inherited wisdom, that they failed to honor the divine heritage from previous generations. After the level of consciousness had decreased over time, now, with the help of the people from Judah, a deep cleansing of the egos and psyches began to awaken the Babylonians, who would start to see the prophets in a renewed light. They were able to renounce their old egoic ways and embrace the conscious awareness of their true divine selves. This heritage was not only meant to benefit Jews but also Gentiles.

Another part of our teachings and beliefs that would prove to be beneficial to the Babylonians were the Psalms of Solomon. Although not all of them can be attributed to King Solomon, as Akhenaten was the author of some of them, we had nonetheless adopted them at the core of our culture. Our people in exile often sang songs from the Psalms of Solomon, which were overheard

by the people of Babylon who liked them so much that they would request them to be sung to them often. It was by this method also that the people of Babylon began to adopt some of our ways and ideas for their own benefit.

But it was not only the Babylonians that were learning new and valuable spiritual information. The exiles from Judah also profited from the inspiration they got from Zoroastrianism, which was at one time one of the world's largest religions and virtually the state religion of Babylon at the time of the exile. Interestingly, Zoroaster was a previous incarnation of Jesus, according to Edgar Cayce. I will expand more on the underlying ideas of Zoroastrianism in the next chapter about Cyrus the Great, who had also been greatly influenced by these teachings.

I respected and benefited from this new information as well, but during the time of my exile I was mostly focused on creating a secret network to preserve the core concepts of Judaism and the methods of the secret training of our prophets and priesthood. This network was also instrumental in the rewriting of the Torah. Many of the books of the prophets from the Old Testament were also begun in this time period. Edgar Cayce would expand on this in one of his trance readings where he said, "Know that the same soul entity that became Jesus born in Bethlehem was Jeshua who reasoned with those who returned from captivity in those days when Nehemiah, Ezra, Zerubbabel were factors in the attempts of the reestablishing of the worship of God, and that Jeshua, the scribe, translated the rest of the books written up to that time."

Jeshua was the high priest who helped organize the return from exile. He would lead the Jews from Babylon to Israel and supervise the rebuilding of the Temple in Jerusalem as recounted in the books of Ezra and Nehemiah. Jeshua rekindled the kingdom of Judah so that the unconsciousness that had existed before the exile would be cleansed; a return to consciousness or divine inspiration was achieved yet again. The people of Judah would slowly rebuild their kingdom and live many centuries in prosperity and relative peace.

Jeshua is claimed by Cayce to have compiled and translated the books of the Bible after Darius defeated the Babylonians and set the Jews free to return to their homeland. According to Cayce, Jeshua had also been Joshua in a previous life, the man to whom I had taught lessons in sacred warfare after the Exodus from Egypt. I would help and work with this same soul again in another lifetime, where he would carry the same name of Yeshua or Jesus, as we know him today.

Throughout lifetimes you are aligning with soul groups to work together to bring in needed energies and abilities to advance your own spiritual development as well as that of a whole group of people. But it doesn't stop within a confined group, as could be seen in this lifetime where two different cultures would meet and learn from each other. It was a challenging lifetime, but also one that would be very helpful in transforming great numbers of people.

We also learned to stay cohesive and keep our culture alive even though on the surface Nebuchadnezzar's army had destroyed most of its former glory. As time went by, many of the Jews had a better life in exile than they did in their homeland, and thus when it was time for us to return, many chose to stay. The ability to survive, adapt, and excel in a hostile environment while still maintaining their traditions has been a trademark for the Jewish people ever since the exile and an example from which all people can learn.

My own life lessons were many as well. I would learn humbleness in adversity and perseverance when things were at their worst. You can always find a way to help and make a positive difference to any situation if you keep your focus on this idea. I would learn how to create a network that would work behind the scenes and often right under the noses of our captors, keeping our culture alive for us and for future generations.

Because of this, it was possible to continue to train more prophets who would later play important roles as spiritual guides. During the exile, an increased awareness of the value of our prophets and their information was to spring forth. I would interact with many of these prophets, such as Habakkuk, Jeremiah, Obadiah, Ezekiel, and Daniel.

Working with them, understanding their needs, and quietly providing them with what they needed imparted an important life lesson that would prepare me very well for my next lifetime, where I would continue to support their righteous mission even though they would be of another culture in that life.

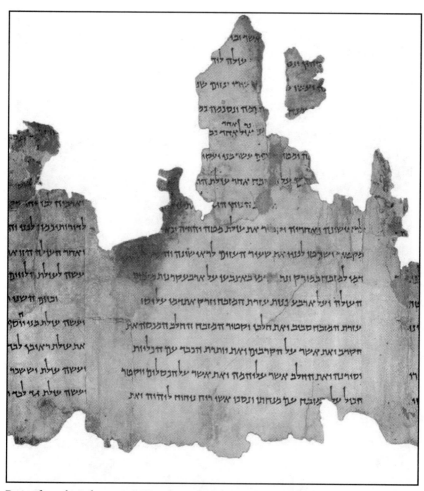

Dating from the 3rd century BCE to the 1st century CE, the Dead Sea Scrolls are considered to be a keystone in the history of archaeology with great historical, religious, and linguistic significance because they include the oldest surviving manuscripts of entire books later included in the biblical canons, along with deuterocanonical and extra-biblical manuscripts which preserve evidence of the diversity of religious thought in late Second Temple Judaism. A view of part of the Temple Scroll that was found in Qumran Cave 11.

The Dead Sea Scrolls are ancient Hebrew religious manuscripts discovered in 1946 and 1947 at the Qumran Caves in what was then Mandatory Palestine, near Ein Feshkha in the West Bank, on the northern shore of the Dead Sea.

This engraving, probably made in the 19th century after the first excavations in the Assyrian capitals, depicts the fabled Hanging Gardens o Babylon, with the Tower of Babel in the background.

The Exodus is the story of the Israelites whose narrative is spread over four books of the Torah (or Pentateuch, corresponding to the first five books of the Bible), namely Exodus, Leviticus, Numbers, and Deuteronomy. This painting called *Departure of the Israelites* was created by David Roberts in 1829.

The word 'Torah' in Hebrew means 'to guide' or 'to teach' The meaning of the word is therefore 'teaching,' 'doctrine,' or 'instruction.' The commonly accepted 'law' gives a wrong impression. The Torah scroll pictured here is in old Glockengasse Synagogue in Cologne, Germany.

"THERE IS A DEEP—AND USUALLY FRUSTRATED—DESIRE IN THE HEART OF EVERYONE TO ACT WITH BENEVOLENCE RATHER THAN SELFISHNESS, AND ONE FINE INSTANCE OF GENEROSITY CAN INSPIRE DOZENS MORE."

◊ *Cyrus the Great* ◊

CHAPTER 14

CYRUS THE GREAT, UNIFIER OF THE PERSIAN EMPIRE, 600-529 BCE

Cyrus II of Persia was the founder of the first Persian Empire and considered the "father of the Iranian nation." From their heartland of Parsua, which was located between the Tigris River and the Persian Gulf, the Persians under Cyrus conquered the Median, Lydian, and Babylonian empires. All of these would be successfully incorporated into the Persian Achaemenid Empire, named after King Achaemenes, who had ruled one hundred years before Cyrus.

At its height, almost half of the world's population lived within this vast empire that reached from the Dardanelles in the west to the Indus River in the east. As the founder of this empire, Cyrus had been an archetypal embodiment of a wise empire builder, which would also earn him the title "the Great." I would have several lifetimes in which this title would be bestowed to me again, and in all of these lifetimes I would essentially emulate the model that I will lay out in this chapter.

Cyrus was the grandson of Astyages, who was the king of Medes. Astyages ruled in alliance with his two brothers-in-law, Croesus of Lydia and Nebuchad-

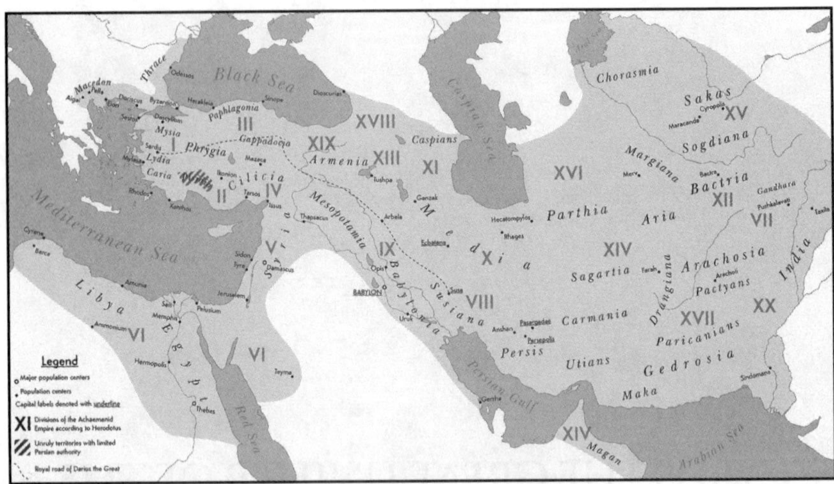

nezzar of Babylon. The reign of Astyages was noted for both its stability and for the growth of Zoroastrianism throughout his empire. Astyages would arrange the marriage of his daughter Mandane to King Cambyses of Anshan, because Astyages considered him to pose no threat to the Median throne. Astyages had a dream that his daughter would one day give birth to one who would rule Asia, but after the birth of her first child, Cyrus, Astyages had another dream that his priest interpreted as a sign that his grandson would eventually overthrow him.

He thus ordered Harpagus, a general of his army, to kill the infant. But Harpagus, morally unable to kill a newborn, summoned a royal bandit herdsman named Mitradates from a nearby mountainous region and ordered him to leave the baby to die in the mountains. Luckily, the herdsman and his wife took pity and raised the child as their own, passing off their recently stillborn infant as the murdered Cyrus.

When Cyrus was ten years old, it became obvious to many that he was not a herdsman's son, because his behavior seemed too noble. This was brought to Astyages's attention, and he decided to interview the boy. Astyages noticed that they resembled each other, so he ordered Harpagus to explain what he had actually done with his grandson. Harpagus confessed that he had not killed the boy, which lead Astyages to have Harpagus's thirteen-year-old son killed, chopped up, broiled, and served to Harpagus, who wasn't told that there was anything extraordinary about his meal.

After the meal, Astyages had a covered basket brought in with Harpagus's dearly beloved son's head in it. As Harpagus removed the lid of the basket, Astyages asked him if he perceived of what animal flesh the meal had been prepared. Keeping his composure, Harpagus replied that he was aware of what he had been eating and that whatsoever the king might do was pleasing to him.

Astyages was more lenient with the young Cyrus and allowed him to return to his biological parents, Cambyses and Mandane. Though his father died in 551 BCE, Cyrus had already succeeded to the throne of Anshan eight years prior, although not yet as an independent ruler. Like his predecessors, Cyrus had to recognize Astyages's status as overlord. Due greatly to his humble upbringing, Cyrus stepped into his new role with great magnanimity. The Greek historian Xenophon quotes him as saying, "When I became rich, I realized that no kindness between man and man comes more naturally than sharing food and drink, especially food and drink of the ambrosial excellence that I could now provide. Accordingly, I arranged that my table be spread everyday for many invitees, all of whom would dine on the same excellent food as myself. After my guests and I were finished, I would send out any extra food to my absent friends, in token of my esteem." Cyrus also made it clear that he greatly appreciated this attitude in others, proclaiming that "men who respond to good fortune with modesty and kindness are harder to find than those who face adversity with courage."

Over time, Cyrus became increasingly dissatisfied with his grandfather's policies as he realized that they were not inspired by the values that Cyrus considered to be essential for the rule of a king. So together with Harpagus, who was still seeking vengeance for the murder of his son, Cyrus rallied the Persian people to revolt against the Medes. The first battles took place in early 552 BCE, and in 549 BCE Harpagus and Cyrus eventually captured Ecbatana, effectively conquering the Median Empire.

With Astyages out of power, Cyrus accepted the crown of Media. He then went on to unite the twin Achaemenid kingdoms of Parsa and Anshan, assuming the title "king of Persia." His uncle, Arsames, who had been the king of the city-state of Parsa under the Medes, therefore had to give up his throne. This transfer of power within the family occurred smoothly, not least because Arsames would still remain the nominal governor of Parsa under Cyrus's authority.

Alarmed by Cyrus's growing influence, the Lydians under King Croesus successfully besieged and captured the Achaemenid city of Pteria in Cappadocia, enslaving its inhabitants. Meanwhile, the Persians invited the citizens of Ionia, who were part of the Lydian kingdom, to revolt against their ruler. The offer was rebuffed, and thus Cyrus levied an army and marched against the Lydians, increasing his numbers while passing through nations in his way. The ensuing battle against the Lydians that again took place at Pteria was effectively a stalemate, with both sides suffering heavy casualties by nightfall.

Croesus retreated to his capital, Sardis, the following morning and sent out requests to his allies to send aid to Lydia, not expecting that Cyrus would pursue him during the harsh winter season. But before the allies could unite, Cyrus pushed the war into Lydian territory and besieged Croesus in Sardis. Shortly before the final battle between the two rulers, Harpagus advised Cyrus the Great to place his dromedaries in front of his warriors to scare the Lydian horses that were not accustomed to the dromedaries' smell. This strategy worked and the Lydian cavalry was routed. Cyrus conquered the Lydian kingdom but kept Croesus as an adviser, as I had described in an earlier chapter.

A Lydian named Pactyas was then entrusted by Cyrus to gather Croesus's riches and send them to Persia, but soon after Cyrus's departure Pactyas hired mercenaries and caused an uprising in Sardis, revolting against the Persian governor of Lydia. To quench the revolt, Croesus recommended turning the minds of the Lydian people to luxury. "By doing this," Croesus advised, "the people will, in a short time, become so enervated and so effeminate that you will have nothing to fear from them." This kind of distraction is a simple and effective tool of mind control to weaken a population, one that we should also be very aware of today where many have become utterly dependent on modern amenities or addicted to an ostentatious entertainment culture.

Cyrus also sent Mazares, one of his commanders, to subdue the insurrection and return Pactyas to him. Upon Mazares's arrival, Pactyas fled to Ionia where he would hire more mercenaries. Nevertheless, Mazares, who also subdued the Greek cities of Magnesia and Priene, eventually captured him. Mazares then continued his conquest of Asia Minor but died during a campaign in Ionia. To complete Mazares's conquest, Cyrus sent Harpagus, who captured Lycia, Cilicia, and Phoenicia using the technique of build-

ing earthworks to breach the walls of besieged cities, a method hitherto unknown to the Greeks.

Though feared in battle, Harpagus followed Cyrus's policy of tolerance and freedom of religion toward those he conquered. Interestingly, there was one city that Mazares entirely spared following Cyrus's order, and that city was Miletus. As you will remember, this was the city where I was living as Thales in a parallel incarnation. Because Miletus had stayed neutral in the war between Croesus and Cyrus, according to Thales's advice, it had earned the favor of Cyrus and was allowed to remain sovereign. Mazares eventually ended his conquest in Asia Minor in 542 BCE, returned to Persia, and was later appointed governor of Asia Minor.

In the year 540 BCE, Cyrus also started a campaign against the Neo-Babylonian Empire under King Nabonidus, capturing Elam and its capital, Susa, north of the Persian Gulf. Following this defeat, Nabonidus ordered many cult statues from outlying Babylonian cities to be taken out of their sanctuaries and brought into the capital of Babylon. This was considered a sacrilege by Cyrus, for whom it confirmed that Nabonidus was unfit to rule. Cyrus's next important battle would be fought near Opis, which was a strategic riverside city on the Tigris, north of Babylon. The Babylonian army was routed and when Cyrus attacked the city of Sippar; it was seized with little to no resistance from the populace as the Babylonian generals ordered their army to stand down to avoid an armed confrontation. Nabonidus was staying in the city at the time but made his escape to Babylon.

Two days later, the Persian troops entered Babylon without any difficulties, owing to the ruse of Croesus who had the idea to divert the flow of the Euphrates River, as I had described in a preceding chapter. Cyrus's troops easily detained Nabonidus, as the Babylonian army would again stand down. Cyrus then returned the statues that Nabonidus gathered in Babylon to their original sanctuaries. Pleased with himself, Cyrus stated, "As for the gods of Sumer and Akkad, which Nabonidus, to the wrath of the lord of the gods, brought to Babylon, at the command of Marduk, the great lord, I caused them to dwell in peace in their sanctuaries, pleasing dwellings. May all the gods I brought to their sanctuaries plead daily before Bel and Nabu for the lengthening of my days, may they intercede favorably on my behalf."

Prior to Cyrus's invasion of Babylon, the Neo-Babylonian Empire had conquered many kingdoms, including Syria, Judea, and Arabia Petraea, all of which would be incorporated by Cyrus into his empire. After taking Babylon, Cyrus proclaimed himself "king of Babylon, king of Sumer and Akkad, king of the four corners of the world," as can be read on the famous Cyrus Cylinder that had been deposited in the foundations of the Esagila Temple dedicated to Marduk, the chief Babylonian god. The text on the cylinder denounces Nabonidus as impious and portrays the victorious Cyrus pleasing the god Marduk. It describes how Cyrus had improved the lives of the citizens of Babylonia, repatriated displaced peoples, and restored temples and cult sanctuaries.

Cyrus was convinced that his empire could only thrive if it would be infused with the spirit of genuine care and mutual respect. He said, "Success always calls for greater generosity—though most people, lost in the darkness of their own egos, treat it as an occasion for greater greed. Collecting booty is not an end itself, but only a means for building an empire. Riches would be of little use to us now except as a means of winning new friends."

The principles according to which Cyrus built his empire were revolutionary in his time and still serve as a reminder today to be humble and considerate in order to create peace among us. At the opening of the first United Nations Conference on Human Rights in Tehran in 1968, Shah Mohammed Reza Pahlavi of Iran even went as far as stating that the guidelines that were inscribed on the Cyrus Cylinder were the precursor to the modern Universal Declaration of Human Rights. "The history of our empire began with the famous declaration of Cyrus, which, for its advocacy of humane principles, justice, and liberty, must be considered one of the most remarkable documents in the history of mankind," he said. Inspired by Cyrus's example, the shah launched a series of economic, social, and political reforms with the proclaimed intentions of transforming Iran into a global power, modernizing the nation by nationalizing certain industries, and granting women suffrage.

However, because of his strong policy of secularization and the atrocities that were committed during his reign, mainly at the behest of the prime minister as the shah's political power was very limited, the clergy and substantial parts of the population overthrew the shah in 1979. Today, when the Iranian government still doesn't acknowledge all of the basic human rights and as Ira-

nians look back at the shah in a more positive light, Cyrus's appeal to hold individual liberty as the greatest good within a society hasn't lost anything of its actuality and importance. Cyrus had made his standpoint perfectly clear by stating, "Whenever you can, act as a liberator. Freedom, dignity, wealth—these three together constitute the greatest happiness of humanity. If you bequeath all three to your people, their love for you will never die."

Cyrus founded his empire as a multi-state empire governed from the four capital cities of Pasargadae, Babylon, Susa, and Ecbatana, allowing a certain amount of regional autonomy in each state in the form of a satrapy system. A satrapy was an administrative unit, usually organized on a geographical basis. A satrap, or governor, was the vassal king administering the region, while a general supervised military recruitment and ensured order, and a state secretary kept official records. The general and the state secretary reported directly to the satrap as well as to the central government. Cyrus also organized newly conquered territories into provinces ruled by satraps, receiving tributes and conscripts from the many areas of his empire. He maintained control over the vast region of conquered kingdoms by flexibly retaining and expanding the satrapies according to the particular circumstances. He also created what was the first pony express system of mail delivery. Through several relay stations his vast empire could receive orders or information within days instead of months as with older methods.

Militarily, Cyrus's leadership was reminiscent of Spartan ideals, which comes as no surprise considering the past lifetime as Lycurgus. Cyrus stated that "brevity is the soul of command. Too much talking suggests desperation on the part of the leader. Speak shortly, decisively, and to the point—and couch your desires in such natural logic that no one can raise objections. Then move on." Through his military expertise, Cyrus created a very organized army including the Immortals unit, consisting of ten thousand highly trained special forces soldiers.

Cyrus also became known for his building projects. He further developed the technologies that he found in the lands he conquered and applied them in new building projects like in the city of Pasargadae. Research on Pasargadae's structural engineering has shown that Achaemenid engineers built the city to withstand a severe earthquake, or what would today be classified as 7.0 on the Richter magnitude scale.

Something that has carried over into my current life is Cyrus's love for gardens. His capital of Pasargadae was the site of two magnificent palaces surrounded by a majestic royal park and vast formal gardens that have been revealed in recent excavations together with a network of irrigation canals. Among these gardens was the four-quartered wall garden of Paradisia with various types of wild and domestic flora and over one thousand yards of channels made out of carved limestone, designed to fill small basins every seventeen yards. The design concept of Paradisia was exceptional and has been used as a model for many ancient and modern parks ever since, and where we get the word "paradise."

His focus on beauty and harmony would enable Cyrus to create an administrative framework that was largely free from corruption and strife, that was relatively peaceful, prosperous, had human rights, justice, an educational system available to the masses, and strong spiritual teachings to genuinely support the spiritual growth of the population. These elements constitute a solid foundation for the advancement of human consciousness, a foundation that I would successfully help to create numerous times throughout history.

While Cyrus had been tolerant toward all religions and sought counsel from a variety of sources, the state religion in his empire was Zoroastrianism, which was founded by the prophet Zoroaster during the reign of King Vishtaspa several hundred years before Cyrus. Vishtaspa had been one of my earlier incarnations. But it can be an illustrative point to mention here because it shows a pattern of incarnations to help achieve altruistic goals for humanity. What we don't accomplish in one lifetime can become the labor of future lifetimes.

As mentioned in the Avesta, which is the primary collection of sacred texts of Zoroastrianism, Vishtaspa would be Zoroaster's patron and instrumental in the diffusion of the prophet's message. He formed the first Zoroastrian community and is described as a righteous king who helped defend the faith. Learning from masters and giving them the ability to teach would be something that I would focus on in many lifetimes, as I will continue to describe in future chapters.

Zoroaster was one of the most influential religious reformers in the history of the world. His monotheistic teachings held Ahura Mazda as the highest god and the creator of heaven and earth, or the spiritual and material world. He is said to be the source of the alternation of light and darkness, the sov-

ereign lawgiver, and the very center of nature as well as the originator of the moral order, the judge of the entire world. If you're seeing similarities to the Abrahamic religions, you are correct. These similarities are no coincidence, because Zoroaster was the reincarnation of Melchizedek, who had taught Abraham, and he would also be Jesus in a future lifetime. In another parallel soul incarnation, Edgar Cayce was the father of Zoroaster, showing the interconnection between Jesus, Cayce, and myself in many supporting incarnations as our souls develop toward mastery.

In Zoroastrianism, it is believed that there is a conflict involving the entire universe between truth and order on one side and chaos, falsehood, and disorder on the other. The religion states that humanity has an active role to play in this conflict, because active participation in life through good thoughts, words, and deeds ensures happiness and keeps chaos at bay. This active participation is a central element in Zoroaster's concept of free will. It is said that the conflict between order and disorder will only be solved when the "bounteous spirit," with which Ahura Mazda originally conceived of creation, ultimately prevails over the "destructive spirit," at which point the universe will undergo a cosmic renovation, and time as we know it will end.

Zoroaster implicitly taught the concept of linear time as opposed to the cyclic or static conceptions of many other ancient cultures, making the idea of progress, reform, and advancement possible. This was a revolutionary approach, because ancient civilizations at that time, particularly the Egyptians, believed that the ideal directive of man had been handed down to the priesthood by the gods during a golden age. Therefore the priests' task was to adhere to the established traditions as closely as possible and make sure that the people did not deviate in any way, because to reform or modify them in any way would be a diminution of the superlative state religion. The freeing of mankind from the priesthood so that they could individually connect with god as Zoroaster taught was an early echo of what would be even more defined in his future incarnation as Jesus.

Cyrus believed that humanity should actively further its own conscious evolution and not trust in outside forces to make the process happen for them. He also considered religions and philosophies to be subject to this process as well. For this reason, he allowed a variety of religious beliefs and practices throughout his empire. This progressive attitude was greatly appreciated by the populace. As the Greek historian Xenophon notes, "And those who were subject to him, he treated with esteem and regard, as if they were his own children, while his subjects themselves respected Cyrus as their 'father.' What other man but Cyrus, after having overturned an empire, ever died with the title of 'the father' from the people whom he had brought under his power? For it is plain fact that this is a name for one that bestows, rather than for one that takes away!"

Cyrus's general policy of religious tolerance throughout his vast empire is well documented in Babylonian texts as well as Jewish sources and many historians' accounts. The Babylonians regarded him as the "liberator," and after his conquest of Babylon, Cyrus's help was instrumental in the return of Jews from Babylon to their homeland. Glorified by Ezra and by Isaiah, Cyrus is said to be the one to whom Yahweh has given "all the kingdoms of the earth."

His treatment of the Jews during their exile in Babylon is also reported in the Jewish Bible, where it is said in Second Chronicles that Cyrus had issued a decree ordering the return of the exiles along with a commission to rebuild the Temple: "Thus saith Cyrus, king of Persia: All the kingdoms of the earth hath Yahweh, the God of heaven, given me; and He hath charged me to build Him a house in Jerusalem, which is in Judah. Whosoever there is among you of all His people—may Yahweh, his God, be with him—let him go there."

This edict is also fully reproduced in the *Book of Ezra*:

> *In the first year of King Cyrus, Cyrus the king issued a decree: Concerning the house of God at Jerusalem, let the Temple, the place where sacrifices are offered, be rebuilt and let its foundations be retained, its height being sixty cubits [one cubit was approximately twenty inches long] and its width sixty cubits; with three layers of huge stones and one layer of timbers. And let the cost be paid from the royal treasury. Also let the gold and silver utensils of the house of God, which Nebuchadnezzar took from the Temple in Jerusalem and brought to Babylon be returned and brought to their places in the Temple in Jerusalem; and you shall put them in the house of God.*

As a result of Cyrus's policies, the Jews honored him as a dignified and righteous king. He is the only Gentile to be designated as the "Lord's Messiah," a divinely appointed leader, in the Jewish Bible in the Book of Isaiah, where it also says, "I will raise up Cyrus in my righteousness: I will make all his ways straight. He will rebuild my city and set my exiles free, but not for a price or reward, says Yahweh Almighty." As the text suggests, Cyrus did ultimately release the nation of Israel from its exile without compensation or tribute. Josephus, the first century CE Jewish historian, relates the traditional view of the Jews regarding the prediction of Cyrus in Isaiah in his *Antiquities of the Jews:*

> *In the first year of the reign of Cyrus, which was the seventieth from the day that our people were removed out of their own land into Babylon, God commiserated the captivity and calamity of these poor people, according as he had foretold to them by Jeremiah the prophet, before the destruction of the city, that after they had served Nebuchadnezzar and his posterity, and after they had undergone that servitude seventy years, he would restore them again to the land of their fathers, and they should build their Temple, and enjoy their ancient prosperity.*
>
> *And these things God did afford them; for he stirred up the mind of Cyrus, and made him write this throughout all Asia: "Thus saith Cyrus the king: Since God Almighty hath appointed me to be king of the habitable earth, I believe that he is that God which the nation of the Israelites worship; for indeed he foretold my name by the prophets, and that I should build him a house at Jerusalem, in the country of Judea."*
>
> *This was known to Cyrus by his reading the book which Isaiah left behind him of his prophecies; for this prophet said that God had spoken thus to him in a secret vision: "My will is, that Cyrus, whom I have appointed to be king over many and great nations, send back my people to their own land, and build my Temple."*
>
> *Isaiah prophesied this one hundred and forty years before the Temple was demolished. Accordingly, when Cyrus read this, and admired the Divine power, an earnest desire and ambition seized upon him to fulfill what was so written; so he called for the most eminent Jews that were in Babylon, and said to them, that he gave them leave to go back to their own country, and to rebuild their city Jerusalem, and the Temple of God, for that he would be their assistant, and that he would write to the rulers and governors that were in the neighborhood of their country of Judea,*

that they should contribute to them gold and silver for the building of the Temple, and besides that, beasts for their sacrifices.

It doesn't seem so strange that Cyrus would be so helpful to the Jews when you take into account how many previous lifetimes this soul had as a Jew, does it? Living within various different cultures can help you develop a love for the entire human race. However, negative experiences in one lifetime can also cause you to develop a subconscious animosity against a certain group of people that you might carry with you over many lifetimes. Regardless of how gruesome some of our past life experiences may be, the only way to overcome the pain that was caused by one's mistreatment is through love and forgiveness. We should never tolerate abusive behavior, but carrying around the pain inflicted on us through many lifetimes will manifest similar experiences until we eventually face the source of why this is happening and process our pain. Learn to forgive whomever or whatever has done you harm in the past. Cyrus was instrumental in triggering such developments within vast groups of people by supporting reconciliation efforts wherever possible.

The higher energies that Cyrus channeled in his political life also came through in his dear love for his wife Cassandane, who loved Cyrus to the point that on her deathbed she is noted as having found it bitterer to leave Cyrus than to depart her life. According to the *Chronicle of Nabonidus,* when Cassandane died, all the nations of Cyrus's empire observed "a great mourning."

Together, Cyrus and Cassandane had four children: Cambyses II, who was the reincarnation of Alexander the Great and would succeed his father and conquer Egypt; Smerdis, who also reigned as the king of Persia for a short time; a daughter named Roxana; and another daughter named Atossa, who would later wed Darius the Great, the first Persian to invade Greece. Atossa played quite an important role in the Achaemenid royal family line, as she bore Darius the next Achaemenian king, Xerxes, who would be the second Persian king to invade Greece, leading the Persian troops in the famous battle at Thermopylae in which I would be involved on the Greek side as the Spartan general Pausanias, which I will describe in a later chapter.

Due in part to the political infrastructure Cyrus created, the Achaemenid Empire endured long after his death, carried on by many of his descendants. Cyrus's conquests began a whole new era in the age of empire building, where a

vast superstate, comprising many dozens of countries, races, religions, and languages, was ruled under a single administration headed by a central government. This system lasted for centuries and was in part retained by the Hellenistic Seleucid dynasty as well as by later Iranian dynasties including the Parthians and Sassanids.

According to Professor Richard Nelson Frye, Cyrus held an almost mythic role among the Persian people, "similar to that of Romulus and Remus in Rome or Moses for the Israelites." Frye writes, "He became the epitome of the great qualities expected of a ruler in antiquity, and he assumed heroic features as a conqueror who was tolerant and magnanimous as well as brave and daring. His personality as seen by the Greeks influenced them and Alexander the Great, and, as the tradition was transmitted by the Romans, may be considered to influence our thinking even now."

Cyrus met his fate in a fierce battle with the Massagetae, a tribe from the southernmost portion of the steppe regions of modern-day Kazakhstan and Uzbekistan, after following the ill advice of Croesus to attack them in their own territory. Cyrus first sent an offer of marriage to their queen, Tomyris, a proposal she rejected. He then commenced his attempt to take her territory by force, beginning by building bridges and towered war boats along his side of the Syr Darya River that separated them. Sending Cyrus a warning to cease his encroachment, in which she stated she expected he would disregard anyway, Tomyris challenged him to meet her forces in honorable warfare, inviting him to a location in her country a day's march from the river where the two armies would formally engage each other.

Cyrus accepted her offer, but learning that the Massagetae were unfamiliar with wine and its intoxicating effects, he set up and then left camp with plenty of it behind, taking his best soldiers with him and leaving the least capable ones. The general of Tomyris's army, who was also her son Spargapises, and a third of the Massagetian troops killed the group Cyrus had left there and—finding the camp well stocked with food and wine—unwittingly drank themselves into inebriation. With their diminished abilities to defend themselves, Cyrus was able to sneak back and overtake them in a surprise attack. They were successfully defeated and Spargapises was taken prisoner. Nevertheless, he managed to commit suicide once he regained sobriety.

Upon learning of what had transpired, Tomyris denounced Cyrus's tactics as underhanded and swore vengeance, leading a second wave of troops into a battle that Herodotus referred to as the fiercest battle of Cyrus's career and the ancient world. Cyrus the Great was ultimately killed and his forces suffered massive casualties. After the battle, Queen Tomyris ordered the body of Cyrus brought to her; she decapitated him and dipped his head in a vessel of blood in a symbolic gesture of revenge for his alleged bloodlust and the death of her son.

My thoughts on Cyrus's death at the hands of a woman are that he had brought this fate upon himself by having become too rigid as a warrior. Every one of us is guided by our internal masculine and feminine qualities—to either ignore or overly focus on one aspect will create problems, making the need for a balancing of these energies evident. If we don't achieve this balance in due time, we will manifest events that will teach us hard lessons in an attempt to achieve balance.

In spite of his inglorious end, Cyrus's achievements sent ripples throughout the ages and all over the world. Alexander the Great, who conquered the Achaemenid Empire two hundred years after Cyrus's death, admired Cyrus from an early age after reading Xenophon's *Cyropaedia,* which describes Cyrus's heroism in battle and governance and his abilities as a king and legislator. Thomas Jefferson, one of the Founding Fathers of the United States of America, was also inspired by the progressive ideas within the *Cyropaedia,* as were several Icelandic writers between the seventeenth and nineteenth century who rewrote the history of Cyrus.

In 2003, in her acceptance of the Nobel Peace Prize, the Iranian lawyer, judge, and human rights activist Shirin Ebadi also evoked Cyrus in her speech:

I am an Iranian, a descendant of Cyrus the Great. This emperor proclaimed at the pinnacle of power 2,500 years ago that he "would not reign over the people if they did not wish it." He promised not to force any person to change his religion and faith and guaranteed freedom for all. The charter of Cyrus the Great should be studied in the history of human rights.

As Cyrus said, "You cannot be buried in obscurity: you are exposed upon a grand theater to the view of the world. If your actions are upright and benevolent, be assured they will augment your power and happiness."

Never underestimate the power and impact of any of your actions, especially if they are infused with courage and love.

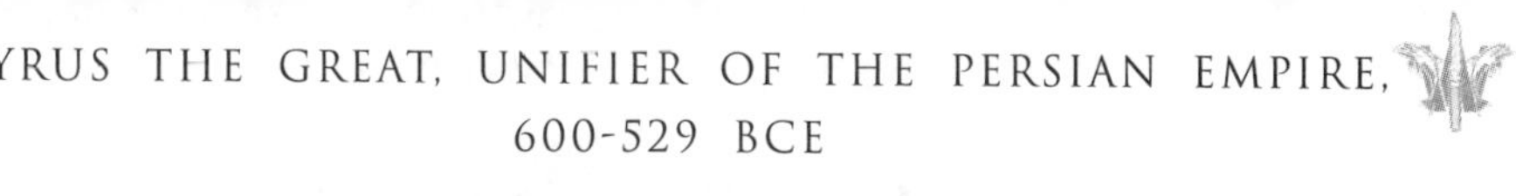

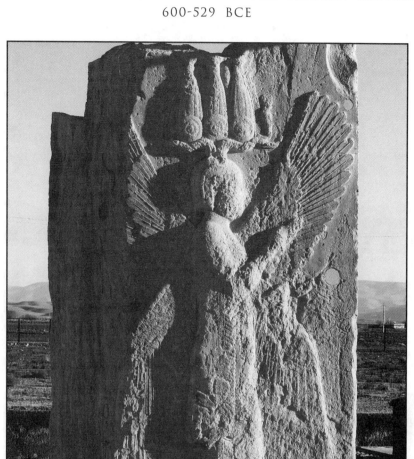

Cyrus the Great is depicted with a Hemhem crown, or four-winged Cherub tutelary divinity, from a relief in the residence of Cyrus in Pasagardae, Iran.

Pasargadae was the capital of the Achaemenid Empire under Cyrus the Great (559–530 BCE), who ordered its construction and the location of his tomb pictured here. Today it is an archaeological site and one of Iran's UNESCO World Heritage Sites, about 55 miles (90 km) to the northeast of the modern city of Shiraz.

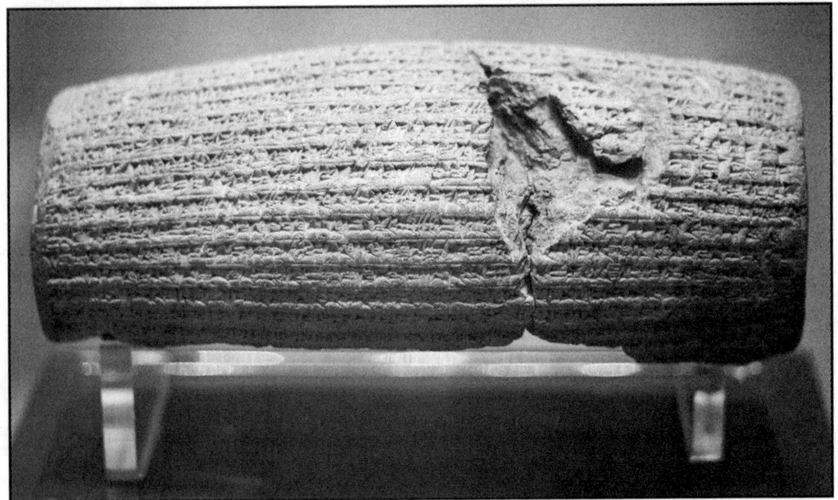

The Cyrus Cylinder is an ancient clay cylinder, now broken into several pieces, on which is written a declaration in Akkadian cuneiform script in the name of Persia's Achaemenid king Cyrus the Great It dates from the 6th century BCE and was discovered in the ruins of the ancient Mesopotamian city of Babylon (now in modern Iraq) in 1879.

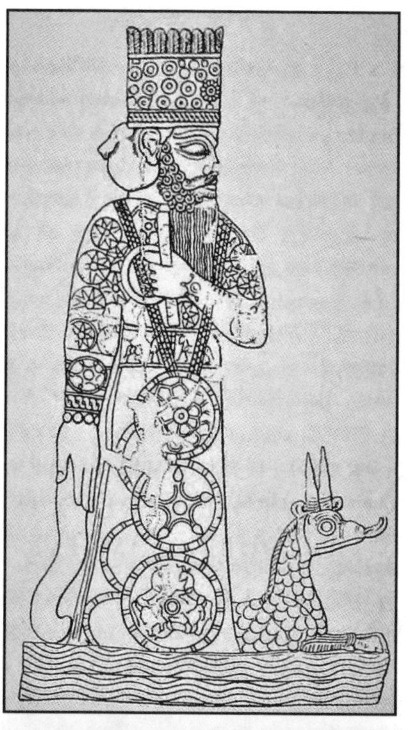

The "Statue of Marduk" depicted on a cylinder seal dates from the 9th century BCE. Babylonian king Marduk had a symbolic animal and servant, whom Marduk once vanquished, is the dragon Mušhuššu. "Marduk" is the Babylonian form of his name.

The Babylonian king Hammurabi (standing), is depicted as receiving his royal insignia from either Marduk or Shamash. The relief on the upper part of the stele is written Hammurabi's code of laws.

"THOUGH ONE MAY CONQUER A THOUSAND TIMES A THOUSAND MEN IN BATTLE, YET HE INDEED IS THE NOBLEST VICTOR WHO CONQUERS HIMSELF."

◊ *Buddha* ◊

CHAPTER 15

ANANDA, PERSONAL ASSISTANT OF THE BUDDHA SIDDHARTHA GAUTAMA, 500 BCE

I had long been intrigued by the story of the Buddha holding up a flower during a sermon. He held the flower in his hand before a group of disciples and just looked at it in silence with an expression of awe and childlike wonder. The whole sermon was conducted in this manner until one of his disciples named Mahakasyapa smiled slightly. The shift within Mahakasyapa signified that he had obtained a direct knowing, which the Buddha confirmed.

For quite a few years I had pondered the idea that I could have been a Buddhist monk, and I even thought that I might have been present at this particular sermon. So it came as no surprise to me when several different psychics told me over a period of several years that I had been a Buddhist monk in some of my past lives. I had never asked any of these psychics if I had been a Buddhist monk, yet several of them shared this piece of information with me, sometimes even without a formal reading involved. These synchronistic events were pointing me to an important lifetime, as I would later learn.

When I asked Ahtun Re during one of our conversations if I had been at the sermon of the flower, he in turn asked me in his typical manner what my

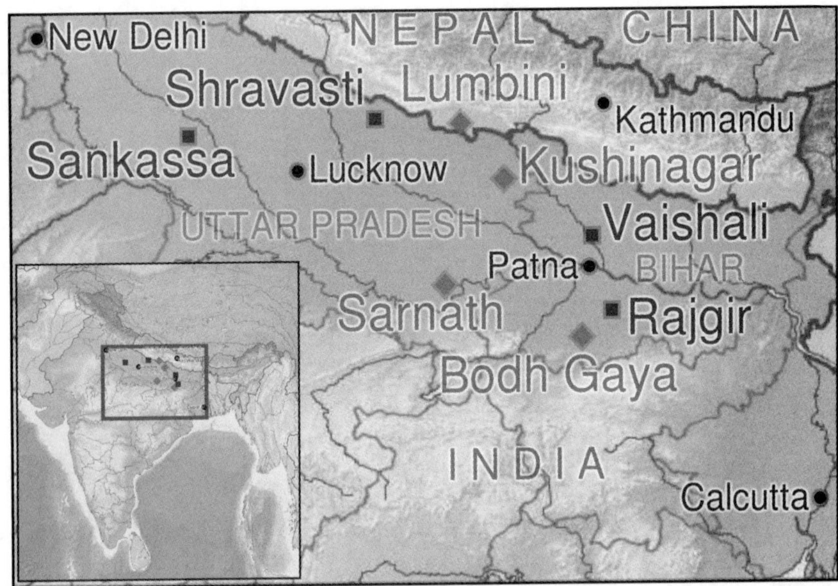

thoughts on the subject were. I told him that I felt like I may have been one of the monks present there, and Ahtun Re went on to tell me quite a bit of information that I had never heard or read before. First of all it was not a one-time event but a recurring sermon. He also said that the color of the flower would determine what particular chakra the Buddha wanted the disciples to focus on.

Each chakra has a particular color and is symbolically described as a flower having a certain number of petals, which was one of the reasons why the Buddha used different flowers for this meditation. By holding up flowers the Buddha would have the disciples focus on the corresponding chakra in their meditative and reflective work. Having a particular flower present could also help to create the atmosphere for what the actual lecture was about to cover. For example, the red color could be about staying grounded in the root chakra, while a green-colored blossom would be related to the heart chakra and be used in a lecture about love and its different meanings as related to human interactions.

"So I was a Buddhist monk who studied under Siddhartha Gautama?" I asked just to confirm. "Yes, you were with the Buddha," Ahtun Re said with a tone almost as if it should have been obvious to me. Ahtun Re is very patient with me, but he likes to make things fun and interesting. He rarely tells me

flat-out what I want to know specifically, thus nudging me to develop my own intuitive perception. His training and insights have been very beneficial and have often stimulated me to awaken memories of past lifetimes. They also motivated me to do the research necessary to find out more about the history of a given lifetime or particular incarnation. All of this extra focus developed my own intuition in finding many lifetimes.

When I tapped into the information of the life with the Buddha, I was almost as amazed as I had been after finding that I had been with Yeshua. However, it was also becoming quite an enigma to me that I had so many lives with such advanced masters. The channeled information of Ahtun Re and the years of work with him and Kevin Ryerson helped me to get further in my research on many of my past lives than I ever would have thought possible on my own. The eventual realization that I had been Ananda, which means "bliss" in Sanskrit, came intuitively after a couple more years during a meditation on my past lifetime as a disciple of the Buddha. It was a knowing that came from the core of my being, and after having relied on intuitive insights for many years in my professional and personal life, I immediately knew that this memory was authentic.

When I started to develop my intuitive abilities, I did it without intricate rituals or formulas, and I still think that simplicity is key in learning and using your intuition. The most important thing is to simply focus on using this natural ability and trusting that you can do it. You can accomplish this in any given situation in order to find an answer to any question you might have. When you train, first get into a meditative state, clear your mind from any chatter, and then ask your question. You need silence of mind before you ask your question to be able to hear the answer that will come from your higher self, which can access the akashic records and provide you with all the information you are looking for. If you practice this over a period several weeks, you will notice that your results will become more accurate and more detailed.

However, there are, of course, also obstacles. The main reasons for getting tainted results are that you are trying to intuit too much too quickly or you haven't gotten into a meditative state first. Sometimes you may have to clear up something in your life or in your mind before you can receive a particular piece of information. In certain instances your higher self may purposefully keep information from you to nudge you to focus on something else. You

may not be ready to handle certain information. It was only after many years of meditation that I received with certainty the information that I had been Ananda, but I believe that it happened at exactly the right time.

When I was born in that lifetime, I incarnated into the same warrior clan as Siddhartha had years earlier and on the exact same day that he attained enlightenment under the Bodhi tree. This day is now celebrated among Buddhists worldwide during the Vesakha festival, which is held at the first full moon in the month of May. My father was a king and brother of Siddhartha's father king, Suddhodana. As was common in the culture I grew up in, he gave me the choice of either serving my clan as a warrior, which was preferred, or serving through religious practices, as a priest. One of my brothers before me had already chosen to serve as a warrior, which made it easier for me to follow my heart and take up a religious life.

Many people don't realize that Siddhartha was from a warrior clan called the Shakyas and that his father had aspirations for him to someday become a warrior king and the unifier and ruler of all of India. Siddhartha was born into a life of abundance and trained as a warrior for much of his life, but after seeing pain and suffering in the world outside his palace he chose to leave and become an ascetic, practicing strict self-denial in order to further his spiritual understanding. In his lifetime, Siddhartha demonstrated a rapid progression through all of the archetypes that I had described in an earlier chapter and eventually became a highly evolved sage, able to call many people to higher states of consciousness.

Siddhartha's divine nature was heralded even before he was born. His parents, Queen Maya and King Suddhodana, did not have children for twenty years into their marriage. Then, during a full moon night, the queen had a vivid dream in which she felt herself being carried away by four spirit beings to Lake Anotatta in the Himalayas. After bathing her in the lake, the spirits wrapped her up in heavenly clothes, anointed her with perfumes, and bedecked her with divine flowers. Soon after that a white elephant holding a white lotus flower in its trunk appeared and went around her three times before he entered her womb. When the queen awoke, she knew that she had been delivered an important message, because in India the elephant has always been a symbol of greatness. And indeed, she became pregnant.

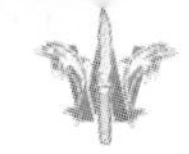

As was the custom of the day, when the time came for the queen to have her child, she traveled to her father's kingdom for the birth. But her birth pains had already begun before she arrived at her destination, and so she asked her handmaidens to assist her to a nearby grove of trees in the small town of Lumbini, where her son would be born. He was named Siddhartha, which means "he who has attained his goals." Sadly, Maya died only seven days after the birth so that Mahaprajapati, his mother's sister, raised Siddhartha.

When King Suddhodana consulted the renowned soothsayer Asita and inquired about the future of his son, Asita proclaimed that he would either be a great king or a great sage and savior of humanity. Suddhodana, eager that his son should become a king like himself, was thereafter determined to shield the child from anything that might result in him taking up the religious life.

Siddhartha was constantly kept in one of their three palaces where he would be surrounded only by beauty and health, not witnessing or experiencing the life of the common people in his father's kingdom. He grew up to be a strong and handsome young man, trained in the art of war as was common for a prince of the warrior caste. When it became time for him to marry, he won the hand of a beautiful princess of a neighboring kingdom by defeating many competitors in a variety of sports. Her name was Yasodhara, and they married when both were only sixteen years old.

Siddhartha lived a life where all material and physical pleasures were satisfied to a blissful level. As Siddhartha continued living in the luxury of his palaces, he grew increasingly restless and curious about the world beyond the palace walls, so he finally demanded that he be permitted to see his people and his lands. The king planned a trip and carefully arranged it in a way that Siddhartha should not see the kind of suffering that he feared would lead him to a religious life, decreeing that only young and healthy people should greet the prince.

As Siddhartha was led through the capital of Kapilavastu, he nevertheless was able to see a couple of old men who had accidentally wandered near the parade route. Amazed and confused, he chased after them to find out what they were. Then he came across some people who were severely ill, and finally he witnessed a funeral ceremony by the side of a river. When he asked his friend and squire Chandaka about the meaning of all that, Chandaka informed him of the simple truths that all of us get old, sick, and eventually die. Later on his trip,

Siddhartha also saw an ascetic monk who had renounced all the pleasures of the flesh. But despite his poverty, the monk had a peaceful look on his face, the memory of which would stay with Siddhartha for a long time to come.

As I began to look deeper into the historical information on Siddhartha, I found that there are some substantial gaps in the accounts of his earlier days. I also saw that there was speculation he may have studied in the universities of Persia. Between 550 and 330 BCE, the Persian Empire had conquered Asia as far as the Indus River, which could have enabled the young Siddhartha to learn about Zoroastrianism in a Persian university. When this new information reached India, it liberated many from the bonds of Hindu religious dogma, because it was declaring the individual as the one responsible for his or her own spiritual enlightenment.

Siddhartha would be vehemently opposed to the Hindu caste system that he grew up in, where one is bound to a particular social class for his entire life. He came to believe that the elimination of suffering from the human condition was an idea that could be incorporated by people from any caste and that enlightenment could be gained by anyone in a single lifetime. All of these ideas were counter to the established ideas of the Hindu priest class, which believed that only through repeated incarnations and climbing through the castes you could eventually attain enlightenment. Siddhartha's response to this idea would be revolutionary and aimed at leading all of mankind toward freedom and enlightenment.

I think it's interesting to note that there are several striking similarities between the lives of Siddhartha and Yeshua, among them miraculous births, gaps in the history from their teenage years to their early thirties, and both with a period of wandering in the wilderness incorporating extreme levels of fasting. Both of them also stood up to the restricting ideas of a priest class in order to teach all of humanity the path to self-empowerment, just as Zoroaster did also (and remember that he had been a previous incarnation of Yeshua). Putting all these pieces together, I believe that Yeshua and Siddhartha were both part of a soul group and working together over many lifetimes to support and awaken each other.

Zoroaster left clues for Siddhartha that guided him on his way to enlightenment, and in return Yeshua found his awakening clues from Siddhar-

tha in a Buddhist monastery when he was a young man. So both men helped awaken and propel each other forward. Neither of them was born with enlightenment, but they had to find it through their own mental, physical, and spiritual challenges.

This process of self-realization can be accelerated with the right information and inspiration. All of us encounter such information during the course of our lives. As Winston Churchill put it, "Men occasionally *stumble* over the *truth,* but most of them *pick* themselves up and hurry off as if nothing ever happened." Finding important information can be as easy as keeping one's eyes open and not merely being focused on the daily routine, but acting upon it takes courage and integrity, because it often involves leaving behind some of what has defined us up to this point in order to step into what we can potentially become.

In my experience, going on a journey with this sentiment and following the clues that synchronistic events present to us is a wonderful and enriching way of life. I think we can all live such lives, if we dare to trust our guidance, protection, intuition, and of course our ability to discern the significance of whatever we encounter, because sometimes important messages are hidden between the lines or under the surface of a seemingly insignificant event.

At the age of twenty-nine, Siddhartha looked closer at what he had witnessed in his life and came to realize that he could not be happy going on living as he had been. He had discovered suffering, and more than anything he wanted to discover how one might overcome suffering. So after kissing his sleeping wife and newborn son, Rahula, goodbye, he snuck out of the palace with his squire Chandaka and his favorite horse, Kanthaka. Later he gave away his rich clothing, cut his long hair, and gave the horse to Chandaka, telling him to return to the palace.

Siddhartha studied for some time with famous gurus of the day, but he found their practices lacking after he realized he had surpassed them in ability and knowledge. He then met five men who had also left a life of luxury to become ascetics. It was at this time that Siddhartha began the practice of severe austerities and self-mortifications. He struggled and tortured his body in an effort to achieve enlightenment and discover liberation while his five friends supported and looked after him. For six years he practiced with a sincerity and intensity so astounding that, before long, the five ascetics became followers of Siddhartha.

Asceticism was believed to burn up negative karma and free a person from the cycle of death and rebirth. It was the ascetics' belief that if they suffered enough in this life, they could perhaps save themselves in the next. So together with his five companions, Siddhartha wore little or no clothing, slept out in the open no matter the weather, and abstained from eating and drinking as much as possible. He lay on the most uncomfortable surfaces and inflicted much suffering on himself, convinced that external suffering would banish the internal suffering forever. Eventually he became very ill, his ribs showing through, until his spine could be felt through his stomach. His hair fell out and his skin became blotched and shrunken.

But still he was plagued with desires and cravings, and the answers to his questions were not forthcoming. He redoubled his efforts, refusing food and water, until he was in a state of near death. As Siddhartha pondered his failure to achieve enlightenment through asceticism, a young girl passed by him and offered him some rice milk. When he drank his fill he realized that these extreme practices were leading him nowhere, that in fact it might be better to find a way between the extremes of the life of luxury and the life of self-mortification. So he cast the ascetic life behind him and ate, drank, and bathed in the river.

The five ascetics saw this and concluded that Siddhartha had given up his desire to reach enlightenment and instead succumbed to the ways of the flesh, so they left him. Meanwhile, Siddhartha slowly nursed himself back to health as he became very conscious of his movements in the world and paid close attention to how he reacted to his environment, observing his thoughts as they passed through his mind. Mindfulness made Siddhartha aware of every craving and of how transitory everything he craved was. He realized that everything changes as it comes and passes and that it is impossible to hold onto something that cannot last—doing so would just inevitably cause suffering.

In the town of Bodh Gaya, Siddhartha decided to sit under a fig tree for as long as it would take for the answers to the problem of suffering to come to him. He sat there for forty-nine days in deep concentration to clear his mind of all distractions, opening himself up to the truth. It is said that he recalled all of his previous lives and saw everything that was going on in the entire universe.

It is said that Mara, the archetypal tempter and evil demon, tried to prevent Siddhartha from bringing this meditation to a conclusion and attaining enlight-

enment. Mara first tried to frighten him with storms and armies of demons. But Siddhartha remained completely calm and without fear, which enabled him to transform the dreadful onslaught into flower petals that gently rained down on him. Then Mara sent his three beautiful daughters to tempt Siddhartha, but again to no avail. Finally, he tried to ensnare Siddhartha in his own ego by appealing to his pride. But Siddhartha conquered all temptations and touched the ground with one hand, asking the Earth to be his witness for his victory over Mara.

On the full moon of May, with the rising of the morning star, Siddhartha finally understood the answer to the question of suffering and became the Buddha, which means "he who is awake." He had achieved his enlightenment at the age of thirty-five and remained seated under the tree—which became known as the Bodhi tree—for many days longer. It seemed to him that the knowledge he had gained was far too difficult to communicate to others. But legend has it that Brahma, the king of the gods, convinced Buddha to teach, saying that some of us perhaps have only a little dirt in our eyes and could awaken if we only heard his story.

Buddha agreed to teach, and the first people he would share his message with were the five ascetics who had abandoned him. He met them at Sarnath near Benares, about one hundred miles from Bodh Gaya. There, in a deer park, he preached his first sermon and set the wheel of teaching in motion, explaining to them the Four Noble Truths and the Eightfold Path. The Four Noble Truths state that there is suffering, that suffering has an origin, that suffering can be ended, and that the way to end suffering is the Eightfold Path.

The origins of suffering have been recognized by the Buddha to be partly inherited and tied to our existence on the physical plane. Getting born, aging, becoming sick, and dying all cause physical discomfort and suffering. Then there is mental and emotional suffering in the form of getting what you don't want, not being able to hold on to what you find desirable, not getting what you want, and being in a general state of dissatisfaction with the impermanence of all things. Interestingly, the Eightfold Path is not primarily focused on changing what happens to us—dying, for example, cannot be avoided. Buddha's way is more about being at peace and focusing on thoughts and actions that do not create negative karma. Thus we can be "in the world, but not of it," as the Islamic Sufis put it. It means that we can get involved in all kinds of beneficial worldly activities

while remaining detached, sovereign, and at peace, regardless of what we may encounter. According to the Buddha, our actions should be following the Eightfold Path's principles: right understanding, right intention, right speech, right action, right livelihood, right diligence, right mindfulness, and right concentration. "Right" in this context means wholesome, balanced, or wise.

Upon hearing Buddha's teachings of the Middle Way, the five ascetics became his first disciples, which marked the beginning of the Buddhist sangha or community of monks. King Bimbisara of Magadha, having heard Buddha's words, then granted him a monastery near his capital for use during the rainy season. This and other generous donations permitted the community of converts to continue their practice throughout the years and gave many more people the opportunity to hear the teachings of the Buddha.

Siddhartha would eventually travel back to his home, and over time members of his family, including his wife, son, father, and aunt, approached him seeking guidance. His son, Rahula, would even become a monk at seven years of age, at which point the Buddha would focus on teaching monastic discipline and building a solid spiritual foundation by explaining to Rahula the importance of truthfulness and self-reflection.

"One should act with body, speech, or mind only after first looking at oneself. Before acting with body, speech, or mind, one should think: 'What I am about to do, will it harm me or others?' If you can answer: 'Yes, it will,' then you should not act. But if you can answer: 'No, it will not,' then you should act. You should reflect in the same way while acting and after having acted. Therefore, Rahula, you should train yourself thinking: 'We will act only after repeatedly looking at ourselves, only after reflecting on ourselves.'"

Rahula would ponder this lesson for eleven years until his training would be intensified. In today's society, we're often very eager to speed up our development in many aspects of our lives, seeking to manifest results on the spot. This enthusiastic energy can be helpful, but without proper grounding and balance it can easily lead to impatience, lack of perseverance, and anger with oneself or others. Not least because of these pitfalls, it was only when Rahula turned eighteen years old that the next important step in his education would be taken, as this was the age determined by the Buddha for monks to become fully ordained. Rahula then received further instructions by his father on how to meditate:

"Rahula, develop a mind that is like the four great elements [earth, water, fire, and air] because if you do this, pleasant or unpleasant sensory impressions that have arisen and taken hold of the mind will not persist. Just as when people throw feces, urine, spittle, pus, or blood on the earth, in the water, in a fire, or in the air; the earth, the water, the fire, or the air is not troubled, worried, or disturbed. So too, develop a mind that is like the four great elements.

"Develop love, Rahula, for by doing so ill will be got rid of. Develop compassion, for by doing so the desire to harm will be got rid of. Develop sympathetic joy, for by doing so dislike will be got rid of. Develop equanimity, for by doing so sensory reaction will be got rid of. Develop the perception of the foul, for by doing so attachment will be got rid of. Develop the perception of impermanence, for by doing so the conceit, 'I am,' will be got rid of. Develop mindfulness of breathing, for it is of great benefit and advantage."

During one of Buddha's travels back to his homeland, my father was afraid that he would also influence me into leaving with him, so he brought me to our palace in Vaisali, trying to keep me in an artificial environment just like Siddhartha's father had tried with him for many years. When the Buddha came to Vaisali, my father sent me back to our palace in Kapilavastu, which was brought to the Buddha's attention. Buddha immediately went to the palace of Kapilavastu, because he was indeed hopeful that I would leave my home with him. He could foresee future possibilities and thought: "If Ananda leaves home, he shall spread Buddha dharma to future generations." As you can tell by the role that I'm playing in my current life and that I have played in my other past lives following this one, you don't have to be a proclaimed Buddhist or an ordained monk to spread the message of Buddha.

When I saw the Buddha in that lifetime, I immediately knew he was enlightened, so I paid my respects to him by using a fan to fan him. I was only nine years old and the youngest of a group of four princes from the Shakya clan that would leave their home to become part of Buddha's blossoming group of monks. Among the monks, our royal descent and the fact that we were cousins of the Buddha didn't affect our status in the sangha. Buddha taught that on the spiritual path it didn't matter what a person's status in the world was, or what their background, wealth, or nationality might be; everyone is capable of becoming enlightened.

There was, for example, Upali, who had been a barber and one of the early monks in the sangha. He was distinguished as being very knowledgeable about the rules of the sangha and even attained nirvana during his lifetime, meaning that he left the cycle of compulsory rebirth as he found stillness of mind after the fires of desire, aversion, and delusion have been finally extinguished. Therefore, even the monks who had been kings looked up to him.

When the Buddha was fifty-five years old, he told the sangha that he needed a new attendant. The attendant's job was a combination of servant, secretary, and confidant. He was supposed to take care of chores such as washing and mending robes so that the Buddha could focus on teaching. He also relayed messages and sometimes acted as a gatekeeper so that too many visitors would not mob the Buddha at once.

Many monks spoke up and nominated themselves for the job. Characteristically for me in that lifetime and this one as well, I remained quiet and observant. When the Buddha asked me to accept the job, however, I accepted—but only under certain conditions. I asked the Buddha to never give me special food, robes, or accommodations, so that the position did not come with material gain. I would also request the privilege of discussing any doubts with him whenever I had them, and I asked him to repeat any sermons to me that I might have to miss while carrying out my duties. The Buddha agreed to these conditions, and from that moment on I served as his attendant for the remaining twenty-five years of his life.

While I was determined to stay humble and follow Buddha's guidance, our princely cousin Devadatta was not humble at all and was a very ambitious man. As a convert and monk, he felt that he should have greater power in the sangha, and he managed to influence quite a few monks to return to extreme asceticism. He had developed some psychic powers but unfortunately was primarily focused on using them to impress and gather a following. Devadatta even asked the Buddha to retire and let him take over the running of the sangha, but Buddha retorted that he didn't even let his trusted disciples Sariputta or Moggallana run the sangha, much less one like him who should be vomited like spittle. Buddha gave a special act of publicity about him, warning the monks that he had changed for the worse.

Seeing the danger in this, Devadatta approached Prince Ajatasattu, who

had become his follower, and encouraged him to kill his father, King Bimbisara. Meanwhile, Devadatta would kill the Buddha so that they could use their combined power to gain more influence. King Bimbisara, however, found out about his plan and gave over the kingdom into the prince's control. Ajatasattu then provided mercenaries to Devadatta who ordered them to kill the Buddha. In an elaborate plan to cover his tracks he also ordered other men to kill the assassins and more men to kill them and so on, but when they approached the Buddha they were unable to carry out their orders and were converted instead.

Devadatta then tried to kill the Buddha himself by throwing boulders at him from on high while the Buddha was walking through a valley. I have memories of this event in which I and the rest of the monks who were accompanying the Buddha ran from the falling boulders to escape certain death. I remember seeing the Buddha moving in a way that seemed to bend time. It was as if he barely moved as boulders fell all around him, but at the same time he appeared to move lightning fast in order to escape being crushed by the boulders.

After the attack, we hurriedly caught back up to the Buddha, and as his new assistant I felt guilty for not staying and providing safety for him. He explained to me that he had indeed bent time by going to a place of no mind. He slipped into a gap between this reality and that of the timeless cosmos, which allowed him to escape the boulders with ease. To me it seemed as if he stood perfectly still, but then in one split second he was in another location. He would later teach this ability and others to me as well, so that I could better protect him.

After our cousin had failed to kill us, he tried another tactic a few weeks later. He conspired to intoxicate an unruly war elephant and let him loose on the Buddha while he was on an alms round. As we came up the street where the elephant was kept in a pen, our cousin opened the gate and out rushed the drunken elephant in a terrible rage. He headed right for our band of monks, who scattered as fast as they could go. Only the Buddha and I stood our ground as the elephant roared and charged down the street with the obvious intent to trample us under his mighty weight.

Remembering my last encounter with what I thought was certain death and how I had run and abandoned the Buddha, I was determined to do a better job this time and moved right in front of him. But he immediately pulled me back and told me to stay back while never taking his gaze from the elephant. I then saw a wave of energy projected from the Buddha toward the elephant that stopped his charge just before reaching our position in the dusty street. The elephant knelt in front of the Buddha who stroked his trunk and commanded him to move back to his walled pen, the gate of which the Buddha shut personally after the elephant had entered. From that point on, the elephant was docile and became a good work elephant for many years afterward.

I asked the Buddha what had he done and was told that the power of his loving kindness had overcome the elephant's rage. Having had a close relationship to animals in many of my past lifetimes before this one, it awakened some of my memories and inspired me to also focus on using the power of love to stop conflicts in the animal kingdom and among humans, something that has become an important part of my current life again.

After all the unsuccessful attempts on the Buddha's life, Devadatta went into the sangha and spread lies, saying that Siddhartha was living in abundance and luxury. Devadatta managed to create a schism and convinced five hundred newly ordained monks, many who had joined the sangha from our warrior clan, to part from the Buddha and his followers. Buddha then sent his two chief disciples, Sariputta and Moggallana, to bring back the erring young monks. Devadatta, however, thought they had come to join his sangha and fell asleep after he asked Sariputta to give a talk. Sariputta and Moggallana used this opportunity to persuade the young monks to return to the Buddha.

It came as a great surprise when the Buddha later informed us during a talk that Devadatta had been his holy teacher in a past incarnation and that it was he who had set him on the path of enlightenment. He made a noteworthy statement about how even Devadatta in time will also become a Buddha.

In the wake of all these events, the Buddha would begin to teach the monks of the sangha the animal forms that would eventually become known as kung fu in China. The animal forms were designed not only as a way for monks to master the physical nature of conflicts and defend themselves from bandits, but also to inculcate the ideals of nature embodied within different animals. The forms were supposed to be used only for protection and only until the monk had mastered the higher levels of consciousness where no physical contact would be needed, just as the Buddha had demonstrated when he pacified the raging elephant.

After a couple of weeks of researching and writing about this lifetime, the following memory came to me. It came unexpected and flooded my awareness one morning as I was coming out of a deep sleep.

At one time, the Buddha and I were traveling alone to a distant city when a mountain thunderstorm approached, so we took shelter under a large Bodhi tree, just like the one that Siddhartha had gained enlightenment under. It was at a time when he was still young looking and lean, with his hair stacked high on his head. We were both quietly meditating as the storm was beginning to let up and pass away into the distance. I could still hear the raindrops falling softly from the leaves and branches of the tree and splashing into small puddles on the ground around us. We were both sitting cross-legged with our backs to the tree and eyes closed.

I asked the Buddha telepathically, as was our way of communicating when alone, how he was able to continue to exist in the world when he was so enlightened. Didn't he find it difficult to be with a mankind that must seem like spoiled, evil children to him? His reply was that his consciousness was like that of a loving parent. When we monks came to him, he simply could not resist helping us through our suffering to gain enlightenment as he had done.

We used telepathic communication because it is purer than verbal communication. It was through my deeper understanding of the Middle Way that I had been able to communicate through this more advanced form of relaying information. Telepathy cancels out any misconceptions of individual words that we may have formed in our minds. Thus when two or more minds communicate directly with each other, all the miscues of verbal inflection, body language, and spoken untruths are being transcended. Only truths can be spoken through telepathy.

Buddha went on to demonstrate to me what beauty lay in enlightenment by having me focus on the sound of a raindrop hitting the water. I was told to go deep into the structure of the water itself until I could touch the consciousness of the individual spark of life that was existent there. It was a beautiful moment as I quietly listened to the water splash. I felt an intense and direct connection with not only the water but with all of life. Tears of happiness welled up in my eyes and began to roll down my cheeks as the connection with the water and the life that was inside my body was now mingling with the water and life outside

of me. Both were at oneness with each other so that there was no separation between us. The connection grew deeper still and I could feel joy flowing through every cell of my body in an indescribably pleasurable, tingling sensation. Buddha's words came gently into my mind as he said, "This exquisite sensation you are experiencing is what enlightenment is like every moment for me."

When Buddha's Aunt Mahaprajapati saw that her foster son had attained enlightenment and that some of the princes had become his followers, she also wanted to leave home and become a nun. Even Buddha's wife asked to be permitted into the sangha, which was originally composed only of men. Mahaprajapati begged the Buddha three different times to permit her to stay in the sangha, but the Buddha refused each time. He believed that permitting women to enter the community would weaken it.

To avoid the frequent begging from his aunt, he went to preach in the Namantini monastery, which was not far from Vaisali. But Mahaprajapati was not deterred and gathered five hundred women of the Shakya clan who had similar thoughts. They all shaved their hair and walked over two thousand miles barefooted to catch up with the Buddha. When they finally reached the monastery where the Buddha stayed, their feet were blistered and bloodied, because none of them was used to walking such a long distance.

They paced outside the monastery tired and haggard but dared not enter. I happened to come out, and when I saw Mahaprajapati and the other women wearing robes and having dust and tears in their faces, I was in shock. I asked them what was going on, to which Mahaprajapati replied, "We left our loved ones and relatives behind and walked all the way here to become nuns. If Buddha refuses us again, we shall die here and never return!" I was so touched by these words that I could not control my tears.

I related the message to the Buddha and begged him to grant the women their wish. But the Buddha refused: "Ananda, I sympathize with them but it is not appropriate to let women enter our community." I didn't understand the reason for this and asked, "Lord Buddha, are men and women different in the Buddha dharma?"

"Ananda, the dharma is the same in heaven or in the world. I do not discriminate against women. I treat all sentient beings as equal. Women can do as the men did, follow my dharma and practice, but they need not become nuns.

This is a question of our system and not whether men and women are equal. Women leaving home are like wild grass in the field that will affect the harvest."

Although the Buddha refused, I nevertheless said in tears, "Lord Buddha, can you bear to see them die. Shouldn't you show them compassion and give them a helping hand?" Buddha was quiet for a while and finally agreed to my request to allow women to enter the sangha. I happily rushed outside to announce the good news to Mahaprajapati and the other five hundred women, who were soon overjoyed with tears. Thus it was due to the persistence of several women of the Shakya clan and Ananda's efforts to convince the Buddha that he would eventually allow his aunt and abandoned wife, Yasodhara, to become the first Buddhist nuns.

You may find Buddha's reluctance to accept women in the sangha irritating, so let me put this in perspective and share my understanding of this event looking at it in hindsight. We had lived in a patriarchal society and culture that for many thousands of years had ranked women far below men in importance. This was inherently abusive, and therefore it was Buddha's intention to first help men develop compassion and wisdom, so that they could do their part to dismantle the patriarchy gently from the inside. You can compare the strict separation of the sexes within the sangha to the incubation periods I had mentioned in earlier chapters. In both cases the desire for seclusion and separation is not motivated by a contempt for others, but because a period of isolation can at times accelerate and support a growth process.

We as humanity are unraveling the patriarchy in an evolutionary process that has been in the process of unfolding over thousands of years. It's like a gigantic alchemic experiment where the most appropriate course of action is determined by the current condition of the potion and the available ingredients and methods of processing. Buddha did what had been most efficient to catalyze humanity's growth process during his lifetime, and while essential parts of his teachings remain unchanged in their value and significance to this day, the idea that women and men should not come together in their spiritual learning is outdated.

As I have mentioned throughout the book, today we are challenged with integrating and balancing the divine masculine and feminine aspects within ourselves as well as collectively. We are moving out of the patriarchy, not to

move into a matriarchy, but to find our balance and transcend the old paradigm of dominance and submission toward a paradigm of mutual appreciation and collaboration. A very good book explaining this ongoing process in great depth is *Unplugging the Patriarchy* by Lucia Rene, who had also studied Buddhism extensively.

Buddha would continue to teach throughout northeast India for a total of forty-five years from the time of his enlightenment. When the Buddha was eighty years old, he informed me that he would be leaving soon, and so it came to be that in Kushinagara, less than hundred miles from his homeland, he ate some spoiled food offered to him by a blacksmith called Cunda and became very ill. Cunda, however, was not to blame for this because he offered the food in good conscience. As Buddha explained to me, "By his deed the worthy Cunda has accumulated merit, which makes for long life, beauty, well-being, glory, heavenly rebirth, and sovereignty." If you focus on supporting others to the best of your knowledge and ability, this is commendable regardless of the outcome.

While lying ill, the Buddha had me gather the monks from the sangha. Much to my protestations he had all of them come by as he lay on his side, and one by one they briefly spoke with him. At this occasion he also prophesied, "Should Ananda die without being fully liberated, he would be king of the gods seven times because of the purity of his heart, or be king of the Indian subcontinent seven times. But Ananda will experience final liberation in this very life."

This suggests that I should have left the cycle of death and rebirth, so you might wonder why I am here again and how I could have had all these other lifetimes that followed my life as Ananda. The answer is very simple; I am here because of my own volition. And in that I am by far not the only one. I believe that quite a few of you reading this don't necessarily have to reincarnate on Earth anymore, but came here to assist humanity to transition into higher consciousness. In my opinion, this is an exciting process and well worth coming back to Earth, even though you don't have to. I have located a couple of kingly lives already and will speak of them in future books.

To put this in perspective, I think it's important to note here that there is a difference between becoming a Buddha and merely leaving the cycle of death and rebirth, which is just one of the attributes of a Buddha or a fully enlightened one. Even after you have reached nirvana and cleared your karma

to a point where you don't have to reincarnate on the physical plane anymore, you're still subject to the law of cause and effect. You will continue to develop as a soul, there will continue to be conflicts, and you will maintain an individual personality. I still learn and grow as a soul in this human body, unlocking my personal human potential and thereby helping to transform humanity as a whole, just as many people currently present on this planet do as well, whether they have a past life history on Earth or whether they came from far distant places within the universe.

Many evolved souls simply consider it their natural responsibility to help and support those who are struggling the most, thereby acting diligently toward their own greater good. The Buddha in his last words also asked for this diligence before he went into a deep meditation and died under a grove of Sala trees:

> *Impermanent are all created things; work out your own salvation with diligence.*

Shortly after the Buddha died, I was called upon to recite many of the discourses that later became the Sutta Pitaka of the Pali Canon. I was asked to do this because I had attended the Buddha personally and memorized many of the discourses he delivered to various audiences, which is why I was also called the "guardian of the dharma" and the one who had "heard much." However, while the benefit of transmitting Buddha's teachings truthfully should be obvious, the Buddha himself advised to rely first and foremost on one's own discernment, to make your own experiences, and to come to your own understanding of any given piece of information. Buddha made this perfectly clear when he addressed his disciples saying, "Do not go by revelation, do not go by tradition, do not go by hearsay, do not go on the authority of sacred texts."

Enlightenment cannot be handed down, thus your personal realization is of central importance. As Buddha said, "No one saves us but ourselves; no one can and no one may. We ourselves must walk the path, but Buddha's clearly shows the way." It can be very advantageous to seek inspiration from teachers, but eventually we must find out for ourselves what "things lead to benefit and happiness, and having undertaken them, abide in them."

As Ananda, I would live a very long life, reaching an age of over one hundred years. Before my final death I was rowed to an island in the center of a river dividing two armies that were about to wage war on each other. When the two armies found that I was on the island they sent representatives begging me to come to their respective side. It would be a recognition and honor for that side and a justification to wage war against the other side. But I refused to take sides in this war and stayed on the island meditating on love and peace until my final death. After my death, my body was burned and the ashes strewn in the water. In the end, my effort to help both sides settle their conflict peacefully had proven to be successful as no war was waged from either side. Thus thousands were saved from death and the trauma of war. In this last act of my life I employed the skills of sacred warfare that I had developed over many lifetimes and that had been refined in my life with the Buddha.

Working toward uniting people, bringing forth spiritual knowledge, and preventing wars is still a main focus in my current lifetime. We still see many wars on the planet as well as hatred based on ignorance, but we can create a better world if we trust our ability to do so and have no fear to fully commit to the struggle for love, truth, and liberty for all.

Fortunately, a rapidly growing number of people understand that the teachings of Buddha, Yeshua, and other teachers throughout time were not meant to divide cultures but to help the individual on the way toward personal empowerment, so that our personal power may be used to create a diverse and harmonious collective on this planet. I believe that a lot of inspiration can be found in virtually any religion and that most religious teachings can be used as tools to help you awaken the divine nature within yourself and develop respect and love for all that is. Because of this, I believe that we will transcend all religions as we know them today and move toward a higher understanding of spirituality that is based on our personal conscious recognition and interaction with the divine. I also believe that at some point religious wars will become a thing of the past, and so too will many of the control mechanisms that for eons were there to divide us and keep us in ignorance of who we really are and what we are capable of as divine creators.

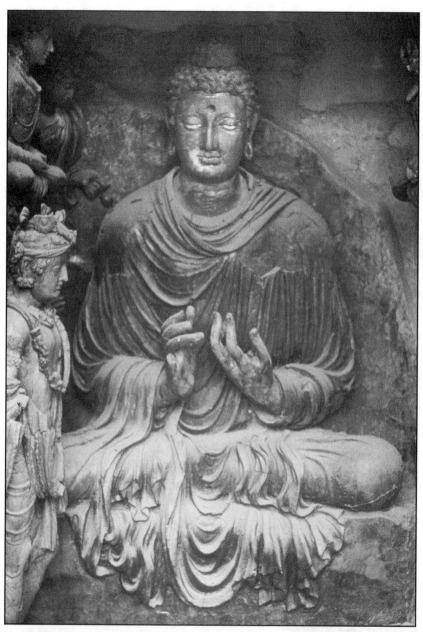

The Buddha also asserted that karma influences rebirth, and that the cycles of repeated births and deaths are endless. This relief carving of "The Buddha" comes from the Tapa Shotor monastery in Hadda, Afghanistan, dated to the 2nd century CE.

Gautama Buddha attained enlightenment (*bodhi*) while meditating underneath a *Ficus religiosa*. According to Buddhist texts, the Buddha meditated without moving from his seat for seven weeks (49 days) under this tree. A shrine called Animisalocana cetiya, was later erected on the spot where he sat. This is a sign at the Bodhi Tree.

Mara is a malignant celestial king who tempted Prince Siddhartha (Gautama Buddha) by trying to seduce him with the vision of beautiful women who, in various legends, are often said to be Mara's daughters. This portrait of "The Demons of Mara" is painted on a palm leaf manuscript from Nalanda, Bihar, India.

The man commonly known as The Buddha was born in Lumbini in what is now Nepal, to royal parents of the Shakya clan The young man Siddhartha Gautama renounced his home life to live as a *śramana*. Leading a life of begging, asceticism, and meditation, he attained enlightenment at Bodh Gaya in what is now India. The Buddha thereafter wandered through the middle Gangetic Plain, teaching a Middle Way between sensual indulgence and severe asceticism, and building a monastic order. Pictured here are monks of a Tibetan Buddhist monastery.

Gautama Buddha believed in the existence of an afterlife in another world and in reincarnation, stating "since there actually is another world (any world other than the present human one, i.e. different rebirth realms), one who holds the view 'there is no other world' has wrong view." This "Seated Buddha" carving dates to 475 CE.

"IT IS ALL ONE TO ME. WHERE I AM TO BEGIN, THERE I SHALL RETURN AGAIN."

◊ *Parmenides* ◊

CHAPTER 16

PARMENIDES OF ELEA, FOUNDER OF THE ELEATIC SCHOOL OF PHILOSOPHY, 515-450 BCE

I have been fascinated by philosophy since I was a little boy. I marveled at the philosophers of ancient Greece and their grasp of complex issues ranging from where human consciousness comes from to which form of government is the best for humanity. Imagine my surprise and delight to trace several of my past lives back to these philosophers. I initially came across Parmenides while reading about the pre-Socratic philosophers.

When I first saw a picture of a statue of Parmenides it was literally like I was looking into a mirror; the facial resemblance is astounding. When I then began to read his biography and writings, I was amazed that he had come up with many of the same ideas that I had focused on during my entire life. This is one of the beauties of past life research, when you find information from your past lives that can help you understand why you think the way you do right now.

Parmenides was born and lived in Elea, a Greek colony in southwest Italy. There he had been influenced by the philosophy of Xenophanes, who argued that the anthropomorphic pantheons of the Greeks and other cultures could well be human-made: "The Ethiopians say that their gods are flat-nosed and

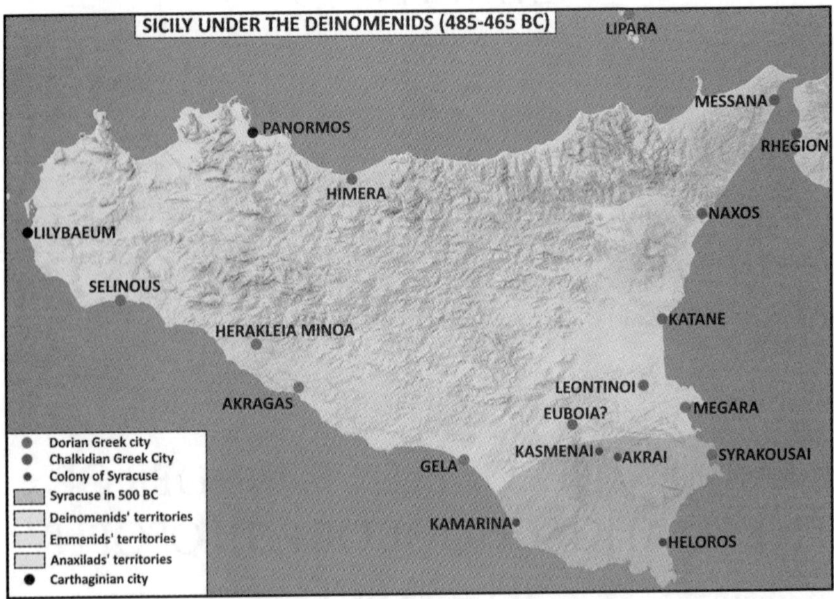

black, while the Thracians say that theirs have blue eyes and red hair. Yet if cattle or horses or lions had hands and could draw and could sculpture like men, then the horses would draw their gods like horses, and cattle like cattle; and each they would shape bodies of gods in the likeness, each kind, of their own."

According to Xenophanes, there is one supreme divine being watching impartially over all of creation, "There is one God, supreme among gods and men, not like mortals in body or thought." I found inspiration in Xenophanes's philosophy because I had always resonated with the idea that there is a supreme force connecting and pervading all of existence. Xenophanes, however, qualified his statements by saying, "Through seeking we may learn and know things better. But as for certain truth, no man has known it, nor shall he know it; neither of the gods, nor yet of all the things of which I speak. For even if by chance he were to utter the final truth, he would himself not know it, for all is but a woven web of guesses." All I can say to Xenophanes's idea that nothing can be known for sure is, if this was true, how would he know?

After Xenophanes was expelled from his hometown of Colophon at the age of twenty-five, the people of Elea would appreciate his presence, just like that of Parmenides, who would even be employed to write a constitution

that was long lasting and would later be regarded as the principal reason for Elea's power. Parmenides is also considered to be the founder of the Eleatic school of philosophy.

Among Parmenides's most notable students was Zeno, who was called the inventor of the dialectic method by Aristotle. Contrary to the classical concept of debating, this method does not primarily focus on persuading an opponent but on coming to a higher understanding of something without attachment to one's initial thought. Zeno's famous paradoxes would also inspire modern quantum physicists, who called the fact that the dynamical evolution of a quantum system can be hindered through observation the "Quantum Zeno Effect," inspired by Zeno's idea that a flying arrow—in every instant in which it can be observed—is never in motion.

Another student of Parmenides who would inspire modern physicists was Leucippus. Together with Democritus, he had been the founder of atomism, a philosophy based on the idea that nature consists of two basic principles: empty space and indivisible parts of matter that in their various combinations and congregations constitute everything within the void. While this theory has been the basis for nuclear physics and enabled many important inventions, even greater inventions will be possible once this theory is transcended.

In my lifetime as Parmenides, I had already expressed that "all is full of what is," hinting at the fact that even what appears to be void is not just empty space.

However, the single biggest contribution that Parmenides made to the evolution of philosophy is probably the introduction of the study of ontology, which is a major branch of metaphysics and concerned with the nature of being, existence, and reality. Parmenides's work is also regarded by some as the foundation of metaphysics, logic, and the methodology of scientific research based upon the principle of invariance, which is the property of remaining unchanged regardless of changes in the conditions of measurement.

Just like in my incarnation as Thales, I would again be drawn to the philosophy of monism. As Parmenides, I formulated the idea that all things are part of a great unity and that everything that can exist already exists, either in thought or materialized, "for it is the same thing that can be thought and that can be." Plato, reverentially referring to Parmenides as "our father Parmenides," expanded on this concept in his Theory of Forms by stating that all

manifest phenomena are merely shadows of the thought forms that precede them, most prominently expressed in his Allegory of the Cave.

Sadly, there is only one work of Parmenides that has survived in fragmentary form. It is a poem called *On Nature,* of which approximately 160 of the original three thousand lines are known today. It is known, however, that the work originally was divided into three parts: a proem introducing the entire work, a section known as "The Way of Truth," and a section known as "The Way of Appearance." The poem is a narrative sequence in which the narrator travels "beyond the beaten paths of mortal men" to receive a revelation from the goddess Persephone on the nature of reality. In Greek mythology, Persephone is the goddess of the soul and possessor of its dark and frightening wisdom, but also the harbinger of spring and a reminder of all the growth and hopes that it brings.

Parmenides's relation from Persephone has even found its way into one of the most famous paintings of all time, *The School of Athens* by the Italian Renaissance painter Raphael. Many of the greats of philosophy are anachronistically gathered in this painting, including Pythagoras, Socrates, Plato, and Aristotle. Parmenides is the first person from the center standing upright on the left bottom side of the painting. Standing just behind him, as he works on a piece of writing and seems to anticipate her next words before continuing, is the only female in the picture. She seems to look into your very being with an expression of calm knowledge, and she is also the only one in the picture who is looking directly at you. I believe that this woman, although officially unacknowledged, is Persephone dictating her knowledge to Parmenides, who then shares it with the world.

In his work, Parmenides tells of a fantastic journey in a horse- drawn chariot, guided by the Heliades, the daughters of Helios, the sun, who guide it to the "gate of night and day." When they reach there, they ask Dike, the gatekeeper and spirit of moral order and fair judgment, to open up and allow their charge to pass through. Parmenides thus manages to enter into the presence of the goddess, who welcomes him and bestows her wisdom upon him.

There are many metaphors in this poem, some of which can only be understood by knowing the imagery of ancient Greece. While driving in his chariot, which is a symbol for the journey of the soul, Parmenides is guided by the Heliades, goddesses related to the light of the sun, who steer him in the right direction. The route here is "the way of the goddess," which takes the "wise man" in the di-

rection of the "ultimate truth." Parmenides's journey leads him to the "gate of day and night," also called the gate of the sun, which had always played a central part in Greek mythology and is identified with the gate of the underworld. Beyond this yawned the abyss, which in Greek was chaos or the world of the dead, the realm of Hades and Persephone, the god and goddess of the underworld.

This focus on Persephone and the underworld is an interesting parallel to my life as Pharaoh Senusret I, who had a strong affinity toward the goddess Isis. I think that throughout time, many of the gods and goddesses in different cultures represent the same archetypes but take on different forms, depending on the particular consciousness of a society, kind of like Xenophanes had described. The Swiss psychotherapist and psychiatrist Carl Gustav Jung had also expressed this idea. Jung founded analytical psychology and developed an understanding of archetypes as being "ancient or archaic images that derive from the collective unconscious." In other words, the gods are part of our own consciousness and ourselves, and we only experience them as being separate from us, but that's an illusion. Jung summarized his theory as follows:

"In addition to our immediate consciousness, which is of a thoroughly personal nature and which we believe to be the only empirical psyche (even if we tack on the personal unconscious as an appendix), there exists a second psychic system of a collective, universal, and impersonal nature which is identical in all individuals. This collective unconscious does not develop individually but is inherited. It consists of preexistent forms, the archetypes, which can only become conscious secondarily and which give definite form to certain psychic contents."

Modern-day comparative studies show many parallels between Greek rituals and that of much older antiquity. For instance, the Minoan fertility cults of Crete and those of Isis and Osiris in Egypt are similar to the Eleusinian cult where Persephone played a major role in helping to elevate the consciousness of humanity. The ceremonies held every year for the cult of Demeter and Persephone, called the Eleusinian Mysteries, are believed to be of considerable antiquity, deriving from religious practice of the Mycenaean period predating the Greek dark ages that followed the Trojan War after the Earth changes that I spoke of in an earlier chapter. The ceremony was intended to help mankind develop its divine potential, or as Carl Gustav Jung might have put it, to make the collective unconscious conscious.

Fittingly, Parmenides was a priest of the Greek god Apollo, who was associated with heightened states of consciousness and accessing the world of oneness. He was said to be able to reveal hidden aspects of the past, present, and future and was also a healer and interpreter of dreams. Interestingly, his sacred bird was the raven—just like that of the Egyptian goddess Isis. The fact that Parmenides was a practicing priest of Apollo is also supported by archaeological evidence from excavations in Parmenides's hometown of Elea, which together with the imagery and wording of Parmenides's poem is a strong indicator for his mystical background connected to the ancient practice of healing and meditation known as incubation.

In my current life I have described in my book *The Intuitive Warrior* how I had an experience with Archangel Michael. When I discovered this lifetime as Parmenides, that mystical experience became more real and alive for me. I have not been a stranger to these experiences throughout time. The shimmering white light and the love that was beaming forth from Archangel Michael was just as incredible as the similar experience for Parmenides was in his day.

On his mystical journey, Parmenides came to the realization that truth is ultimately changeless, whole, unborn, immortal, and one. Change and separation are merely appearances. Socrates has often misunderstood this aspect of Parmenides's teachings. Most prominently, Socrates perceived Parmenides as the only philosopher who flat-out denied the idea that "everything flows/changes," as Heraclitus of Ephesus, a contemporary of Parmenides, put it. Truth cannot change, but the mind wants to believe that it can and will. This causes confusion within the mind. By focusing on truth, the mind is stilled and calmed. The ego part of us wants to constantly busy itself with keeping up with unceasing and formless changes. The still beatific side of us wants only the stillness and calm of truth.

While the ubiquitous change that Heraclitus and Socrates observed does exist at a superficial level, the animating force that brings everything into being is whole, timeless, and immutable—nothing can ever be taken away from it or added to it. I believe that it is our inherited responsibility to become increasingly aware of both of these fundamental facts of existence, just as Persephone told Parmenides, "You must learn all things, both the unshaken heart of persuasive truth, and the opinions of mortals in which there is no true warranty."

Once we realize that there are these two realms of volatile appearance

and of unchanging oneness, the next step is to bring our interactions with both into balance, because we cannot escape either one of them. This approach to embrace all of our experiences while remaining detached and rooted in our higher understanding of the true nature of everything exactly mirrors the teachings of the Buddha that I was exposed to in a parallel lifetime. You can see how the same information came through at the same time in multiple places on Earth; it was just channeled into different expressions.

The fact that one and the same truth can be received, comprehended, and expressed in different ways is probably the most common source of misunderstandings among humans. Socrates accusing Parmenides that he denied the idea of change altogether is just one example. I believe most of us have experienced situations where you have been in an argument with a person and both of you eventually came to the conclusion that you tried to articulate the same thing, even though for some time you assumed that you were expressing different or even contradicting points of view.

Our understanding of any given fact or situation happens first on an intuitive level before we even start to mentally put anything into words. I mentioned in the previous chapter that verbal communication is a comparatively inefficient way to communicate; words are shadows at best. But while we are still partly dependent on them, our intuition can help us discern the underlying energy and intent of what is being communicated.

I believe that the vast majority of misunderstandings between humans who genuinely desire to come to an accepting of the "unshaken heart of persuasive truth" arise because you can so easily get lost in the unclear "opinions of mortals." If we acknowledge this obstacle and strengthen our connection to our higher selves, we will be able to see beyond the mere appearance of opinions and avoid many unnecessary arguments. We will then create more harmony in any situation and maximize our efficiency when working together.

The philosopher life is just one of many aspects of expressing and experiencing the human experience. I think we all embrace an attribute of the philosopher in ourselves at some point in our lifetime. Some of us devote entire lives to it. The reward and carry-through into other lives is part of the ongoing process toward the divine and angelic self within us all.

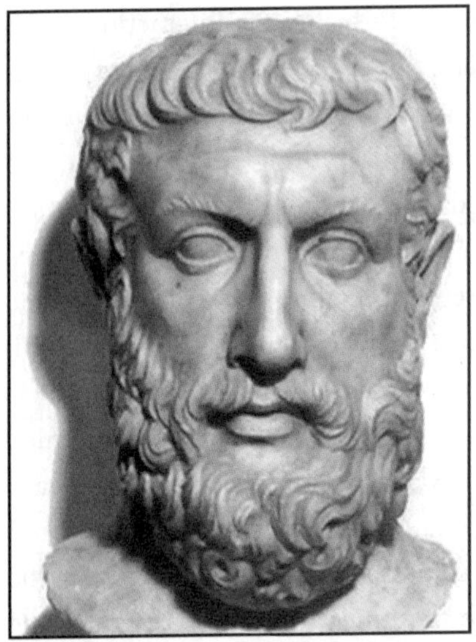

Head from a herm discovered at an excavation in Velia in 1966. The body of the herm had been discovered in 1962, with the inscription "Parmenides the son of Pyres the natural philosopher."

Persephone was the Greek queen of the underworld. She was the goddess of spring, the dead, destruction, life, grain, and nature.

Aristotle (384–322 BCE) was a Greek philosopher and polymath during the Classical period in Ancient Greece. Taught by Plato, he was the founder of the Peripatetic school of philosophy within the Lyceum and the wider Aristotelian tradition. His writings cover many subjects.

"The School of Athens" is a fresco by the Italian Renaissance artist Raphael. The fresco was finished in 1511 as a part of Raphael's commission to decorate the rooms now known as the Stanze di Raffaello, in the Apostolic Palace in the Vatican. It depicts a congregation of philosophers, mathematicians, and scientists from Ancient Greece, including Plato, Aristotle, Pythagoras, Archimedes, and Heraclitus. The Italian artists Leonardo da Vinci and Michelangelo are also featured in the painting, shown as Plato and Heraclitus respectively.

Carl Gustav Jung (1875 – 1961) was a Swiss psychiatrist and psychoanalyst who founded analytical psychology. Jung's work has been influential in the fields of psychiatry, anthropology, archaeology, literature, philosophy, psychology, and religious studies. When Jung worked as a research scientist at the Burghölzli psychiatric hospital, in Zurich, he came to the attention of Sigmund Freud, the founder of psychoanalysis. The two men conducted a lengthy correspondence and collaborated, for a while, on a joint vision of human psychology.

“I NEVER LEARNED HOW TO TUNE A HARP OR PLAY UPON A LUTE, BUT I KNOW HOW TO RAISE A SMALL AND INCONSIDERABLE CITY TO GLORY AND GREATNESS.”

◊ *Themistocles* ◊

CHAPTER 17

THEMISTOCLES, GREEK POLITICIAN AND GENERAL, 524-460 BCE

I first connected with this lifetime after I had already written the next chapter on the Spartan general Pausanias, who was the leader of the Greek army that defeated the Persians on land a year after the Persian fleet had been defeated by Themistocles at the Battle of Salamis. In these two simultaneous lifetimes, I would help ensure that the Persians did not reverse the flowering of consciousness that was happening in Greece, the long-term effects of which would affect all of humanity. It is interesting, however, that both Themistocles and Pausanias would fall out of favor with their respective city-states after their successful military campaigns. Both would be accused of siding with the Persians in a plot hatched by astute politicians in Athens and Sparta that sought to advance their own selfish goals.

It would be during this time and in this region of the Earth that the idea of democracy would gain momentum and transform Greece, which resulted in the notion of Greece being the "cradle of democracy." If we look at the work of the historians of that period, we can see in their accounts that Themistocles was imbued with a very strong desire and interest in public affairs even at an

early age. Together with my past life experience, this keen interest would help me challenge the authoritarian form of government that had been firmly established in Athens over a very long period of time.

I was determined to create a government by and for the people. Because of these progressive views, Themistocles would encounter much resistance and opposition from the hitherto most powerful and influential leaders in the city, as would be expected during a period of intense change. His influence would nevertheless increase and people would be stirred to new kinds of enterprises and innovations across a broad spectrum of human endeavors. His friend Pericles, who is credited as the greatest and longest-lasting leader of this

time frame, would eventually follow in his footsteps, but for all of that to happen, the Persian invasion had to be stopped first.

The Persian Empire that I had founded in my lifetime as Cyrus had morphed from a culture of universal human rights to one that was bringing slavery to the cultures it conquered, but the people of Greece were determined to put a stop to these injurious expansionist policies. History shows us that cultures focused on developing their consciousness and living a simple and harmonious life would be invaded by empires with superior military forces that would destroy them. This is why throughout all of my lifetimes I continually kept my focus on developing and promoting spirituality and physical vigilance side by side.

The Greeks had been in conflict with the Persians for many years already when I and the other Athenian military strategists determined that we needed to make proactive moves in anticipation of a Persian invasion. We came to the conclusion that our best chance to defeat and turn back the invading Persian army was to meet them east of Athens at their landing site at Marathon. We had previously received assurances from the Spartans that they would send their forces, which we believed would make a critical difference in the battle, as they were considered to be the best fighting force that Greece had to offer.

When the Spartans had not yet arrived shortly before the battle began in 490 BCE, I was among the generals who decided to send a professional runner named Pheidippides to Sparta to urge them to dispatch their troops. Many would wonder why a horse wasn't used, but over very long distances a well-trained human beats a horse in stamina. The 140-mile course was very mountainous and rugged, but spurred on by the desire to help save Athens, Pheidippides ran the entire distance in about thirty-six hours.

The Spartans agreed to help, but religious laws did not allow their army to march toward Marathon right away. This was very frustrating for the Spartan forces, but ten years later this negative experience would cause their King Leonidas to override a similar restriction to facilitate a timely response when they needed to depart for Thermopylae. However, at the Battle of Marathon the missing support from Sparta would leave the Athenians alone to fight the Persian army.

After the dejected but still determined Pheidippides brought the disappointing news to Athens, the small Athenian army immediately marched to the plains of Marathon to prepare for battle. Although the Athenian army was out-

numbered four to one, we launched a surprise offensive thrust, which at the time appeared suicidal to the Persians. But by day's end, close to seven thousand Persian bodies lay dead on the field while only 192 Athenians had been killed. The surviving Persians fled to their ships and headed south to Athens where they hoped to attack the city before the Athenian army could reassemble.

Pheidippides was again called upon to run the twenty-six miles to Athens to carry the news of the victory together with a warning about the approaching Persian ships. Despite his fatigue after his recent runs and having fought all morning at Marathon in heavy armor, Pheidippides rose to the challenge. Pushing himself past normal limits of human endurance, he reached Athens in about three hours and delivered his message in time. Sadly, Pheidippides died shortly thereafter from exhaustion. It was this type of selfless dedication by Pheidippides that was a mind-set of every Greek. Throughout history, highly developed cultures would achieve this ideal level of consciousness. More than two thousand years later his epic feat would also inspire Michel Break He suggested that the Olympic committee include the long-distance run known today as the marathon in the first Olympic Games in modern times, which were held in 1896 in Greece.

When Sparta and the other Greek allies arrived at Marathon soon after the battle, they found the great number of killed Persians, which were a testament to our victory. They quickly marched on to Athens, where we arrived before the Persians, blocking their safe landing and turning back the Persian attempt to conquer Greece. The Battle of Marathon was important for all Greeks because it showed us that we could defeat the mighty Persians. Our dedication, advanced battle tactics, and cutting-edge technology in armor and weaponry had played a decisive role in securing our victory.

Many were of the opinion that after the Battle of Marathon the war with Persia was over, but I estimated that we had only seen the first phase of a much greater conflict, so I put my focus on building up our defenses and keeping Athens in continual readiness. After a very profitable silver mine had been found thirty miles southeast of Athens at Laurium, I was able to convince the Athenians to use this wealth to build two hundred trireme ships. The trireme ship derived its name from the three tiers of oars on each side of the ship, with a total of 170 oars that accelerated the ship up to a speed of eight knots. Its most powerful weapon was an underwater ram that would be used to devastate the larger and slower Per-

sian ships. Thus triremes were like reusable surface-skimming missiles that could ram, back out, maneuver, pick up speed again, and quickly ram another ship.

Because Themistocles was convinced that the Persians would attack again and because he knew that on land the Athenian army was inferior to the Spartan forces, he would purposefully draw Athens's attention toward the sea and build a large harbor facility in nearby Piraeus to house the naval fleet that was tripling in size.

Darius indeed planned to quickly launch another war against Greece but was restrained by a revolt against the Persians in Egypt. He died while preparing to march on Egypt and the throne of Persia was passed on to his son Xerxes, who crushed the Egyptian revolt and very quickly restarted the preparations for the invasion of Greece, which would begin ten years after the Battle of Marathon.

When the forces of Xerxes approached Greece, Themistocles proposed to block the advance of the Persian army at the pass of Thermopylae and simultaneously block the Persian navy at the Straits of Artemisium. A naval force of 271 triremes was therefore dispatched to await the arrival of the Persian navy. Fortunately, the Persian navy would already be decimated on their way to Artemisium as they were caught in a gale off the coast of Magnesia and lost about four hundred of their twelve hundred ships. After arriving at Artemisium, the Persians sent a detachment of two hundred ships around the coast of Euboea in an attempt to trap the Greeks. The god of the sea, Poseidon, was apparently on the side of the Greeks once again when these elements of the Persian fleet were caught in another storm and shipwrecked. When the Persians eventually engaged the Greek navy in a battle that would last three days, both sides would suffer roughly equal losses—about half of the allied Greek fleet would be destroyed.

At the third day, Themistocles received news of the defeat of the allied army at Thermopylae, and since the allied fleet was badly damaged and no longer needed to defend the flank of Thermopylae, they retreated from Artemisium to the island of Salamis in the Saronic Gulf near Athens. Meanwhile, the Persians overran central Greece and captured the now-evacuated Athens.

According to Plutarch in his parallel lives work on Themistocles, he stated that the Greek admiral wrote messages on the stones around potential landing and berthing sites for the Persians. He asked that Greeks fighting for the Persians to come over to the Greek side in the next battle.

Although heavily outnumbered, Themistocles persuaded the Greek allied forces to bring the Persian fleet to battle again in the hope that a victory would prevent naval operations against the last bastion of Greece, the Peloponnesian peninsula where Sparta was located. His idea was to lure the Persians into the narrow Straits of Salamis to have a tactical advantage over the larger Persian ships. Themistocles sent a servant, Sicinnus, to Xerxes with a message proclaiming that Themistocles was "on the king's side and prefers that your affairs prevail, not the Hellenes." Themistocles claimed that the allied Greek commanders were infighting, that the Peloponnesians were planning to evacuate that very night, and that to gain victory all the Persians needed to do was to block the Greek fleet.

Because Xerxes was anxious for a decisive battle, he indeed ordered his ships to attack the Greek navy in the Straits of Salamis while blocking both entrances. But in the cramped conditions the great Persian numbers were an active hindrance, as ships struggled to maneuver and became disorganized.

Queen Artemisia I of Caria was a Greek who had been forced to side with the Persians. She brought five ships into the Persian fleet and was considered their best warrior. When Artemisia spied the notes from Themistocles, she planned to turn against the Persians when the timing was right. On her ships she ordered that they carry flags of both the Persians and the Greeks, and on her signal the Persian flags were to be switched.

Artemisia was my twin soul as I've covered in her life as Queen Hatshepsut. This is a perfect example of twin souls supporting each other on a larger scale throughout time. During the Battle of Salamis she would change out her flag and ram a Persian ship and then leave the battle with her ships. Xerxes had come to witness the battle from his throne atop Mount Egaleo. He witnessed Artemisia attacking and sinking what he thought was a Greek ship. Xerxes then quipped sarcastically, "My men have become women, and my women men."

Seizing the opportunity of the Persian fleet's confusion, the Greek fleet scored a decisive victory, sinking or capturing at least three hundred Persian ships. Since it was Themistocles's long-standing advocacy of Athenian naval power that enabled the allied fleet to fight at all, and because it was his stratagem that brought about the Battle of Salamis, Plutarch noted that Themistocles "is thought to have been the man most instrumental in achieving the salvation of Hellas."

Through more subterfuge from Themistocles, Xerxes became fearful

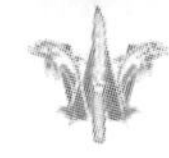

of being trapped and quickly retreated to Asia, leaving the remainder of his forces with his general, Mardonius, to finish up Greece. Mardonius, however, would be defeated a year later by the allies under the leadership of Spartan General Pausanias. Themistocles tried to persuade the Greeks to cut off Xerxes's retreat into Asia at the Dardanelles, but being unsuccessful he again sent Sicinnus to Xerxes, claiming that he had dissuaded the Greeks from pursuing him and thus saving his life.

In the wake of the war, the Spartans carried Themistocles with them to Sparta where he was rewarded for his wisdom and conduct with a crown of olive. He was presented with the best chariot in the city, and the three hundred knights of the royal bodyguard escorted him to the confines of their country—an honor never awarded to anyone other than the king of Sparta before or afterward. Plutarch notes that when Themistocles entered the stadium at the next Olympic Games, "the audience neglected the contestants all day long to gaze on him, and pointed him out with admiring applause to visiting strangers, so that he too was delighted, and confessed to his friends that he was now reaping in full measure the harvest of his toils in behalf of Hellas."

Themistocles continued with his policy of establishing Piraeus as the main harbor of Athens. He saw the great natural advantage of its locality and desired to use it for the benefit of the Athenians. This was a reversal of what the ancient Athenian kings had established, endeavoring to turn their subjects from the sea to planting and tilling the earth. Themistocles created a whole new middle class by empowering the mariners, and he also turned Athens into a major sea power and successful trading empire.

In an effort to further protect Athens, Themistocles would be responsible for the construction of the Long Walls, which were four miles long and joined Athens with the new harbor of Piraeus and the ancient harbor of Phalerum in a single system of defenses. The Spartans had insisted that no fortifications be built outside the Peloponnese for fear that if the Persians would ever come back and manage to capture fortified cities, this would give them too much of an advantage. When the Spartans protested about the fortification of Athens, Themistocles was sent to Sparta to discuss the matter. Meanwhile, Pericles was rushing the people of the city to build the foundations and part of the walls.

Themistocles told the Athenians not to send any other envoys until the walls were at a reasonable height, but once he got to Sparta he refused to open discussions until his fellow envoys arrived. When they finally did arrive, he suggested that a delegation of the most eminent Spartans trusted by both sides accompanied by the Athenian envoys be sent to investigate the matter. The Athenians then refused to let the Spartan delegation leave until Themistocles was safely home. During all these delaying tactics, the walls were built to such a height that the Spartans could no longer prevent the Athenians from finishing their defensive works.

Unfortunately for Themistocles, his bold actions would eventually come to haunt him as some Athenians grew increasingly jealous of his success and power. So less than ten years after the Greek victory in the Straits of Salamis, they exiled Themistocles by popular vote for ten years. Themistocles really hadn't done anything wrong; his ostracism "was not a penalty, but a way of pacifying and alleviating that jealousy that delights to humble the eminent, breathing out its malice into this disfranchisement," as Plutarch notes. The Athenians ordinarily did this with all whom they considered too powerful, or, by their fame, disproportionate to the equality thought requisite in a popular government.

Themistocles went to live in Argos between Athens and Sparta, but as if exiling him wasn't enough, the Spartans would send a delegation to Athens accusing Themistocles of being involved in a conspiracy along with Spartan General Pausanias to hand over Greece to the Persians. Keeping in mind that both Pausanias and Themistocles were both heavily responsible for successfully fighting off the Persian attack, their subsequent vilification and persecution is an inglorious but impressive example of the potential for the excesses of democratic mob rule. One hundred years later, the great philosopher Plato would declare that "tyranny naturally arises out of democracy," which is why the United States of America was initially founded as a constitutional republic where even 99 percent of the population couldn't take away any basic rights from anybody—an achievement that Americans should cherish and defend.

Despite the preposterousness of the claim that Pausanias and Themistocles were involved in a conspiracy against Greece, the Athenians gladly chose to believe the Spartans. They found Themistocles guilty in absentia, and an order was passed that he be put to death. Meanwhile, Pausanias was recalled to Sparta, where he would be wrongly accused and murdered. Understandably, Themistocles didn't feel safe in Argos anymore and took refuge with Admetus,

king of Molossia. Admetus refused to give up Themistocles when Athens and Sparta demanded his surrender, but he also pointed out to Themistocles that he could not guarantee his safety in case of a joint Athenian-Spartan attack. He did, however, give Themistocles an armed escort to Pydnus.

From there, Themistocles took a ship for Ephesus on the west coast of present-day Turkey. He had a narrow escape at Naxus, where the Athenian navy was stationed at the time, but the captain of the ship that Themistocles was traveling on refused to let anyone leave the ship, and so he arrived safely in Ephesus. From there Themistocles took refuge with Artaxerxes, the son of Xerxes, claiming that Artaxerxes owed him a favor since he had been responsible for his father getting home safely from Greece. Themistocles asked for a year to learn Persian and promised that after this period he would help Artaxerxes conquer Greece.

Artaxerxes danced with joy after hearing this. He praised the gods and asked them that the Greeks continue to ostracize their best and brightest so that he could have them for his own empire. In an effort to express his hospitality and gratitude, Artaxerxes would go on to assign the revenues from Magnesia to Themistocles to fund his bread, those from Lampsacus for his wine, and those from Myus for his household.

It is, however, reported by Athenian General Thucydides that Themistocles died shortly thereafter at the age of sixty-five at Magnesia near Ephesus. Thucydides would later be instrumental in restoring Themistocles's reputation, saying that he was "the best judge in those sudden crises which admit of little or of no deliberation" and "whether we consider the extent of his natural powers, or the slightness of his application, this extraordinary man must be allowed to have surpassed all others in the faculty of intuitively meeting an emergency."

Rumor even had it that Themistocles didn't die of natural causes but poisoned himself by drinking the blood of a bull. This was thought to be because he was unwilling to help King Artaxerxes crush an Athenian revolt against the Persians in Egypt, as is reported by Plutarch.

My thoughts, however, are that true to his ability at subterfuge, Themistocles deceived Artaxerxes both with his initial promise to help him conquer Greece and also with his feigned death. My belief is that I had planned to go into hiding all along when I had asked for a year to learn Persian and that I continued my life in a secret location.

In Ancient Greece, the history of running can be traced back to 776 BCE. Running was important to members of ancient Greek society, and is consistently highlighted in documents referencing the Olympic Games. The Olympic Games hosted a large variety of running events, each with its own set of rules. The ancient Greeks developed difficult training programs with specialized trainers in preparation for the Games.

Themistocles was an Athenian politician and general. He was one of a new breed of non-aristocratic politicians who rose to prominence in the early years of the Athenian democracy. As a politician, Themistocles was a populist, having the support of lower-class Athenians, and generally being at odds with the Athenian nobility.

In the Olympics, there was a race in armor, the hoplitodromos, which reflected the games' origins as a means of training for warfare. The torch-relay race was added to entertain the crowds. This event was run the night before the ancient Olympic Games began. Today we honor this tradition with the Olympic torch.

A *trireme*, literally "three-rower," was an ancient vessel and a type of galley that was used by the ancient maritime civilizations of the Mediterranean Sea, especially the Phoenicians, ancient Greeks and Romans. This is an image of a fleet of *triremes* ready to engage in a sea battle.

Poseidon was the protector of seafarers, and of many Hellenic cities and colonies. Homer and Hesiod suggest that Poseidon became lord of the sea following the defeat of his father Cronus, the world was divided by lot among his three sons; Zeus was given the sky, Hades the underworld, and Poseidon the sea, with the Earth and Mount Olympus belonging to all three.

"I SHALL SHOW THAT IT ISN'T POSITIONS WHICH LEND MEN DISTINCTION, BUT MEN WHO ENHANCE POSITIONS."

◊ *King Leonidas* ◊

CHAPTER 18

PAUSANIAS, SPARTAN GENERAL AND REGENT, 480 BCE

In 2007, when the movie *300* by director Zack Snyder hit the big screen, the story of a tiny band of Spartan warriors fighting to defend their freedom against the mighty Persian army received wide attention even among those who had not been familiar with this episode of Greek history before. The movie, which is an adaptation of a comic series by Frank Miller, accurately depicts many important details surrounding the involvement of the three hundred warriors of the Spartan royal guard in the Battle of Thermopylae and impressively conveys the fundamental values of ancient Sparta such as honor, courage, and discipline. However, some of the known historical facts would be changed in order to create an even more idealized account of what had happened. I'm very excited to relate to you what I have remembered from my lifetime as Pausanias during the reign of King Leonidas, including some hitherto unknown details about the Battle of Thermopylae.

I had been fascinated with this part of Greek history since I first heard of it, and more than two decades ago, while I was an assault team operator in SEAL Team Six, the first memories of this particular incarnation began to

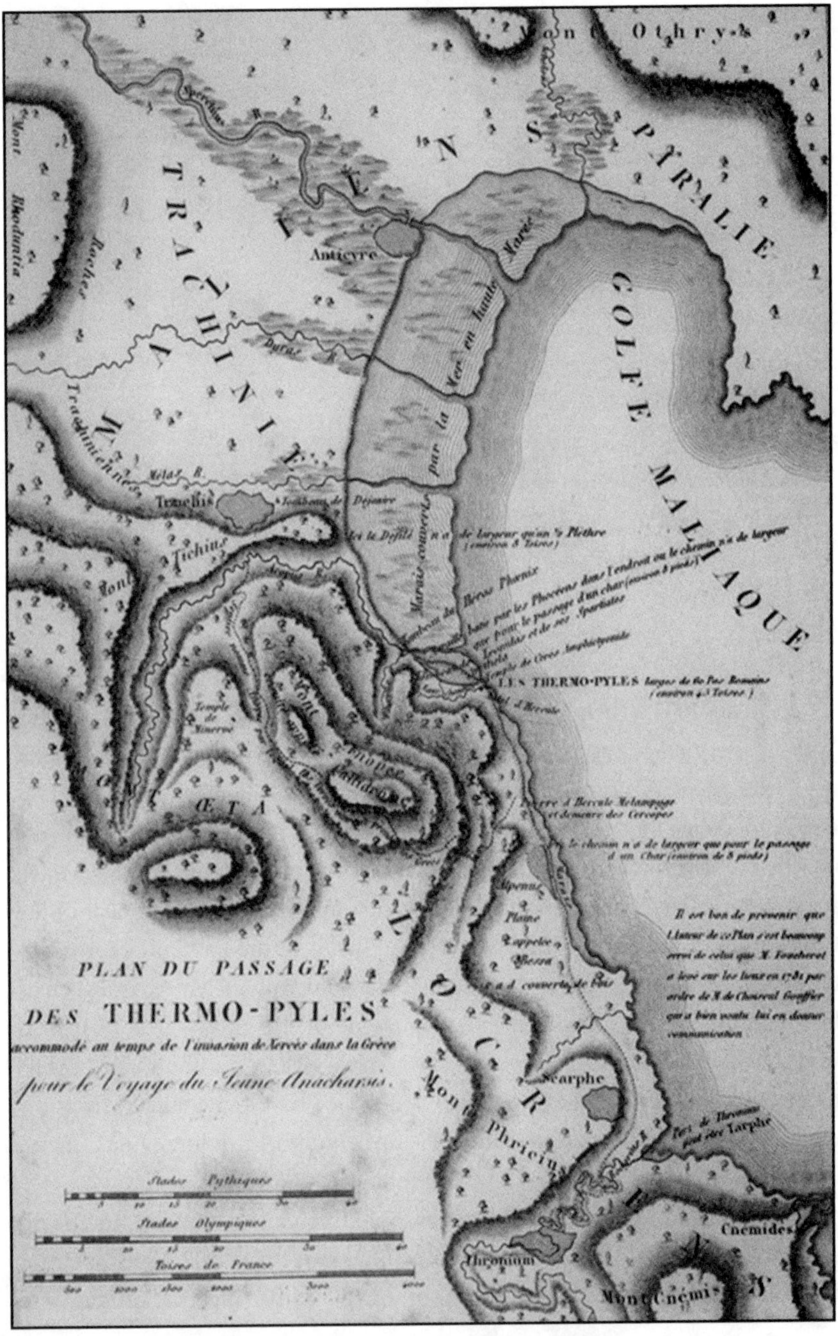

PLAN DU PASSAGE
DES THERMO-PYLES
accommodé au temps de l'invasion de Xercès dans la Grèce
pour le Voyage du Jeune Anacharsis.

Il est bon de prévenir que
l'Auteur de ce Plan s'est beaucoup
servi de celui que M. Foucherot
a levé sur les lieux en 1781 par
ordre de M. de Choiseul Gouffier
qui a bien voulu lui en donner
communication

Mont Othrys
PARALIE
GOLFE MALIAQUE
TRACHINIE
Anticyre
LES THERMO-PYLES
ŒTA
Scarphe
Mont Phricium
Thronium
Cnemides
Mont Cnemis
Stades Pythiques
Stades Olympiques
Toises de France

surface. At first, I just felt strongly that I had been at the Battle of Thermopylae. The next wave of memories finally came in during my very first past life regression with Rebecca Shaw, the owner and director of the Charleston Hypnosis Center in Charleston, South Carolina. Rebecca expertly led me in a deep meditative session and had me go to the past life that I was most drawn to explore. I was conscious as an observer while scenes from a past life as a Spartan warrior during the time frame of King Leonidas appeared before my mind's eye.

I was greatly surprised at the amount of emotion that was stirred up during this process as tears started streaming down my face. Only later I would learn that it's very common for people to experience these intense emotional releases during past life regressions. I would have several more sessions with Rebecca, and each one was instrumental in recovering more memories and developing my intuitive abilities. Rebecca, who is a very gifted intuitive in her own right, told me that she believed I would be channeling and accessing past life memories independently within the next few years.

Time would prove her right, as I grew more confident in my ability to connect to the memories of my previous lifetimes, whether spontaneously or during my meditations. Interestingly, when I'm traveling to one of my past lives it's like entering a theater where I'm one of the actors and the action seems to be happening *right now.* We tend to believe that linear time is the only way to experience reality. After many years of exploring past life information, I've come to the conclusion that all time exists simultaneously and our ability to channel information from different lifetimes is in fact the ability of our consciousness to transcend the restricting boundaries of linear time. I estimate that in the future we will all channel our past lives as I can already see a rapidly increasing number of people that are waking up to this ability.

During the many occasions when I regressed to my lifetime as Pausanias, I have recognized several of my friends from the SEAL teams. This makes perfect sense to me, because both the ancient Spartan societies as well as the SEAL community have a lot of common characteristics. These similarities include the devotion to rigorous training and the mental discipline to persevere and adapt even to the harshest of challenges. The ability to unwaveringly carry on with a mission in the face of insurmountable odds and the threat of physical annihilation is second nature to any SEAL just as it had been to Spartan warriors.

As Pausanias I would be born into the royal house of the Agiads, who were descendants from Heracles and conquered Sparta two generations after the Trojan War. Because I excelled during my training in the *agoge*—the Spartan system of education that I had described in the chapter about Lycurgus—I would eventually be selected to be one of the three hundred Spartan warriors of the royal guard. After several years of performing admirably and even saving the king's life during a battle, I would eventually be chosen to join an advanced scout unit consisting of twenty-one warriors. Everybody within this scout unit was a battle- tested former member of the three hundred and recommended by our peers with the king having the final say on who would be selected.

All of us strongly felt the responsibility that we had as the protectors of Sparta. We routinely assessed the possible threats to our city and determined that the Persian Empire, now under the rule of Xerxes, still had the power and ambition to launch another massive campaign against Greece. We knew that the Persian Empire extended from Asia over Egypt to what is now Turkey and was able to draw vast amounts of men and material from its subjects, keeping an army that we estimated to number close to a million men. A revolt among his subjects in Egypt kept Xerxes busy for some time, but it came as no surprise for us when we eventually heard that the Persian army approached the Greek heartland, making rather leisurely progress through Thrace and Macedon. It was said through witnesses that the army was so big that it drank rivers dry and left the landscape behind it barren.

Earlier in the year, the Oracle at Delphi warned us with the following prophecy:

> *People of Sparta, either your city is destroyed by the Persians or it is not, and Lacedaemon will mourn a dead king of Heracles's line. For the might of bulls and lions will not stay the enemy in battle; he has Zeus's might. And I say that he will not stop until he has destroyed one of these two.*

This prophecy reinforced our confidence in our ability to defend Sparta against the greatest army on the face of the Earth at the time, even under the prospect that Leonidas, who was my uncle in that lifetime, might be killed in the process. Sparta had two hereditary kings at a time, one from the Agiad and one from the Eurypontid dynasty, and as a king from the Agiad line, Leonidas was fully aware that this prophecy referred to him.

Finally, in mid-August of 480 BCE, news of the imminent Persian invasion reached Greece thanks to a Greek spy. It was at this time of the year that all Spartans were celebrating the festival of Carneia. Spartan law forbade military activity during the festival, which had been the reason why the Spartans missed the Battle of Marathon ten years earlier. It was also the time of the Olympic Games, and therefore it would have been doubly sacrilegious for the whole Spartan army to march to war, breaking the Olympic truce during the festival of Carneia.

However, the memory of how we had been late at the Battle of Marathon was still alive in our minds when we realized the great danger that we were in now. We felt that we had to move out immediately. Being aware of our determination, the Ephors—five annually elected citizens who were too old to fight and meant to be a counterbalance to the king, acting as governors when the king was leading the army in battle—decided that the urgency was sufficiently great to justify a limited advance expedition. They allowed Leonidas to take with him the three hundred men of his personal guard, the twenty-one men of the scout unit, and the so-called hippeis, a cavalry unit that also consisted of three hundred warriors. Additionally, one thousand Phoceans and a large number of helots, or unfree men, drawn from other parts of Lacedaemon, accompanied us.

During our rapid transit to Thermopylae, our scout force and the hippeis moved ahead to alert our allies along the way, asking them to join us. But because several of the cities and towns were already deserted, we were reinforced by a smaller contingent than anticipated and numbered no more than seven thousand by the time we arrived at the pass of Thermopylae, which literally translates to "hot gates," deriving its name from the hot sulfur springs close by.

Leonidas, under the scout team's advice, chose to camp at the narrowest part of the pass, which had a sheer mountain face on one side and a cliff heading straight down to a rocky coastline on the other. A mere thousand men standing side-by-side could physically reach from one end to the other.

In preparation for the battle we would further fortify a wall that had been built some time before and also practice our battle formations, especially the phalanx. This formation was designed so that our interlocking shields formed a single line uniformly deep in files of seven to ten or more men who were pressing from behind, thus creating an impenetrable wall. Our heavily armored infantry warriors, the so-called hoplites, would attack with eight-foot-long spears from behind this wall, decimating an enemy force that was less disciplined and armored.

Many years of constant drill and superb discipline made the Spartan phalanx much more cohesive and effective than any other of the Greek armies, which were similarly equipped but trained and formed only when the need arose. In contrast, the Spartan army never stood down, and when it wasn't at war it was training for it. During the next few days, the phalanx led by the Spartans would prove itself to be almost invincible in the confined space of the pass.

We determined that the Spartans would be the first to fight in the front line with the allies moving up and replacing us in several waves. Each group being replaced would fall back in reserve until it was its turn to push to the front again. Initially, there would be four phalanx groups of over one thousand men each. A reserve of over a thousand would be ready to support any group that was faltering. The rest would man the wall and be the last line of defense. We knew that over time our numbers would be decreased, so our plan was to hold the line for as long as possible while the Greek fleet under Themistocles confronted the Persian fleet. We estimated that if we held up their land force in one spot for a protracted period of time while our fleet destroyed large parts of the Persian navy, their mighty land force would be shocked, isolated, and more vulnerable.

Before their main force was even visible, the Persian cavalry approached our position, but we easily turned them back because they had no maneuverability in the confined pass. In an attempt to persuade us to let the Persian army march through, Xerxes sent a messenger delivering a letter to Leonidas saying, "It is possible for you, by not fighting against God but by ranging yourself on my side, to be the sole ruler of Greece." But rebuking the hubris of Xerxes, Leonidas wrote in reply, "If you had any knowledge of the noble things of life, you would refrain from coveting others' possessions. But for me to die for Greece is better than to be the sole ruler over the people of my race." When Xerxes sent his messenger a second time with the mere demand that we should hand over our arms, Leonidas replied with "*molon labe*" or "come and take them." As a symbol of determination and defiance, these words have inspired countless individuals and combat units ever since; even today they are being repeated by pro-Second Amendment activists in the United States.

For several days we watched the Persian army move into position north of our stronghold in the pass. Our scout team did a reconnaissance of the surrounding area, noting that there was a mountain track above and behind our position, which could be used to outflank us. I intuited that we would need to position a large response force on the mountain track to protect our rear, because even a small force coming from behind would preclude our ability to form a phalanx. Holding the pass hinged on our ability to form the phalanx, so Leonidas agreed with my assessment and stationed our scout force along with several hundred Phoceans and a group of helots on the heights to prevent such a maneuver.

After it appeared that the Persians had settled their main force with Xerxes's tent in view in the distance, we moved up into the mountain trail where we had earlier found a perfect spot for an ambush. On their way over the mountain, the Persians would have to move through a narrow rock formation that allowed barely two abreast to walk through. This path led toward an open field that we assumed would serve as a rally and formation point. One side of this field had sheer cliffs dropping down several hundred feet so that it could only be left safely after crossing the field and moving down the narrow pathway.

To maximize our ability to rally, motivate, and direct the warriors who accompanied us on the mountain trail, we split our scout force into three groups of seven. I would close and hold the rock formation, or "door" as we called it, through which the Persians would enter the open field. The leading officer of our group would command the largest force, which would be concealed at the side of the open field where a small mound rose. This would allow our men to crouch without being seen. The second senior enlisted and his group would be positioned farther down to prevent anyone from leaving the open field and continuing farther down the mountain trail toward our position at the hot gates. We planned to spring our trap after the Persians had come through the door and formed up to continue their movement to the rear of our encampment.

We set up our formations and practiced our maneuvers so that we could perform them with precision even during the night, which we anticipated we would have to do. As Spartans we were trained to fight in any weather or terrain and perform complex movements even in the darkest of nights. Training others to do the same in a short amount of time was also part of our expertise as every Spartan in the *agoge* was trained to be a leader from the earliest age.

Anticipating a force of possibly several hundred to as many as one thousand Persians, we had already set up lookout posts reaching far up the trail that could alert us secretly through a relay system day or night. We expected that some if not all of this force would consist of warriors of the Persian imperial guard, the "Immortals," which presumably was more than ten thousand men strong.

It was late one evening when we decided to suspend our training and eat our meal. For a few hours we would rest under the stars with full armor and weapons ready to spring up at any moment, so when the signal was given that a large force was moving in our direction everyone was fully awake and in position. Silently we awaited the force of unknown strength and ability.

First, an advance group moved through the gap in the rocks and indicated for the rest of the force to follow. The Persians came through in the hundreds and set up a formation in the field just as we had expected. It took almost two hours for the whole force to quietly move into position in the field, and the faint light of dawn was beginning to glow in the east. At last, the final warriors moved through the slit, and a few minutes later the lead group started to move out again.

Around a bend and down a slope—far enough away from the eyes and ears of the soldiers in the open field—we had a force of twenty men ready to quietly spring on their scouts. Only several minutes after this group had been taken care of, the rest of the main body also started to move out two abreast down the path. We would let them get as far as the point where our rear group could spring out and block their passage.

When the signal was given, both pathways leading out of the open field were slammed shut as Greeks rushed out and formed phalanx walls bristling with long spears. The surprise was complete and many in the Persian ranks were cut down by spear thrusts before they could lift so much as a shield to protect themselves. The cries of the wounded and dying quickly began to fill the air in the enclosed killing field. Some of the Persians immediately shouted commands to form up the survivors into coordinated groups. Although we had instantly reduced more than a hundred Persians in the first few thrusts of our spears we were now fighting an organized and determined force. The killing began to happen on both sides now.

Combat is extreme, uncivilized brutality. I had experienced this kind of warfare in many campaigns over thirty years during that lifetime up to this

point. In the heat of the battle my survival instincts and routine training made me perform in a very professional and focused manner. I knew that I had to kill as many of the enemy as quickly and efficiently as possible until there would no longer be anyone left on the Persian side who would be willing or able to fight.

During the wild, chaotic close-in fighting at the front of the shield wall I would thrust my eight-foot-long spear into eye sockets, as this was a vulnerable spot unprotected by helmets. A spear thrust into an eye would easily penetrate through the soft tissue of the brain and into the brainstem causing instant death. The spear point had to be quickly extracted or it would be pulled down and the shaft would be yanked out of your hand by a falling body with the spear still stuck in the skull. The Persian Immortals were a fierce adversary but died as any other man when struck with a killing blow.

I thrust my highly sharpened spear designed with multiple blade edges into a piercing point at throats that would then erupt in geysers of shooting blood. I often had to duck to the side or hike my shield to keep the hot sticky blood from causing me irritating and burning blindness. The blood soon covered our shields and began to muddy the soil so that it crept over my sandals and onto my feet. Puddles of blood began to form on the ground and in the dim light of the stars looked black.

If I could not easily penetrate into an unprotected throat or eye because of an upraised shield I would use all of my strength to thrust through it into the enemy. The shields the Persians carried were made of wicker or of light wood and could be penetrated by a powerful spear thrust. Several spears up and down the line had several wicker shields in a line stuck to them yet they continued to thrust and jab adding more shields to the count.

In contrast, the Spartan shields were made of oak several inches thick and covered in polished bronze. We would protect ourselves with our shields but also use them as weapons as we crashed their metal fronts into unarmored bodies. This shock would often cause the light Persians to fall and then we'd drop the heavy weighted edges of our shields onto the prostrate faces and bodies on the ground. Skulls and bones would crunch and snap with a sickening sound that was repeated up and down the line.

I could make out what I knew were Persian nobles with tiaras on their heads directing their dwindling number of warriors into the fray. I focused on

them exclusively now as several Spartans began to coalesce on either side of me so that we would fight as a unit just as we had trained to do all our lives. We moved as one, intuitively knowing what each other was doing by the slightest movement in the shield wall. My spear was shivered into pieces along its shaft by a sword. I instantly went for my *xiphos,* a two-foot-long double-edged stabbing sword. I began thrusting upward into the bellies and groins of my opponents. Sometimes I'd perform an overhead stab over my shield at an unprotected head if it presented itself when I slammed my shield against a body. I would re-sheath my *xiphos* back into the shoulder sling over my left shoulder and pick up one of the many weapons that were strewn across the battlefield, preferably javelins as I could immediately throw them at exposed combatants. The coppery smell of blood filled the air. Excrement and the contents of half-digested food from stomachs assailed my nostrils as men suffering from disembowelment slashes screamed and writhed on the ground in their own waste.

We started to gain the upper hand and went on to do a series of maneuvers that I'd trained our group in. Although the movements required a high level of skill and finesse, they were performed expertly. Using the phalanx formation, we would shield-press the Persians in front of us until the resistance became fierce and then fall back as if in retreat. This maneuver caused our opponents to charge after us in disarray because they thought we were vulnerable. But to their surprise we would quickly reverse ranks again as the warriors who had been in the front line ran back through the long single-spaced lines of our second line. A new phalanx wall was quickly formed after the last man ran through.

We were as good fighting at night as we were in the day, having practiced our maneuvers into the darkness on many occasions. We could all move as one even if blindfolded. Most armies were untrained for night fighting and so we had the upper hand. The orders for maneuver were called on the flute and we moved as one.

With this tactic we would devastate the Persians as they rushed surprised into our amassed and ready weapons. The group charging behind them forced the soldiers trying to stop into our razor-sharp spears. I remember seeing the terror in the faces of many of the Persian nobles when they were attacked in this manner. I immediately knew that they had not trained for this kind of combat, and I felt an instant of pity for these men, many of whom were likely princes and

related to Xerxes. I quickly looked across the field and saw dwindling pockets of resistance. I saw Greeks in a phalanx formation as they pushed several Persians over the cliff and another line that was slowly moving to our position in the field pushing before them the remnants of our battle- weary foes. We had little resistance left in our portion of the field so we also began to move toward the advancing group across the body-strewn field. Their fear was heavy in the air.

I knew that once the Persians realized that they would suffer a defeat on the mountain trail they would fight like demons to make their way back through the door and inform Xerxes. This could not be allowed because a larger force would instantly be sent. To prevent any Persian from alerting their main force, we had a twelve-man group positioned on the other side of the door that would immediately kill anyone who tried to escape through the tight rock formation. The dead, stacked bodies of our enemies had already physically closed the door. If anyone should be so lucky to tear a hole in the corpse wall, twelve simultaneously thrusting spears from our guard from the other side would send them to Hades.

The Persians fought to the last man, which was well and good because we were not willing to spare the men to watch prisoners or take Persians to our camp as there was the risk that one could escape or be seen by their main force. We wanted the Persians to be completely unaware of what had happened to their expeditionary force. For all they knew their group could have been lost and wandering around in the mountains. This no doubt would buy not only us but also the Athenian fleet under Themistocles more time. It would also show the rest of the Greeks that the seemingly invincible Persians could be held up for several days by a vastly smaller Greek force.

When the battle on the mountain trail was over, I would learn that there were only five left of our scout unit, two men and myself from my group and two from the other flank. Our leader and all of the men from the middle group had been overwhelmed and killed. Although all survivors from our scout unit including myself had sustained some type of wound, we were still in fighting shape. The Spartan-trained helots that were promised their freedoms if they would fight honorably in battle were of great support, but nevertheless over half of their number had been killed. Of the Phoceans there were less than one hundred left alive of which only fifty were still able to fight. Altogether, there were only a little over one hundred Greeks left alive. On the other side, we estimated that well over a thousand of the Persians had fought and died in the blood-soaked field. Even the rock walls that had quietly stood sentinel around us were splashed high up their faces with the blood and gore of the combatants.

While the majority of the survivors remained on the mountain pass, I left with a small force to report back to Leonidas and help the wounded return to our camp. Leonidas was astonished that the Persians had sent such a large force and pleased that we had annihilated so many of their best men. I relayed to him that our battlefield tactic of pressing shields in a phalanx formation followed by quickly retreating and immediately reforming had been instrumental in our victory. I had a close relationship with Leonidas and we would converse often. We had a mutual respect and noticed the intuitive abilities in each other that transcended the instinctual and analytical abilities that all advanced Spartan warriors possessed.

Leonidas sensed that it was the right time now to announce that he was bestowing the honor of generalship over the armies of Sparta to me. As a general I would still answer to the king but also have the right to make unilateral decisions to implement his directions. It would be an honor and a fortunate decision, as I would later lead our forces to one of the greatest victories on the battlefield that Sparta and all of Greece would ever see.

Our annihilation of the Persian force on the mountain trail had undeniably earned us time as Xerxes would not send any more troops for another two days. But when he gave up on hearing back from his advance force he eventually ordered his main force to move forward and confront us at the hot gates. We Spartans had lived and trained our whole lives for the kind of battle that was now upon us. We would march out into the mountains around Sparta where we would exercise for several days straight in the worst of conditions imaginable to prepare for any battle hardships that we might have to face. We had trained to fight in all weather conditions all day long and could perform advanced maneuvers on the move, delaying tactics, advancing tactics, and many more without food or water for extended periods of time. The Persian forces on the other side had not been exposed to such conditions and were ill suited to meet an army with advanced armor, tactics, and stamina.

It was a slaughter as wave after wave of different formations advanced toward us during the long hot day. As a general now, I would call out the forma-

tions to the flute players who would then pipe the melodies to set the cadence, formations, and maneuvers like the one where our phalanx would perform an organized retreat and quickly reform. Leonidas particularly wanted me to use this one because of our previous success on the mountain trail. This tactic would again prove itself effective as we would destroy several formations of several thousand men each, advancing our line back up each time to where we had started and repeating the process. Some of the Persian units sent to our position put up a better fight than others, but none were our equal.

It was already late when a phalanx of Greeks that had sided with Xerxes approached us and gave us one of the toughest fights of the day. The fighting was brutal and we had difficulty making progress. The Persians became exhausted and realized that they could not defeat us. It was at this point that we started breaking through their line in several places until eventually the entire line collapsed. At this point many Greeks surrendered and we took some of our first prisoners of the day. Xerxes would not send any further units, probably also because a storm had been building up all day with lightning bolts striking all around us. We intuitively saw that as a good omen right when it happened. It became apparent later how good an omen it was when we learned that the Persians lost a great number of ships and men during this particularly violent storm.

As no more Persian units were approaching us it was decided that we would use the storm as a cover for a secret operation during the night. Our bold plan was to use the mountain trail ourselves to get behind enemy lines. During the battle three days earlier I could witness that even the Persian Immortals were very much dependent upon their officers to make decisions. We had seen several of the formations that approached us literally being whipped to the battle lines. Unlike Spartan warriors, who were all trained to be leaders, the Persian forces seemed to be ineffective without their officers. Therefore, we agreed that by killing Xerxes, their commander-in-chief, their motivation and drive for continuing the war would most probably evaporate and the army before us would crumble and disperse.

We formed a small group made up of the survivors of our scout unit and a handful of other skilled climbers to retrace the mountain trail to a known point and scale down a cliff face, inserting ourselves into the Persian encampment. Several of the Greek deserters informed us about the layout of the camp and how we could find the palatial tent of Xerxes. Because there were still many more Greeks in the camp, our plan was to use the armor and blue cloaks of some of the Greeks who had deserted as a cover for our movement. Additionally, we would keep one Spartan dressed in a red cloak and our signature armor to act as a prisoner. We would then escort this prisoner in haste to see the king because he allegedly knew a way over the mountain pass that he was willing to divulge only to the king, as he wanted a ransom for his information.

We suited up in armor and weapons and quickly moved out under the raging storm. Our sentries on the mountain pass helped guide us and after a few hours of slogging through mud and mountain streams we found the place where we needed to climb down the cliff. We had a lot of experience in finding ways to move through the mountainous Greek terrain, leading our army on paths that would surprise our enemies, but even though all the members of our scout unit were skilled rock climbers and mountaineers, this cliff turned out to be very difficult to climb down in the rain even for us. But spurred on by our desire to put an end to the invasion of Greece, our group finished the descent within just one hour. As we reached the bottom of the mountain we placed our decoy in the center of our formation and started marching toward Xerxes's tent.

We encountered several sentry positions in concentric rings around our target in the sea of tents, but the downpour and the very late hour had dulled the attentiveness of the entire armed forces. It was really not that much of a challenge for us to point to our prisoner and gesture about our intent that got us all the way up to an entrance to the royal tent. We presented our preplanned story to an Immortal soldier guarding the tent, and under a suspicious glare we were made to wait.

Not much time would pass before several more of the king's guard came to surround our group of thirteen and escort us unwittingly into the tent. The Immortals led us through several large rooms before we entered a cavernous chamber in which a golden throne encrusted with jewels was placed on a wooden platform in the back of the room. Behind it was a leather wall imbedded with metal points and a heavy wooden door, which opened as we approached the throne platform. Several more Immortals were streaming out of the door and taking up positions on the platform while we were made to wait at a position several yards back from the steps to the raised platform.

A few minutes later, Xerxes entered the room escorted by a contingent of even more Immortals and an individual who was probably his chief councilor to the throne. One of our men spoke Persian and began conversing with the councilor as we sized up the forces around us. We were outnumbered three to one and our chances of fighting through this many men seemed to be very thin. The Immortals that intently watched our every move were much larger than the average Persian and appeared to be stronger and more focused than the warriors we had encountered so far.

We had predetermined that three of us would throw javelins at Xerxes if it didn't look like we could get close enough to attack him with our swords, so I gave the signal for the rest of our men to lash out at the guards around us while three of us threw spears at the king. Our surprise attack nearly succeeded but several of the Immortals quickly stepped in front of Xerxes with shields raised. Two of the spears pierced through their wooden shields killing the Immortals behind them and one of the spears only narrowly missed the king's head as he was shoved off the throne and into his secure chambers.

Even though we were able to strike down several more of the royal guard with our javelins, we knew that our chance to kill Xerxes was gone as the heavy door was shut behind him. The room erupted into screams and curses as all entrances were spilling Persians into the room as if the outside storm had started a flood of Immortals. We could not possibly withstand this onslaught so we dashed for one of the walls, slashing through the cloth that separated the rooms and escaping through the slit. We had already lost several of our men during the fighting and several more were wounded as we broke through the last wall and into the downpour.

Fortunately, the Persians seemed to stay right by their king's side and didn't pursue us with full force, allowing us to disappear into the darkness as the sound of shouting died away behind us. We quickly reformed as if in typical detail and when asked about what was happening we simply shrugged and pointed back toward the royal tent saying that someone had tried to kill the king. We usually got muttered sounds with scowls in reply clearly indicating to us that many of the Persian soldiers secretly hoped that the attempt had been successful.

We made our way back to the cliff but were unable to climb back up the same way with our wounded. Therefore we decided to ditch all of our armor

and weapons except our short swords and wade along the banks of a mountain stream that poured through one of the valleys. It was tedious and we even lost one of the wounded in the stream, but six of our group were able to make it back to the mountain pass as the first light of dawn began to break.

When we arrived at the hot gates our king was pleased with how close we had come to ending the reign of Xerxes. Leonidas predicted that this event had so unnerved the Persian king that it would take little more for him to withdraw from the campaign. Leonidas ordered that nothing be said of this event to the rest of our warriors lest they become too emboldened by our near success.

The next day saw even more intense combat than we had seen the day before. Although we were systematically defeating every single unit that was sent against us, it was beginning to take its toll on our numbers. We were nearly at half strength from the many casualties we had suffered over the last two days. Even though the number of enemy dead was over ten times the number we had lost, we would not be able to hold out much longer. Every available man was sent into the front lines including Leonidas and myself. We would join the phalanx together on the right flank, which was the most crucial part of the entire line. Individual hoplites carried their shields on their left arm, protecting not only themselves but also the warrior to their left. A phalanx would thus tend to drift to the right as the hoplites sought to remain behind the shield of their neighbor, which is why the most experienced warriors were usually placed on the right side of a phalanx.

During this final phase of the battle we would learn from Greeks who had deserted the Persian army and joined our ranks that a huge reward had been offered to anyone who could lead the Immortals over the mountain pass and toward our rear. Apparently a Greek by the name of Ephialtes from Malis took the bait and agreed to guide the Persians along the mountain path.

I was called to Leonidas soon after this news began to spread and was told that I must return to Athens and gather Queen Gorgo and his son Pleistarchus and escort them back to Sparta by ship. As the king's representative, Gorgo was helping to coordinate the alliance between Athens and Sparta. Leonidas told me to leave at once with the last few men of the scout unit, so I embraced my uncle and wished him well, fully knowing that this would be the last I would see of him. Leonidas would also send most of the remaining forces with the wounded

back to their respective cities so that they could pass on the word of what we had done here—we had held up the mightiest army on Earth for several days with only a few thousand Greeks, inflicting enormous casualties on the enemy. The remainder of the three hundred warriors of the royal guard refused to flee and stayed along with the Thespians and four hundred Thebans to continue to delay the Persian advance so that we could gain some distance on the Persian cavalry.

Together with the other three remaining members of my scout unit I moved out through the night and arrived at the walls of Athens by late morning the next day. The city was already being evacuated as we moved to the villa where Queen Gorgo was staying. I had been to Athens before accompanying the royal couple as an adviser so I knew exactly where to find the villa where we used to stay. As we rounded the last corner in the diplomatic enclave we saw the queen together with Pleistarchus being pulled away from the villa's front door by a band of Persians. They had infiltrated into the city in the confusion and turmoil and were now trying to capture diplomats for ransom. We immediately fell upon the group with our spears and swords and even though they were skilled fighters we quickly neutralized their entire group of eight. We took the queen and her son and made haste to the docks where the Spartan ships had been made ready to quickly cast off for Sparta.

While we had been traveling to Athens during the night, Ephialtes was leading the way for a much larger group of Immortals along the mountain track. The Greek forces at the hot gates would thus be encircled at last. Herodotus gives the following account of the ensuing battle:

> *The Persian commanders armed with whips urged their men forward with continual blows. Many were thrust into the sea and there they perished. Their own soldiers trampled a still greater number to death; no one heeded the dying. For the Greeks—reckless of their own safety and desperate since they knew that as the mountain had been crossed their destruction was nigh at hand—exerted themselves with the most furious valor.*
>
> *Here on a little hill they resisted to the last with their swords, if they had them, and, if not, with their hands and teeth until the Persians, coming on from the front over the ruins of the wall and closing in from behind, finally overwhelmed them with missile weapons.*

Xerxes proceeded to pass through the slain and finding the body of Leonidas, whom he knew to have been the Lacedaemonian king and captain, he ordered that the head should be struck off and the trunk fastened to a cross. This proves to me most clearly what is plain also in many other ways—namely that King Xerxes was more angry with Leonidas, while he was still in life, than with any other mortal.

The resistance at Thermopylae had indeed achieved what Leonidas had hoped it would as the Athenians had time to flee their city before the Persian army reached it. My wise uncle had thus saved his wife and son by his sacrifice as well.

When we finally reached Sparta we told the story of how Leonidas with his illustrious three hundred and the other Greeks had performed at Thermopylae. The stories of the defenders' courage began to spread quickly, positively affecting the morale of all Greeks. As decreed by Leonidas, the helots who had fought alongside us were given freedom for valiant fighting. I confirmed his decree and pointed out that without the helots we would not have done as well as we had.

As the new head general of Sparta and eventually all allied Greek forces, I immediately began the fine honing of all our warriors in the battle strategies and tactics that I had learned from my recent combat experience. Because Leonidas's son was very young, I would also be regent until he reached the age of ten.

To improve Sparta's defenses I would initiate the process of fortifying a wall across the entrance into Lacedaemon called the Isthmus of Corinth, a narrow land bridge about four miles wide. Although during my lifetime as Lycurgus I had emphasized that the prowess of our warriors would be more important than the construction of defensive structures, I now had the belief that it would be most expedient to combine both of these elements.

While I put my focus on strengthening our position on land, Themistocles would resoundingly defeat the Persian navy in the Straits of Salamis. Mardonius, Xerxes's top general who had convinced Xerxes to begin the campaign against Greece to begin with, now attempted to convince Xerxes to stay nevertheless and fight yet another campaign. This time, however, Mardonius could not persuade him. Xerxes had witnessed how a relatively small Greek force had fought at Thermopylae where he had almost been killed during our nightly raid that had penetrated his heavily guarded lines. Fearing that he

could be captured or killed if the unopposed Greek fleet blocked his escape route through the Dardanelles, Xerxes took one-third of his army and headed back toward Persia. His forces would suffer heavy losses as they marched back over lands that had already been stripped of their resources.

Mardonius was allowed to stay in Greece and was made governor of those parts of Greece that had been conquered by the Persians. He offered to return Athens, help rebuild the city, and give it autonomous rule and more lands—all under the condition that the Athenians would accept a truce. Fortunately, the Athenians rejected this so the Persians would not have enough time to build up their foothold in Greece. The Spartans and the other allied Greeks had proven their commitment to support the Athenians. It was decided to continue the fight against the Persian invaders.

Mardonius prepared to meet the allied Greek force on the plains of Plataea with his force of nearly three hundred thousand. During the summer of 479 BCE, we marched out with the mightiest Greek army in history numbering slightly more than one hundred thousand and positioned ourselves in the hills near the city of Plataea. Again, we were outnumbered but better trained and armed than our opponents.

Over the next several days, both armies would try to entice the other to move into a disadvantageous position. The Persians had superior cavalry and numbers of men at arms, therefore they wanted to lure us onto the open plain where they could work our flanks and rear with their cavalry and use their superior numbers to wear us down. We knew of that and were determined to deny the Persians this advantage and instead meet them where our hoplite formations would have the greatest leverage. My plan was similar to what had worked in the mountains above Thermopylae and down at the hot gates: we would form a phalanx and quickly retreat to have them chase us thinking we were panicked, disorganized, and poorly commanded, just to let them run right into our newly formed phalanx wall.

During almost two weeks of limited engagements, our troops were gaining confidence and more Greeks were joining our lines. We would eventually lure the Persians into chasing us in larger numbers and encircle them by pulling back the center of our formation quite far while our flanks—controlled by the Spartans on the right and the Athenians on the left—would retreat only

slightly. It was during one of these false retreating maneuvers that Mardonius joined the fight from his fortified camp in his chariot.

The terrain was sloping and rough, which prevented the Persian cavalry from fully forming into a tight charging formation that could have broken our shield walls, but nevertheless Mardonius thought that he was going to gain victory on this day. Up until that point I had not joined the fight on the front lines, but I knew that by killing Mardonius we could end the conflict and expel the Persian force once and for all.

When I spotted Mardonius I immediately led a Spartan contingent toward his position, first cutting off his possible retreat route and then fighting our way through the units surrounding him. As his driver was wheeling the chariot around trying to escape I threw a javelin at him killing the driver while the Spartan next to me threw his javelin and killed Mardonius. Soon after this, the Persian resistance collapsed and their army began to retreat back over the Asopus River with the entire Greek force in hot pursuit. The fortifications of their encampment were no match for our onslaught as we took it by storm until only forty thousand Persians were left and became our prisoners.

After the defeat of the Persian army we decided to have the Persian cooks have a cook-off with us. They would prepare the usual banquet meal for their officers served on golden plates under ornate tents while we would prepare our normal Spartan meal of barley grains and pig's blood. History would record that once the meals were served I would laugh and remark that "the Persians must be greedy when—having all this—they come to take our barley cakes." I would let the Spartan helots who had fought with us eat the Persian meal and gather much of the wealth for themselves. Keeping to a Spartan tradition of not indulging in material gain after a decisive battle, I and the other Spartans would eat our normal meal and not loot the battlefield.

While we were defeating Mardonius and the Persian ground force, the allied Greek fleet sailed to Samos where the demoralized remnants of the Persian navy were based. The Persians, seeking to avoid a battle, beached their fleet below the slopes of Mycale in present-day western Turkey where they had built a palisaded camp. The Greek commander Leotychides decided to attack the Persians anyway, landing the fleet's infantry units to do so. Although the Persian forces put up stout resistance, the heavily armored

Greek hoplites again proved themselves superior in combat and eventually routed the Persian troops. The Ionian Greek contingents in the Persian army defected and the rest fled to their camp, which would then be assailed and a large number of Persians slaughtered. The Persian ships were captured and burned, which marked the complete destruction of the Persian navy. Along with the destruction of Mardonius's army at Plataea, this decisively ended the invasion of Greece.

After Plataea and Mycale, the Persians made no more attempts to conquer the Greek mainland and the allied Greeks would eventually take the offensive. The battles of Salamis and Plataea thus marked a turning point in the course of the Greco-Persian Wars as a whole. A number of historians believe that a Persian victory would have hamstrung the development of ancient Greece—and by extension Western civilization—which has led them to claim that Salamis and Plataea were among the most significant battles in human history.

It's interesting that after my lifetime as Cyrus the Great, who had been the greatest emperor that Persia had ever seen, I would reincarnate as Pausanias, who was the commander of the greatest Greek army the world had ever seen and one of the few Greeks to defeat an imperial Persian army in open battle. Cyrus had been stopped as he overreached in his efforts to expand his empire, and now as his reincarnation I had been instrumental in stopping another unjust expansion of the Persian Empire, thus fulfilling karma from a previous lifetime and helping history to unfold in a positive way.

After the Greek victory I would commission the construction of the so-called Serpentine Column, which featured three intertwined serpents with the top of their heads holding a golden tripod. Constantine the Great, who would be another of my incarnations, which I will talk about in my next book, would later take this monument from Delphi and bring it to the Hippodrome of Constantinople where it still stands today. Reincarnating as Constantine again shows the continuity of soul development and the attraction the soul has to places, ideas, and artifacts connected to former lifetimes. The Serpentine Column originally had the following inscription:

> *Pausanias, commander-in-chief of the Greeks, when he had destroyed the army of the Medes, dedicated this memorial to Phoebus.*

Phoebus is the god of light and another appellation of the god Apollo. The inscription would later be changed and my name deleted as many influential Spartans gradually lost their trust in me and as Sparta devolved into a paranoid police state. Not only were decision makers in Sparta afraid that the other Greek city-states or other countries could potentially become a powerful threat, they also feared that some of their own citizens could become too powerful, just like the Athenians would view Themistocles at the end of my parallel lifetime. As Pausanias, I would be suspected of conspiring with the Persians and recalled to Sparta. But because there was no sufficient evidence to back up this claim, I was acquitted and left Sparta of my own accord, taking a trireme from the town of Hermione to lead the Greek military coalition.

Shortly after the Greek victories at Plataea and the Battle of Mycale, the Spartans had lost interest in liberating the Greek cities of Asia Minor, but when it became clear that Athens would dominate the Hellenic League in Sparta's absence, I would be sent out to lead the allied forces. After we successfully captured Byzantium, I began to make peace negotiations with Xerxes hoping to end the war between Persia and Greece for all time. I even started to adopt Persian customs and expressed a desire to marry the king's daughter, as marrying into a royal bloodline has been a way to cement ties and create peace between two previously warring groups throughout history.

The Spartans recalled me once again because of suspected Persian sympathies, and upon my arrival in Sparta the Ephors had me imprisoned but would later release me after I explained my intentions. On another front they suspected me to be instigating a revolt among the helots. I had long propositioned for the freedom of Sparta's helot community as the helots grew the food and fought in all of Sparta's wars, but it was never my intention to lead or instigate a violent revolution among the helots. I simply was of the opinion that by all Greek standards the helots should have been free and given the opportunity to join the ranks of Spartan citizenry a longtime ago. Unfortunately, the helots far outnumbered the Spartans and a deeply ingrained mutual distrust had been growing over time.

As nobody had enough evidence to convict me of disloyalty, it was decided to forge evidence. A group of helots were convinced to testify that I had offered certain other helots their freedom if they joined me in a revolt. I would

also be accused of conspiring with Xerxes to foment insurrection among the helots and install myself as a tyrant over Sparta. One of the helot messengers that Xerxes and I had relied upon in our communications with each other even provided contrived written evidence to the Ephors supporting that claim, which was the final piece that was needed to formally prosecute me.

The Ephors planned to arrest me in the street, but I was warned of their plans by one in their party and escaped to a temple of Athena. The Ephors walled up the doors, put sentries outside, and proceeded to starve me out. Only when I was on the brink of death did they carry me out so I could die outside the temple, which prevented my death from becoming an act of ritual pollution.

When the helots learned of my betrayal, a group of them indeed revolted and took over a temple of Poseidon. After several days of negotiations, the Spartans would set an example for how rigorously they intended to deal with the helots and defiled the temple, massacring all the helots in and around it. It wouldn't be long after this event that a massive, catastrophic earthquake would shake Sparta as if in retaliation. Contemporary sources estimated the dead at twenty thousand. The helots took advantage of this moment to rise in rebellion once again.

A number of Greek city-states sent troops to help put down the rebellion, among them Athens, which sent approximately four thousand hoplites. But when the Athenians expressed outrage that the Spartans treated what should have been Greek citizens as slaves, this contingent was sent back to Athens out of concern that the Athenians would switch sides and assist the helots. The Athenians were insulted and therefore repudiated their alliance with Sparta. Once the uprising was put down, some of the surviving rebels fled to Athens, which settled them at Naupactus on the strategically important Corinthian Gulf.

The great alliance that had driven off the Persians would never be revived again as disagreements between Sparta and Athens would continue to intensify. The animosity between the two city-states would eventually lead to the outbreak of the Peloponnesian War. I would again experience parallel lifetimes as an Athenian and Spartan. Athenian General Thucydides would record the war for posterity. Spartan Admiral Lysander would be instrumental in ending the long and brutal war.

This 1891 painting of the Priestess of Delphi by John Collier, showing the Pythia sitting on a tripod with vapor rising from a crack in the earth beneath her.

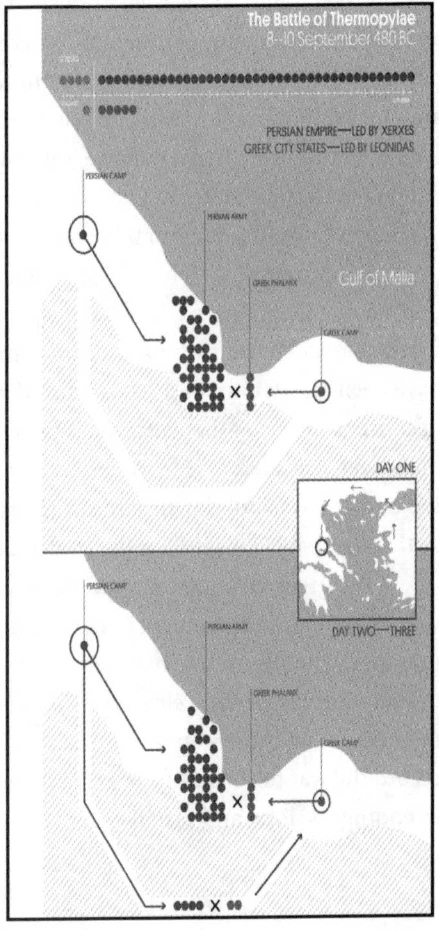

The engagement at Thermopylae occurred simultaneously with the Battle of Artemisium: between July and September 480 BCE. The second Persian invasion under Xerxes I was a delayed response to the failure of the first Persian invasion, which had been initiated by Darius I and ended in 490 BCE by an Athenian-led Greek victory at the Battle of Marathon. This is a flow map of the famous 3-day battle.

Pausanias like all Spartan citizens, would have gone through intense training from the age of seven and was required to be a regular soldier until the age of thirty. Pausanias was from the royal house of the Agiads. Yet this did not exempt him from going through the same training as every other citizen as every male Spartan citizen earned their citizenship by dedicating their lives to their *polis* and its laws.

A modern recreation of a hoplite. Hoplite soldiers used the phalanx formation to be effective in war with fewer soldiers. The formation discouraged the soldiers from acting alone, for this would compromise the formation and minimize its strengths.

Rock relief of an Achaemenid king, most likely Xerxes I, located in the National Museum of Iran. Xerxes I is notable in Western history for his invasion of Greece in 480 BCE. His forces temporarily overran mainland Greece north of the Isthmus of Corinth until losses at Salamis and Plataea a year later reversed these gains and ended the second invasion decisively.

"WHERE IT IS EASY FOR ONE MAN TO CLIMB, IT CANNOT BE HARD FOR MANY TO CLIMB ONE BY ONE, AS THEIR NUMBERS WILL GIVE THEM CONFIDENCE AND MUTUAL SUPPORT."

◊ *Marcus Furius Camillus* ◊

CHAPTER 19

MARCUS FURIUS CAMILLUS, SECOND FOUNDER OF ROME, 446-365 BCE

During the course of my research on past lives, I have often found valuable information in the *Lives of the Noble Greeks and Romans* from the Greek historian Plutarch. His analysis of the parallels in the character traits and accomplishments of influential Greeks and their Roman counterparts has pointed out many similarities that awakened past life memories. This life is one of them. He would always compare two lives at a time, and eventually I began to intuit that Plutarch—whether he was aware of it or not—was tracking reincarnations. When I did further research on Plutarch I found that he was a believer in reincarnation and that we had many similarities between us as well.

To give you an example of Plutarch's work, I had lifetimes with both Alexander the Great and Julius Caesar, and seeing the similarities between them I felt very strongly that Caesar could be a reincarnation of Alexander. When I asked Ahtun Re if they were indeed the same soul, he confirmed my intuition. Other examples of accurately traced reincarnations in Plutarch's work are the parallel biographies of Numa Pompilius and Lycurgus, and those of Themis-

tocles and Marcus Furius Camillus. In fact, I found the life of Camillus after reading Plutarch's biography of Themistocles, whom I had previously connected with on my own. As if Plutarch did some of the investigative work for me, he presented these particular lives right next to each other, so that when I read about them I immediately recognized the soul connection.

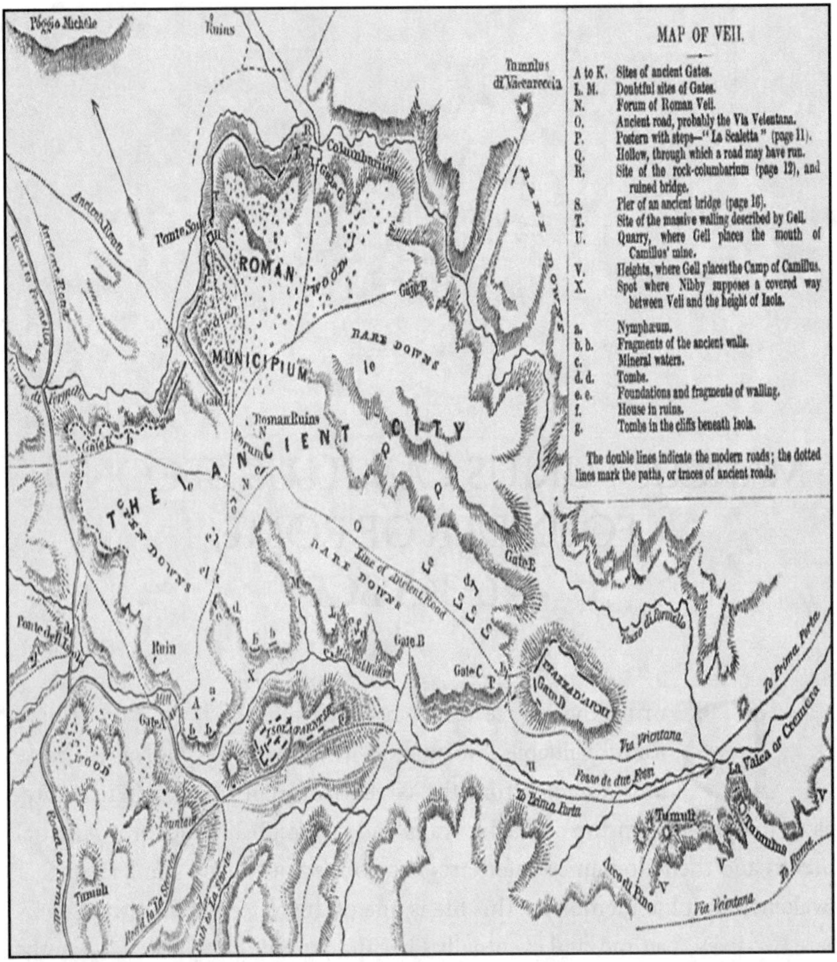

If I could have written a book in the past leaving clues for my future incarnations, then Plutarch's work was perfect. I wasn't all of the incarnations he wrote about, and I'm sure his intent was to also help others reconnect with their former life streams to better inform their current lives. I would eventu-

ally discover that I was Plutarch in a past life. When I saw a statue of Plutarch I felt like I was staring at myself. I will write of Plutarch's life in my next book.

Throughout this chapter, as I outline the life of Marcus Camillus, I will include parallels to Themistocles. In both of these lifetimes I have helped to bestow equal rights to poor and rich alike while having been a nobleman myself. This has met with resistance, and in both lives I would at times be exiled from my hometown despite the great services I rendered as a trailblazer in the development of the Athenian democracy and as the second founder of Rome.

Marcus Camillus came from a prominent family named Furius. His family line was distinguished for rising to power during troubled times as military men. His older brother, Lucius, had a remarkable career serving as consul and tribune for many years. After the Roman monarchy was abolished in 509 BCE, most of the powers and authority of the king were given to two consuls who were usually elected on a yearly basis. Tribunes had the power to convene the *concilium plebis,* the people's assembly, and to act as its president, which also gave them the right to propose legislation before it. The *concilium plebis* functioned as a legislative assembly through which the commoners could pass laws, elect magistrates, and try judicial cases. Another important function of the tribunes was to protect the commoners from the power of the upper class, whose members were called the patricians.

Marcus received an education in religious matters early in his lifetime as a priest's assistant, which earned him the surname Camillus. This period would also help him develop the traits of humility and dignity that would serve him well in his later life—but also offend some of his more worldly associates, as could be observed after his first major military victory against Veii.

Veii was a large and fortified city situated on a rocky plateau about ten miles north of Rome. Both cities had already fought two long wars against each other as they both sought to control the lower region of the Tiber River. This time Rome took the initiative, something that was only possible because the internal social and class struggles had lost their energy thanks to the work of the Furius family. However, as the Romans were unable to put up a blockade and starve the enemy into surrender, the war that had begun in 406 BCE had already lasted ten years when two Roman military tribunes were defeated, which caused a severe crisis. Rome was almost bankrupt and desperate for victory.

It was in times like these that the Romans often appointed a dictator for a six-month term. The word "dictator" literally means "one who composes something" or "one who gives orders." The negative connotation of a dictator being cruel or tyrannical is a later development. Although there were more experienced commanders, like Marcus's older brother, Lucius, Marcus was chosen to be dictator because he had not only shown himself to be an excellent commander but was also seen as a pious man. Once appointed dictator, Marcus made a promise to rebuild the Temple of Juno, which had been destroyed in an earthquake, if he would be successful in the war against Veii. Juno was the wife of Jupiter, the chief deity of the Romans. As the queen of heaven, Juno chiefly presided over every aspect of female life from marriage to childbirth and was referred to as the goddess of love.

In his campaign against Veii, Marcus first marched to Nepete, north of Veii, where he would defeat its allies. Finally, he attacked Veii itself and captured it after diverting a river that ran through an artificial tunnel into the city, similar to what I had done during my incarnation as Thales. Through this tunnel the troops were able to insert into Veii, where they came up inside the Temple of Juno located in the city's citadel. Juno was the main deity of Veii, but in his prayers Marcus asked her to abandon Veii for Rome. The Roman soldiers fought their way through the surprised city and flung open the gates so that the rest of the troops could rush in. The city was quickly sacked afterward, just as the Oracle of Delphi foretold it after Roman delegations had been sent to inquire about the outcome of the long war. Like Themistocles, Marcus won a great military victory that would be a major turning point for his city. The celebration following the capture of Veii lasted four days, and Camillus would return to Rome in a triumphal procession.

Drunk with the success and wealth accumulated from the conquest of Veii, the tribunes of the people's assembly urged a war with the Faliscans, and to ensure victory Camillus was appointed military tribune. Plutarch notes that "the emergency was thought to demand a leader with the dignity and reputation which experience alone could give. After the people had ratified the election, Camillus, at the head of his army, invaded the territory of the Faliscans and laid siege to Falerii, a strong city and well equipped with all the munitions of war." However, it was not through a frontal assault that Marcus would be

victorious, as has been written by Plutarch:

> *The Falerians, relying on the great strength of their city at all points, made so light of the siege that, with the exception of the defenders of the walls, the rest went up and down the city in their garb of peace. The boys went to school as usual and were brought by their teacher along the walls outside to walk about and get their exercise. For the Falerians, like the Greeks, employed one teacher in common, wishing their boys from the very start to bond with one another and grow up together.*
>
> *This teacher, then, wishing to betray Falerii by means of its boys, led them out every day beyond the city walls, at first only a little way, and then brought them back inside when they had taken their exercise. Presently he led them, little by little, farther and farther out, accustomed them to feel confident that there was no danger at all, and finally pushed in among the Roman outposts with his whole company, handed them over to the enemy, and demanded to be led to Camillus.*
>
> *So led, and in that presence, he said he was a boys' school-teacher, but chose rather to win the general's favor than to fulfill the duties of his office, and so had come bringing to him the city in the persons of its boys. It seemed to Camillus, on hearing him that the man had done a monstrous deed, and turning to the bystanders he said: 'War is indeed a grievous thing and is waged with much injustice and violence. But even war has certain laws, which good and brave men will respect, and we must not so hotly pursue victory as not to flee the favors of base and impious doers. The great general will wage war relying on his own native valor, not on the baseness of other men. Then he ordered his attendants to tear the man's clothing from him, tie his arms behind his back, and put rods and scourges in the hands of the boys, that they might chastise the traitor and drive back into the city.*
>
> *The Falerians had just become aware of the teacher's treachery, and the whole city, as was natural, was filled with lamentation over a calamity so great. Men and women alike rushed distractedly to the walls and gates, when lo! There came the boys, bringing their teacher back stripped, bound, and maltreated, while they called Camillus their savior, their father, and their god.*

On this wise not only the parents of the boys but the rest of the citizens as well, when they beheld the spectacle, were seized with admiration and longing for the righteousness of Camillus. In haste they held an assembly and sent envoys to him, entrusting him with their lives and fortunes. These envoys Camillus sent to Rome.

Standing in the Senate they declared that the Romans, by esteeming righteousness above victory, had taught them to love defeat above freedom—not so much because they thought themselves inferior in strength, as because they confessed themselves vanquished in virtue. On the Senate's remanding to Camillus the decision and disposition of the matter, he took a sum of money from the Falerians, established friendship with all the Faliscans, and withdrew.

But the soldiers thought to have had the sacking of Falerii, and when they came back to Rome empty-handed, they denounced Camillus to the rest of the citizens as a hater of the common people and as begrudging to the poor the enjoyment of their rightful booty. And when the tribunes once more put forward the law for the division of the city and summoned the people to vote upon it, then Camillus, shunning no hatred or any boldness of utterance, was manifestly the chief one in forcing the multitude away from its desires.

Therefore, they did indeed reject the law, much against their will, but they were wroth with Camillus, so that even when he met with domestic affliction and lost one of his two sons by sickness, their wrath was in no wise softened by pity. And yet he set no bounds to his sorrow, being by nature a gentle and kindly man, but even after the indictment against him had been published, he suffered his grief to keep him at home, in close seclusion with the women of his household.

Well, then, his accuser was Lucius Apuleius, and the charge was theft of Tuscan goods." It was said,"forsooth, that certain bronze doors belonging to the booty had been seen at his house. But the people were exasperated and would plainly lay hold of any pretext whatever for condemning him.

So then he assembled his friends and comrades in arms, who were many in number, and begged them not to suffer him to be convicted on base

charges and to be made a laughing-stock by his foes. When his friends had laid their heads together and discussed the case, they answered that, as regarded his trial, they thought they could be of no help to him; but if he were punished with a fine, they would help him pay it. This he could not endure and in his wrath determined to depart the city and go into exile.

Accordingly, after he had kissed his wife and son good-bye, he went from his house in silence as far as the gate of the city. There he stopped, turned himself about, and stretching his hands out toward the Capitol prayed the gods that—if with no justice, but through the wantonness of the people and the abuse of the envious, he was now being driven from his country—the Romans might speedily repent and show to all men that they needed and longed for Camillus.

The exile of Camillus is a major parallel with my lifetime as Themistocles, where I was also exiled because too many people became jealous of my influence and status. But as if the soul of Camillus had learned from his previous life, he would later turn the tables in his favor.

Soon after Marcus's exile, the Gauls under their king, Brennus, invaded Italy and made their way south toward Rome. The Gauls were a people who lived in the region roughly corresponding to what is now France and extending beyond its present-day eastern boarders. An army was formed to counter the threat, but in 387 BCE it was completely defeated and routed. The way to Rome was open for the invaders, who sacked the city and besieged the Capitoline Hill where the Sabines had held up in Rome's citadel well over three hundred years earlier. On top of this most famous of Rome's seven hills was also the newly refurbished temple of Juno that Marcus had completed before his exile.

Seven months passed during which the Gauls kept the rest of the city occupied. They also looted the surrounding countryside, spreading fear across many regions of Italy. In the small town of Ardea, however, where Camillus was exiled, he banded together the local men who were of fighting spirit and trained them in guerrilla warfare. Marcus began to destroy some of the raiding parties and quickly aroused the interest of other neighboring towns to join his cause. The remaining Roman army that had held up in the ruins of Veii wanted to elect him and no other as their general, but the Senate had to consent.

A volunteer named Pontius Cominius secretly penetrated the Gaulic lines around Rome to deliver their plea for Camillus to the remaining senators under siege on the Capitoline Hill. In a dangerous night journey he stole through the enemy's lines and climbed up to the Capitol on a secret route. Camillus was then voted not only to be the general of all forces, but he was also given dictatorial powers. It was after this decision that tens of thousands joined Camillus, swelling his ranks to a number that could easily defeat the Gauls if led properly.

The Gauls saw and heard nothing of the stealthy coming and going of Pontius during the night, but the following morning one of them found tracks and scratches down the cliff that clearly indicated a way to gain entrance to the Capitol. That night a large band of Gauls crept silently up the cliff to attack the unsuspecting Romans. Plutarch described the events in this way:

> *They climbed on all fours over places which were precipitous and rough, but which yielded to their efforts better than they had expected, until the foremost of them reached the heights, put themselves in array, and had all but seized the outwork and fallen upon the sleeping watch.*
>
> *Neither man nor dog was aware of their approach. But there were some sacred geese near the Temple of Juno, which were usually fed without stint, but at that time, since provisions barely sufficed for the garrison alone, they were neglected and in evil plight. Geese are naturally sharp of hearing and alert of every noise, and these, being specially wakeful and restless by reason of their hunger, perceived the approach of the Gauls, dashed at them with loud cries, and thus awakened the garrison.*
>
> *At once the Barbarians, now that they were detected, spared no noise and came on more impetuously to the attack. The defenders, snatching up in haste whatever weapon came to hand, made the best shift they could. Manlius first of all, a man of consular dignity, mighty in body and exceeding stout of heart, confronting two of the enemy at once, cut off the right hand of one of them with his sword as he was lifting his battle-ax, and dashing his shield into the face of the other tumbled him backward down the cliff. Then, taking his stand on the wall with those who ran to his aid and formed about him, he repulsed the rest of the enemy, who*

> *had reached the top in no great numbers and showed no prowess to match their daring. So, the Romans escaped out of their peril.*

The Temple of Juno had housed the Romans' gold, silver, and copper coins for safekeeping during the siege. Now, in appreciation of the safety the sacred geese of Juno had wrought, a new honor was bestowed on the goddess. She was henceforth known as the protector of the Romans' coins, and a new temple named Juno Moneta would be built near the Temple of Juno to house and mint Roman coins. The epithet *moneta* derives from the Latin word *monere,* which means "to warn" or "to advise," in recognition of her role in the protection of the treasure stored in her temple. The English word "money" also has its roots here.

The energy that people in Roman times associated with money was considered sacred and kept safe by Juno, while today many people see money as something inherently evil. It is not and never has been evil in and of itself. Money is energy and when you acquire some it is through the energy you have exerted for good or bad. How money is utilized at that point is also up to the entity that came upon it.

In Rome, with supplies running out, disease spreading in their ranks, encamped within ruins, and with no hope of restocking their supplies through raiding parties because of Camillus, the Gauls decided to make a break from Rome. In the middle of the night, Brennus broke camp and abandoned the city with his whole force. After a slow march, because of all the booty they were trying to haul, they covered only about eight miles. Thereupon they encamped in exhaustion and were hunted down by Camillus, as Plutarch relates:

> *At break of day Camillus was upon him, in glittering array, his Romans now full of confidence, and after a long and fierce battle routed the enemy with great slaughter and took their camp. Of the fugitives, some were at once pursued and cut down, but most of them scattered abroad, only to be fallen upon and slain by the people of the surrounding villages and cities.*

After the battle, Camillus celebrated the triumph and the Romans returned to their devastated city. Many resisted the idea of restoring Rome and wanted to abandon the city instead, but inspired and motivated by Camillus, the citizens began to rebuild what was to become one of the greatest cities in history. It was through this achievement that Marcus was named the "second founder of Rome." This is also another parallel to the life of Themistocles, who had reoccupied Athens after the Persians had abandoned it and motivated the Athenians to rebuild the city along with a strong protective wall.

It is through a resurrection in consciousness, which precedes truly uplifting physical actions, that any city throughout history would be rebuilt, whether it had been devastated by natural disasters or human- made calamities. This is also what can happen in many cities in the so- called Third World, in war-torn cities of the Middle East, or in impoverished cities in Western countries such as Detroit. We can see the emergence of many inspiring and empowering projects like large-scale urban farming initiatives to revive and cultivate plots of land that have fallen victim to economic downturn. The recipe for success is always the same; it is the love and the willingness of the population to become creators and stewards of their own habitat, as the people of ancient Rome demonstrated after the Gaulic invasion.

Marcus would continue to serve Rome and its people for many years well into advanced age. In 381 BCE, he was again elected as military tribune together with his nephew Lucius Furius Medullinus, who had a strong following with the younger men of the army. As happens often with the youth, Lucius and many of his soldiers were eager to engage in combat when a conflict arose with the coalition of the Volsci.

According to the Roman historian Livy, Lucius Furius was impatient to begin the battle, and referring to Camillus said that "war was the province of youth, and that men's minds flourished and withered, together with their bodies; that he, who certainly had been a most active warrior, was become a mere drone; and though it had been his custom immediately on coming up with an enemy to snatch from them the possession of their camps and cities at the onset; yet now he wasted time, lying inactive within the trenches. And what accession to his own strength, or diminution of that of the enemy, did he hope for? What opportunity, what season, what place for practicing stratagem? The old man's schemes were too cold and languid. Camillus, for his own part, had enjoyed a sufficient share both of life and of glory; but where was the propriety of suffering the strength of the state which ought to be immortal, to sink into the debility of old age, together with one mortal body?"

Marcus realized that neither Lucius nor the large part of the army that was eager to attack could be held back. If he'd tried to stop them nevertheless, it would have weakened the morale of the Roman forces and left the city more vulnerable to an attack. Hence, intending to both allow Lucius to advance but also remaining prudent in his own actions, Marcus argued that "in all wars which, to that day, had been waged under his singles auspices, neither himself nor the Roman people had found reason to be displeased, either with his conduct or his fortune.

"At present, he was sensible that he had a colleague, in command and authority equal to himself, in vigor of age superior. In regard to the troops, he had always been accustomed to rule, not to be ruled. But his colleague's right of command he could not call in question. Let him do, with the favor of the gods, what he thought the commonwealth required. He would even request so much indulgence to his age, as he should not be in the front line. That whatever duties in war an old man was qualified for, in these he would not be deficient."

Marcus would thus sit back with a reserve force as the rest of the army set off. The provocations from the coalition forces had the desired effect, and relying on his impulses more than on reason and experience, Lucius severely misjudged the enemy. Subsequently, the Roman army was routed all the way back to the camp, so Camillus had no other choice but to rally the men. Leading from the front, he turned the enemy away and drove them completely from the field, nearly annihilating them. Even at an advanced age he was still a great warrior and commander. Fortunately, Lucius also survived and went on to become a great commander and later a consul.

As I write this, I am well over fifty years of age, just as Marcus had been in that battle. I also still actively serve my country. After twenty- four years of active duty as a Navy SEAL, I have now spent over ten years as a security professional protecting government officials in combat zones all over the world. The men that I work with, many of whom are half my age, are not just colleagues to me but potentially men I have fought with throughout the ages. I have caught glimpses of some of these men in past lifetimes where we fought countless battles together. I have no doubt that many who will read these chapters are famous warriors in their own right that history remembers. If I haven't served with you in battle, I have more than likely at some point in history served you by protecting your right to life and freedom.

Marcus Furius Camillus from Guillaume Rouillé's *Promptuarii Iconum Insigniorum* in the 16th century. Camillus was a Roman soldier and statesman of patrician descent.

Juno was an ancient Roman goddess, the protector and special counselor of the state. A daughter of Saturn, she is the wife of Jupiter and the mother of Mars, Vulcan, Bellona and Juventas.

Livy was a Roman historian who wrote a monumental history of Rome and the Roman people, titled *Ab Urbe Condita*, meaning "From the Founding of the City." The history included the period from the earliest legends of Rome before the traditional founding in 753 BCE through the reign of Augustus in Livy's own lifetime.

This is an engraving of Camillus arriving in Rome. There is a facial and physical similarity to Michael Jaco.

Le Brenn et sa part de butin "Brennus and His Share of the Spoils," also known as "Spoils of the Battle," painting by Paul Jamin, 1893. An argument about the weights of his spoils had delayed matters that the exiled dictator Marcus Furius Camillus had extra time to muster an army, return to Rome and expel the Gauls, thereby saving both the city and the treasury.

"THE BRAVEST ARE SURELY THOSE WHO HAVE THE CLEAREST VISION OF WHAT IS BEFORE THEM, GLORY AND DANGER ALIKE, AND YET NOTWITHSTANDING GO OUT TO MEET IT."

◊ *Thucydides* ◊

CHAPTER 20

THUCYDIDES, ATHENIAN GENERAL AND HISTORIAN, 460-411 BCE

During the so-called Classical Period of Greek history in the fifth and fourth century BCE, Athens was at the pinnacle of its might and prestige. The Parthenon, Athens's most famous landmark, was built on the Acropolis, and Socrates defined his method of philosophy, whereby one would continually ask questions and look for inconsistencies in mental concepts, both in one's own thinking and in dialogues. Besides his philosophical activity, Socrates also fought on the front lines of several battles during the Peloponnesian War. He said that "no man has the right to be an amateur in the matter of physical training" and that it is "a shame for a man to grow old without seeing the beauty and strength of which his body is capable." His student Plato would later expand on this idea, saying that "in order for man to succeed in life, God provided him with two means, education and physical activity. Not separately, one for the soul and the other for the body, but for the two together. With these two means, man can attain perfection."

Greece would be a focal point where a huge number of very powerful souls would come together to stimulate each other and all of humanity. As one of these

The Athenian Empire at the brink of the Peloponnesian War (431 BCE)

Aegina (456)
• City-state (date captured)
★ Cleruchy (Athenian garrison) (date)
Rebellion against Athens (date)
Athenian territory
Territory of allied city-states
(I) Thrace district
(II) Hellespontic district
(III) Ionic district
(IV) Carian district (joined with ionic after 438)
(V) Islands district

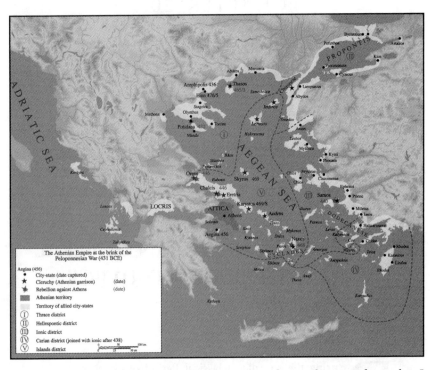

souls, I would have many important incarnations during that time frame, but I also want to emphasize that I only write about selected lives in this book and leave out many lifetimes as obscure people where I would also learn valuable lessons. While these people have never been recorded in the books of history, in the case of Thucydides I even had the opportunity to examine an actual marble bust modeled after him. When I first looked at it, it was like looking at myself in the mirror—just with a beard. I had similar experiences when I discovered marble busts of some of the other Greeks that I incarnated as during this time frame.

Of course, our parents' DNA determines to a great extent how we look physically, but it also seems that distinct physical features are being carried over throughout many lifetimes. We can see it in our daily lives in how our moods affect our appearance and how over time our mental, emotional, and spiritual states affect permanent physical features such as our postures or furrows in our brow. Just as we develop our physical appearance during the course of one lifetime according to both our inner and outer bearings, I think certain characteristics at a soul level shape each physical body in very distinctive ways.

THUCYDIDES, ATHENIAN GENERAL AND HISTORIAN, 460-411 BCE

To find out the truth about my past lifetimes, I determined that I would investigate as much of the available information as I possibly could, whether it would pertain to a person's appearance, writing style, or life purpose. Helpful clues can be found in the most unlikely of places, especially if you follow your intuition and examine your findings diligently with an open mind as you venture to uncover the truth, whatever it may be.

Such diligence was characteristic for Thucydides, who is known as the father of scientific history because of his meticulous research, documentation, and evaluation. Thucydides's account of the "war between the Peloponnesians and the Athenians"—today known as the *History of the Peloponnesian War*— set new standards and paved the way for the modern school of political realism, which views the relations between nations as based on might rather than right. Thucydides placed a very high value on eyewitness testimony and writes about many events in which he personally took part. He assiduously consulted written documents and interviewed participants about the events that he recorded.

Thucydides had been taught by the Sophists in Athens not to accept things at face value but to question all things. The Sophists were a category of teachers who specialized in using the tools of philosophy and rhetoric, an art that aims to improve the facility of speakers or writers who attempt to inform, persuade, or motivate particular audiences in specific situations. The Sophists' ultimate purpose of teaching was called *arete,* meaning excellence or virtue, and was taught predominantly to young statesmen and nobility. In its earliest appearance in Greece, this notion of excellence was ultimately bound up with the notion of the fulfillment of one's life purpose or function, the act of living up to one's full potential.

Because he was born into old Thracian nobility, Thucydides used to live in both Athens and Thrace, where his influential family owned gold mines on the coast opposite the island of Thasos, the northernmost of the Greek islands. Through his family, Thucydides was connected to the Athenian general Miltiades and his son Cimon, leaders of the old aristocracy supplanted by the radical democrats. Interestingly, it was Cimon who had led Athens in the ostracizing of Themistocles. Also among the friends of Thucydides was the great statesman Pericles, whom history considers one of the first and most famous rulers of a new form of government, democracy.

Pericles was part of the same soul stream as the Spartan king Leonidas, whose wife, Gorgo, would also join him in this lifetime as his wife, Aspasia. She was called the "female Socrates" by Socrates himself and influenced Pericles in his orations, which would in turn inspire future leaders like Abraham Lincoln. Parts of his Gettysburg Address, which he delivered in 1863 during the American Civil War, have striking similarities to Pericles's funeral oration. In it, he commemorated the dead of the war and praised the achievements that had been made in Athens at that time, "for I wanted to show that for us there is more at stake than there is for others who do not enjoy our privileges. And at the same time, I wanted to provide clear proof of the reality on which I based my praise."

In a display of the way soul groups shift and assume different roles, Gorgo and Aspasia are incarnations of my soul mate. Pharaoh Amenhotep III, Leonidas, and Pericles were all the same soul incarnation. After his life as Pericles, he is reputed to have ascended and assumed the role of the Ascended Master Serapis Bey.

When the Peloponnesian War began in 431 BCE, as a result of the growing distrust between Athens and Sparta, Thucydides was in his twenties. Sparta saw Athens in a dark light. Athens, they believed, was trying to gain control over a growing number of city-states in the region. Meanwhile, Athens saw Sparta as resisting what they thought was their manifest destiny to rule. Early on in the war while herded and confined in their city walls by a Spartan land blockade, Thucydides contracted and miraculously survived the plague that would ravage Athens between 430 and 427 BCE. Most Athenians would suffer in one form or another and thousands would die, including Pericles. Thucydides gives a detailed description of Athens during the plague when people in their great distress and during their fevers would throw themselves in the water cisterns of the city, unwittingly increasing the spread of the disease.

One of the most remarkable battles of the war was the Battle of Sphacteria in 425 BCE, seventy-two days after the Battle of Pylos. The island of Sphacteria is located at the west coast of the Peloponnesian peninsula and separates the Bay of Pylos from the Adriatic Sea.

The previous Battle of Pylos began after a storm forced the Athenians to rest in the bay of Pylos; Demosthenes encouraged the stranded warriors to fortify the peninsula. Within six days, basic structures were built, and Demosthenes was allowed to stay behind with hoplites, archers, and three ships while the other Athenian commanders moved on with the majority of the fleet.

When the Spartans found out about this, they immediately sent out sixty ships and almost one thousand hoplites to attack the Athenians in Pylos. But although the Athenians were outnumbered, they could easily repel the Spartans, who approached the rock on the only two available pathways, both of which were narrow and steep. The Spartan fleet was of no help in this situation because the high surf allowed landing only at one very disadvantageous spot. Only the Spartan war hero Brasidas would dare to land at the beach of Pylos, but he was severely wounded and lost his prized bronze shield. The Spartans would eventually retreat from Pylos and occupy the castle rock of Sphacteria instead.

Before the battle, right after Demosthenes had become aware of the imminent Spartan arrival, he dispatched two of his ships to alert the commanders that had been part of his group before. When Eurymedon and Sophocles arrived with fifty ships a couple of days later, they saw that Sphacteria was occupied and decided to spend the night at the nearby island of Proti, which was uninhabited. The next morning, they found the entrances to the Bay of Pylos unguarded by the Spartan ships, which were lying idle before Sphacteria. The Athenians were quick to take advantage of the situation and managed to capture five ships. The Spartans would save the rest, but all of them would be heavily damaged because of the attacks they suffered when they were being pulled onto the shore.

The Athenians started patrolling around the island to isolate and starve out the Spartans, who were secretly provided by divers with honey and linseed. When the Spartans sent an emissary to negotiate a truce, a full surrender of their fleet was demanded. The Spartans agreed, but when their emissary came to Athens, the Athenians found excuses to delay and eventually cancel the peace negotiations. Seventy- two days after the Battle of Pylos, the Athenians would start attacking the Spartans on Sphacteria, as was described by Thucydides in a detailed and riveting account.

The Athenians used archers to wear out and whittle down the numbers of the Spartans, who thought that archers were unmanly. Unfortunately for the Spartans, their method of relying solely on hop- lite formations was outdated and employed only because of a stubborn determination to hold on to old ways. The Athenians quickly encircled the Spartan warriors and, seeking to take prisoners, asked the Spartans to surrender—to which the Spartans surprisingly agreed.

This would be a shock to the entire Greek world. Spartans, it was strongly believed, would never surrender. It would be the psychological effect of the capture of almost three hundred hoplites by Athens that radically shifted the balance of power in the war for some time. Athens now threatened to execute the prisoners if Sparta continued to invade the Athenian territories like they had since the beginning of the Peloponnesian War. Thus they brought the annual invasions to a halt, and for the first time since the beginning of the war they could farm their crops securely. At Pylos, a Messenian garrison was installed, from which many raids into the country were launched, inflicting significant damage to the Spartans and instigating the desertion of numerous helots.

However, the Athenian superiority would not last for too long as Sparta worked aggressively to tip the scales in the war. Following the defeat at Sphacteria, Spartan General Brasidas would lose no time in heading east with a force to launch a surprise attack on Amphipolis on the Thracian coast. Less than a year earlier, Thucydides had been given command of a squadron of seven ships forty miles east of Amphipolis on the island of Thasos. When the news of the Spartan approach reached Eucles, the Athenian commander at Amphipolis, he immediately dispatched a ship to request assistance from Thucydides.

Aware of Thucydides's presence on Thasos and his influence with the people of Amphipolis, Brasidas was quick to offer mild terms for a surrender of the city. Everyone who wished to stay was allowed to keep their property, and safe passage was offered to those who wanted to leave. Despite protests from Eucles, Amphipolis surrendered. The city would be lost, but Thucydides arrived in time to defend the nearby city of Eion with help from those who had just left Amphipolis.

Amphipolis was of considerable strategic importance, so news of its fall caused great consternation in Athens, where Thucydides's enemies would successfully put the blame on him. Thucydides would be recalled to Athens, tried, and banned. However, as an exile with great wealth to fund his travels and focus on his writing, Thucydides would later say, "It was also my fate to be an exile from my country for twenty years after my command at Amphipolis; and being present with both parties, and more especially with the Peloponnesians by reason of my exile, I had leisure to observe affairs somewhat particularly."

The Athenians would send a strong force to regain control of Amphipolis. Brasidas, who would die in a crucial engagement, would soundly defeat them. One of Sparta's bravest and ablest warriors did not die in vain as a peace treaty

was signed by war-weary Athens in 421 BCE. I was Brasidas in this lifetime in a parallel life. Throughout history I will often work on both sides to keep the madness of war to a minimum or win decisive battles to end a conflict.

In 416 BCE, the Athenians wanted to conquer the small island of Melos east of Sparta to intimidate the Spartans. Melos had been free, independent, and neutral during every conflict for over seven hundred years. Thucydides would include the communications between Athens and Melos in his *History of the Peloponnesian War,* not as a literal transcription but as a crystallized version of the actual negotiations, giving the reader deeper insights into the minds of ancient movers and shakers.

To no avail, the Athenians tried to reason with, humiliate, and threaten Melos through envoys. Eventually, the Athenians demanded that the Melians surrender their city and pay them tribute—or face the destruction of their city. The Melians claimed their right to remain neutral and appealed to the Athenians' sense of decency and mercy toward a small, peaceful, and defenseless city. However, not yielding the slightest, the Athenians sternly replied that questions of justice did not arise between unequal powers. They proceeded to lay siege to Melos and in a brutal display of abuse of power killed all the men of Melos, enslaved the women and children, and resettled the island with Athenians. According to Thucydides, the lesson learned for the Melians would be that "the strong do what they have the power to do, and the weak accept what they have to accept."

In the twenty-seven-year-long struggles, both sides would implement this type of intimidation, subjugation, and merciless warfare against those that would not join them as allies; for example, Sparta would demand the surrender of Plataea, which had been the scene of victory against the Persians during the second Persian invasion of Greece. The Plataeans argued that they had helped both the Spartans and the Athenians during the battle against the Persians and should be allowed to remain neutral, but Sparta reasoned that because it had been more than a generation ago it was no longer valid. Neither side would move in this matter. Eventually, the Spartans would destroy Plataea and massacre all the defenders.

In the seventeenth year after the start of the war, Thucydides wrote one of his most renowned accounts, the story of the tragic defeat of an Athenian expeditionary force to Sicily. The expedition was hampered from the outset by uncertainty in its purpose and command structure, particularly due to the political maneuvering between the "peace party" led by Athenian General Nicias, who had previously brokered a peace between the two warring factions, and a "war party" led by Alcibiades. The party led by Alcibiades was more popular and had more adherents in the military; therefore, Nicias would deliver an emphatic appeal to the Athenian Senate in which he urged the senators to pursue a nonaggression policy, as has been recounted by Thucydides:

> *Against your character, any words of mine would be weak enough, if I were to advise your keeping what you have got and not risking what is actually yours for advantages which are dubious in themselves, and which you may or may not attain. I will, therefore, content myself with showing that your ardor is out of season, and your ambition not easy of accomplishment. I affirm, then, that you leave many enemies behind you here to go yonder and bring more back with you.*

Alcibiades replied before the Senate to influence the senators' opinions in favor of war:

> *Men do not rest content with parrying the attacks of a superior, but often strike the first blow to prevent the attack being made. And we cannot fix the exact point at which our empire shall stop; we have reached a position in which we must not be content with retaining but must scheme to extend it, for, if we cease to rule others, we are in danger of being ruled ourselves. Nor can you look at inaction from the same point of view as others, unless you are prepared to change your habits and make them like theirs.*

The Senate would affirm the war plans, and an initial lightweight force of twenty ships swelled into a massive armada of 134 triremes ready to depart to Sicily. Thousands of hoplites, missile troops, and cavalry were added to the force, increasing its number way beyond what had initially been planned.

But the night before the expedition was about to begin, something unexpected happened. A mysterious group carried out the coordinated destruction of stone markers devoted to the god Hermes, which were situated on the boundaries and crossroads of Athens. The stones were considered sacred protectors, and therefore many people saw the desecration as a bad omen for the expedition and as evidence of a revolutionary conspiracy to overthrow the government. The political enemies of Alcibiades immediately came forward

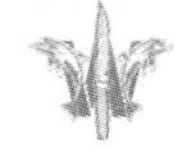

to blame the destruction on him and his friends, but Alcibiades was ready to stand trial as he insisted on his innocence. However, because the trial had to be prepared first, Alcibiades was allowed to depart to Sicily for the time being.

The expedition was sent off with great fanfare, leaving the port of Athens with the grandiose idea and conviction that they would expand the empire of Athens. Alcibiades had convinced the Athenians that Sicily was only the beginning of a greater campaign that would eventually include the Carthaginian Empire in Northern Africa, but within a few weeks of the expedition departing, a ship arrived from Athens to escort Alcibiades back to stand trial. Without the troops, Alcibiades was not able to stand a chance in the trial—his enemies would simply overwhelm the vote against him.

Because a conviction would have been his death, Alcibiades escaped to the Spartan side. He revealed the entire Sicilian expedition plan and much more to the Spartans, but the expedition still achieved early successes under Nicias. Syracuse, the most powerful state in Sicily, responded exceptionally slowly to the Athenian threat and was almost completely besieged when Spartan General Gylippus arrived at the scene. Gylippus galvanized the inhabitants of Syracuse into action, and from that point forward the Athenians ceded the initiative to their newly energized opponents.

Nevertheless, the Athenians would briefly get the upper hand once more when a massive reinforcing armada requested by Nicias arrived together with Demosthenes. The latter would launch a surprise attack, which was going exceedingly well until a portion of the Spartan contingent discovered the secret code word that the Athenian force was using to identify each other during the nightly attack. With that code word, the Spartans infiltrated into the Athenian lines whereupon they created confusion and turned the battle.

Many Athenians would be forced off a cliff and killed in the battle as they fled back down the slope toward their defensive lines. The devastating failed assault on a strategically important point and several crippling naval defeats would damage the besiegers' fighting capacity and morale so much that they planned to abandon the campaign and return to Athens.

But fate would have it that there was a lunar eclipse just as the Athenians were preparing to sail home. When Nicias, described by Thucydides as a very superstitious man, asked the priests what he should do, they suggested that the Athenians should wait for another twenty-seven days before departing—Nicias agreed to do so. The Syracusans took advantage of the delay, and seventy-six of their ships attacked eighty-six Athenian ships in the harbor. The Athenians were soundly defeated and their General Eurymedon was killed in battle. Many of the ships were pushed onto the shore where Gylippus was waiting. His forces killed some of the crews, and eighteen beached ships were captured before a force of Athenians and Etruscans pushed Gylippus back. However, the Athenians were now in a desperate situation as the Syracusans completely blocked the entrance to the port, trapping the Athenians inside.

The Athenian ships were extremely cramped and had no room to maneuver. Collisions were frequent, and the Syracusans could easily ram the Athenian ships head-on without the Athenians being able to move to ram them broadside. Javelin throwers and archers shot from each ship, and the Syracusans thwarted the highly successful Athenian technique of using grappling hooks by covering their decks with animal hides. The battle went on for some time with no clear victor, but the Syracusans eventually pushed the Athenian ships toward the coast, causing the Athenian crews to flee to the camp behind their wall.

Demosthenes suggested that they man the ships again in an attempt to force their way out as both fleets had only lost about half of their ships, but Nicias wanted to find refuge on land. The Athenians were eventually forced to attempt a desperate overland escape from the city they had hoped to conquer, but even that last measure failed and nearly the entire expedition surrendered or was destroyed in the Sicilian interior. If we were to look at the lunar eclipse that preceded this disaster in hindsight, we could interpret it as a warning of a possible eclipse of Athenian might.

In one of his stirring accounts, Thucydides relates how the Athenians in a desperate attempt to outdistance their foes left their wounded behind and the dead unburied. The survivors, including all the noncombatants, numbered forty thousand, and some of the wounded crawled after them as far as they could go. As they marched they defeated a small Syracusan force guarding the River Anapus, but Syracusan cavalry and light troops would continually harass them. Near the Erineus River, Demosthenes and Nicias became separated, at which point Demosthenes was again attacked by the Syracusans and forced to surrender his six thousand troops. The rest of the Syracusans followed Nicias

to the Assinarus River, as has been described by Thucydides:

> *As soon as it was day Nicias put his army in motion, pressed, as before, by the Syracusans and their allies, pelted from every side by their missiles, and struck down by their javelins. The Athenians pushed on for the Assinarus, impelled by the attacks made upon them from every side by a numerous cavalry and the swarm of other arms, fancying that they should breathe more freely if once across the river, and driven on also by their exhaustion and craving for water. Once there they rushed in, and all order was at an end, each man wanting to cross first, and the attacks of the enemy making it difficult to cross at all; forced to huddle together, they fell against and trod down one another, some dying immediately upon the javelins, others getting entangled together and stumbling over the articles of baggage, without being able to rise again.*
>
> *Meanwhile the opposite bank, which was steep, was lined by the Syracusans, who showered missiles down upon the Athenians, most of them drinking greedily and heaped together in disorder in the hollow bed of the river. The Peloponnesians also came down and butchered them, especially those in the water, which was thus immediately spoiled, but which they went on drinking just the same, mud and all, bloody as it was, most even fighting to have it.*

Nicias personally surrendered to Gylippus, hoping that he would remember his role in the earlier peace treaty between Athens and Sparta. But against the order of Gylippus, both Demosthenes and Nicias were executed. The prisoners, numbering about seven thousand, were held in the stone quarries near Syracuse, as there was no other room for them. After ten weeks, all but the Athenians, Italians, and Sicilians were sold as slaves. The remaining Athenians were left to die slowly of disease and starvation in the quarry. Only some of the very last survivors managed to escape and eventually trickled back to Athens, bringing first-hand news of the disaster.

In Athens, the citizens did not, at first, believe the defeat. Plutarch recounted how the news reached the city:

> *It is said that the Athenians would not believe their loss, in a great degree because of the person who first brought them news of it. For a certain*

stranger, it seems, coming to Piraeus, and there sitting in a barber's shop, began to talk of what had happened, as if the Athenians already knew all that had passed; which the barber hearing, before he acquainted anybody else, ran as fast as he could up into the city, addressed himself to the rulers of the city, and presently spread it about in the public place.

On which, there being everywhere, as may be imagined, terror and consternation, the rulers of the city summoned a general assembly, and there brought in the man and questioned him how he came to know. And he, giving no satisfactory account, was taken for a spreader of false intelligence and a disturber of the city, and was, therefore, fastened to the wheel and racked a long time, till other messengers arrived that related the whole disaster particularly. So hardly was Nicias believed to have suffered the calamity, which he had often predicted.

When the magnitude of the events became evident, there was a general panic. Attica seemed free for the taking. The defeat caused a great shift in policy for many other states as well. States that had previously been neutral joined with Sparta, assuming that the defeat of Athens was imminent. Many of the Athenian allies in the Delian League also revolted, and although the city immediately began to rebuild its fleet there was little they could do about the revolts for the time being.

Athens's enemies on the mainland and in Persia were encouraged to take action. Rebellions broke out in the Aegean, and Persia joined the war on the Spartan side through the influence of Lysander, whom I will speak of next. Some ten thousand Athenian hoplites had perished, but even though this was a huge blow, the real concern was the loss of the thirty thousand experienced oarsmen that were lost in Sicily. Now Athens had to rely on ill-trained slaves to form the backbone of its new fleet. Thucydides observed that contemporary Greeks were shocked not that Athens eventually fell after the defeat, but rather that it was able to continue to fight on for as long as it did, so devastating were the losses suffered.

Following the advice of Alcibiades, the Spartans began to fortify and eventually maintain a year-round presence in Decelea, ten miles north of Athens. From there, Spartan patrols would strain the Athenian cavalry and curtail the ability of Athens to grow crops, which forced Athens to import

all of its food. Athens was also forced to discontinue exploiting the Laurium silver mines in southeastern Attica that were an important source of income. Thucydides estimated that about twenty thousand Athenian slaves, many of them skilled workers, escaped to Decelea.

Revolts of several Athenian subjects occurred either at Alcibiades's suggestion or under his supervision. Nevertheless, Alcibiades would later fall out of grace with the Spartan leaders, partly because he seduced the wife of the Spartan king Agis II. Offering his services first to the Persians and later to the Athenians, he would eventually be able to side with the radical democrats who sought to topple to Athenian oligarchy, which had risen to power in 411 BCE after a coup. Once the oligarchy was replaced and Alcibiades's status restored, he played a crucial role in the Athenian victory at the Battle of Cynossema.

Ironically, this battle was won against a combined Spartan and Syracusan fleet. Alcibiades's military and political talents frequently proved valuable to whichever state currently held his fickle allegiance, but his propensity for making powerful enemies ensured that he never remained in one place for long. By the end of the war that he had helped rekindle, his days of political relevance were a bygone memory.

Thucydides would end his narrative abruptly after Alcibiades rejoined the Athenian side and led them to the victory at the Battle of Cynossema, which suggests that Thucydides died unexpectedly. The very last lines of his chronicles state, "When the winter after this summer is over, the twenty-first year of this war will be completed." According to the first century BCE Greek geographer and historian Pausanias, someone named Oenobius was able to get a law passed allowing Thucydides to return to Athens, but that he was murdered on his way back.

Before I even read of the possible murder of Thucydides, I had memories of being killed before my return to Athens. My activity as a historian had sufficiently angered a good portion of my old political enemies who saw my work as a threat to their position and power.

However, all efforts to suppress the truth and the genuine empowerment of humanity invariably backfire in the end, and life always finds a way to balance injustice. Any person or group opposed to truth and justice will have to suffer the consequences, or as Socrates put it during the trial in which he was sentenced to death twelve years after the assassination of Thucydides, "If you kill a man like me, you will injure yourselves more than you will injure me." My next chapter will illustrate this concept.

Today, Socrates is renowned as one of the founders of Western philosophy, and Thucydides's work is being studied at advanced military colleges worldwide. Athens began its descent as a world power and center for art and advanced thought during this time frame in history. Fortunately for the world, the golden age of Athens in terms of its creativity and philosophy would be preserved and passed on for posterity by key players in history.

In 415 BCE, Alcibiades deployed his influence and money to convince the Athenians to embark on an expedition to Sicily, a venture that turned out disastrously and marked the end of Athenian supremacy. In retaliation, Alcibiades enemies hired false witnesses and conspired against him to condemn him to death. This is called *Alcibiades Being Taught by Socrates*, a painting from 1776 by François-André Vincent.

Like the Greek and Roman orators before him, the "prairie lawyer" Abraham Lincoln was an expert public speaker. Before the advent of amplified sound and the mass media the spoken word was the only effective form of communication to large groups of people. Proficient speaking skills was usually the basis for a rise in political power. This 1958 postage stamp commemorates the Lincoln and Douglas debates.

The Parthenon is a former temple on the Athenian Acropolis, in Greece. It was dedicated to the goddess Athena during the 5th century BCE. Its decorative sculptures are considered some of the high points of Greek art, an enduring symbol of Ancient Greece, democracy and Western civilization.

The Sicilian Expedition was an Athenian military expedition to Sicily, which took place from 415–413 BCE during the Peloponnesian War. This battle was between Athens on one side and Sparta, Syracuse and Corinth on the other. The expedition ended in a devastating defeat for the Athenian forces, severely impacting Athens. This image depicts the destruction of the Athenian army at Syracuse.

"THERE IS SMALL RISK A GENERAL WILL BE REGARDED WITH CONTEMPT BY THOSE HE LEADS, IF, WHATEVER HE MAY HAVE TO PREACH, HE SHOWS HIMSELF BEST ABLE TO PERFORM."

◊ *Xenophon* ◊

CHAPTER 21

XENOPHON, GREEK HISTORIAN, AUTHOR, PHILOSOPHER, AND GENERAL, 430-355 BCE

When you work to unravel a lifetime, at first there is often a subtle fear of confronting the unknown or forgotten parts of your past. It's like opening the door to a darkened room in which you feel something profound and life changing is awaiting you. Eventually, as you bravely cross the threshold with apprehension and excitement, the numinous nature of reconnecting to a forgotten part of your soul history will invariably send waves of emotion throughout your entire being. As you lighten up the room you may begin to notice wondrous things; perhaps there are treasures that only you can enjoy, but they are treasures nonetheless. This is the way that I feel when I find a past life match. It is wonderful and exciting, like diving down to the bottom of the ocean after perceiving a scarcely audible sound emanating from a sunken chest that remained there until its owner returned one day to discover its hidden treasures.

The lifetime of Xenophon is one of these treasures that had called out to me to be recognized for a long time. I had been strangely attracted to his book *Anabasis* whenever I found a reference to it during my research into Greek his-

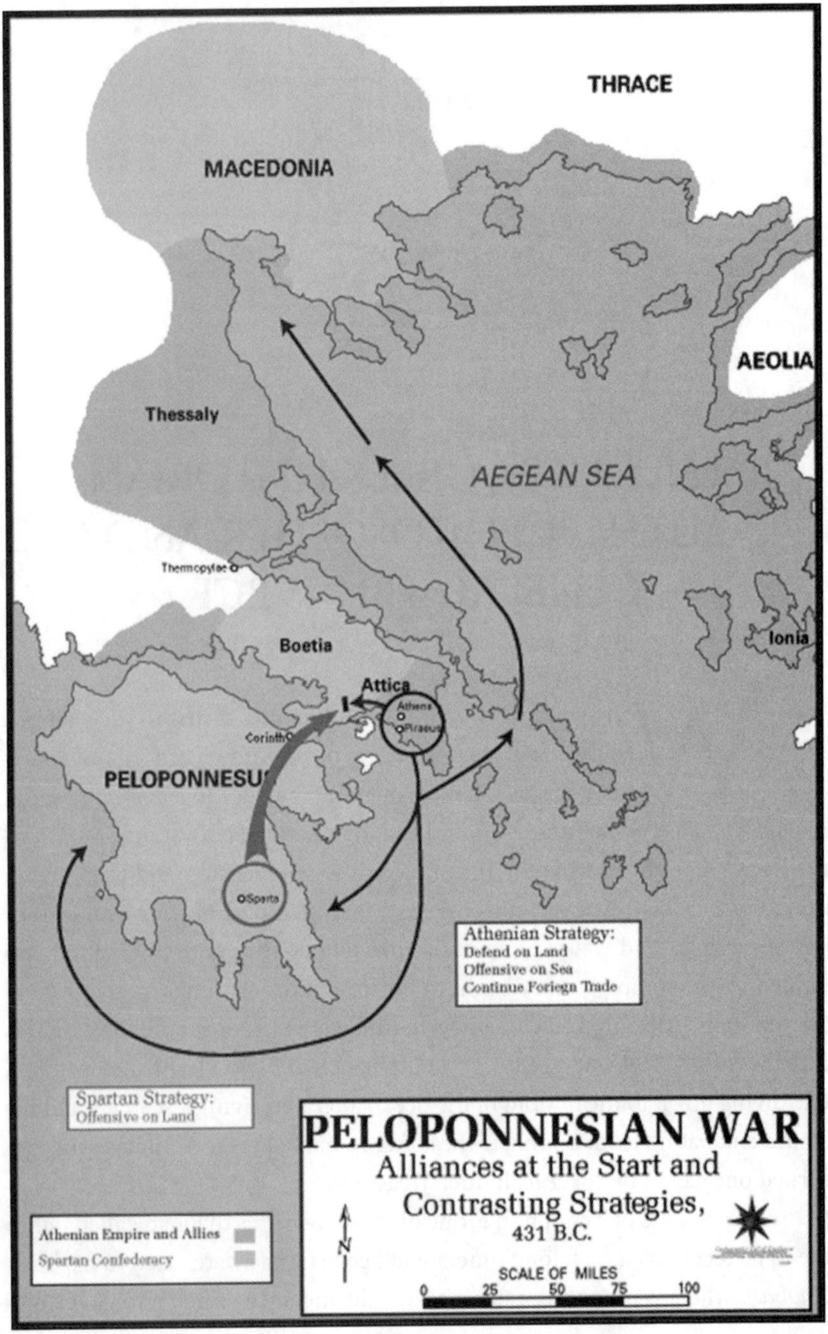

THRACE

MACEDONIA

AEOLIA

Thessaly

AEGEAN SEA

Thermopylae

Boetia

Attica

Athens

Piraeus

Corinth

Ionia

PELOPONNESUS

Sparta

Athenian Strategy:
Defend on Land
Offensive on Sea
Continue Foriegn Trade

Spartan Strategy:
Offensive on Land

PELOPONNESIAN WAR

Alliances at the Start and Contrasting Strategies, 431 B.C.

N

Athenian Empire and Allies

Spartan Confederacy

SCALE OF MILES

0 25 50 75 100

tory. The name of the book literally means "going up" and describes the movement of an army that starts at the coast and proceeds farther inland. It tells the story of the attempt of Cyrus the Younger to overthrow Artaxerxes II, his despised older brother and king of Persia. To accomplish this, Cyrus hired the "Ten Thousand," which were Greek mercenaries numbering a little more than ten thousand. They would join his Persian troops on their march from Sardes in present-day western Turkey into the heart of the Persian Empire. Xenophon personally participated in this expedition, but only after Cyrus agreed to meet him first. Not only did the two meet, but they would become friends.

Cyrus the Younger was the reincarnation of Cambyses II, my son in my lifetime as Cyrus the Great. I would connect again with this soul in both my lifetimes as Lysander and as Xenophon, and in both lives I would immediately feel a strong affection for Cyrus. As Xenophon, I would speak highly of Cyrus's excellence:

> *In this courtly training Cyrus earned a double reputation; first he was held to be a paragon of modesty among his fellows, rendering an obedience to his elders that exceeded that of many of his own inferiors, and next he bore away the palm for skill in horsemanship and for love of the animal itself. Nor less in matters of war, in the use of the bow and the javelin, was he held by men in general to be at once the aptest of learners and the most eager practicer.*
>
> *As soon as his age permitted, the same preeminence showed itself in his fondness for the chase, not without a certain appetite for perilous adventure in facing the wild beasts themselves. Once a bear made a furious rush at him, and without wincing he grappled with her and was pulled from his horse, receiving wounds the scars of which were visible through life. But in the end he slew the creature, nor did he forget him who first came to his aid, but made him enviable in the eyes of many.*

Seven year prior to the events described in the *Anabasis,* after the victories of Athenian General Alcibiades during the Peloponnesian War, Darius II of Persia decided to give strong support to the Spartans. He sent his son Cyrus the Younger into Asia Minor, where he would meet Spartan General Lysander and endow him with funds to build up the Spartan fleet. In 404 BCE, Darius fell ill and called his twenty-year-old son to his deathbed. Cyrus put all his available means and money over to Lysander and went to Susa, the capital of Persia, anticipating that he would be proclaimed the new king. Darius, however, made his elder son, Artaxerxes, his successor. Notwithstanding, Cyrus remained satrap of Lydia, Phrygia, and Cappadocia.

Soon after Darius died, a Persian named Tissaphernes told Artaxerxes that Cyrus planned to assassinate his older brother. It should be noted that Tissaphernes was previously removed as military commander of Asia Minor and satrap of Lydia, because he showed himself unwilling to support Sparta in the Peloponnesian War as had been ordered by Darius. Tissaphernes had been replaced by Cyrus, so it seems likely that for this reason Tissaphernes was still holding a grudge against Cyrus when he informed Artaxerxes about Cyrus's alleged plans, which Tissaphernes certainly did not hear about from Cyrus himself. Still, Tissaphernes's warning was considered reason enough for Cyrus to be captured and brought to Artaxerxes. Only by the intercession of their mother would Cyrus would be pardoned and sent back to Asia Minor. According to Plutarch, "his resentment for his arrest made him more eagerly desirous of the kingdom than before." I think history could have taken a different course if the two brothers would have been more cooperative from the start and if Tissaphernes would have refrained from contributing to their mutual distrust, but unfortunately this was not the case.

When the Peloponnesian War was over, Cyrus managed to gather a large army, which he used to attack Tissaphernes, who was still satrap of Caria. Cyrus also pretended to prepare an expedition against the Pisidians, a mountainous tribe that was never obedient to the Persian Empire, but in reality he began to move with his army toward the Persian heartland. At Tarsus, the soldiers became aware of Cyrus's plans and as a result refused to march on. However, Spartan General Clearchus convinced the army to continue with the expedition. Clearchus had fallen out of grace with the Ephors in Sparta despite his previous military victories, and so he gladly accepted Cyrus's proposal to join with the Ten Thousand as a general.

The newly formed army would advance far into Babylonia before it met with an enemy. Only at the last moment had Artaxerxes been warned by Tissaphernes, and he gathered an army in haste. Nevertheless, his army of one

hundred thousand was about four times larger than that of Cyrus, who arrived with more than ten thousand Greek hoplites under Clearchus, two thousand five hundred light infantry soldiers, and approximately ten thousand soldiers under his second-in-command, General Ariaeus. In October of 401 BCE, the two armies met at Cunaxa on the left bank of the Euphrates River, forty-five miles north of Babylon.

Cyrus determined that the outcome depended on the fate of the king; he therefore wanted the force led by Clearchus to join him at the center of the formation where he intended to engage Artaxerxes personally. Clearchus refused, however, because the position of honor for the Greeks was the right flank. They wanted to dominate this position first because they were skeptical that the makeshift army of Cyrus would be capable of holding its position if they didn't. Cyrus would nevertheless be in the center, as it was the custom of Persian nobles leading an army.

The Greeks easily routed the left wing of the Persians along the bank of the Euphrates, causing the Persians to flee in terror before they were even within bowshot. They then swung around to engage the center of the Persian army where Cyrus impetuously threw himself into the fray and came very close to killing Artaxerxes but was in turn slain by his bodyguard.

I believe that Cyrus could have won the battle if he had allowed the Greek warriors more time to work their way through to him. This was a soul lesson that would be learned, and when Cyrus reincarnated as Alexander the Great he would be far more successful at defeating the Persians. I would also incarnate during that time as his bodyguard and childhood companion Leonnatus, a lifetime of which I will speak in my next book. If we are sufficiently advanced enough as souls, we will play out subordinate roles in following lifetimes to help guide and evolve other souls.

Because Cyrus had been killed, the success of the Greeks would be rendered irrelevant and the expedition a failure. Cyrus's army found itself in the middle of a very large empire with no food, no employer, and no reliable friends. The considerable money that Cyrus had promised them would not be seen. Even worse, once it was learned that Cyrus was dead, the rest of his forces surrendered and switched sides to Artaxerxes. The unprotected Greek camp was raided and destroyed by the Persian cavalry.

Shortly thereafter, Tissaphernes invited Clearchus to a peace conference, where, alongside four other generals and many captains, he was betrayed and beheaded. The Ten Thousand found themselves without their former leadership, far from the sea, deep behind enemy lines. They elected new leaders, including Xenophon himself, who would use his rhetorical abilities to motivate the survivors, because in his opinion it was a question of honor "to make an effort to return to Hellas and to revisit our hearths and homes, if only to prove to other Hellenes that it is their own faults if they are poor and needy." It was my desire to inspire our forces to live on as shining examples of what can be achieved through willpower, discipline, and determination. Since our former leaders had been betrayed and killed, I appealed to our forces so that each warrior could call upon the greatness and leadership abilities within himself:

> *You see, the enemy did not dare to bring war to bear upon us until they had first seized our generals. They felt that whilst our rulers were there and we obeyed them, they were no match for us in war. But having got hold of them, they fully expected that the consequent confusion and anarchy would prove fatal to us. What follows?*
>
> *This: Officers and leaders ought to be more vigilant ever than their predecessors, subordinates still more orderly and obedient to those in command now than even they were to those who are gone. And you should pass a resolution that, in case of insubordination, any one who stands by is to aid the officer in chastising the offender. So the enemy will be mightily deceived, for on this day they will behold ten thousand Clearchuses instead of one, who will not suffer one man to play the coward.*
>
> *And indeed, the Greek forces would fight their way through hostile territory to Trapezus on the coast of the Black Sea. Their journey is recounted in the Anabasis in vivid detail, like this episode of their passage through the deep snows of central Turkey:*
>
> *Soldiers who had lost the use of their eyes through snow-blindness or whose toes had dropped off from frostbite were left behind. It was a relief to the eyes against snow-blindness if one held something black in front of the eyes while marching, and it was a help to the feet if one kept on the move and never stopped still and took off one's shoes at night. If one slept*

with one's shoes on, the straps sank into the flesh and the soles of the shoes froze to the feet. This was the more likely to happen since, when their old shoes were worn out, they had made themselves shoes of undressed leather from the skins of oxen that had just been flayed. Some soldiers who were suffering from these kinds of complaints were left behind.

From Trapezus, they would make their way westward, back toward Greece. During the entire journey Xenophon would keep his focus on reminding the troops of the honorable conduct that must be upheld in order to keep the enemy at bay, demonstrating to whomever they would encounter "that you are of a better sort, and prove to the enemy that battle with the undisciplined is one thing, but with men like yourselves another." Keeping up this discipline was a tough challenge and would be put to a serious test when the troops were betrayed by Spartan Admiral Anaxibius, who was stationed at Byzantium and refused to furnish the troops with the funds for their needed provisions that he had promised if they would continue their journey toward Thracia.

The Greek soldiers were infuriated and demanded that Xenophon lead the attack against the city of Byzantium, but Xenophon managed to help them discharge their emotions, which might have caused great problems if they had been acted upon without restraint. As the troops were gathered and ready to storm Byzantium, he delivered the following speech:

Soldiers, I am not surprised at your wrath, or that you deem it monstrous treatment so to be cheated. But consider what will be the consequences if we gratify our indignation and, in return for such deception, avenge ourselves on the Lacedaemonians here present and plunder an innocent city. We shall be declared enemies of the Lacedaemonians and their allies.

And what sort of war that will be, we need not go far to conjecture. I take it you have not forgotten some quite recent occurrences. We Athenians entered into war against the Lacedaemonians and their allies with a fleet consisting of not less than three hundred line-of-battle ships, including those in dock as well as those afloat. We had vast treasures stored up in the city and a yearly income, which was derived from home, or foreign sources, amounted to no less than a thousand talents. Our empire included all the islands, and we were possessed of numerous cities both in Asia and in Europe. Amongst others, this very Byzantium, where we are now, was ours. And yet in the end we were vanquished, as you all very well know.

What, must we anticipate, will now be our fate? The Lacedaemonians have not only their old allies, but the Athenians and those who were at that time allies of Athens are added to them. Tissaphernes and all the rest of the Asiatics on the seaboard are our foes, not to speak of our archenemy, the king himself up yonder, whom we came to deprive of his empire and to kill, if possible. I ask then, with all these banded together against us, is there anyone so insensate as to imagine that we can survive the contest?

For heaven's sake, let us not go mad or loosely throw away our lives in war with our own native cities—nay, our own friends, our kith and our kin, for in one or other of the cities they are all included. Every city will march against us, and not unjustly, if, after refusing to hold one single barbarian city by right of conquest, we seize the first Hellenic city that we come to and make it a ruinous heap.

For my part, my prayer is that before I see such things wrought by you, I, at any rate, may lie ten thousand fathoms under ground! My counsel to you, as Hellenes, is to try and obtain your just rights through obedience to those who stand at the head of Hellas. And if so be that you fail in those demands, why, being more sinned against than sinning, need we rob ourselves of Hellas too?

At present, I propose that we should send to Anaxibius and tell him that we have made an entrance into the city, not meditating violence, but merely to discover if he and his will show us any good. For if so, it is well, but of otherwise, at least we will let him see that he does not shut the door upon us as dupes and fools. We know the meaning of discipline; we turn our backs and go.

By this time the troops were pacified, and as Anaxibius would not change his mind, they eventually moved on toward Thracia. Anaxibius, however, would recall them one more time, but when Xenophon found out that he only did so because he was deposed as admiral and sought

support against the new authorities of Byzantium, Xenophon decided to leave the city behind and join Seuthes II instead, who asked for support to expand his Odrysian kingdom in Thrace. This would be accomplished, but when Seuthes, who was surrounded by advisers who became increasingly jealous of Xenophon, also refused to pay the promised rewards, Xenophon would once again be the voice of reason as he spoke to the king:

The country is now yours, and from this time forward you have to make provision for what is yours. And how will you best secure it immunity from ill? Either these soldiers receive their dues and go, leaving a legacy of peace behind, or they stay and occupy an enemy's country, whilst you endeavor, by aid of a still larger army, to open a new campaign and turn them out. And your new troops will also need provisions. Or again, which will be the greater drain on your purse; to pay off your present debt, or, with that still owing, to bid for more troops and of a better quality?

Seuthes would agree to grant the troops their pay, and about two years after they departed with Cyrus, the remaining six thousand warriors of his army would arrive in the heartland of Greece. They had marched from Sardis to Cunaxa and back north through what is today eastern Turkey to the Black Sea, and from there back along Turkey's north coast to Greece. The total marching distance they covered amounted to more than two thousand miles.

Their achievements demonstrated the potential superiority of Greek soldiers over their Persian adversaries. It is believed that this was why Philip II of Macedon formed his strategy for defeating the Persian Empire by means of a compact and well-trained army, a feat accomplished by his son, Alexander the Great. It is known that Alexander used the *Anabasis* as a field guide during the early phases of his expedition into Persia, which is another instance that shows how souls support each other not only directly but also through the legacies they leave behind.

After his return to Greece, Xenophon would become an ally of Spartan King Agesilaus II, whom Xenophon valued greatly, considering him as an unsurpassed example of all the civil and military virtues. Because of a war that broke out between Athens and Sparta in 394 BCE, Xenophon would therefore be exiled from Athens just like Thucydides, who was killed before he finished his *History of the Peloponnesian War.* As Xenophon, I would pick up where Thucydides left off and finish the rest of the account of the Peloponnesian War. Xenophon's meticulous documentation would resemble that of Thucydides, but his work would have a unique style, as each incarnation has its own personality and unique traits.

Xenophon's decision, whether intentioned or not, to continue the work of Thucydides illustrates how we will incarnate in follow-on lives to carry on work started in previous lives. Imagine Xenophon making the connection to the life as Thucydides and making it a point to finish the work that he had started. Look at your own life now and think of possible parallels with past lives you may be continuing the work of. If you made the connection would that get you more excited about a particular project or life path?

Throughout the rest of his life, Xenophon would be a prolific writer, and much of his work has still survived to this day. He made important contributions to the fields of philosophy and economics. Moreover, he is the author of the *Cyropaedia,* which was both a historical account of the education of Cyrus the Great and an instruction manual for military commanders, rulers, and governments. Xenophon was using Cyrus's lifetime as an example that he had set in a previous incarnation. Do you have important figures in history to whom you are unusually drawn over others? Perhaps the influence they have on you goes much deeper than you think. My next incarnational threat would be the force behind ending the Peloponnesian War.

This original bust of Thucydides is a Roman copy from 100 CE, copied from an early 4th Century BCE Greek original. It is on display in Holkham Hall in Norfolk, UK.

Xenophon dictating His History, illustration from Hutchinson's 1915 book "History of the Nations." Xenophon's *Anabasis* recounts his adventures with the Ten Thousand while in the service of Cyrus the Younger, Cyrus's failed campaign to claim the Persian throne from Artaxerxes II of Persia, and the return of Greek mercenaries after Cyrus's death in the Battle of Cunaxa. Anabasis is a unique first-hand, humble, and self-reflective account of a military leader's experience in antiquity.

The Greek military leader, philosopher, and historian Xenophon of Athens established precedents for many logistical operations, and was among the first to describe strategic flanking maneuvers and feints in combat.

Anabasis and Xenophon's other book *Cyropaedia* inspired Alexander the Great and other Greeks to conquer Babylon and the Achaemenid Empire in 331 BCE. By the age of thirty, Alexander had created one of the largest empires in history, stretching from Greece to northwestern India. He was undefeated in battle and is widely considered to be one of history's greatest and most successful military commanders.

After defeating the Greek city-states of Athens and Thebes at the Battle of Chaeronea in 338 BCE, Philip II led the effort to establish a federation of Greek states known as the League of Corinth, with him as the elected hegemon and commander-in-chief of Greece for a planned invasion of the Achaemenid Empire of Persia. However, his assassination by a royal bodyguard, Pausanias of Orestis seen here, led to the immediate succession of his son Alexander, who would go on to invade the Achaemenid Empire in his father's stead.

The Achaemenid Empire (559–330 BCE) was the first of the Persian Empires to rule over significant portions of Greater Iran. The empire possessed a "national army" of roughly 120.000-150.000 troops, plus several tens of thousands of troops from their allies. The various uniforms of the Persian warriors are seen in this relief carving from Persepolis, in present-day Iran.

“TRUTH IS BETTER THAN FALSEHOOD, BUT THE WORTH AND VALUE OF EITHER IS DETERMINED BY THE USE TO WHICH IT IS PUT.”

◊ *Lysander* ◊

CHAPTER 22

LYSANDER, SPARTAN ADMIRAL DURING THE PELOPONNESIAN WAR, 405 BCE

Lysander grew up as a *mothakes,* which was a term used for a particular sociopolitical class in ancient Sparta. The *mothakes* were primarily either offspring of Spartan fathers and helot/slave mothers or children of impoverished Spartans. *Mothakes* were not able to contribute to *common meals* in the corps and were thus not allowed to maintain an "equal" status. They were, however, permitted to fight in the Spartan army just like the *perioeci,* who were members of an autonomous group of inhabitants of the city that had no formal citizenship but were allowed to travel to other cities, while the Spartans had to ask for permission. The *mothakes* were not citizens either, but were brought up alongside Spartan boys as their foster brothers and would also train in the *agoge.* Warrior training has served me well in many lifetimes and would also help Lysander to rise in prominence during the long war with Athens.

Following the destruction of the Sicilian Expedition, Sparta encouraged the revolt of Athens's tributary allies, and many Athenian allies rose in revolt. The Syracusans sent their fleet to the Peloponnesians, and the Persians promised to support the Spartans with money and ships. Revolt and faction

also arose in Athens itself, but nevertheless the war would not be brought to a conclusion until many years later, because the Persians were slow to furnish promised funds and ships, and Corinth and Syracuse along with the other Spartan allies were also slow to bring their slave fleets into the Aegean. When the Ionian states didn't receive any support or protection as they began to revolt, many of them rejoined the Athenian side.

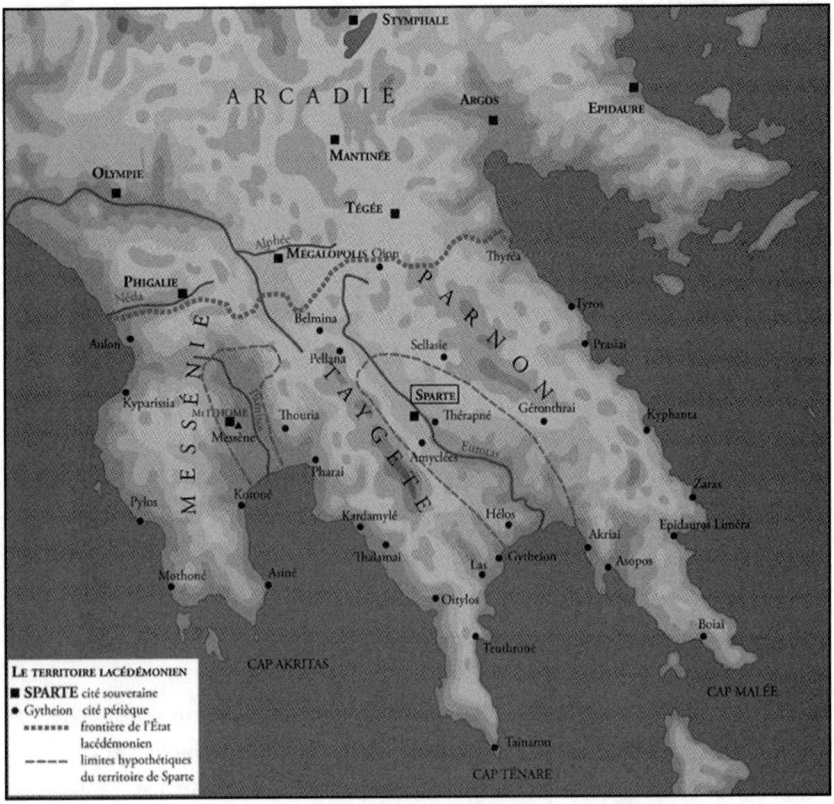

At the start of the Peloponnesian War, the Athenians had prudently put aside some money and one hundred ships that were to be used only as a last resort. These ships would now be released and served as the core of the Athenians' fleet throughout the rest of the war. In 411 BCE, this fleet engaged the Spartans at the Battle of Syme with neither side claiming victory. Out of desperation, Alcibiades would be appointed the new leader of the Athenian fleet. Alcibiades, as you may remember, was accused as a traitor in absentia during the disastrous

Sicilian Expedition. However, he still carried weight in Athens, as his military expertise could not be denied. Alcibiades would persuade the Athenian fleet to attack the Spartans at Cyzicus, where the Athenians obliterated the Spartan fleet and succeeded in reestablishing the financial basis of their empire through the silver mines in the area that had previously been captured by the Spartans.

Between 410 and 406 BCE, Athens won a continuous string of victories and eventually recovered large portions of its empire. All of this was due, in no small part, to Alcibiades's leadership. Alcibiades had lived among the Spartans for many years and had learned much about them that was now useful in defeating them, much to their dismay. The Spartans were rapidly losing territory and allies and after several battles were on the verge of capitulation, when Lysander came onto the scene, as has been recounted by Plutarch:

> *The Lacedaemonians were frightened again. Summoning up fresh zeal for the war, which required—as they thought—an able leader and a more powerful armament, they sent out Lysander to take command upon the sea. Lysander was chosen as the ablest leader for the job of defeating the Athenian navy.*
>
> *When he came to Ephesus, he found the city well-disposed to him and very zealous in the Spartan cause, although it was then in a low state of prosperity and in danger of becoming utterly barbarized by the admixture of Persian customs, since it was enveloped by Lydia, and the king's generals made it their headquarters. He therefore pitched his camp there, ordered the merchant vessels from every quarter to land their cargoes there, and made preparations for the building of triremes. Thus he revived the traffic of their harbors, the business of their market, and filled their houses and workshops with profits, so that from that time on and through his efforts the city had hopes of achieving the stateliness and grandeur that it now enjoys.*

Remember from the life of Pausanias, the Spartan general, that he was vilified and forced into starvation for associating with the Persians, which was considered inappropriate because they were seen as barbarians and beneath the dignity of Greeks. But afraid of their own annihilation, the Spartans would now look the other way and allow Lysander, the reincarnation of Pausanias, to continue his work, as he would connect with Cyrus the Younger, who was the reincarnation of Cambyses II, son of Cyrus the Great. The two souls that had worked together in many lifetimes would meet again, and this time Cyrus, in his function as military commander of Asia Minor, would help Lysander.

An idea of Lysander was discussed by the two in which Lysander's sailors would be given one-third more pay than those serving on Athenian ships. Sailors in any given age are notorious for going where the money is, and this time was no different. The city of Ephesus would also support Lysander, giving him proceeds to fund his fleet and more ideas for attracting Athenian sailors. The plan worked, but Athens could not man up all the ships of its fleet because of the flood of experienced seamen cross-decking to Spartan warships. The superior land force of the Spartans was now matched with an experienced naval force that was superior to that of the Athenians, who had strategically relied on their dominant naval force throughout the war.

The tide of the war was turning, but still, Lysander was observant and calculating. He had put a dent in the capabilities of the Athenian navy, but he waited for the correct opportunity and was not easily led into a battle, not least because Alcibiades still had a greater number of ships and up to that time had been victorious in all his battles. From Samos, Alcibiades moved toward Ephesus, where the Spartan fleet stayed safely moored. He hoped Lysander would respond to this approach, but nothing happened, and the Athenians retreated to nearby Notium.

When Alcibiades departed for Phocaea on business, he left Antiochus in command of the fleet with strict orders not to start an attack on the Spartan fleet in his absence. Antiochus, however, as if in bold mockery of Lysander, put in to the harbor of Ephesus with two triremes and had them row provocatively past the Spartan ships, which were lying drawn up on shore. Lysander was incensed as the triremes passed with loud noise and laughter, but at first he cautiously sent only a few of his triremes to pursue the Athenians. However, when he saw that other ships were coming to their rescue, he realized that this was no sophisticated trap but a poorly led flaunt of power by someone other than the skilled Alcibiades. Lysander quickly manned more ships and managed to capture fifteen triremes from the Athenians, who would retreat to Samos with the rest of their fleet.

When the people of Athens heard of the disaster, they turned into a passionate mob as their democracy was devolving to its lowest point. They voted to depose Alcibiades from his command, and even the soldiers at Samos turned against him. Even though he had previously turned around the fortunes of Athens in the war and was not personally responsible for the defeat in the Battle of Ephesus and Notium, the Athenians would drive out one of their most able commanders. Alcibiades had no other choice but to leave, so he sailed off to the Thracian Chersonese where he settled and built a castle.

Despite having won a victory, the elite in Sparta determined that Lysander had won through less than honorable means as he dealt with the Persians and did not win by meeting the enemy in a classical battle formation. So, not to be outdone by poor decision making, the Spartans decided to replace Lysander with another admiral named Callicratidas, who was of noble birth and in favor with the elite of Sparta. I have memories of being informed that Callicratidas would assume command. When I met him, he was not open to my ideas of leadership, so instead of creating conflict I chose to depart. On my way home, I returned the unused monies for the fleet that I had received from Cyrus, whom the Spartan nobles and Callicratidas so despised.

Interestingly, after realizing that all of the traditional means of acquiring funds to build up a fleet still did not work, Callicratidas would also seek support from Cyrus just as I had done. Cyrus, however, refused to even see Callicratidas, knowing that he held strong prejudices against all Persians. Incensed that he would not be given audience, Callicratidas shouted for all to hear that he would return to Greece and reconcile all Greeks, so that they may work together to never need the wealth of the barbarians again and thereafter never have any more dealings with them. This is important to note, because, in a future incarnation of Cyrus the Younger as Alexander the Great, he would have no dealings with the Spartans! It is another instance where we can see how unresolved issues can influence decisions over the course of several lifetimes.

Callicratidas was forced to assemble his fleet from the remnants of Lysander's fleet and the meager contributions from Sparta's already sorely tasked Greek allies. In the end, he was able to piece together a fleet of 170 triremes. The new Athenian commander, Conon, could only muster seventy out of one hundred available ships because of the loss of able-bodied seamen that went over for

Lysander's increased wages. When the two forces clashed and Conon lost thirty ships, he was forced to flee south of the Hellespont to the harbor of Mytilene on the island of Lesbos. The Athenians were now clearly inferior at sea and blocked and besieged by land. For the first time since Themistocles and Pericles had outwitted the Spartans and built a wall around Athens and its harbor to secure its naval superiority, Athens would be unable to protect its vital shipping lanes.

Because Athens depended on the grain shipments that came through the Hellespont, Conon sent out a ship to inform Athens of his plight. This was difficult to accomplish, because Callicratidas had left fifty ships to keep Conon's force bottled up. Fortunately for Athens, the messenger ship would make it through nevertheless. Upon its arrival, an assembly quickly approved drastic measures to build and man a relief force. Golden statues of Nike, the victory goddess, were melted down and used to fund the construction of new vessels. To ensure enough loyal crewmen for the fleet, citizenship was granted to thousands of slaves. Over a hundred new ships were rapidly built, and allies contributed another fifty.

The new fleet was commanded in a radical new way by eight generals who collaboratively controlled their own portions of the 150 triremes. They would meet Callicratidas's fleet of 140 triremes east of the island of Lesbos near the islands of Arginusae. Experimenting with new tactics, the Athenian commanders outwitted Callicratidas, who was a traditionalist and inflexible in his battle tactics. They added a second line of ships to counter the Spartan tactic of passing between two ships and wheeling quickly around to strike the Athenian ships in the side. This second line of ships would be able to defeat this tactic and inflict severe losses on the Spartan fleet.

Another technique that led to victory was to deploy an extended right flank well past the line of Spartan ships. When the Spartans became engaged, this extended line of ships performed a flanking maneuver. This is one of the most effective tactics for defeating any force on land or at sea in general. By attacking the flank of a formation, you catch the enemy where they are less able to support each other and usually not prepared to meet an attacking force. Battles are often won when a flanking movement is performed swiftly and with precision. A flanked military force will often collapse and be driven into chaotic retreat, making easy prey for annihilation.

Callicratidas would be killed in the Battle of Arginusae, and half of the ships of his fleet were lost before the remaining seventy retreated. The Athenians lost only twenty-five ships and decided to send the major portion of their fleet to destroy or drive out the Spartan ships that were blockading Conon, leaving only a small contingent behind to rescue the sailors who were either floating in the water or caught on disabled ships. When they departed, however, a storm quickly gathered, and the two separate Athenian forces were forced to return to port.

A messenger ship brought news of the victory to the relief of the citizenry of Athens, but the merriment was cut short when another group of ships brought news of the loss of the sailors at sea who could not be rescued. In the bitter rhetorical battle that would ensue over who was responsible, the leaders of the rescue ships were acquitted of any wrongdoing. The public anger, spun up by opportunistic politicians, would turn on the eight generals who had won the victory. The generals were deposed from their offices and ordered to return to stand trial.

Six of the eight returned believing that they could clear themselves of the allegations. After all, they had just saved Athens from starvation and won a great victory. They tried to win an even greater victory by freeing the captured ships of the Athenian fleet, and even Socrates argued in their favor. It was decided that they did not act irresponsibly and could not be held accountable for the death of their fellow shipmates who had perished in the storm. The generals—one of whom was Pericles the Younger, the son of Pericles and Aspasia, who is my wife, Tracy, in my current life—were thus found not guilty.

A festival was held after the trial, and the dead from the battle were mourned. It happened that during this highly emotional time a politician called for another trial outside the normal court system. The six generals were tried again and now found guilty and executed. When the Athenian democracy had devolved to the point where an immoral opportunist could so easily manipulate the Athenians, logic and justice no longer applied. After the citizens realized the folly of what they had done, there was an outrage against this particularly manipulative politician, who thereupon also fled together with the others who had advocated in favor of the execution of the generals. Of course, the responsibility for the execution of the six generals did not solely rest with these few politicians, but also with the citizens' unbridled emotions.

In Sparta, the stunning defeat of Callicratidas was discouraging, and Sparta's allies were calling for the return of their favorite general, Lysander. But instead of appointing a leader who could win the war but was unpopular with the Spartan elite, they offered to surrender their fort at Decelea in return for peace. The fort at Decelea had been used to keep Athens behind their walls and dependent on their fleet for food shipments, but the Spartan elite argued that the surrender of the fort would cause no tactical disadvantage as the Athenians were going to get their food anyway because of their regained maritime superiority. Nevertheless, such an offer was highly unusual for Sparta, whose allies would be losers by this political move because Athens would be free to once again to pursue an aggressive policy to dominate the lands surrounding the Aegean and Mediterranean Seas.

Athens, however, foolishly refused the offer of peace terms from the Spartans. The Athenians were flush with victory and were convinced they would completely defeat the Spartans. The Spartan elite was forced to once again consider Lysander for a leadership role. With increasing pressure from the allies and Cyrus the Younger, the hand of the political despots in Sparta was called. They found themselves in a tricky situation not only because of their bias against Lysander, but also because of a law that forbade an admiral from achieving the highest rank for a second term. To overcome this restriction they made an agreement with Lysander that he would be nominally second in command, but in practice all-important decisions concerning the war with Athens would be made by him.

As the old and new commander of the Spartan navy I went back to my friend Cyrus, where I was warmly greeted and offered enough money to re-establish the Spartan fleet. This would be the last time that I would see Cyrus, who died in October 401 BCE during the Battle of Cunaxa, which I spoke of in the previous chapter.

Because the odds were still stacked against me, I searched for the perfect opportunity to engage in a battle and maneuver my opponents into a situation that would assure naval victory, just like in my life as Themistocles and during my previous command in this life. My Spartan enemies tried to undermine me by saying that the descendants of Heracles should not wage war by deceit, but true to the Spartan wit and ability to formulate a succinct repartee, I replied,

"Where the lion's skin will not reach, it must be patched out with the fox's." The skin of the lion, hard won and worn by Heracles, was a symbol of greatness and honor. I approved of these qualities but argued that they should be complemented by cleverness, symbolized by the skin of a fox.

I initially chose to fight a guerrilla war raiding coastal cities loyal to Athens. Later I would pull my fleet up on the coast close to Athens and join with the Spartan army at the Fort of Decelea. With news of the approach of the Athenian fleet, this was a short-lived show of force, but it also was an excellent boost to the morale of the Spartan forces. My game was to eventually lure the Athenian fleet into the confined area of the Hellespont where numerical superiority would be less of a factor. This mirrored the tactic of Themistocles at the Battle of Salamis, but this time there would be an interesting twist.

Finding the vital Hellespont unguarded, we immediately attacked the city of Lampsacus, which was located north of the former city of Troy. We'd take this important trading city by storm, and it would be here that our trap for the Athenians would be set.

Upon learning that Lampsacus was taken, the Athenian fleet of 180 triremes docked directly across us at the port city of Aegospotami, three miles west of Lampsacus. They planned to engage my fleet the next morning, but before the Athenians set sail I had already ordered our fleet into battle formation while remaining within the confines and protection of the harbor. I gave strict orders that no ship was to row out to meet the Athenians, and three ships rowed up and down the line to ensure that no one disobeyed the command. When the Athenians arrived, they drew up in battle formation within view of us, but we would just sit there until midafternoon, whereupon they went back to Aegospotami and disembarked their ships. I sent a single ship to make sure they had settled down for the day and then retired the Spartan fleet.

We would perform this exact same drill for four consecutive days. On the fifth day, I gave orders to the spy ship to let us know as soon as the Athenians disembarked by racing back into view and hoisting a polished bronze shield. The Athenians had become bold and contemptuous of us, thinking we were cowards and would not dare to leave the harbor.

During the previous days we had observed that when they beached their ships they left and went into the city for provisions and entertainment. The city was a distance away from the ships, and so many men were scattered about the countryside while other sailors were asleep in their tents or cooking their evening meals. When our ship alerted us we began to row with all our might across the channel and caught the unsuspecting Athenians away from their ships.

Only eight ships were able to stealthily escape, and Conon was on one of them. These eight ships would eventually land on the Peloponnesian coast, where all sailors would be killed by our local forces. At Aegospotami, 172 triremes and over three thousand men were captured with barely a struggle. Plutarch would sum up the action in his *Life of Lysander:*

> *He had wrought a work of the greatest magnitude with the least toil and effort and had brought to a close in a single hour a war which, in length and the incredible variety of its incidents and fortunes, surpassed all its predecessors. Its struggles and issues had assumed ten thousand changing shapes, and it had cost Hellas more generals than all her previous wars together. Yet it was brought to a close by the prudence and ability of one man.*

I would go back to the cities surrounding Athens and tell all the Athenian citizens living there that they could go back to Athens now or they would be killed. This drove a vast multitude into the city and strained the resources and food stores very quickly. Our fleet stopped all grain shipments, and the Spartan army surrounding the walls prohibited any food from coming into the city by land. Disease, hunger, and death would slowly gnaw at the citizenry and turn them against the political elite. The Athenians would capitulate in 404 BCE, less than a year after their defeat at Aegospotami.

After its surrender, Athens was stripped of its walls, its fleet, and all of its overseas possessions. Corinth and Thebes demanded that Athens should be destroyed and all its citizens enslaved. I refused, however, and in agreement with humble and grateful Spartan policy makers chose not to destroy a city that had done a good service at a time of great danger to Greece during the war with Persia. We sought to make Athens our ally once again, so it may "have the same friends and enemies" as Sparta. By doing so, the victorious Spartans proved to be the most clement state that fought Athens, and at the same time we turned out to be its savior as neither Corinth nor Thebes could challenge our decision. Spartan honor was never to follow and attack an enemy on the

battlefield that was in full retreat and capitulation. We held to the same standards in our political dealings as well. Athens would never again rise to prominence as a strong leader in the world.

Unfortunately, when my friend Cyrus was killed a few years later as he tried to overthrow his brother Artaxerxes II, my attempts to lead a Spartan force to defeat him instead would be thwarted by the Spartan elite. Many years later in 395 BCE, I tried to nip a Theban revolt in the bud, but I would be killed because the Thebans had intercepted a communication requesting Spartan support. The Thebans laid an ambush inside the city's walls and only had to wait for the right moment to rush out and surprise my unsuspecting force. I was in charge of a group that was not Spartan; otherwise the outcome would have probably been different. The campaign stalled after my death and grew into a larger conflict called the Corinthian War, which would last eight years.

In the beginning of his commentary on Lysander, Plutarch noted, "The treasury of the Acanthians at Delphi bears this inscription: 'Brasidas and the Acanthians, with spoil from the Athenians.' For this reason many think that the marble figure standing within the edifice by the door is a statue of Brasidas. But it really represents Lysander, with his hair very long, after the ancient custom, and growing a generous beard."

But how could the two be mistaken? It was because I was also Brasidas and, like I have said before, we often have a very similar physical appearance in many of our lifetimes. As you may remember, Brasidas would use new strategies of war such as launching surprise attacks to take a city without force or invading areas controlled by Athens that supplied the city with lumber and silver. The old Spartan tactics called for direct engagement of soldiers, but after Pericles refused to meet the Spartan army in the open, Brasidas's unconventional invasions of the sister states of Athens brought the war to a close, albeit briefly.

As I have been stating throughout this work, we often will return to complete unfinished business or return to a work in progress. Lysander completed the work of Brasidas and did it with little loss of life. He also kept Athens from being completely wiped off the face of the map of Greece. History would be much different if he hadn't been there. Whether Cyrus the Great or Lysander, I have given you an example of a soul that has benefited countries or city-states where that soul was intimately involved in former incarnations. Cyrus saved Israel and

Lysander saved Athens. This pattern will continue throughout many incarnations for thousands of years to the present, as I'll bring up in following books.

Saving Athens from annihilation would be important for the history of the Western world. When you think of Greek art, philosophy, or government, which city-state comes to mind? Although Sparta had the military might to defeat Athens, it would be a cold, dark world today if Athens had not been able to pass on its superior ideas. My thoughts are that some souls have the capacity to gain a bigger picture of what's ahead for humanity's future and position themselves in lifetimes to help keep us on track for greater possibilities. The work you started in one lifetime can be continued in follow-on lives, as I'll point out in the next life.

Finding and expressing the divine gifts within myself and helping others to find them in themselves are what fill every moment of my life with a sense of magic, fellowship, challenge, and accomplishment. I think that all of us are on a path of self-realization as we venture to become awakened, bringing forth what is within us. On that path- keeping in mind that we invariably stumble and fall every so often—it's our willingness to learn from our experiences and pick ourselves up time and again that eventually determines our trajectory. Therefore, let us be persistent as we stand up for what we determine to be true and precious, and let us be humble in recognition of the fact that we're all fallible.

This is what I have learned through remembering and reflecting on the experiences I have gone through as a soul. For my future, I wish to continue on the path that I'm on, supporting the empowerment of all life, just like I feel a growing number of souls currently present on Earth intend to do. Considering the immense transformative efforts that are happening around the world and that I am very glad to be involved in, it really seems to me like one of most auspicious periods in all of human history. I am very confident that humanity is going to move forward in a more enlightened way after all.

But wherever the path may lead us, I want to sincerely thank you for being in this great adventure with me—may your days be blessed and your lives be full of love, courage, and happiness!

LYSANDER, SPARTAN ADMIRAL DURING THE PELOPONNESIAN WAR, 405 BCE

Lysander of Sparta outside the walls of Athens, ordering their destruction. 19th century lithograph depicting the conclusion of the Peloponnesian War, which reshaped the ancient Greek world. On the level of international relations, Athens, the strongest city-state in Greece prior to the war's beginning, was reduced to a state of near-complete subjection, while Sparta became established as the leading power of Greece.

The Peloponnesian War (431–404 BCE) was an ancient Greek war fought between Athens and Sparta and their respective allies for the hegemony of the Greek world. The war remained undecided for a long time until the decisive intervention of the Persian Empire in support of Sparta. Led by Lysander, the Spartan fleet built with Persian subsidies finally defeated Athens and started a period of Spartan hegemony over Greece. The Battle of Potidaea in 431 BCE of Athenians against Corinthians was a turning point. In this scene from the battle Socrates can be seen saving Alcibiades.

The assassination of the exiled Athenian general Alcibiades was organized by Pharnabazes, at the request of Lysander. The stories of the Peloponnesian War and ancient Greek history remained of great interest to Europeans for thousands of years. This painting by Philippe Chéry dates from 1791.

This image shows the encounter between Cyrus the Younger (left), Achaemenid satrap of Asia Minor and son of Darius II, and Spartan general Lysander (right) in Sardis. The encounter was related by Xenophon. This is a 17th century painting of Francesco Antonio Grue.

The Spartan army stood at the center of the Spartan state, citizens trained in the disciplines and honor of a warrior society. Subjected to military drills since early manhood, the Spartans became one of the most feared and formidable military forces in the Greek world, attaining legendary status in their wars against Persia. At the height of Sparta's power – between the 6th and 4th centuries BCE – other Greeks commonly accepted that "one Spartan was worth several men of any other state." This Spartan helmet is on display at the British Museum. The helmet has been damaged and the top has sustained a blow.

AFTERWORD

The goal of this work has been to inform and inspire. I believe that anyone can find evidence of past incarnations through his or her own strong interests. I hope that my research into my own past lives has convinced you of the reward and thrill that can be found in doing your own past life investigations. It is like a mystery game where you are intimately involved, not just as an observer but also as an exciting participant.

As I've found in more recent lifetimes, I've been able to actually visit places where I've lived and worked. At first it is like the greatest deja vu experience you could ever imagine. After several past life connections with places I've lived, I'm still awestruck when I encounter them now. I look and feel for deeper insights when I'm in places I know I've lived and walked because I know these can inspire and inform my development in countless ways.

Future books will follow my life stream as I experienced lives with Alexander the Great and with Julius Caesar, who was the same soul as Achilles. Would it surprise you to find out that Cleopatra reincarnated as Marilyn Monroe? I will relate my memories of Jesus when I was a Roman centurion and how I studied with him and helped his Disciples after his death. We will explore lives together when I was the historian Plutarch, Roman Emperor Marcus Aurelius, Saint George, Constantine the Great, Saint Althanasius the Great, Theodosius the Great, Saint Augustine, and Justinian the Great.

You may be familiar with many of these names. History for you can become vividly alive and exciting as never before when you hear it from an actual participant.

Other lifetimes we will explore in following books will include the beginning of the foundation of European empires as I delve into lifetimes as Sir Lionel with King Arthur, and as William the Conqueror of England. I will explore many lifetimes as kings of England, including Aldfrith of Northumbria, Alfred the Great, Henry I and II, Edward I and III, Henry V, and many others up to more recent times. My current wife joined me in virtually all these lives as my queen. Remember my comments about lifetimes incorporating bows and arrows? Many of the kings above used longbow men as major deciding factors in battles against overwhelming odds.

I will explore lifetimes as Frederick the Great, king of Prussia, and King Ludwig II, who was a castle builder in Bavaria, as were many of the kings of England I mentioned above. I was a castle builder in a more recent life as William Randolph Hearst, the publishing magnate. You can visit a castle in San Simeon, California, that he built. The Hearst castle is open to the public and filled with ancient art that he probably remembered from past lives, many of them that I've mentioned in this book. As an example of a past life connection, on the grounds of Hearst castle are Egyptian statues of the goddess Sekhmet. I mentioned Sekhmet in Chapter 6 during the life as a Nubian warrior sage for Pharaoh Hatshepsut. When I saw the statues during a tour of the castle in my current life, I had a deja vu moment and linked to both past lives and many others in a flood of memories.

In many of these past lives, I was a law bringer, as I have mentioned in several of the lifetimes in this book. Art, music, more freedoms for the general population, and the start of educational institutions were all common in many of these lifetimes.

I would not limit myself to incarnating in one location but would be all over the world map. I was Saint Louis IX of France, Charlemagne the Great and Otto the Great of Germany, Ashoka the Great and Kanishka the Great of India, and Dazu Huike, the second patriarch of Chinese Buddhism. I would be Viking kings as Rollo, first duke of Normandy, and Harald Fairhair, first king of Norway; William the Conqueror; and many others.

Discovering your past lives can open doorways not just for yourself but can also have a ripple effect for the rest of humanity as well. When I finally worked through the trauma of my past life as King Richard III of England and felt the wounds he received after being the last king of England to die in battle, a floodgate of past lives as England kings poured into my consciousness over the next year. The day after working through the pain and frustration of that lifetime, the remains of Richard III were discovered under a parking lot in England. The misinformation about his life fomented by the Tudor line that usurped the throne of England became apparent to many after this discovery.

A short time after this, I discovered and confirmed a life as King Alfred the Great, and his remains were also soon discovered. I'm still piecing together the magnitude of these events, but it is obvious that our own healing through past life discovery can also be a healing event and discovery for the rest of the world. Never sell yourself short on your own personal power or your own unique abilities to make a difference in the world.

It's also not all about the grand lives. Sometimes you need to get down in the weeds as common folk, as I am in my current life. I even have memories as slaves. The hard, serious soul work gets done in these lives as well as the grand lives. By getting down to earth in the dirt, your next incarnation can grow strong and have maximum impact. Think of your hard challenges and hard labor as time for reflection and appreciation for the simple pleasures.

Don't ever consider yourself as a noncontributing soul entity if you don't find grand lives at first or at all. The true work is in discovering what your soul desires and needs to develop and flourish. The journey of the soul is often more important, exciting, and fulfilling than the arrival at the actual destination. I didn't personally believe it was possible that I had any life of importance other than a contributory role for decades of past life research.

I would discover that I not only fought in the American Revolution but also in the American Civil War as generals on both sides of the conflict. It's not always about glorious long lifetimes. I have memories of being in World War I in Patton's first tank corps in France, where my tank was engulfed in flames and I burned alive. In World War II as a Tuskegee airman I was shot down over Germany by the first jets used in combat. I have memories of not being able to exit the cockpit and crashing. Thankfully, it's not always about war. I have also had many lives as spiritual masters and philosophers. We balance throughout our lifetimes between the things we want and the things we need to advance our soul development.

All the lives I've mentioned show multiple common threads that are easily discernible, as I will continue to point out in future books. Your own lives will offer common themes to you as you begin to uncover them. One of the most startling things that can happen is for you to see your own likeness staring back at you from a long-ago age. Similarities in facial features are often carried forward in future incarnations.

Another great pleasure in past life recall is finding beloved family members, friends, and coworkers from past lifetimes reincarnated into your current lifetime. My current wife and children have been in many of my past

lives. Finding that my wife and I have been in countless lives together brings a deeper level of connection and fealty to our lives. It's especially rewarding to go to past life locations and walk together as we did long ago and stir up happy memories once again. I can see the development over time of different aspects of my family members and friends. Now when I meet or see someone new and feel like I already know him or her, I'm no longer confused by this occurrence. It's often someone that I've known from past lives. If the feeling is not a positive one, then I know that I need to be watchful of our interactions together.

Why do we incarnate and not remember our past lives to begin with? Are we not immortal souls that never die? I think we wouldn't even attempt our new lives if we had to carry with us the entire trauma we have experienced in all of our previous lives. It would be overwhelming. There is the business of living and adapting to our new incarnation that must be managed first. It would also not be conducive to working through some of the challenges we have decided to task ourselves with in our current life. Some people regrettably get so wrapped up in the living that they have no time for reflection. I believe we all get glimpses or deja vu moments that give pause even to the heavy doubters.

I do at times see some sweet innocent children who remember the beautiful memories of the life between lives, though. My own daughter used to ask me repeatedly in private moments all the way up until she was seven years old if she would ever get her wings again and be able to fly. I would smile at her and tell her that we are all angels waiting to rediscover who we truly are. When the time is right, rediscovering your own past lives is like earning your wings once again.

Michael Jaco
June, 2022

History repeats many centuries later. In 1799, Napoleon Bonaparte violated his oath of fidelity to the Republic's Constitution, overthrowing the directory in a coup, assumed full powers, and ending the Revolution. General Napoleon Bonaparte to power as First Consul of France and ended the French Revolution, which lead to the Coronation of Napoleon as Emperor.

This is a photo from the 1940s showing U.S. veterans of four different wars, that lived in the same town of Geary, Oklahoma.

Letters of the historical runic alphabet and the modern Armanen runes have been used by Nazism and neo-Nazi groups that associate themselves with Germanic traditions, including the "Black Sun" used by Esoteric Nazi circles and other neo-Nazi groups.

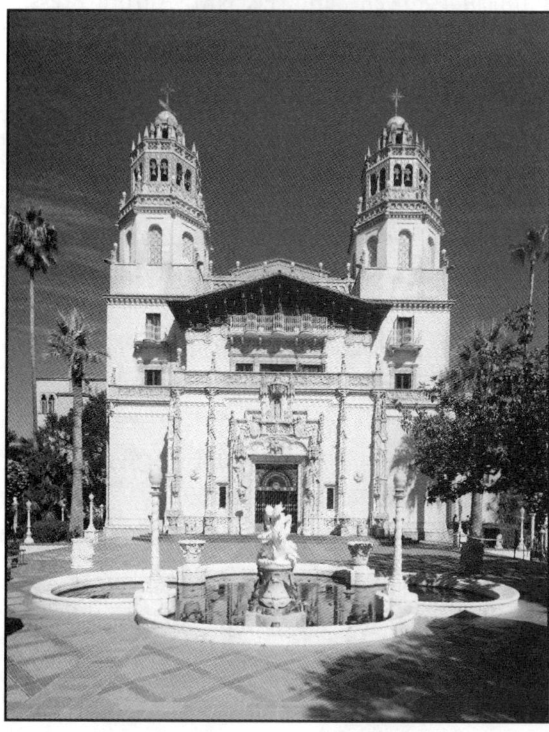

A dedicatory plaque at the Hearst Castle reads: "La Cuesta Encantada presented to the State of California in 1958 by the Hearst Corporation in memory of William Randolph Hearst who created this Enchanted Hill, and of his mother, Phoebe Apperson Hearst, who inspired it."

WORKS CONSULTED

Bailey, Alice. *The Consciousness of the Atom.* Cheshire, UK: A&D Publishing. September 22, 2013.

Bauval, Robert; Gilbert, Adrian. *The Orion Mystery: Unlocking the Secrets of the Pyramids.* New York: Crown. November 3, 2010.

Buck, William. *Mahabharata.* Delhi: Motilal Banarsidass, September 1, 2000.

Buck, William. *Ramayana.* (Thirty-fifth anniversary edition). Berkley: University of California Press. June 12, 2012.

Cannon, Dolores. *Between Death and Life.* Huntsville, AR: Ozark Mountain Publishing Inc. January 1, 1993.

Cannon, Dolores. *The Convoluted Universe: Book One.* Huntsville, AR: Ozark Mountain Publishing Inc. November 1, 2001.

Chia, Mantak. *Awaken Healing Energy Through the Tao: The Taoist Secret of Circulating Internal Power.* Santa Fe, NM: Aurora Press. June 1, 1983.

Dunn, Christopher. *The Giza Power Plant: Technologies of Ancient Egypt.* Rochester, VT: Bear & Company. August 1, 1998.

Eadie, J. Betty. *Embraced by the Light.* Seattle: Onjinjinkta Publishing. November 7, 2012.

Griaule, Marcel. *Conversations with Ogotemmeli: An Introduction to Dogon Religious Ideas.* Oxford, UK: Oxford University Press. November 6, 1975.

Hancock, Graham. *Fingerprints of the Gods: The Evidence of Earth's Lost Civilization.* New York: Three Rivers Press. September 19, 2012.

Hancock, Graham. *Underworld: The Mysterious Origins of Civilization.* New York: Three Rivers Press. November 18, 2009.

Hancock, Graham. *The Sign and the Seal: The Quest for the Lost Ark of the Covenant.* New York: Crown. September 19, 2012.

Heartsong, Claire. *Anna, Grandmother of Jesus.* S.E.E. Publishing. October 3, 2002.

Hermes. *The Emerald Tablets of Thoth the Atlantean.*

Herodotus. *The Histories.* London: Penguin. January 30, 2003.

Homer. *Iliad.* London: Penguin. July 1, 1991.

Homer. *Odyssey.* London: Penguin. November 1, 1997.

Jaco, Michael. *The Intuitive Warrior: Lessons from a Navy SEAL on Unleashing Your Hidden Potential.* CCC Publishing: Michael Jaco. July 1, 2022.

Josephus, Flavius. *Antiquities of the Jews.* Oxfordshire, UK: Acheron Press. October 14, 2012.

Josyer, G. R. *Vaimanika Shastra.* Sacred Texts website: 1973.

Justin, Daria. *Angels Whisper to Us: Decoding the Messages in Daydreams.* Iuniverse.com: iUniverse. November 24, 2008.

Lloyd, Andy. *The Dark Star: The Planet X Evidence.* Timeless Voyager Press. July 1, 2013.

Machiavelli, Niccolo. *The Prince.* Waxkeep Publishing. January 26, 2013.

MacLaine, Shirley. *Out on a Limb.* London: Bantam. July 27, 2011.

MacLaine, Shirley. *The Camino:A Journey of the Spirit.* New York: Atria Books. May 16, 2000.

Melchizedek, Drunvalo. *The Ancient Secret of the Flower of Life: Volume 1.* Flagstaff, AZ: Light Technology Publishing. April 27, 2012.

Nabonidus Chronicle, an ancient Babylonian text. Wikipedia 2014.

Newton, Michael. *Destiny of Souls: New Case Studies of Life between Lives.* Woodbury, MN: Llewellyn Publications. May 8, 2000.

Newton, Michael. *Journey of Souls: Case Studies of Lives Between Lives.* Woodbury, MN: Llewellyn Publications. June 30, 1994.

Newton, Michael. *Journey of Souls: Evidence of Life between Lives.* Woodbury, MN: Llewellyn Publications. July 1994.

One Thousand and One Nights. Amazon Digital Services.

Osman, Ahmed. *The Hebrew Pharaohs of Egypt: The Secret Lineage of Patriarch Joseph.* Rochester, VT: Bear & Company. September 19, 2003.

Parmenides. *On the Order of Nature.* Aurea Vidya. April 15, 2009.

Pliny, Gaius. *Natural History.* London: Penguin. February 5, 2004.

Plutarch. *Lives of the Noble Greeks and Romans.* Amazon Digital Services.

Ryerson, Kevin, & Harolde, Stephanie. *Spirit Communication: The Soul's Path.* London: Bantam. August 1, 1989.

Scranton, Laird. *The Science of the Dogon: Decoding the African Mystery Tradition.* Inner Traditions. September 22, 2006.

Semkiw, Walter. *Return of the Revolutionaries: The Case for Reincarnation and Soul Groups Reunited.* Charlottesville, VA: Hampton Roads Publishing. April 1, 2003.

Siculus, Diodorus. *Library of History.* Cambridge, MA: Harvard University Press. January 31, 1933.

Sitchin, Zecharia. *The 12th Planet.* Rochester, VT: Bear & Company. May 1, 1991.

Sugrue, Thomas. *Story of Edgar Cayce: There Is a River.* (Revised edition). A.R.E. Press. January 1, 1997

Talbot, Michael. *The Holographic Universe: The Revolutionary Theory of Reality.* New York: Harper Perennial. September 6, 2011.

Tellinger, Michael. *Slave Species of god: The Secret History of the Anunnaki and Their Mission on Earth.* Rochester, VT: Bear & Company. September 14, 2012.

Temple, Robert. *The Sirius Mystery: New Scientific Evidence of Alien Contact 5,000 Years Ago.* Rochester, VT: Destiny Books. October 1, 1998.

Terminator 2: Judgment Day. Director: James Cameron; Writers: James Cameron, William Wisher Jr.; Stars: Arnold Schwarzenegger, Linda Hamilton, Edward Furlong. 1991.

The Kolbrin Bible. Your Own World Books. August 1, 2013.

The Tale of Sinuhe and Other Ancient Egyptian Poems 1940-1640 B.C.E. Oxford, UK: Oxford University Press. May 15, 2009.

Thucydides. *History of the Peloponnesian War.* London: Penguin. February 28, 1974.

Velikovsky, Immanuel. *Worlds in Collision.* Paradigma Ltd. September 26, 2012.

Velikovsky, Immanuel. *Ages in Chaos.* Paradigma Ltd. December 1, 2012

Waddell, L. A. *Makers of Civilization in Race and History.* Norfolk, UK: Whitley Press. April 20, 2011.

Wallis, Budge. *The Book of the Dead.* Benediction Books. September 29, 2010.

Weiss, L. Brian. *Many Lives, Many Masters: The True Story of a Prominent Psychiatrist.* New York: Touchstone. May 1, 2012.

Weiss, L. Brian. *Same Soul, Many Bodies: Discover the Healing Power of Future Lives through Progression Therapy.* New York: Free Press. November 3, 2004.

Wilcock, David. *The Source Field Investigations.* Plume Books. July 31, 2012.

Xenophon. *Anabasis.* Amazon Digital Services.

Xenophon. *Cyropaedia: The Education of Cyrus.* Amazon Digital Services.

Xiru, Liu. *Yellow Emperor's Canon of Medicine: Spiritual Pivot.* World Book Press. November 1, 2008.

ABOUT THE AUTHOR

Michael Jaco was born and raised in Columbia, South Carolina. He enlisted in the United States Navy in November 1978 and started his career as a Navy Hard Hat Diver. He volunteered for Basic Underwater Demolition/Sea Air and Land (BUD/S) training in August 1981. He completed BUD/S training 6 months later with class 116 in February 1982. He served with distinction as a Navy SEAL with the following commands:

UDT-12, SEAL TEAMS – 3, 4, 5, & 6 Naval Special Warfare Development Group Naval Special Warfare Training Center (BUD/S/1st Phase); Naval Special Warfare Training Center (Advanced Training); Naval Special Warfare Unit - 1 (Guam); United States Naval Academy. Upon leaving the US Navy in December 2002 he has served as a High Risk Security Contractor for over 8 years. Providing security leadership for 40 different contracts in the most violent war torn areas of the world.

Navy Seal Team Six operator and CIA security operative with expert intuitive abilities developed over 35 years of extensive combat experience.

With over 20 years of experience as an Intuitive, Remote Viewer and Remote Influencer in diverse environments including combat Michael has expertly honed his skills in the higher consciousness realms.

As a master training specialist Michael has trained thousands of people in extremely high levels of personal development.

Michael's mission and life focus is to help anyone quickly and easily develop the skills for success in all aspects of human achievement.

Connect with Michael online at:
http://www.michaeljaco.com

LEO ZAGAMI BOOKS FROM CCC PUBLISHING

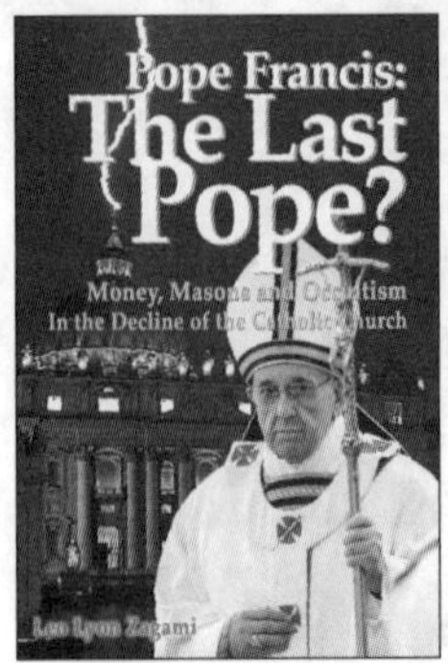

***Pope Francis: The Last Pope?**: Money, Masons and Occultism in the Decline of the Catholic Church*

– by Leo Lyon Zagami

Perfect for anyone interested in prophecies about the end times, Pope Francis: The Last Pope reveals the truth about the last Pope and the darkness that may follow him; fascinating investigations into the gay lobby; Freemasonry; the Jesuit agenda; and, the legend of the White Pope, the Black Pope, and how Benedict's resignation may fulfill an ancient prophecy.

$16.95 :: 224 pages **paperback 978-1888729542**

... all eBooks priced $8.99

Kindle: 978-1888729566; PDF: 978-1888729559
ePub: 978-1888729573

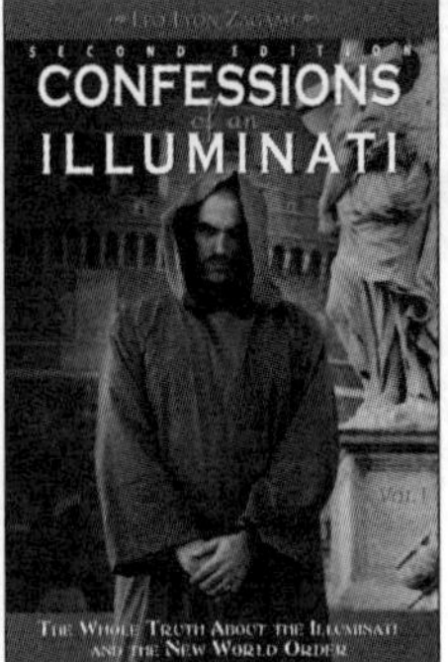

***Confessions of an Illuminati, Volume I:** The Whole Truth About the Illuminati and the New World Order*

– 2nd EDITION; by Leo Lyon Zagami

From the OTO's infiltration of Freemasonry to the real Priory of Sion, this book exposes the hidden structure of the New World Order; their occult practices; and their connections to the intelligence community and the infamous Ur-Lodges.

$17.95 :: 408 pages **paperback 978-1888729870**

... all eBooks priced $9.99

Kindle: 978-1888729894; PDF: 978-1888729887
ePub: 978-1888729900

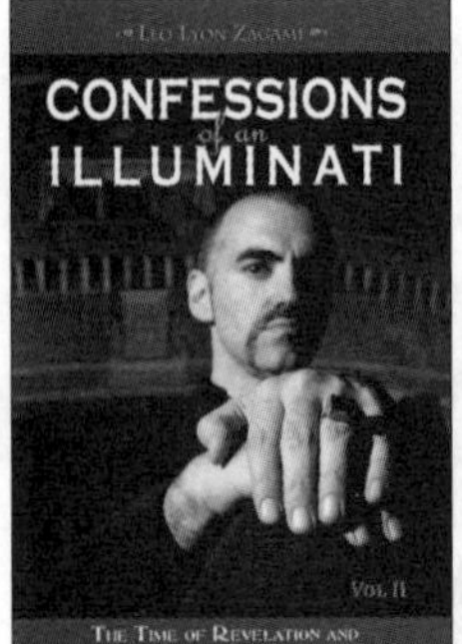

***Confessions of an Illuminati, Volume II:** The Time of Revelation and Tribulation Leading up to 2020*

– by Leo Lyon Zagami

Since the Second Vatican Council, the hierarchy of power emanating from the Jesuits in Rome and the Zionist's in Jerusalem, united by a secret pact, have been manipulating world powers and using economic hitmen to create a unified one-world government.

$17.95 :: 380 pages **paperback 978-1888729627**

... all eBooks priced $9.99

Kindle: 978-1888729658; PDF: 978-1888729634
ePub: 978-1888729641

***Confessions of an Illuminati, Volume III:** Espionage, Templars and Satanism in the Shadows of the Vatican*

– by Leo Lyon Zagami

Take a unique and personal journey into the secretive world of the Dark Cabal. Explore a variety of cryptic topics and learn the truth about the mythical Knights Templars, the Jesuits, and their mastery of the Vatican espionage game.

$17.95 :: 336 pages **paperback 978-1888729665**

... all eBooks priced $9.99

Kindle: 978-1888729696; PDF: 978-1888729672
ePub: 978-1888729689

The Invisible Master: Secret Chiefs, Unknown Superiors, and the Puppet Masters Who Pull the Strings of Occult Power from the Alien World

– by Leo Lyon Zagami

Leo Zagami's groundbreaking study of aliens and UFOs explores where we come from and which mysterious figures have guided humanity's political and religious choices. From the prophets to the initiates and magicians, all ages have drawn from a common source of ultra-terrestrial and magical knowledge, passed down for millennia. This text reveals the identity of the unknown superiors, secret chiefs, and invisible masters who have guided Freemasonry, the Illuminati, and others.

$17.95 :: 380 pages **paperback 978-1888729702**

... all eBooks priced $9.99

Kindle: 978-1888729733; PDF: 978-1888729719
ePub: 978-1888729726

Sacred Places North America: *108 Destinations*

– 2nd EDITION; by Brad Olsen

This comprehensive travel guide examines North America's most sacred sites for spiritually attuned explorers. Spirituality & Health reviewed: "The book is filled with fascinating archeological, geological, and historical material. These 108 sacred places in the United States, Canada, and Hawaii offer ample opportunity for questing by spiritual seekers."

$19.95 :: 408 pages **paperback: 978-1888729139**

... all Ebooks priced at $9.99

Kindle: 978-1888729252; PDF: 978-1888729191
ePub: 978-1888729337

Sacred Places Europe: *108 Destinations* – by Brad Olsen

This guide to European holy sites examines the most significant locations that shaped the religious consciousness of Western civilization. Travel to Europe for 108 uplifting destinations that helped define religion and spirituality in the Western Hemisphere. From Paleolithic cave art and Neolithic megaliths, to New Age temples, this is an impartial guide book many millennium in the making.

$19.95 :: 344 pages **paperback: 978-1888729122**

... all Ebooks priced at $9.99

Kindle: 978-1888729245; PDF: 978-1888729184
ePub: 978-1888729320

Sacred Places of Goddess: *108 Destinations* – by Karen Tate

Readers will be escorted on a pilgrimage that reawakens, rethinks, and reveals the Divine Feminine in a multitude of sacred locations on every continent. Meticulously researched, clearly written and comprehensively documented, this book explores the rich tapestry of Goddess worship from prehistoric cultures to modern academic theories.

$19.95 :: 424 pages **paperback: 978-1888729115**

... all Ebooks priced at $9.99

Kindle: 978-1888729269; PDF: 978-1888729177
ePub: 978-1888729344

Sacred Places Around the World: *108 Destinations*

– 2nd EDITION; by Brad Olsen

The mystical comes alive in this exciting compilation of 108 beloved holy destinations. World travelers and armchair tourists who want to explore the mythology and archaeology of the ruins, sanctuaries, mountains, lost cities, and temples of ancient civilizations will find this guide ideal.

$17.95 :: 288 pages **paperback: 978-1888729108**

... all Ebooks priced at $8.99

Kindle: 978-1888729238; PDF: 978-1888729160
ePub: 978-1888729313

World Stompers: *A Global Travel Manifesto*

– 5th EDITION; by Brad Olsen

Here is a travel guide written specifically to assist and motivate young readers to travel the world. When you are ready to leave your day job, load up your backpack and head out to distant lands for extended periods of time, Brad Olsen's "Travel Classic" will lend a helping hand.

$17.95 :: 288 pages **paperback: 978-1888729054**

... all Ebooks priced at $8.99

Kindle: 978-1888729276; PDF: 978-1888729061
ePub: 978-1888729351

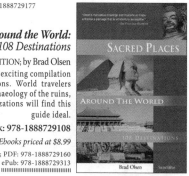

Beyond Esoteric:
Escaping Prison Planet

– by Brad Olsen

Nothing in this world works the way we are led to believe it does; there is always more to the story. Be aware that there is a war being waged for your body, mind and soul. Owners of corporations have taken over governments in a new form of Fascism that now incorporates high technology and artificial intelligence. The survival of the human race may depend on breaking the Truth Embargo, that is, exposing the Big Lie.

$19.95 :: 480 pages; paperback: 978-1888729740

... all eBooks priced $9.99

All ebook ISBN versions: 978-1888729757

Modern Esoteric:
Beyond our Senses

– 2nd EDITION; by Brad Olsen

Organized into three sections (Lifeology, Control and Thrive), Modern Esoteric: Beyond Our Senses by World Explorer magazine editor Brad Olsen examines the flaws in ancient and modern history, plus explains how esoteric knowledge, conspiracy theories, and fringe subjects can be used to help change the dead-end course we humans seem to be blindly running ourselves into.

$17.95 :: 480 pages; paperback: 978-1888729504

... all eBooks priced $9.99

Kindle: 978-1888729856 • PDF: 978-1888729832 • ePub: 978-1888729849

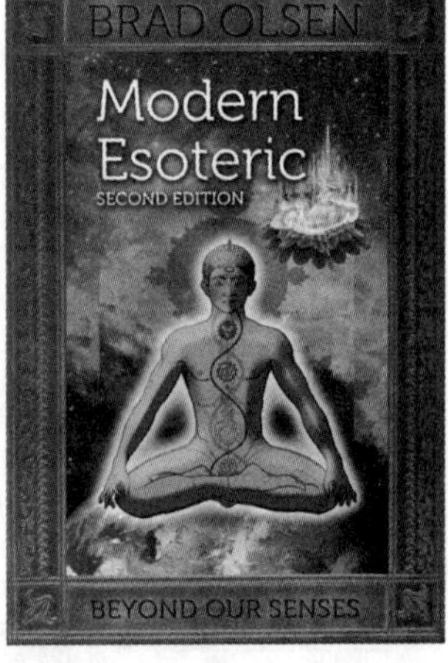

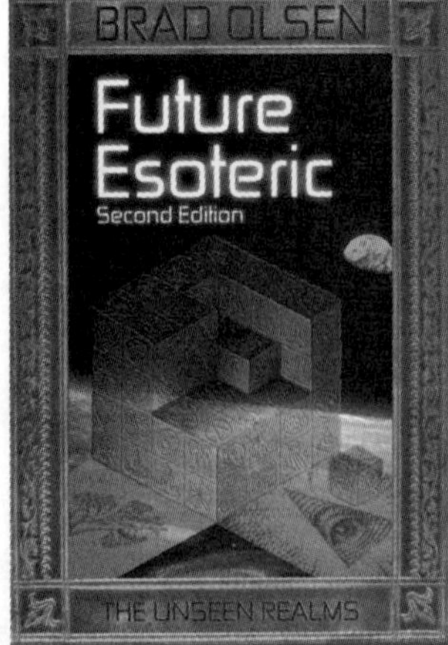

Future Esoteric:
The Unseen Realms

– 2nd EDITION; by Brad Olsen

Things are not always as they appear. For the past century forbidden subjects such as UFOs, human abductions, secret space programs, suppressed free energy devices and other fantastic notions have tested the human mind, forcing it to decipher fact from fiction. But is there a common thread? As sites like WikiLeaks and their founders try to unveil war secrets and covert black operations, international governments have little-by-little begun exposing what they've tried for years to keep hidden. Chronicling what he calls the "alternative narrative," Brad Olsen gets down to the middle of it all.

$17.95 :: 416 pages; paperback: 978-1888729788

... all eBooks priced $9.99

Kindle: 978-1888729801 • PDF: 978-1888729795 • ePub: 978-1888729818

CCC Publishing is distributed by Independent Publishers Group (800) 888-4741, www.IPGBook.com
Follow us on: www.EsotericSeries.com & www.Facebook.com/ccc.publishing • www.CCCPublishing.com
features the content of all of our books online, plus blogs, ebooks & discounts

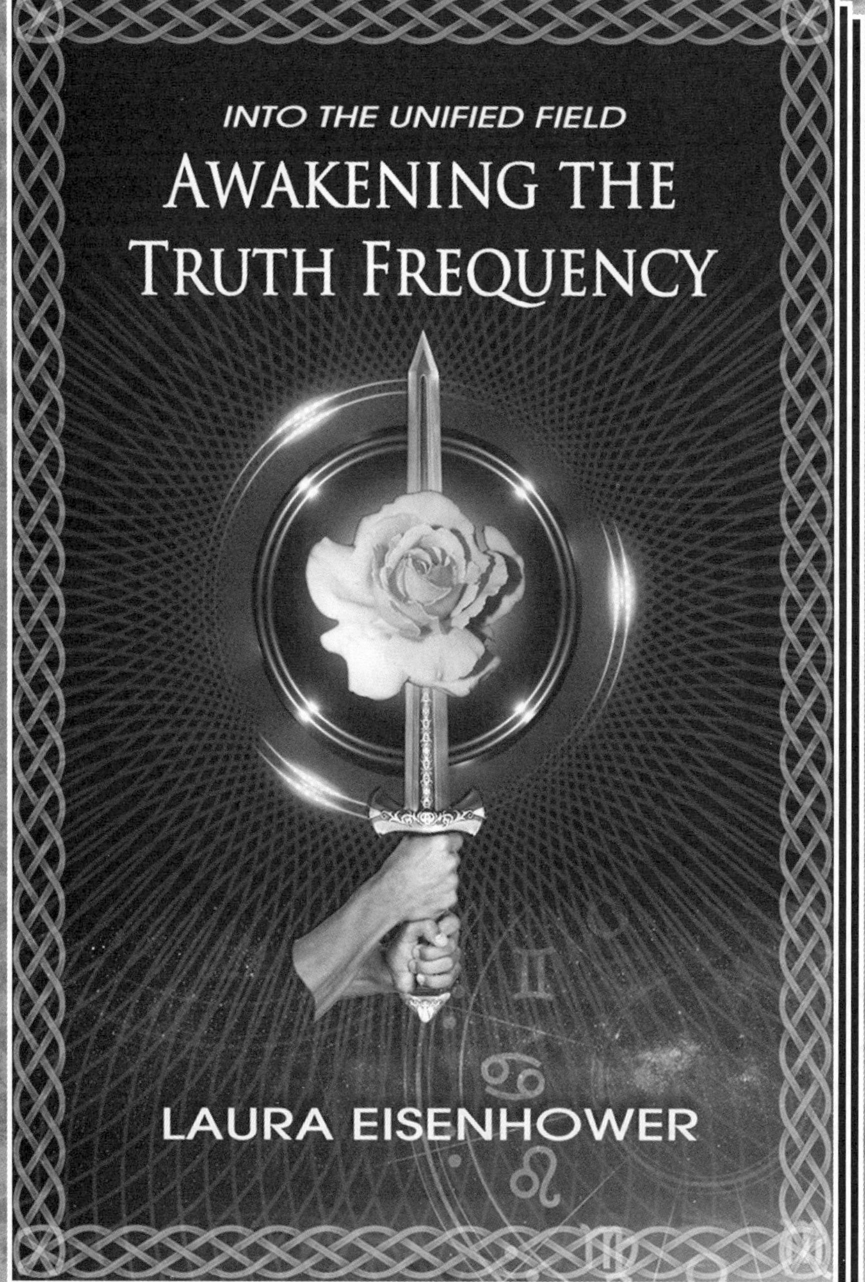
INTO THE UNIFIED FIELD
AWAKENING THE TRUTH FREQUENCY
LAURA EISENHOWER

ANOTHER IMPORTANT BOOK BY
MICHAEL JACO

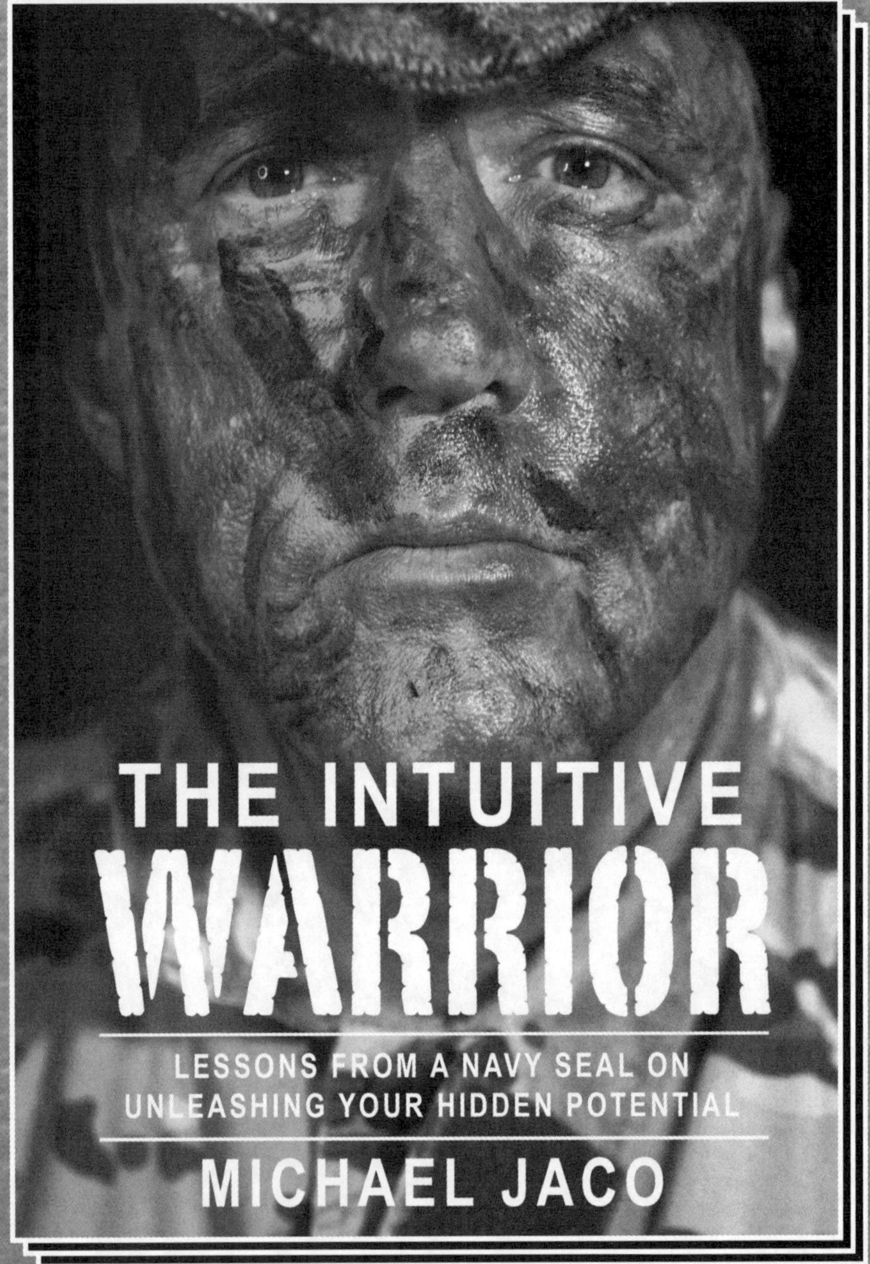

ISBN 13: 978-1-888729-92-4 · PAPERBACK · $16.95